→ Typology
and Early
American
Literature

edited by Sacvan Bercovitch

The University of Massachusetts Press 1972

Library of Congress
Catalog Card Number
74–181362

Set in Linotype Electra
and printed in the
United States of America
by Connecticut Printers, Inc.

Designed by
Richard Eckersley

For Everett Emerson

Introduction

Sacvan Bercovitch

Typology and Early American Literature

Introduction

What else is the Old Testament but the New foreshadowed? And what other the New than the Old revealed? St. Augustine

The whole cultus of the law, taken literally and not as shadows and figures corresponding to the truth, will be utterly ridiculous. . . . Until Christ was manifested in the flesh all signs shadowed him.   Calvin

There are christoi, anointed prophets, priests and kings in the Old Testament, christianoi in the New Testament, but only depending upon and proceeding from the fact that there is a unique Christos, the Lord of the covenant attested to in the Old and New Testaments . . . the proper Christos, of whom they are but types.   Karl Barth

Typology
and Early
American
Literature

Introduction

Sacvan Bercovitch
Columbia University

Nothing more clearly reveals the parochialism of colonial studies than the fact that in 1948, when introducing Jonathan Edwards' *Images or Shadows of Divine Things*, Perry Miller felt it necessary to explain the nature and meaning of typology, a branch of hermeneutics which had figured in doctrinal development from the Church Fathers through the Reformation, which had informed the major creative works of medieval and Renaissance Europe— *Pilgrim's Progress* and *Paradise Lost* no less than the *Divine Comedy*—and which, from the Enlightenment into our own times, had been the subject of religious controversy and of literary, philological, and historical analysis. Moreover (as Miller himself failed to recognize), the typological approach held far-reaching significance for the seventeenth-century settlers. They had brought it with them from England, where it permeated the literature of all factions of Puritanism, and they proceeded to use it explicitly from one generation to the next as an integral part of their outlook: in their histories and diaries, poetry and polemics, jeremiads and discourses on grace. Almost a decade before Edwards was born, Gurdon Saltonstall of Connecticut, surveying the theocracy's prospects from the election-day pulpit by way of various 'typical' places and persons, could confidently declare that 'These Figurative Terms . . . are obvious; and need not much to be said for their Explication.'[1]

1. *A Sermon Preached before the General Assembly* (Boston, 1697), p. 11.

The startling oversight of our intellectual historians suggests a number of basic methodological difficulties. One of these lies in the formidable demands inherent in any interdisciplinary undertaking, especially perhaps where they entail unfamiliar patterns of theology. Another stems from the chronic resistance of Americanists, in their zealous search for National Character, to give due attention to 'foreign' influences. Still another difficulty arises from the notion that the New World Puritans were Ramist-bound scholastics who denigrated the imagination, reducing metaphor and parallel, type and trope, to an ornamental gateway into the precise logical structure of their thought. Surely the most salient effect of the burgeoning interest in typology would be to broaden our knowledge in all these areas. The essays in this volume diversely attest to the creative energy of early New England writing, to the remarkable new avenues of interpretation opened by an awareness of exegetical traditions, and to the need for viewing the culture within its Christian-European context. In particular they demonstrate that now, some twenty-one years after Miller's seminal introduction, the study of typology in colonial America has come of age and that it has proved beyond any doubt an invaluable addition to our knowledge of the period.

What these essays offer, then, is, in the richest sense of the word, a guide to a recently established field of growing importance in American intellectual, cultural, and aesthetic history. They constitute at once a fulfillment of over two decades of promising research and a stimulus for future investigations. Professor Thomas Davis unravels a wide variety of exegetical problems in his detailed and comprehensive exploration of the long foreground to New England typology; he also sets out a number of intriguing questions: the role of typology in the disputes over baptism and in the evolution of covenant theory, for example, or the relation of the 'apologetic' link between the two Testaments to the interpretations of the Apocalypse, that 'heavenly book,' as Samuel Torrey put it, wherein 'all the universal verities . . . [are] under pleasant types and tropes decided.'[2] Professor Stephen Manning—taking up, as it

2. *An Exhortation Unto Reformation, Amplified* (Cambridge, Mass., 1674), p. 1.

were, the connection that Davis establishes between Catholic and Protestant exegesis—elucidates the intertwined-yet-different levels of medieval figuralism. The framework he proposes for distinguishing between modes of expression (historical and pseudo-historical, theological and allegorical, natural and arbitrary) challenges further application and seems as relevant to the American colonists as to the earlier poets and theologians he treats.

The value of such application, indeed, is amply evident in the essays that follow. Professors Jesper Rosenmeier and Mason Lowance reveal not only the centrality but the subtlety of typological thought in the leader of the Plymouth migration and the representative third-generation Massachusetts theocrat. Their studies combine broad learning with astute biographical and imaginative insight in developing what are surely authoritative statements about some key documents in the literature. They also serve heuristically to highlight the need for a full-length analysis of the typologists who may be seen to link the two Puritans; I refer to the founders of the Bay church-state, Bradford's congregationalist contemporaries, and Mather's actual and spiritual forebears. Several scholars have discussed John Cotton in this regard; we still await an adequate overview of men like Shepard, Davenport, Bulkeley, Richard Mather, Norton, and Hooker, each of whom contributed crucially, though differently, to the formulation of the New England Way, and all of whom held that 'the truths of Christ are laid up under the types,' sharing as they did the Reformation belief that 'the thing signified by the words of Scripture is but one, namely, that onely which the Literal Sense exhibits, which propounds the Type,' and that, accordingly, 'as the New Testament giveth light unto the Old, so the Old Testament giveth light unto the New. 'Tis the same *Christ* and the same *Gospel* which is held forth in both. . . . Promises given unto the Saints in the Old Testament belong unto believers living under the New Testament . . . not onely David, but also . . . us.'[3]

3. John Norton, 'The Evangelical Worshipper,' in *Three Choice and Profitable Sermons* (Cambridge, Mass., 1664), p. 33; John Wilson, *The Scriptures Genuine Interpreter* (Cambridge, Mass., 1678), p. 90; John Norton, *The Heart of N-England Rent* (Cambridge, Mass., 1659), pp. 19–20. These statements express the oft-misunderstood Reformation attack upon the

These beliefs clearly inform the greatest single body of poetry of early New England. Ever since his manuscripts were discovered in 1939, critics have noted Edward Taylor's 'fondness for types.' Professors Ursula Brumm, Karl Keller, and Robert Reiter go further than that. Their readings are model examples of the specific illuminations that sophisticated and sensitive figural explication can provide. More impressively still, they show how Taylor fuses typology and poetry, transforms hermeneutic into aesthetic, in a way that suggests marked continuities with Transcendentalism. In so doing, they encourage further study into the development of American symbolism and of corresponding themes and modes of the national culture. And in terms of Puritanism itself, they invite new speculation on still dimly understood issues, both practical and theoretical, with regard (for example) to the relation of aesthetics and theology in sermons, narratives, and biographies, as well as to the use of modern techniques—archetypal, psychological, anthropological—in defining the anatomy of the American Puritan imagination.

The remaining two essays bring the development since 1948 full circle by wide-ranging revaluations of Roger Williams and Jonathan Edwards. Professor Reinitz proves that the former's method, far from being eccentric or anachronistic as Perry Miller contended, reflects that of a popular movement in England and on the continent, one which demands a more comprehensive treatment than we have had to date in terms of Separatist thought and of Congregationalism as a whole; and the questions he raises concerning the causal relation between politics and hermeneutics reminds us that the political function of typology, intrinsic to its history from the earliest anti-Jewish polemics to the theological controversies in Nazi Germany, has gone largely unexamined. Professor Lowance places *Images or Shadows of Divine Things* against its complex seventeenth- and eighteenth-century background in a bal-

---

Roman Catholic multi-levelled exegesis; for a typical English Puritan statement on the subject, see William Perkins, *The Arte of Prophesying*, trans. T. Tuke (London, 1607), p. 30; see further John Cotton, *The Keyes of the Kingdom* (London, 1660), *passim*; and cf. Benjamin Keach on 'the wrangling of critics' over 'THE DIVISION OF TYPES,' in *Tropologia* (London, 1681), p. 228.

anced, illuminating critique of Miller's position. His inquiry leads through the whole range of Edwards' work, detailing the intricacies of Edwards' exegesis and showing their connection with Platonic and Lockeian epistemology. If he does not deal with the parallels between Edwards' typology and that underlying revivalist millennialism and German pietism, he provides a viable context within which such issues may be discussed, and which extends beyond Locke and the Great Awakening to the Romantic nineteenth-century belief (shared by the leading figures of the American Renaissance) that 'Nature itself is but a system of types—the translation of what is invisible and divine into material forms'—in order to 'make plain unto us lessons otherwise obscure.'[4]

4. Joseph A. Seiss, *Holy Types* (Philadelphia, 1866), p. 25; Milton Bales, *Types of the Holy Spirit* (New York, [18—]), p. 3. Cf. Perry Miller's 'Introduction' to Jonathan Edwards, *Images or Shadows of Divine Things* (New Haven, 1948), pp. 141–42: 'A study of . . . typology in Protestant countries during the seventeenth century would . . . make a substantial contribution to an understanding of modern literature.' A key aspect of such an undertaking would deal with the transformations in the concept of types through the nineteenth-century theologians who respond to Enlightenment and Romantic modes of thought. Thus George Townsend sets antiquarian research, naturalism, literary technique, and common-sense experience under the category of 'type,' together with prophecy, trope, and emblem. The phrase 'fishers of men,' he writes (*The New Testament* [London, 1825], I, 152–53), 'typifies' the 'design of Revelation,' the order of a world where 'all that can or shall take place is known to God,' the meaning of 'both covenants' (via Cocceius), and 'a great number of prophecies, . . . fulfilled, . . . now fulfilling [and] . . . to be accomplished.' When 'Christ assured his disciples that they should become fishers of men,' He meant it as a type— which is to say, first 'as a metaphor' pertaining 'literally' to their own lives, and secondly as a prediction that 'the Apostles on a future day [will] bring many myriads into the Church of God.' Then, drawing upon the 'imagination,' Townsend notes 'the several objects, means, and terms, which are used by fishermen, and concerning fish, were interpreted by the ancients in an emblematical sense, and similar interpretations may be found in the talmudic writers.' In this volume, Professors Brumm, Keller, and Lowance make a significant contribution toward a special study of the course of typology in the modern world, a development especially relevant to American literature, in which (as in Townsend) *figura* and symbol, nature and Scripture, fact and promise, exegesis and interpretation, have traditionally been closely interwoven.

Finally, the Bibliography is intended as a map outlining these many areas of typological study. The territory is immense, encompassing as it does the explorations of two millennia of theologians, scholars, critics, and historians; and I have restricted myself to only the important landmarks, with emphasis on the formative early writings, on the Reformation and Renaissance (especially the seventeenth century), and on the twentieth century (especially literary criticism). I claim no more than to have suggested the scope and sustained vitality of the subject, and at best to have opened certain new prospects for consideration. For the rest, I am more than content to refer students and teachers to the essays themselves. The authors have set out to show the significance of typology for American studies, to delineate the major fields of concern, and to provide a fuller appreciation of the works and themes they discuss. It is an ambitious plan, but I believe that they have succeeded.

Acknowledgments

The essays by Professors Ursula Brumm and Jesper Rosenmeier appear in this volume for the first time; all other essays appeared in *Early American Literature* in substantially the same form: Professor Lowance's (on Cotton Mather) in Volume IV (1969), the rest in the special typology issue, Volume V (Spring, 1970). The bibliography appeared, in a considerably more compact version, in Volumes V and VI of the same journal.

I would like to express my gratitude to H. M. Bercovitch, Benson Bobrick, Ursula Brumm, Thomas Davis, Alan Heinert, Paul Korshia, Richard LeVine, Mason Lowance, William Madsen, Niki Plumstead, Lawrence Rosenwald, and Roba Schori for their generous and valuable help in this venture. My largest debt, to *Early American Literature* and its superb editor, is expressed in the dedication.

The
Exegetical
Background

The
Traditions
of Puritan
Typology

Scriptural
Exegesis
and the
Literary
Critic

Lex antiqua novam firmat,
veterem nova complet:
In veteri spes est, in novitate fides,
Sed vetus atque coniungit
gratia Christi.   Paulinus of
Nola

Sic igitur est lex nova in
veteri sicut fructus in spica;
omnia enim quae credenda traduntur in novo testamento
explicite et aperte, traduntur in
veteri testamento, sed implicite sub figura.   Vincent of
Beauvais

Dominus qui est plentitudo
. . . veritatem praefiguratae
imaginis adimplevit.   St.
Cyprian

The Traditions of Puritan Typology

Thomas M. Davis
Kent State
University

Only recently have students of New England Puritanism focused upon the Puritan's widespread interest in typology. When noticed at all, typology has been generally viewed as an aspect of the regrettable Puritan flirtation with allegory, and, as such, has been seen as a naive and inhibiting characteristic of an already rigidly limited aesthetic. Several recent studies, however, have called attention to the relationship of typology to the Puritan view of history, to the covenantal structure of the New England theocracy, and to the basically analogic character of the Puritan poetic, demonstrating that an understanding of typology is central to reading Puritan texts and to identifying the references of Puritan imagery.[1] As recent studies have also indicated, the type-antitype construct is far more complex than at first appears and to be unaware of typological traditions is to distort basic Puritan beliefs. Several critics, for example, have suggested that the taint of unorthodoxy

---

1. See, for example, Perry Miller, 'Introduction,' in Jonathan Edwards, *Images or Shadows of Divine Things* (New Haven, 1948); Sacvan Bercovitch, 'Typology in New England: The Williams-Cotton Controversy Reassessed,' *AQ*, XIX (Summer 1967), 165–91; Mason I. Lowance, Jr., 'Typology and the New England Way: Cotton Mather and the Exegesis of Biblical Types,' *EAL*, IV (Spring 1969), 15–37, and 'Introduction,' in Samuel Mather, *The Figures or Types of the Old Testament* (New York, 1969); and Thomas M. Davis, 'Edward Taylor and the Traditions of Typology,' *EAL*, V (Winter 1970), 27–47.

hovers about the 'Meditations' of Edward Taylor in part because the poems are 'quite literally redolent of altar incense' and the images of the 'altar censer, incense, and offerings' evoke a 'curiously Catholic response.' Such imagery is, of course, not at all 'strange . . . in a Puritan context,' for the references are to the typological significance of Hebrew ceremonial ritual. Such imagery appears in discussions of typology from the Epistle to the Hebrews to John Calvin and is standard fare in such typological studies as Thomas Taylor's *Moses and Aaron, or the Types and Shadows* and Samuel Mather's *The Figures or Types.*[2]

Nor is the Puritan preoccupation with typology simply a seventeenth-century phenomenon. The roots of the Puritan practice of typological exegesis are deep in the traditions of the Church Fathers. Neither were the 'great Protestant Reformers . . . explicit in their condemnation of the typological method.'[3] The Reformers were, in fact, among the most earnest practitioners of typology, and the Puritan practice is clearly based on Reformational precedent. Even though the 'establishment of historical connexions between certain events, persons or things in the Old Testament [the type] and similar events, persons or things in the New Testament [the antitype]'[4] may have led to the regrettable excesses (from the Puri-

2. The first comment occurs in *The Puritans*, ed. Perry Miller and Thomas H. Johnson (New York, 1963), II, 652; the second in Mindele Black, 'Edward Taylor: Heavens Sugar Cake,' *New England Quarterly*, XXIX (June 1956), 175–76. As a matter of fact, Taylor himself makes the identification clear; in Meditation 23 (2), for example, he notes:

> Lord let my Soule the Vessell be of thine . . .
> Sweet incense burn with Altars fire Divine
> To Typify the Incense of thy Prayer
> Perfuming of thy Service thou didst beare.

(*The Poems of Edward Taylor*, ed. Donald E. Stanford [New Haven, 1960], p. 123. Subsequent references are to this edition.)

3. Perry Miller, *Roger Williams: His Contribution to the American Tradition* (New York, 1953), pp. 34–35.

4. G. W. H. Lampe, 'The Biblical Origins and Patristic Development of Typology,' in *Essays on Typology*, Studies in Biblical Theology, No. 22 (Naperville, Ill., 1957), p. 39.

tan point of view, at any rate) of Catholic exegetes, the Puritan experiment in New England and the most central points of its theology were based too fully on the Old Testament to discard a traditional method of exegesis which provided impeccable biblical authority for the New England Way. From John Cotton's slightly unwarranted application of typical symbolism to New England events to Jonathan Edwards' adaptation of the analogic character of typology to his imagistic views of nature, the structure of the type-antitype construct pervades nearly all aspects of Puritan thought. The purpose of this paper, then, is to trace the development of the principles of typological exegesis from the New Testament through the early Greek and Latin Fathers to the works of Tyndale, Luther, and Calvin, indicating the complexity of the exegetical traditions which inform Puritan typology.

Typology proper begins with the work of the authors of the New Testament books. As with much of Christian thought, however, certain Jewish and Greek traditions contributed to the framework of the typological approach. Until the fourth century, there was no clearly established New Testament canon; 'scripture' meant the Old Testament, particularly the Greek version, the Septuagint. The development of any typology meant, then, that the identification of the type depended upon Hebrew Scripture and the Messianic traditions of prophecy. One of the major characteristics of the numerous rabbinical commentaries was the futuristic character of Messianic prophecy. A new Messiah would come; there would be a new and eternal House of God, superior to Solomon's Temple; there would be a new Exodus, a new Jerusalem, a new and eternal covenant, and the final deliverance of God's people from their enemies. For the early Christian ministers and the authors of the New Testament, ready at hand lay a Jewish method of interpretation which implied that an historical event would find its fulfillment in the future, a 'greater than David would come.' Such visionary dreams of the glorious age of a New Israel were also a part of Jewish liturgical materials, in addition to the traditions of prophecy, further extending the habit of mind which saw history as a series of integrated steps culminating in a grand, triumphant design.

In addition to the traditions of prophecy and liturgy, Jewish and Hellenistic allegorical habits also contributed to the development of typological exegesis. Homeric studies of pagan texts had introduced an allegorical method of reading certain passages in the epics which scholars felt were unworthy of Homer, or which required allegorical readings to discover their true meanings. Hermeneuticists are generally agreed that Alexandrian Jews adopted many of the pagan techniques in their exposition of unclear or immoral passages of the Hebrew Scriptures. The leading Jewish scholar whose allegorical interpretations most influenced the subsequent tradition of Christian exegesis was Philo of Alexandria (ca. 20 B.C.– 40 A.D.), who represents the culmination of these traditions in Jewish thought.[5] Typology in the canonical authors of the New Testament is relatively limited in scope; Philo influenced none of the New Testament writers, except perhaps the author of the Epistle to the Hebrews.[6] But through the influence which he had on Origen, and Origen's subsequent authority in medieval exegesis, Philonian allegory was extended throughout the Middle Ages.

What had originally been a method of explaining unclear passages, justifying anthropomorphic descriptions of God, and relieving scripture of the charges of immorality in a relatively few places, Philo applies indiscriminately to all of scripture. He did not deny that scripture had a literal and historical meaning; occasionally his commentary on specific passages begins with an exposition of the literal meaning of the text, using a standard formula to indicate the movement to an allegorical reading: 'This is the literal meaning. But as for the deeper meaning. . . .' The literal meaning is not unrelated to the allegorical meaning, but, as Philo commonly phrases it, only as the body is related to the soul, or the shadow of truth to the reality. But 'Philo does not . . . wait for the text to present obstacles to literal interpretation, or suggestions at a hidden meaning

---

5. For a discussion of Philonian exegesis, see Sidney G. Sowers, *The Hermeneutics of Philo and Hebrews: A Comparison of the Interpretation of the Old Testament in Philo Judaeus and the Epistle to the Hebrews*, Basel Studies of Theology, No. 1 (Zurich, 1965).

6. *Ibid.*, p. 62.

before he allegorizes it.'[7] Individuals in the Old Testament are taken as personifications of abstractions—Moses is intelligence, Aaron speech, Enoch repentance, Noah righteousness, Abraham is virtue acquired by learning, and so on. Philo's discussion of the 'deeper meaning' of the furniture of Solomon's Temple indicates his allegorical methods. The Temple Court, he notes, represents 'the objects of sense . . . , the Sanctuary, the objects of thought. . . . The five pillars of the porch indicate the senses which have relations both outwards and inwards. The fourfold fabric of the veil [indicates] the four elements, and . . . the seven lamps of the Candlestick . . . the planets with the Sun in the midst.'[8] In essence, Philo's methods discard the historical context of the Scripture, focusing upon the 'under-senses' of the text. Philo notes, for example, that there was 'probably . . . an actual man called Samuel; but we conceive of the Samuel of the scripture, not as a living compound . . . , but as a mind which rejoices in the service and worship of God and that only.'[9] As Beryl Smalley comments: 'The abstraction which Samuel signifies is more real . . . than the historical Samuel'; in Philo's approach to scripture, 'the distinction between reality and imagery is melted' (p. 3).

Although many of Philo's allegorical interpretations are incorporated in the allegorical readings of the Church Fathers, he is not a typologist. Even the limited 'typology' of the Jewish traditions of Messianic prophecy has only a minor place in Philo's approach to the Hebrew Scriptures. Moreover, his allegorical readings are 'essentially distinct from Christian typology, which always implies that the two events, promise and fulfillment, have taken place in time as real, historical facts.'[10] Yet, Philo's 'two-level' approach to

7. Ibid., p. 26.

8. Cited in Brooke Foss Westcott, The Epistle to the Hebrews (London, 1892), p. 239.

9. Cited in Beryl Smalley, The Study of the Bible in the Middle Ages (Oxford, 1941), p. 3.

10. Johan Chydenius, 'The Typological Problem in Dante: A Study in the History of Medieval Ideas,' Commentationes Humanarum Litterarum, Societas Scientiarum Fennica, No. 1 (Helsingfors, 1958), XXV, 23.

scripture was adopted by the earliest Christian apologists; further, Philonic allegory, combined with Alexandrian principles of exegesis, dominated Patristic interpretations for over 1000 years. Although there were several Fathers (Diodorus, Theodore, Chrysostom, and others) who denounced the allegorical methods of Philo —and Origen—and insisted on a literal reading of scripture, by the end of the fifth century, allegorical exegesis dominated Patristic hermeneutics.

Philo's significance to the early development of typology, however, is best seen in relation to the typology of the New Testament authors. Typology occupies a relatively limited place in the New Testament because the primary concern of the canonical authors is Christological: the acts and person of Christ provide the substance of their message, and typology is only of secondary importance. Christ's own references to his typological significance are few and occur mostly in Matthew, the Gospel most clearly designed to appeal to Jewish readers. In Matthew 12:40, for example, Christ says: 'For as Jonas was three days and three nights in the whale's belly; so shall the Son of man be three days and three nights in the heart of the earth.' In the same context, he refers to Solomon, saying 'a greater than Solomon is here.' In addition to the specific parallels which Christ draws, Matthew characterizes Christ as fulfilling certain promises of the Old Testament; the infant Jesus, for example, is taken to Egypt so that the prophecy of Hosea, 'Out of Egypt I have called my son,' might be fulfilled. Neither Mark nor Luke refers explicitly to Christ's fulfillment of Old Testament prophecies, and in John's Gospel, only one mention is made of Christ's typological significance: 'And as Moses lifted up the serpent in the wilderness, even so must the Son of man be lifted up ...' (3:14). Although the term *typos* is not used, by associating the person and work of Jesus with events and persons in the Old Testament, Matthew and John represent an intermediate stage between the prophecies of the Old Testament and the fuller typological readings of St. Paul and the author of Hebrews.

St. Paul uses various terms to describe the typological event: in Gal. 4:22–24, for example, he interprets the fact that Abraham had two wives as an *allegoroumena* of the two covenants; in I Cor. 10:11, he refers to certain events in the Old Testament as *skia* or 'shadows' of the reality that came in Christ. In the same context, however, Paul first uses the term which indicates an event which adumbrates another event—*typos:*

> . . . *I would not that ye should be ignorant, how that all our fathers were under the cloud, and all passed through the sea;*
> *And were all baptized unto Moses in the cloud and in the sea;*
> *And did all eat the same spiritual meat;*
> *And did all drink the same spiritual drink: for they drank of that spiritual Rock that followed them: and that Rock was Christ.* . . .
> *Now all these things happened unto them for ensamples* [typoi]; *and they are written for our admonition.* . . . (*I Cor.* 10:1–4, 11)

He also uses the same term in Rom. 5:14 with the same meaning: 'Nevertheless, death reigned from Adam to Moses . . . who is the figure [*typos*] of him that was to come.' But the New Testament writer who assigns the most importance to typological interpretation is the author of the Epistle to the Hebrews. In fact, the Epistle is founded upon typology, for the writer's purpose is to demonstrate to a Jewish audience that the men and institutions of the Old Covenant have been excelled and abolished by the New. The terminology is not consistent, using *skia, hypodeigma* (pattern), *parabole*, as well as *typos* to describe the historical event in the Old Testament, although, as the context makes clear, the various terms are synonymous.

Although the references to typology in the Gospels and Epistles indicate that the terminology for describing the typical event has not been completely established, the basic concepts of typology are clearly illustrated. Writing before there is any New Testament canon, the authors view the Old Testament in the light of divine history. The Hebrew Scriptures, they believe, are not simply the sacred books of the Jewish people, and, as such, to be read in reference to that faith alone; they are the records of God's dealings with his people, and in these relationships, the advent of his divine Son is foreshadowed. To the New Testament authors, typological exegesis is a method of reading history; it is centrally rooted in history itself. Even in the limited typological exegesis of New Testament authors, however, are the seeds of a more individualistic approach to scripture; for, divorced from the literal sense and modified by the allegorical methods of Philo and hermeneutic principles of Origen, the typology of Old Testament history is transformed into the relatively subjective allegorical interpretations of Origen and the Alexandrian school of exegetes.[11]

The fact that 'Origen divided the interpretation of Scripture into three senses is almost as well known as the fact that Caesar divided Gaul into three parts.'[12] Origen does not deny that there is a literal sense of scripture; like Philo, however, Origen rarely comments upon the literal level. He asserts that there are three 'graduated' (*teleois*) levels; of these, the literal is the least important. In connection with his extensive production of Homilies, Origen develops a second, higher level of interpretation, which he calls 'moral' exegesis. And finally, for those who have been endowed by God with a special gift of grace, there is a 'spiritual' or 'mystical' level. Origen supports his threefold schema with citations from the New Testament. In II Cor. 3:6, for example, Paul writes that 'the letter killeth, but the Spirit giveth life'; in Eph. 5:32, he speaks of Christ's relation to the church as a bridegroom's relation to his bride, and declares that this is a 'great mystery.' In addition, Origen frequently cites Prov. 22:20, where the mistranslated verse in the Septuagint,

11. The development of allegorical interpretations between Philo and Origen may be seen in the anonymous *The Epistle of Barnabas* (*The Apostolic Fathers*, trans. Edgar J. Goodspeed, New York, 1950), and in Justin Martyr, *Dialogue with Trypho*. With regard to my discussion of Pauline typology, above, it should be noted that there are several other, less explicit, typological references in the Gospels and Epistles; these, however, ordinarily do not employ the terminology of typology, but of Hebrew prophecy. Yet, quite early in Christian interpretation, such passages as John 6: 47–50, are incorporated in typological interpretations:

Verily, verily, I say unto you, He that believeth on me hath everlasting life.
I am that bread of life.
Your fathers did eat manna in the wilderness, and are dead.
This is the bread which cometh down from heaven, that a man may eat thereof, and not die.

12. R. P. C. Hanson, *Allegory and Event: A Study of the Sources and Significance of Origen's Interpretation of Scripture* (Richmond, Virginia, 1959), p. 235.

'Have I not written unto thee a triple way?', implies a threefold
scriptural signification.[13] In addition to adducing scripture to vali-
date his textual approach, Origen, directly influenced by Philo's
tripartite division of man into body, soul, and spirit (which Philo
acquired from the Neo-Platonism of the Alexandrian interpreters),
accepts the Greek concept of the faculties as a testimony from the
Hellenistic traditions to the legitimacy of a multi-level reading of
scripture. In the *Homily on Leviticus*, for example, Origen comments:

*The words of Scripture should be printed in the soul in one of three
ways. The uneducated should be edified by the letter itself, by what
we call the obvious meaning. People at a higher level should find
edification for their souls. The perfect should be edified by the spiritual Law, as it contains the shadow of the blessings to come. Man
is composed of body, soul and spirit, and the structure of Scripture
has been planned by God for man's salvation in the same way.*[14]

It would be incorrect to say that Origen completely abandons
traditional Christian typology in developing the moral and spiritual
levels of interpretation; remnants of the kind of typology practiced
by the canonical authors are retained in numerous exegetical passages. But in his *Commentary on John*, and in other passages as
well, Origen asserts that with the coming of Christ, types had been
done away with; though they still might foster the faith of the beginning Christian, they had in fact lost their significance to the
mature believer. Given this assumption, as Hanson notes, it is quite
simple for Origen to ignore the 'fairly broad and recognizable path
of traditional Christian typology . . . [and] indulge in an allegory of
a basically Philonic, Hellenistic' character (p. 253).

Origen's threefold level of interpretation and his subordination
of the typology of the New Testament to his bent for allegory can
best be illustrated by one of the earliest baptismal type-antitype
identifications. In I Pet. 3:20–21, Noah's sojourn in the ark is iden-

13. Hanson, p. 236. Ironically, however, the Septuagint translation of the
Hebrew incorrectly renders the original, which, properly translated, reads,
'Have I not written unto thee excellent things.'

14. Cited in Jean Daniélou, *Origen* (New York, 1955), p. 188.

tified as a type of Christian baptism: '. . . God waited in the days of
Noah, while the ark was a preparing, wherein [a] few . . . were saved
by water. The like *typos* whereunto even baptism doth also now
save us.' Because the gnostics, particularly the disciples of Marcion, had questioned the credibility of the Noah account, Origen is forced to defend the historicity of the text more fully than
he ordinarily does. The story of the ark is, Origen asserts, literally
true; there was a real ark which did once float upon the waters. But
he immediately adds that the 'truer'. meaning of the account lies
in its spiritual import: '. . . we call upon him who alone can lift the
veil in our reading of the Old Testament, [and] we will try to see
what this building of the ark contains for our spiritual profit.'[15]
Allegorically speaking, Origen notes, the Flood 'is an image of the
true and final end of this world'; as Noah was instructed to bring
into the ark various animals, so the true Noah, 'Our Lord Jesus
Christ, is told by his Father . . . to construct an ark of measurement
full of heavenly *sacramentis*' (pp. 105–06), and to people it with
'those who are saved through the Church.' Because the animals
were divided among the various compartments, thus signifying various degrees of perfection, 'this shows that in the Church also,
though all share the same faith and are washed by the same baptism, all do not equally advance and each one remains in his own
class' (p. 107). In interpreting the extended description of the
measurements of the ark, Origen moves beyond the relatively
simple moral lessons which dominate the first part of his analysis.
One example will suffice to indicate the tenor of this rather lengthy
passage. The length of the ark was 300 cubits, uniting, according to
Origen, the mystical numbers of 100 and three. The number 100
indicates fullness and

*contains the mystery of the totality of the Spiritual creation, as we
read in the Gospel, when it is said that a man have a hundred sheep
and losing one of them left the ninety-nine others and went to seek
the lost one. . . . [However,] this 'hundredth,' the fullness of Spiritual creation, does not subsist of itself, but proceeds from the Trinity and receives from the Father, through the Son and Holy Spirit,*

15. This quotation and the ones from the *Second Homily* which follow are
cited in Daniélou, and page numbers refer to his text (p. 105).

the length of life, that is the grace of immortality; it is because of this multiplied by three, so that having fallen, from 'hundred' through ignorance, it is restored in the three hundred by the knowledge of the Trinity (p. 109).

Origen further interprets the remaining dimensions of the ark and labels his analysis a penetration of the 'mystical' sense. 'The ark,' he asserts, 'is the faithful soul. It should be coated with bitumen within and without, that is, perfect in knowledge and works.' The 'clean' animals are 'memory, culture, understanding, reflexion and judgment upon what we read'; the 'unclean' animals are 'desire and anger' (p. 110). Further, the clean animals also signify the seven powers of the soul (the five senses, speech, and the generative faculty); the unclean animals are the ill uses that man can make of the powers of the soul.

Even though a typological identification provides the point of departure for Origen's interpretation, this is not typology. 'The type exists in history and is factual,' as Perry Miller notes in another context. 'By contrast, the allegory, the simile, the metaphor have been made according to the fancy of men, and they mean whatever the brain of the begetter is pleased they should mean.'[16] Or, as Samuel Mather puts it: 'It is not safe for Men to form *Allegories* out of their own Fancies. . . .'[17] Yet, in Origen's use of the typical event, the framework for future expositors is established; the 'typology' of Origen is the typology of the Latin Fathers, with relatively few modifications, from Augustine to Aquinas: 'to write a history of Origenist influence on the west,' Miss Smalley notes, 'would be tantamount to writing a history of western exegesis' (p. 14). Types continue to appear, of course, in the works of succeeding commentators, particularly in relation to the literal sense. In general, however, the typological reading is allotted only a minor role in such exegesis; further, when related to the 'higher' senses of scripture, it is ordinarily subordinated to the 'spiritual' interpretation or so completely absorbed in it, that, in fact, typology ceases to exist, in the historical New Testament pattern at any rate.

16. *Images or Shadows*, p. 4.

17. *The Figures or Types*, p. 129.

In his interpretation of the Flood, Origen touches on one aspect ('an image of the . . . final end of this world') which, although not developed, anticipates the fourth level of interpretation which will be partially systematized 150 years later by St. Jerome and St. Augustine, and codified in the fifth century by John Cassian: 'anagogical.' Although not too systematic, Jerome generally adopts Origen's threefold division, citing the same texts which Origen uses to support the threefold approach. Yet Jerome makes two changes in Origen's system. First, Jerome introduces the term *tropologiam* which had been used by Origen about allegorical and typological interpretation in general; with Jerome it assumes the exclusive meaning of moral signification. Moreover, in the *Second Commentary on Amos* Jerome introduces an additional level of meaning which was to assume later the restricted meaning of anagogical: 'We must interpret the sacred Scriptures first, according to the letter . . . , according to allegory . . . , [and] according to the bliss of things to come.'[18] The eschatological implications of the 'bliss of things to come' anticipates, as does Origen's interpretation of the Flood as an image of the end of the world, the anagogical level of interpretation. Jerome's influence on typological exegesis was slight, for from Origen he inherited a fairly well-established tradition which had already assigned typology to a minor role in scriptural interpretation. Further, as Wolfson makes clear, 'Jerome believed that with the coming of Christ only the moral commands of the Old Testament . . . were still to be obeyed . . .' (p. 67). Hence, in many cases the type-antitype construct testified only to the predictive character of the Old Testament; it might also be related to the moral and allegorical senses, but only occasionally, and then peripherally.

Augustine was even less systematic in his exegesis than Jerome, although Augustine is often mistakenly identified as the exclusive author of the fourfold sense of interpretation. Augustine 'favours fourfold classifications of various kinds.'[19] In several instances, he speaks of a fourfold method identical to the one Jerome presents in

18. Harry Austryn Wolfson, *The Philosophy of the Church Fathers* (Cambridge, 1964), I, 66.

19. Wolfson, p. 68.

the *Second Commentary on Amos;* in *De Utilitate Credendi,* however, Augustine says that 'all Scripture . . . is handed down fourfold . . . , according to history, according to aetiology, according to analogy, [and] according to allegory.'[20] And in *De Vera Religione,* as Wolfson notes, Augustine enumerates, in addition to the literal sense, four kinds of allegory: the allegory of history (*historiae*), the allegory of facts (*facti*), the allegory of discourse (*sermonis*), and the allegory of rites (*sacramenti*) (p. 69). Erich Auerbach is misleading when he asserts that Augustine 'emphatically rejected the purely allegorical interpretation of the Holy Scriptures and dismissed the notion that the Old Testament was a kind of hermetic book that became intelligible only if one discarded the literal historical meaning. . . .'[21] Augustine did insist on the historicity of the literal text:

Before all things, brethren, we admonish and command you in the name of the Lord, that when you hear an exposition of the mystery of the Scriptures telling of things that took place, you believe what is read to have actually taken place as the reading narrates; lest, undermining the foundation of actuality, you seek as it were to build in the air.[22]

Yet, Augustine's insistence, taken within the context of his debt to Origen and Jerome, and within the context of his own description of the differing allegorical senses, is not as emphatic as Auerbach implies. Moreover, Augustine's practice indicates that any passage which does not, from his point of view, measure up to the requirements of ·the Faith, can be interpreted according to a 'deeper' meaning. In trying to explain the various immoral episodes in Samson's life, for example, Augustine, following Origen and Jerome, discards the literal meaning of the text. Samson lied to his friends; he also lay with a harlot. Such actions are hard to reconcile with Samson's role as a prefiguration of Christ. Augustine notes, how-

20. Cited in Wolfson, p. 68.

21. Erich Auerbach, *Scenes from the Drama of European Literature* (New York, 1959), p. 39.

22. Cited in Auerbach, p. 39.

ever, that 'the justice of this man lies hidden in the depths.' Since
it is written that 'he submitted to the charms of women and that
he went to a harlot, his righteousness must indeed appear dubious
to those who are only *partially aware of the secrets of the truth.'*[23]
Augustine then discards the literal sense, using a standard formula
which he commonly applies in such cases: 'We can say that in the
Old Testament such things were neither criminal nor worthy of
censure, for whatever was done or said was prophecy.'

Augustine's exegetical principles are directly traceable to Jerome
as his are traceable to Origen. In the light of previous typological
identifications, Augustine's *Contra Faustum* and his various incidental typological interpretations are largely a summary of the
statements of previous exegetes. Although the fourfold system
generally governs Augustine's exegesis, the system which dominated the next 1000 years of biblical exegesis was not formalized by
either Jerome or Augustine. John Cassian is apparently the first
Patristic commentator to append to the work of Jerome and Augustine a complete terminology.

The first sense he [Cassian] terms historia, *employing an expression
which had been used in reference to the literal sense ever since
Origen. The second, the moral sense, which had already been discerned by Origen, Cassian calls* tropologia, *using a term that was
given this signification by Jerome. The third sense . . . is called*
allegoria *by Cassian, who in this follows the example of Jerome.
Finally, the fourth sense is that which refers to eternal things. It
had first been discerned by Origen, and later by Jerome. Now
Cassian gives it its own name, that of* anagoge.[24]

In a climate such as this, the relatively limited use of the typology
of the New Testament could not flourish as a distinct means of
exegesis; types became so completely subordinated to the more

23. 'On Samson: Judges 13–16,' *Selected Sermons of St. Augustine,* trans.
Quincy Howe, Jr. (New York, 1966), pp. 118 ff. Italics added.

24. Chydenius, p. 34. The same point is made by Harry Caplan, 'The Four
Senses of Scriptural Interpretation and the Mediaeval Theory of Preaching,'
Speculum, IV (July, 1929), 285–86.

spiritual levels of interpretation that the basic distinctions between typology and allegory were no longer observed. In its general framework, then, the principles of typological exegesis reflected in Augustine are those of the Middle Ages.

It should be noted, however, that a number of early Church Fathers were quite displeased—as the Puritans were later to be—with the allegorical interpretations associated with Origen and the School of Alexandria. In the first decade of the fourth century, the 'school' at Antioch was 'founded . . . in direct opposition to the excesses and fantasies of the allegorical method of Origen. . . .'[25] St. Basil, called the 'Father of Orthodoxy,' was a member of the Council which condemned Origen as an heretic; he makes clear in his commentaries on Genesis, *In Hexameron*, that allegory has no place in scriptural interpretation:

> *I know the laws of allegory, though not from my own works but the works of others. Some preachers do not concede the ordinary sense of the Scriptures. They will not call water water, but something else. They interpret a plant or fish as their fancy wishes. They change the nature of the reptiles and wild beasts to fit their allegories, like those who explain . . . dreams to suit their own ends. When I hear the word grass, I understand that grass is meant.*[26]

Such Fathers as Basil, Cyril of Jerusalem, Eusebius, Chrysostom, and others insist upon the historicity of the Old Testament and the necessity of avoiding allegorical 'fancies,' focusing instead on the literal and typological meaning of the text. Chrysostom, the last major exponent of the Antiochene principles, attempted to establish general principles of typological exegesis which would combat the extravagances of Alexandrian allegory. Because all commentators after Christ are in possession of the 'reality,' Chrysostom insists that there is the temptation to read into the type the full details which can only be ascertained by a knowledge of the anti-

---

25. Johannes Quasten, *Patrology: The Golden Age of Greek Patristic Literature, From the Council of Nicaea to the Council of Chalcedon* (Westminster, Maryland, 1963), III, 121.

26. Cited in Quasten, II, 217.

type. But the type, he asserts, does not possess 'all the exactness of the reality';[27] ignoring this principle, he argues, leads to the exegetical subjectivism of Alexandrian allegory.

The conflict between the exegetical schools of Antioch and Alexandria was resolved in the fifth century, for the two schools could not long exist together. Although there was broad agreement on certain aspects of traditional exegesis, the proponents of the different schools were themselves convinced of an irreconcilable contradiction in their approaches:

At Antioch the object was to find in Holy Writ its most obvious meaning; at . . . Alexandria the search was for figures of Christ. The one side accused allegory of destroying the value of the Bible . . . , of travestying it into mythological fable; the other dubbed 'carnal' all who clung to the letter. . . . Origen discovers types not just in certain episodes, but in every detail of the inspired words. Each line is filled with mystery. On the other hand Antioch made it a fundamental principle to see figures of Christ just occasionally, not always, in the Old Testament. . . . Types were the exception, not the rule; the Incarnation was everywhere prepared, but not everywhere prefigured.[28]

The development of the fourfold levels of interpretation presupposed a much broader approach than the Antiochenes could accept. Further, allegory encouraged the tendency for exegesis to be used as a support for dogma. Church Tradition was gradually being formed in the third and fourth centuries, based in large part on the sacramenti of the Bible; and the rationalistic tendencies of the Antiochenes were directly opposed to its development. Two individuals ultimately contributed to the disrepute of the School of Antioch. One of the first pupils of Lucian, one of the founders of the school, was Arius. The rationalistic tendencies of the school, exaggerated in Arius' teaching, led to the disapproval of the Church councils, and, in the Council of Nicaea, to the designation of Arianism as heresy. The second person was Augustine.

27. Cited in Jean Daniélou, *From Shadows to Reality: Studies in the Biblical Typology of the Fathers* (Westminster, Maryland, 1960), p. 191.

28. Quasten, II, 122.

Augustine viewed himself as a reconciler between the two traditions; as a matter of fact, however, his exegetical principals predisposed him to the Origenistic approach and his actual practice demonstrates his commitment to it. In *The City of God*, Augustine appears to support a position which would encompass the principles of both schools:

No one ought to suppose . . . that these things were written for no purpose, or that we should study only the historical truth, apart from any allegorical meanings; or, on the contrary, that there are only allegories, and that there were no such facts at all, or that, whether it be so or no, there is here no prophecy of the church.

His next sentence, however, indicates that the real significance of scripture lies beyond 'bare historical facts':

For what right-minded man will contend that books so religiously preserved during thousands of years, and transmitted by so orderly a succession, were written without an object, or that only the bare historical facts are to be considered when we read them.[29]

The purpose for which Scripture was written, the object which underlies it, is the indication of the 'prophecy of the church.' In 'On Christian Doctrine,' Augustine again returns to the same points:

When what is said figuratively is taken as if it were said literally, it is understood in a carnal manner. And nothing is more fittingly called the death of the soul than when that in it which raises it above the brutes, the intelligence, namely, is put in subjection to the flesh by a blind adherence to the letter.[30]

Such a principle is, as Chrysostom makes clear, inimical to typology, for the relatively disparaging attitude toward the literal sense provides less precise exegetes an open license for subjective interpretation. It is true that Augustine insisted that allegorical readings

29. 'The City of God' in *The Nicene and Post-Nicene Fathers*, ed. Philip Schaff (Grand Rapids, Michigan, 1956), II, 307.

30. 'On Christian Doctrine,' in *The Nicene and Post-Nicene Fathers*, II, 559.

should be based on the literal sense; but when it 'came to practical application, he was swayed by the thought of his times. . . . He often went too far, almost to the point of panallegorism.'[31] In the process, as in Jerome and Origen's practice, typology is identified with a 'blind adherence to the letter,' and is subordinated to more 'spiritual readings' so much as to become a very minor mode of exegesis. Auerbach is incorrect when he asserts that 'the only reason [*typos*] fell behind *figura* is that it was a foreign word' (p. 48). *Typos* is the term invariably used in the interpretations of the school of Antioch, for its connotations were those of the *koiné* Greek of the New Testament. *Figura* (the term which Augustine normally uses), as Auerbach correctly observes, 'more or less consciously evoked all the notions involved in its [classical] history' (p. 48). One of the 'notions' the term evokes is Greek allegorism, and subsequently the allegory of Philo, Origen, Jerome, and Augustine.

Allegorical readings, based on Alexandrian precepts, dominate medieval exegesis. Ordinarily, the type provides only the original identification and has little relationship to the extensive allegorical interpretations; before Protestant typology could develop, therefore, it was necessary to re-establish the primacy of the literal sense, eliminating the accrued interpretations of Patristic allegory which had become a major part of Church Tradition. The rehabilitation of New Testament typology was, perhaps, only a by-product of the more central concerns of the Reformation. Yet, when the Reformers denied the validity of the Church and its Councils, when they insisted on a faith founded upon *Scriptura sacra* alone, and when the vernacular translations of the Bible which were deemed necessary to the Protestant cause led exegetes back to the original Greek and Hebrew texts, it was inevitable that typological exegisis would find its way into the Reformers' treatises. Moreover, once the distinction between typology and Alexandrian allegory had been re-established, for a brief time typology became almost as important a method of biblical exegesis as medieval allegory had been to the Scholastics.

31. A. D. R. Polman, *The Word of God According to St. Augustine* (London, 1961), p. 96.

In assessing the role which typology plays in the works of the Reformers, Perry Miller asserts that 'the great Protestant reformers had been very explicit in the condemnation of the typological method along with every other variant of the allegorical.' Moreover, he continues, 'the English Reformers . . . were furiously hostile to all typological speculations.' As an example of this 'hostility,' Miller cites Tyndale's statement in *The Obedience of a Christian Man*: 'Such allegory proveth nothing, it is a mere simile. God is a Spirit, and all His words are spiritual, and his literal sense is spiritual.'[32] Miller's statements are incorrect and his citation of what he takes to be Tyndale's exegetical principles is misleading; for unlike Miller, Tyndale clearly distinguishes between Patristic allegory and typology, accepting the typology of the New Testament, and recognizing the use of allegory in the Scriptures themselves and in the interpretation of certain passages. Moreover, these distinctions occur in the same context as Miller's citation, as well as in Tyndale's numerous prefaces to his translations and in other essays. By the fifteenth century, from Tyndale's point of view, the allegorizing of the Fathers as represented in the glosses had obscured and distorted the scriptural text:

The greatest cause of . . . captivity and the decay of the faith, and this blindness wherein we now are, sprang first of allegories. Origen and the doctors of his time drew all the scripture unto allegories whose ensample they that came after followed so long, till they at last forgot the order and process of the text, supposing that the scripture served but to feign allegories upon; insomuch that twenty doctors expound one text twenty ways. . . . Then came our sophisters with their anagogical and chopological sense, and with an anti-

32. Perry Miller, *Roger Williams*, pp. 35–36. Miller's citation from *The Obedience* is incorrect; the first sentence ('Such allegory proveth nothing, it is a mere simile') does not occur in the same context as the second, but two pages earlier in relation to a fictitious allegory which Tyndale presents as an example of the methods of Patristic allegorizing. See *The Work of William Tyndale*, ed. G. E. Duffield, The Courtenay Library of Reformation Classics (Appleford, Berkshire, 1964), I, 345. Subsequent citations refer to Vol. I of this edition.

theme of half an inch, out of which some of them draw a thread of
nine days long (p. 343).

In contrast to indiscriminate allegorizing, Tyndale insists that because 'allegories prove nothing . . . they are to be used soberly and
seldom, and only where the text offereth thee an allegory' (p. 343).
As he makes quite clear, allegories divorced from the literal sense
do not prove anything; when they are justified by the literal sense,
however, when allegories alone are not presented as a sole basis for
doctrinal proof, then 'doth the literal sense prove the allegory, and
bear it, as the foundation beareth a house' (p. 343). Therefore, all
interpretations—including typological and allegorical—must arise
from the literal sense and be proved by it.

Tyndale does not attack allegory per se; he attacks the allegorizing of the Church Fathers which discards the literal sense in favor
of a spiritual reading. Neither in *The Obedience* itself, from which
Miller quotes, nor in any other work does Tyndale condemn allegory itself, but the use to which allegory had been put in the interpretations of the Church Fathers; moreover, his condemnations
invariably appear in relation to the *glossia* in general or to some
specific interpreter.[33] And it is in *The Obedience* that Tyndale
makes clear that allegories and 'similitudes' are to be used when
'we preach, [or] when we expound the scripture.' Only the literal
text may be used as doctrinal proof, but figurative language leads to
a clearer understanding of the literal sense:

. . . similitudes prove nothing, but are made to express more plainly
that which is contained in scripture, and to lead thee into the spir-
itual understanding of the text: as the similitude of matrimony is

33. See, for example, the prologue to his translation of the New Testament,
'A Pathway into the Holy Scripture': '. . . our great pillars of holy church
. . . have nailed a veil of false Glosses on Moses's face' (p. 24); the preface
to Genesis: '. . . in times past [they] were wont to look on no more scripture
than they found in their Duns . . .' (p. 31); the preface to Jonah where
glosses are called 'juggling hypocrisy' and 'juggling allegories' (pp. 86, 89);
the prologue to the First Epistle of St. John: the Scriptures are corrupted
with a 'leaven of false glosses . . .' (p. 173); the prologue to the Exposition
of Matthew V, VI, VII: '. . . by such glosses . . . have we Christians lost
Christ . . .' (p. 183); and so on.

*taken to express the marriage that is between Christ and our souls,
and what exceeding mercy we have there, whereof all the scriptures
make mention. . . . That preacher therefore, that bringeth a naked
similitude to prove that which is contained in no text of scripture,
nor followeth of a text, count a deceiver . . . (p. 348).*

Yet Tyndale clearly distinguishes between the allegories of men
and those contained in the Scripture; to understand scriptural allegories is to understand the literal sense even though it is phrased in
figurative language:

*Thou shalt understand . . . that the scripture hath but one sense,
which is the literal. And that literal sense is the root and ground of
all, and the anchor that never faileth, whereunto if thou cleave,
thou canst never err or go out of the way. And if thou leave the
literal sense, thou canst not but go out of the way. Neverthelater
[emphasis added], the scripture useth proverbs, similitudes, riddles, or allegories, as all other speeches do; but that which the prov-
erb, similitude, riddle, or allegory signifieth, is ever the literal sense,
which thou must seek out diligently . . . (p. 340).*

Tyndale's position is generally the position of Luther and Calvin—
and the Puritans: Alexandrian allegorical interpretations are the
'fancies' of men; some texts, however, necessitate an allegorical
reading; although figurative, allegory elucidates the literal sense;
moreover, scripture itself utilizes similitudes and allegories to clarify the literal sense. And in Tyndale's work, 'types' are similitudes.

   Neither in his translations nor in the prefaces added later does
Tyndale use the term *typos* or any of its cognates; because of the
excesses of medieval allegory, it seems clear that Tyndale wished to
avoid any of the medieval connotations associated with a theory of
types. In contrasting the promises of the Old Law with its fulfillment in Christ, he uses the awkward term 'fore-rehearsed' to express the typical relationship between the testaments.[34] In 'A Pathway into the Holy Scripture' he also uses the phrase 'promises rehearsed' in a typological sense:

When Christ is thuswise preached, and the promises rehearsed,

34. See 'A Pathway into the Holy Scripture,' p. 15.

which are contained in the prophets, in the psalms, and in divers places of the five books of Moses . . . , then the hearts of them which are elect and chosen begin to wax soft and melt at the bounteous mercy of God . . . (p. 15).

In the 'Prologue to the Book of Leviticus,' however, Tyndale is more direct: he explains that the rites and ceremonies of the Hebrew faith are 'shadows' of the promises fulfilled in Christ; moreover, he makes explicit that these promises are expressed in 'allegories, similitudes, or examples':

. . . though sacrifices and ceremonies can be no ground or foundation to build upon; that is, though we can prove nought with them, yet when once we have found out Christ and his mysteries, then we may borrow figures, that is to say allegories, similitudes, or examples, to open Christ, and the secrets of God hid in Christ. . . . For similitudes have more virtue and power with them than bare words, and lead a man's wits farther into the pith and marrow and spiritual understanding of the thing, than all the words that can be imagined (p. 60).

In relation to the prefigurations of Christ in the Old Testament, Tyndale makes clear that 'similitudes' or 'examples' (the two terms he uses in his translations as a substitute for typos) lead one further into the 'marrow of sacred divinity' than 'bare words' alone. Although some types are unclear in their meaning and only 'shadow forth' Christ, some are as clear as the 'light of broad day':

. . . all the ceremonies and sacrifices have, as it were, a star-light of Christ, yet some there be that have, as it were, the light of the broad day . . . and express him, and the virtue of his death so plainly, as if we should play his passion on a scaffold, or in a stage-play, openly before the eyes of the people; as the scape-goat, the brasen serpent, the ox burnt without the host, the passover lamb, &c: insomuch that I am fully persuaded, and cannot but believe, that God had shewed Moses the secrets of Christ, and the very manner of his death beforehand. . . . And I believe also that the prophets, which followed Moses to confirm his prophecies, and to maintain his doctrine unto Christ's coming, were moved by such things to search farther of Christ's secrets . . . (p. 60).

The scapegoat, brazen serpent, sacrificial ox and lamb are, of course, traditional typological identifications of the Passion; as such, they testify to the typological unity of the two testaments, and to the necessity of setting the 'promises rehearsed' before the eyes of the people. Such type-antitype identifications are not unusual in Tyndale's writing, particularly when one recognizes that he often uses the term 'ensample' as a substitute for type.[35]

Luther's use of typology—and allegory—is far more extensive than Tyndale's,[36] and his discussion of his early predilection for allegorical readings indicates how deeply embedded in his thought typological exegesis is. In the 'Lectures on Genesis,' Luther comments on his earlier captivation by allegorical renderings and enunciates his 'Protestant' hermeneutic principles. After presenting his interpretation of the first three chapters of Genesis, Luther asserts that he has

created all these facts in their historical meaning, which is their

35. In discussing Tyndale's attitude toward typology, I have limited my analysis to those works which deal specifically with principles of exegesis and translation, works published primarily before the development of Tyndale's theology of the 'contract.' In *A briefe declaration of the sacraments* (London, 1548), however, the dominant mode of exegesis is typological, and Tyndale presents an elaborate series of typological identifications.

36. One hesitates to belabor Miller's inaccuracies in relation to the Reformers' use of typology; yet his comments have been widely accepted and, hence, have led to a misunderstanding of the nature of Puritan typology. According to Miller, after the disciples of Bonaventure had formulated an eightfold sense of scriptural interpretation, 'Luther thought it time to call a halt and assert: "The literal sense of Scripture alone is the whole essence of faith and of Christian theology." ' Miller continues: 'Each passage, Luther declared, has one clear, definite and true sense of its own; allegories are empty speculations, "and as it were the scum of Holy Scripture" ' (*Roger Williams*, p. 35). In several places, Luther does insist that the literal sense contains the sum of faith; his exegetical principles, however, are not that simple. His comments in relation to New Testament typology are invariably favorable. Moreover, in the most obvious places, Luther defends allegory, properly used, and practices typological exegesis (the Preface to the Old Testament, for example). There are numerous, and quite obvious, places in the *Works* where Luther practices allegorical and typological interpretation. It is difficult to reconcile Miller's statements with such extensive evidence to the contrary.

real and true one. In the interpretation of Holy Scripture the main task must be to derive from it some sure and plain meaning, especially because there is such a variety of interpreters—Latin, Greek, and Hebrew too. Almost all of these not only do not concern themselves with the story but bury it and confuse it with nonsensical allegories.[37]

Luther then identifies the original sources of 'nonsensical allegories': Origen and Jerome. 'Everywhere,' he says, 'they depart from the historical account, which they call the "letter that kills" and "the flesh"; and they bestow lofty praise on the "spiritual meaning," of which they have no actual knowledge. In fact, Jerome followed Origen as his teacher' (I, 232). As the context makes clear, Luther condemns 'nonsensical allegories' which he expressly associates with the Alexandrian school of interpretation. In the same context, he characterizes Scholastic interpretations of his own time as the contemporary extension of Alexandrian allegory. He then comments upon his own earlier use of this mode:

When I was a young man, my own attempts at allegory met with fair success. It was even permissible to come up with foolish ideas, since these great teachers of the churches, such as Jerome and Origen, had at times given wide range to their imagination. . . . Augustine, too, was led astray . . . , and, especially in the instance of the Psalms, he disregards the historical sense and has recourse to allegories. They were all convinced that, especially in the historical accounts of the Old Testament, the allegories represented the spiritual meaning; but the historical account itself, or the literal sense, represented the carnal meaning (I, 232).

Luther asserts, again in relation to Alexandrian allegory, that such procedures are a 'desecration of the sacred writings,' and he recommends that beginning students of the Scriptures read the Church Fathers with discretion. As a young man, Luther continues, he lacked that discretion; hence, he was 'led astray.' He then begins to define his 'mature exegetical' principles:

37. 'Lectures on Genesis,' *Luther's Works,* ed. Jaroslav Pelikan (St. Louis, 1958), I, 231. Unless otherwise noted, subsequent references to Luther's writing are to this edition.

Ever since I began to adhere to the historical meaning, I myself have always had a strong dislike for allegories and did not make use of them unless the text itself indicated them or the interpretations could be drawn from the New Testament [emphasis added] (I, 232–33).

He then returns to his earlier captivity by the allegorical interpretations of the Origenistic mode:

But it was very difficult for me to break away from my habitual zeal for allegory; and yet I was aware that allegories were empty speculations and froth, as it were, of the Holy Scriptures. It is the historical sense alone which supplies true and sound doctrine. After this has been treated and correctly understood, then one may also employ allegories as an adornment and flowers to embellish or illuminate the account. The bare allegories, which stand in no relation to the account and do not illuminate it, should simply be disapproved as empty dreams. This is the kind which Origen and those who followed him employ (I, 233).

He then concludes:

There is no need at all for dwelling at greater length on this matter of allegory. Let this reminder suffice: that those who wish to make use of allegories, make use of those which the apostles point out and which have a sure basis in the words themselves or in the historical account (I, 234).

Luther does not condemn allegory per se, any more than Tyndale does. Luther does condemn Alexandrian allegory, yet he makes clear that allegorical interpretation is a part of the apostles' methods, that allegories are in the texts themselves, and that allegories are a part of the literal sense and historical account. Such distinctions which Luther makes in the *Commentary on Genesis* are reiterated in nearly every major work.

Unlike Tyndale, however, Luther does not insist that the literal sense is also the spiritual sense; on the contrary, Luther consistently interprets scripture according to a twofold sense: literal and spiritual. Because of its unique message, the Old Testament not only deals with the experiences of the Hebrew people but also looks for-

ward to Christ; the Old Testament 'law and way of life must therefore be seen in two ways.'[38] Luther consistently calls the two levels
of scripture the literal and spiritual meanings. In the 'Preface to the
Old Testament,' for example, Luther explains that as a history of
the Hebrew people and an expression of their faith, the Old Testament Scriptures 'are not to be despised, but diligently read'
(XXXV, 236), for the Old Testament is the 'ground and proof' of
the New and is to be 'highly regarded.' On the other hand, however, beyond the literal meaning of Old Testament events and rites
is a 'spiritual meaning' (XXXV, 247), for Moses and the prophets
'are nothing else than administrators . . . bringing everyone to
Christ through the law.' To interpret the Old Testament 'well and
confidently,' Luther asserts, one must 'set Christ before you, for he
is the man to whom it all applies, every bit of it' (XXXV, 247).
Luther expressly distinguishes his 'spiritual' reading from the allegorical interpretations of Origen and Jerome, and 'many other
distinguished people' (XXXV, 235), for such interpretations are
not based upon the literal meaning of the text and by their very
nature ignore the historicity of the Old Testament. In contrast to
this approach, Luther argues that he respects the historical experiences of the Hebrew people because in Christ the history of the
Old Testament actually reaches the goal which God had planned
for it. As a result, 'Luther can thus place the original literal meaning and the spiritual interpretation beside each other and bring
them into a vital relationship to each other through his concept of
"sign" or "type." '[39]

Luther's typological identifications are extensive; in numerous
instances, the type-antitype construct is basic to his view of the
sacraments, and typological analysis occupies a central part of his
theology.[40] In addition, throughout his writing, types are referred

38. Paul Althaus, *The Theology of Martin Luther* (Philadelphia, 1966),
p. 95. I am indebted to Althaus' discussion of Luther's hermeneutic principles.

39. Althaus, p. 97.

40. In the sacramental controversies of 1524–27, for example, Luther carefully distinguishes among the different terms which are used to explain
Christ's statement, 'This is my body.' Because of his developing theory of

to in the most casual manner, indicating the central place which typology occupies in his thought. In the early 'Lectures on Genesis,' Luther uses *typos*, *schema*, and *figura* as generally synonymous; in his later writings he ordinarily uses the terms *figure* and *type*, quite often together as if to restrict the meaning of the Latin term to its original significance in Greek. Yet Luther is not consistent, using *picture*, *example*, and *image* in the typical sense; because he clearly distinguishes between Alexandrian allegorizing and typology, he apparently sees no need for a precise terminology. Moreover, typology is so much a part of his exegesis that, regardless of which term he uses, the context makes clear that the various terms are used in a typological sense. And his assumption that 'every bit' of the Old Testament applies to Christ leads inevitably to numerous typological identifications. David is a 'type of Christ, as are Solomon, Aaron, and all the other figures of the Old Testament';[41] twenty-seven psalms are interpreted in a typical sense;[42] Melchizedek, the Red Sea, the crossing of the River Jordan, manna, water from Horeb's rock, the brazen serpent, and so on, all have typological significance.

For all his use of typology, however, Luther is not simply a medieval allegorist in the robes of a Reformer. It is true that he does not escape making typical identifications closely associated with Alex-

---

consubstantiation, Luther insists that there is a literal equation of the bread and Christ's flesh. Several of his opponents had interpreted the text to read, 'This is the *figura* of my body,' using the term to mean the 'real essence.' Luther's answer to this point indicates in a specific and concrete way his knowledge of New Testament typology and his rejection of the Alexandrian connotations of *figura*: '. . . *figura* is an obscure and ambiguous word. Of course, he [Oecolampadius, Luther's opponent] would like to interpret it to mean parable, type, or interpretative sign, just as one describes the stories in the Old Testament as figures of the New, as Adam is called a figure or type of Christ, or as a bride is called a type or figure of the Church. But *figura* in the Latin language does not mean that kind of type; the word *figura* is misused in such an instance' (Luther, *Works*, ed. Pelikan, XXXVII, 109).

41. *Luther: Early Theological Works*, ed. James Atkinson (Philadelphia, 1962), p. 335.

42. Heinrich Bornkamm, *Luther und das Alte Testament*, cited in Althaus, p. 94.

andrian allegory, for Luther knew the commentaries too well to avoid being influenced by them. It is also true, however, that he recognized and condemned the interpretations of the Alexandrians, particularly as they found their way into the works of the Scholastics. Moreover, he repeatedly insists that biblical interpreters 'should strive, so far as possible, to get one, simple, true, and grammatical meaning from the words of the text; and when we have it, then nothing prevents us from seeking figures and allegories in the text' (VIII, 146).

Like the authors of the New Testament, Luther's theology is Christological; Christ is presented in the Gospel as the culmination of the prefigurations of the Law; typology, in this sense, is the literal meaning of the Scriptures.

Tyndale's use of typology is cautious and restrained; in Luther's writing, typology is only one of numerous exegetical methods and is ordinarily incidental to the main point at issue. Without typology, however, Calvin would not be Calvin; for typology occupies a central and significant role in his theology. More emphatically than either Tyndale or Luther, Calvin insists that many passages must be interpreted typologically: 'the whole cultus of the law, taken literally and not as shadows and figures corresponding to the truth, will be utterly ridiculous.'[43] In the *Institutes*, for example, Calvin argues that the infinite majesty of God makes direct communication with him impossible; the references in the Old Testament to individuals who beheld God 'face to face' should not be taken to mean that they saw God as 'he really is,' but only 'as far as he can be beheld by mortal man.'[44] In order to reveal himself,

43. John Calvin, *Institutes of the Christian Religion*, The Library of Christian Classics, ed. John T. McNeill (Philadelphia, 1960), I, 249. All page references to the *Institutes* refer to this edition. As my citations indicate, Calvin uses 'image,' 'figure,' 'foreshadow,' 'shadow,' and 'promises' (in reference to the Old Testament) as synonymous with 'type.' In discussing the 'Peculiarities in Calvin's Exegesis,' H. Jackson Forstman calls attention to the typological meaning of these terms and notes that Calvin had a 'weakness for typology' (*Word and Spirit: Calvin's Doctrine of Biblical Authority* [Stanford, 1962], p. 106).

44. *Commentary on Ezekiel*, cited in Ronald S. Wallace, *Calvin's Doctrine of the Word and Sacrament* (Grand Rapids, Mich., 1957), p. 2. I am indebted to Wallace's excellent analysis of Calvin's doctrine of Revelation.

then, it was necessary for God to 'veil' his majesty in signs and symbols which man could comprehend. Hence, Revelation involves an original 'veiling' and necessitates a subsequent 'unveiling.' If God were only a single entity, he would forever remain hidden to the eyes of men; from the beginning, however, God planned for a Mediator between himself and man in the Old Testament: the Word of God, the second Person of the Trinity. According to Calvin, the frequent appearance of the Angel of the Lord in the Old Testament is, in reality, the record of the veiled appearance of 'God's only-begotten Son, who was afterwards manifested in the flesh. . . .'[45] In his appearance in the Old Testament, however, Christ was veiled in 'shadows,' for 'until Christ was manifested in the flesh all signs shadowed Him. . . .' God's revelation, even through the office of the Mediator in the Old Testament, was, as Calvin notes in the *Commentary on Hebrews*, by the 'circuitous course of types and figures' (p. 98). Hence, the Old Testament, far from being solely a history of the Hebrew people and a 'book of law,' is a 'book of promises' which find their realization in Christ. Calvin insists, however, that there is a substantive difference between the 'nature or quality of the promises' of the Old Testament and the promises of the New: 'the gospel points out with the finger what the law foreshadowed under types' (*Institutes*, I, 426). Therefore, Calvin warns his readers 'to remember to open up their way with [typology,] the key' to understanding the Old Testament and its relationship to the New.[46]

Calvin's extensive typological identifications are based upon his conviction that Christ is everywhere revealed in the Old Testament, not in his full glory, of course, but in 'types and shadows' which are intimations of future fulfillment. According to Calvin, all of the Old Testament represents the 'letter' of the Law; the New Testament presents the 'spirit' of the New Law. Paul's state-

---

45. 'Commentaries on the Four Last Books of Moses,' *Calvin's Commentaries* (Grand Rapids, Michigan, 1956), I, 248. Unless otherwise noted, all citations to the commentaries refer to this edition.

46. Calvin's identification of typology as the 'key' to 'open up' the Old Testament is found in the *Institutes*, Book II, p. 447. My discussion is a brief summary of the principles which Calvin develops at length in Book II of the *Institutes*.

ment that the 'letter killeth but the spirit giveth life' refers, in Calvin's view, to the essential differences between the shadowed revelations of the Old Testament and the typological reality of the New. But in order to make certain that those under the Law were continually aware of the future promises, God 'foreshadowed spiritual happiness by . . . types and symbols,' in 'figures,' and in the 'image and shadow' of the future reality. These promises, Calvin asserts, are 'mentioned almost wherever the New Testament is contrasted with the Old' (*Institutes*, I, 452–53). Hence, typology is the single most important method for interpreting the Old Testament, for types provide New Testament authors—and all Christians as well—with a 'key' to understanding the promises of Christ in the Old Testament. Moreover, as types indicate, the children of Israel did not live under the irrevocable sentence of the Law, but in continual awareness of a greater life to come. For Abraham, Jacob, Joseph, Moses, Joshua, and all of the prophets, repeatedly foreshadow the promises made manifest in the flesh: 'it was always their custom to describe through the types of their own time the truth which has been revealed by the gospel' (*Institutes*, II, 1433). Typology, then, is the handwriting of God; in its 'shadowy forms' it reveals the presence of God, as much as his presence can be revealed before the sum of all types 'became flesh and dwelt among us.'

Calvin is less severe in his condemnation of allegory than are Tyndale and Luther. He invariably condemns the excesses of Origenistic allegory, yet he often accepts the allegorical readings of 'les Docteurs anciens' if the text supports such readings. In discussing Paul's assertion that Abraham's wives are to be interpreted as an allegory of the two covenants, for example, Calvin clearly distinguishes between legitimate allegory and 'subtle frenzies':

He [Paul] says that what is here read, was written allegorically: not that he wishes all histories, indiscriminately, to be tortured to an allegorical sense, as Origen does; who, by hunting every where for allegories, corrupts the whole Scripture; and others, too, eagerly emulating his example, have extracted smoke out of light. . . . The design of Paul was, to raise the minds of the pious to consider the secret work of God, in this history; as if he had said, What Moses relates concerning the house of Abraham belongs to the spiritual kingdom of Christ; since, certainly, that house was a lively image of the Church.[47]

In this passage, and others as well, although Calvin condemns Alexandrian allegory, he accepts without question the restricted application of allegorical interpretation. Moreover, he asserts that what has been said of the house of Abraham (the Jewish nation) is a type ('lively image') of the church. On the other hand, in discussing the distinctions made in the ceremonial law between clean and unclean animals, Calvin accepts with little hesitation the allegorical interpretations of 'les Docteurs anciens' as found in the Glossa Ordinaria:

Whilst I fear that but little confidence can be placed in allegories, in which many have taken delight; so I do not find fault with, nor even refuse that which has been handed down from 'les Docteurs anciens,' viz., that by the cleaving of the hoof is signified prudence in distinguishing the mysteries of Scripture, and by the chewing of the cud serious meditation on its heavenly doctrines; although I cannot approve of the subtlety which they add, viz., that those 'rightly divide the word' who have known how to elicit mystical senses from its letter; because hence it has come to pass that they have allowed themselves in all sorts of imaginations. I therefore embrace the more simple notion, that they who only have a taste for the carnal sense, do not divide the hoof. . . . The chewing of the cud ought to follow, duly to prepare and digest the spiritual food; for many gulp down Scripture without profit. . . .[48]

It would be misleading to assert that this kind of interpretation is common in Calvin; it is equally misleading to say that he condemns out of hand either allegorical or typological readings.[49]

47. Commentary on Genesis, I, 545.

48. 'Commentaries on the Four Last Books of Moses,' II, 61–62.

49. Calvin's assumption that everything in the Old Testament foreshadows Christ occasionally leads to rather extravagant identifications. One should note, however, that unlike most of medieval allegory, Calvin's 'excesses' arise from an attempt to make sense of the literal meaning of the Hebrew rites and ceremonies. Moreover, Calvin's predicament is based upon his con-

In discussing the idea of reform in the early church, Gerhart B. Ladner suggests that

the greatest contribution, perhaps, of the Old Testament to Christian ideology of reform was through prophecy and 'typology.' The prophets not only foretold the coming of Christ, but they also are the great exemplars of all authentic reformers within the Church. . . . Furthermore, all through Christian history, typology, the sacramentum futuri, the mystery of the expectation and anticipation of Christ and the Church in the Old Testament, acted as a stimulus for further reform in the spirit of the Gospel: the sequence of creation, Incarnation and reform is a fundamental pattern in early Christian and mediaeval historical consciousness and theology of history.[50]

One cannot say with certainty whether typology was an impetus to reform or simply a by-product of the larger concerns of the Reformation. It is certain, however, that typology, isolated from Alexandrian allegory and divorced from the extravagances of medieval Scholasticism, is a central part of the Reformers' approach to the

---

viction—shared by the Puritans—of the absolute authority of all Scripture; to admit that certain aspects of the ceremonial regulations are only reflections of the peculiarities of Jewish worship in a specific historical period would open the door to human decisions concerning the validity of any portion of Scripture, Old or New Testaments, and effectively destroy the sole authority of the Bible.

In this context, Calvin asserts (as Miller cites in *Roger Williams*, p. 35), that 'it is better to confess our ignorance than indulge in frivolous conjectures.' The passage in which this citation occurs is Calvin's discussion of the dimensions and ceremonial significance of the Tabernacle ('Commentaries on the Four Last Books of Moses,' p. 174). The Tabernacle, Calvin notes, was not to be viewed as an end in itself, for '. . . the people should not rest their attention on the visible tabernacle, but with the understanding of faith should penetrate to heaven, and direct their minds to the spiritual pattern, the shadows and types of which they behold' (p. 174). Calvin then proceeds to interpret the Tabernacle, its furniture, and the garments of the High Priest typologically.

50. *The Idea of Reform: Its Impact on Christian Thought and Action in the Age of the Fathers* (Cambridge, Mass., 1959), p. 53.

Scriptures. This is not to say that Protestant typologists consistently avoid superimposing allegorical readings upon type-antitype identifications; it is to insist, however, that Protestant allegory is not simply a re-worked version of Origenistic practice. There are two significant differences.

First, the allegory of Protestant typologists is informed by a twofold sense of biblical hermeneutics; it does not attempt to determine tropological and anagogical readings beyond the literal and spiritual levels. Such readings occur, but they are viewed as part of, not in addition to, the spiritual or Gospel interpretation. The distinction, to the Puritans particularly, is not simply an artificial one; for from their point of view, any additional reading is twice removed from the literal sense and is a distortion of it. All passages have a literal and spiritual meaning; the spiritual meaning may have, and often does have, moral and eschatological implications, but in every case these arise from the literal level. Second, Protestant allegory, unlike Alexandrian allegory, is based upon an extensive analysis of the typical event. Alexandrian allegory essentially subordinates types, relegating them exclusively to the literal sense or discarding them entirely. In Protestant allegory, however, typology becomes of crucial significance; for types are one of the two central methods by which the Old and New Testaments are related. Hebrew prophecy is the second; and from the work of the earliest biblical authors, prophecy, after its fulfillment in Christ, becomes part of the typological message. Prophecy implies future fulfillment; typology asserts that the consummation has occurred. Hence, Protestant allegory, based on typical identifications, limits the vehicle of allegory to the Old Testament and its tenor to the New.

Origen's allegorical interpretation which identifies the clean animals in the Ark with 'memory, culture, understanding, reflection and judgment upon what we read' and the unclean animals with 'desire and anger'; or, the clean animals as also signifying the seven powers of the soul and the unclean animals representing the ill uses which man too often makes of the powers of the soul, is a clear extension beyond the confines of Scripture. To Samuel Mather, however, the clean and unclean beasts signify that *in the Church there are both Saints and Hypocrites: Hypocrites are unclean Beasts. A Cham in the Ark; a Judas, a Devil in Christ's own Family. In the visible Church there be sometimes Wolves within, and Sheep without: Tho' they are Wolves in Sheeps clothing; for prophane Persons may, and should be kept out; but close Hypocrites cannot. As in the Ark tho' there were ravenous Beasts; yet their Natures were restrained; So in the Church, such as are Beasts by nature; yet the Corruption of their Natures is restrained, there is restraining Grace upon Hypocrites in the Church, as well as renewing Grace in the Saints* (Figures or Types, p. 75).

Both Origen and Mather interpret the Ark as a type of the church and the deluge as a type of baptism. Beyond this typological identification, however, Origen sees a 'deeper mystery' which can only be understood by moving beyond the limits of the Bible to subjective allegorism. Mather also allegorizes the same passages; in each case, however, the type-antitype construct limits his allegory solely to the relationship between the two testaments. It would be misleading to assert that the differences between the two approaches are always this explicit. Augustine also interprets the clean and unclean beasts as a sign that 'good and bad take part in the sacraments of the Church,'[51] avoiding in this instance the allegorical abstractions of Origen; and at times Mather's allegorizing is hard to distinguish from Origen's practice. In most cases, however, the distinctions are clear, and it is the relative importance allotted to typology which marks the line between Patristic and Protestant allegory.

The ultimate significance of typology lies beyond the theological idiom in which it is expressed. Regardless of how much theorists of typology might insist, as Samuel Mather does, that '. . . *all this typical Dispensation is expired and abolished by the exhibition of Jesus Christ the Truth and Substance and Scope of all*' (pp. 539–40), the peculiar circumstances of the New England experiment—the New Exodus, the journey through the Wilderness, the establishment of a New Israel, and so on—provided the Puritan with a continuous analogy to the great biblical dramas. At every point in his

---

51. 'Contra Faustum Manichaeum,' in *The Nicene and Post-Nicene Fathers,* IV, 789.

life, and in the life of the New England theocracy, his experiences reflected what must have seemed to be a divinely constituted series of parallels to the recorded acts of God's providence to the Hebrews. Thus an imagistic consciousness based upon typology pervaded Puritan thought. The cloud by day and the pillar of fire by night which had guided the Hebrew children through their wilderness wanderings prefigured Christ's guiding role to his church. And that church was part of the divine plan which New England fulfilled in the history of Christianity. To someone like Edward Taylor, then, the parallels between his 'wilderness wanderings' and the experiences of God's first Chosen People were irrefutable testimony that history—and New England history in particular—was in fact the handmaiden of the Lord. Hence, such imagery made even more real the 'shadow' of the living Messiah in the Westfield minister's study:

Then lead me, Lord, through all this Wilderness
   By this Choice shining Pillar Cloud and Fire.
By Day, and Night I shall not then digress.
   If thou wilt lead, I shall not lag nor tire
   But as to Cana'n I am journeying
   I shall thy praise under this Shadow sing.[52]

52. Poems, ed. Stanford, p. 187. It may be added that the identifiable typologically oriented Patristic treatises from which Edward Taylor cites indicate a very sophisticated knowledge of typological traditions: Justin Martyr, Dialogue with Trypho; St. Basil, De Baptismo; Theodoret, Ecclesiasticae Historiae; Chrysostom's commentaries on Romans and Philippians and his Homily on Romans; Clement, Stromata and Paedogogus; Tertullian, De Anima; Origen, De Principiis and Contra Celsum; Augustine, Contra Faustum; and unidentifiable citations to Jerome and Gregory of Nyssa.

Scriptural Exegesis and the Literary Critic

Stephen Manning
University of Kentucky

To negotiate the historical and the aesthetic approaches to literature is not easy for the medievalist, least of all where typology and such related concepts as allegory and analogy are concerned. It is probably no easier for the specialist in early American literature. The very notion of typology, for instance, obviously assumes different shapes for the early theologian and for the modern literary critic, but reconciling such differences—indeed merely identifying them—requires great care. Even from a purely historical point of view, important distinctions must be carefully sifted. The concept of typology is certainly not identical for the medieval and for the Puritan theologian; for that matter, it was not identical for all medieval theologians. We might well succeed in patiently separating some strands of medieval typology, yet we are left with what seems like a hopeless tangle. Although the Reformation also reformed typology, it did inherit enough of the medieval tangle as perhaps to make some observations about typology in medieval exegesis and literature relevant to a study of Puritan literature in America.

The fourfold method of exegesis has had its share of doubters in literary studies; for example, W. K. Wimsatt reminds us that 'The poetic universal is of a different sort from the historic and Incarnational';[1] and Morton Bloomfield similarly objects to such a sym-

---

1. 'Two Meanings of Symbolism: A Grammatical Exercise,' *Renascence*, VIII (1955–56), 16.

bolic approach, not because it finds a Christian *sententia*, but because 'it assumes that this symbolic method is unique to the period and that there is no essential difference between literary works and theological or pastoral works. It misunderstands the nature of meaning and of literature.'[2] Nor does historical perspective clear the confusion: St. Thomas reserves the fourfold method for the theologian, not the poet; Boccaccio interprets the poetic fiction of Perseus on four levels; and Dante, who distinguishes 'allegory of theologians' from 'allegory of poets,' apparently invites a reading of his *Commedia* which is theologically allegorical.[3] St. Thomas, of course, speaks as theologian and not as poet; Boccaccio's fourfold interpretation does not accord with what we might call the 'classical' tradition of scriptural exegesis; and critics are still arguing over what to do about Dante.

It seems perfectly logical that the thousand years—give or take a few—during which typology held sway would weigh heavily upon a poetry that was tradition-minded and religion-oriented. But the fourfold method has built-in difficulties for poetic translation: the literal level points to actual events, not to imagined ones, and gives rise to a sequence of spiritual meanings which interlock. All four levels are multiple expressions of the same basic reality, representing four successive stages of the human condition 'ante legem, sub lege, sub gratia, in pace,' thus connecting a twofold past with the present and the future. This basic reality, visible everywhere throughout Scripture, distills into Jesus Christ and his act of redemption so that he becomes both Exegesis and Exegete.[4] This Christological foundation and the consequent centrality of the al-

2. 'Symbolism in Medieval Literature,' *MP*, LVI (1958), 75.

3. On the question of fourfold interpretation of secular literature, Bloomfield cites for the negative Aquinas, Conrad of Hirsau, Hugh of St. Victor, and John of Salisbury, p. 77. The passage in Boccaccio is *Genealogia Deorum Gentilium*, I.iii; in Dante, *Convivio*, II.i.

4. Henri de Lubac, *Exégèse médiévale*, (Paris, 1959–64), I, 323–24. The Latin quotation is from Hugh of St. Victor, cited III, 342. For a good definition of typology, see I, 352–53, in a discussion of why de Lubac dislikes the term. The standard works on typology and medieval literature are those by D. W. Robertson, esp. 'Historical Criticism,' in *English Institute Essays*

legorical level give the faith from which the tropological level of charity and the anagogical level of hope evolve. This is what we have called the 'classical' tradition of typology, and it is difficult to transpose it all into a poetic key.

Nor is the task simplified when we examine the fourfold method from a historical perspective. We can understand why St. Thomas and others reserved it for theologians, and we can realize more fully the implications of Dante's 'allegory of theologians' when we recognize that for the same thousand years of typological reign, biblical exegesis *is* theology. St. Bonaventure opens his *Breviloquium* by referring to 'the origin, development, and end of Holy Scripture, which is called theology.' He later presents Scripture as a cross, commenting: 'If we are to understand this cross, we must know God, the Principle of beings; we must know how these beings were created, how they fell, how they were redeemed through the blood of Jesus Christ, reformed through grace, and healed through the sacraments; and, finally, how they are to be rewarded with eternal pain or eternal glory.'[5] Moreover, this exegesis-theology developed as a bulwark against heresy: hence the insistence on a spiritual understanding of the letter, in which the 'perfidious' Jews were bogged down.[6] At the same time it was vitally necessary to emphasize the reality of the letter and to distinguish *allegoria in factis* from *allegoria in dictis*: the Bible recounts actual events, not fictions. The consequence of the Alexandrine tradition of a Philo Judaeus would be to reduce the whole meaning of history to nothing; as St. Thomas reports: 'The Manicheans said that God's Son assumed not a real, but a phantasy, body; thus, He could not be a true man, but only an apparent one. Consequently, the things He did as man—such as being born, eating, drinking, walking, suffering, and being buried—were done not in truth but in a kind of false appearance. Thus, clearly, they reduce the whole mystery of

---

1950, ed. Alan S. Downer (New York, 1951), pp. 3–31, and *A Preface to Chaucer* (Princeton, 1962).

5. *Works of Bonaventure*, trans. José de Vinck (Paterson, N.J., 1963), II, 1, 21. For further discussion of exegesis as theology, see de Lubac, I, 59–60, 111–14; II, 478.

6. *Ibid.*, III, 99–181.

the Incarnation to a fiction.'[7] Hence the sharp distinction between theology-exegesis and poetry.

Another difficulty for the fourfold method, especially when applied to a specific literary text, is the problem of ambivalence on any one given level of the four. This ambivalence takes many forms and needs fuller exploration than it has been granted. One form is the 'subjectivity' of interpretation; this whole matter becomes more acute from the twelfth century on, as we shall note later. St. Bernard, a transitional figure in this particular historical aspect, presents the problem with great clarity:

I know that I have explained this passage more fully and in another sense in my book upon the Love of God, and if it shall please any of you to read that, he can decide whether of the two is to be preferred. A prudent person will not, I think, condemn the giving of two senses to the same passage, provided that each appear to be grounded in truth, and that charity, which is the rule in interpreting Scripture, shall edify the more persons, inasmuch as there are a greater number of truthful senses, which each may apply to his own special need. For why should that be found faulty in the interpreting of Scripture, which we see is industriously practised in other things? To how many different bodily uses (only to take one thing for an example) do we put the element of water? In the same way a person is not to be blamed who gives divers senses, fitted to the various needs of souls, to a passage of Scripture.[8]

And if one saint can offer two different interpretations, what do you do when St. X says one thing and St. Y another, and they both meet the Augustinian touchstone of charity? Certain interpretations, of course, become standard, but that kind of solution does not really dispose of the alternates.

Then there is a basic problem of distinguishing the spiritual sense from the literal—more of a problem than it might seem. St. Thomas says that if the literal level speaks of future glory, the pas-

7. *Summa contra Gentiles*, trans. Charles J. O'Neil, IV, 29 (Garden City, 1957), p. 149.

8. *Life and Works of Saint Bernard*, ed. John Mabillon (London, 1896), IV, 310, cited by John P. McCall, 'Medieval Exegesis: Some Documents for the Literary Critic,' Supplement IV to William F. Lynch, *Christ and Apollo* (New York, 1963), p. 237.

sage is to be interpreted only on the literal level. St. Bonaventure says that if the literal level speaks of faith or of charity, then we needn't seek further for typological meaning. Nicholas of Lyra says that it is useless to seek under the letter of Psalm 67 for a second sense, because the literal sense of the psalm is already spiritual.[9] The implications of such statements for literature are certainly complex: no wonder Dorothy Sayers had some difficulty with the anagogical level of the *Commedia*. And what of the relationship between literal and anagogical in the Middle English dream-vision, *Pearl?* Since the narrator beholds the heavenly Jerusalem in his dream, should we follow St. Thomas and say that because the dream speaks of future glory, it is to be interpreted only literally? There is also a long tradition of two kinds of anagogical meaning— 'open' vs. 'mystical,' according to a late anonymous treatise.[10] Perhaps 'surface' meaning and 'spiritual' meaning are what the author means; his examples gloss 'Blessed are they that wash their gowns in the blood of the Lamb' (Rev. 7:14). 'Openly,' this means 'Blessed are the clean of heart, for they shall see God'; 'mystically,' it means 'Blessed are they who purify their thoughts that they may see Jesus Christ.' A similar tradition exists on the tropological level, although the examples given in the same treatise refer to two different passages: thus *openly*, 'Just as David conquered Goliath, so ought humility to conquer pride,' and *mystically*, 'Let thy garments be white' (Eccl. 9:8) means 'At all times let thy deeds be clean.' The 'open' or 'natural' meaning is thus the moral lesson which can be deduced from the straightforward teaching of the text, such as when it proposes good example or makes us detest evil.[11] Stephen Langton's term for this meaning is *moralitas secundum litteram*.[12] The other, 'mystical' meaning applies more sharply to the life of grace within the soul and is thus properly a spiritual interpretation. With this kind of distinction, how to interpret the morality of such

9. Aquinas, *Quodl.* 7, q.6, a.15, ad.5; Bonaventure is cited by de Lubac, IV, 271; Nicholas, *ibid.*, 348.

10. Described by Harry Caplan, 'The Four Senses of Scriptural Interpretation and the Mediaeval Theory of Preaching,' *Speculum*, IV (1929), 283.

11. *Ibid.*; de Lubac, II, 554.

12. Beryl Smalley, *The Study of the Bible in the Middle Ages* (Notre Dame, 1964), p. 234.

a work as *Patience?* Is its morality on the literal level, or on the tropological? The problem becomes particularly acute since it is a 'secular' work, and although secular works may be interpreted on various levels, all additional meanings are part of the literal level.[13] In Scripture alone is there a spiritual level, divisible into three.

The tropological level receives special emphasis in the thirteenth century. Since the allegorical level emphasizes faith, and since all now believed, attention turned to tropology and yielded interpretations which got more and more involved with matters of politics and of secular government. This kind of interpretation seems to have been encouraged by the availability of Aristotle's *Politics.* Miss Smalley records some of the concerns:

Hugh of St. Cher illustrates the text A just king setteth up the land *(Prov. 29:4) by the example of Philip Augustus setting up the realm of France. . . . Then for the first time we find short treatises on the duties of kingship inserted into commentaries. 'John of Varzy,' the Dominican commentator on Proverbs, takes the opportunity offered him by his text to set forth the obligations of a good ruler to the commonwealth. . . . Another postillator on Proverbs . . . applies the teaching of Pseudo-Dionysius' De coelesti hierarchia to the text Prov. 8:15–16:* By me kings reign, and lawgivers decree just things etc. *He adapts the concept of hierarchy, an essential ingredient of medieval thought, to the political order with unusual concreteness. . . .*[14]

Again, the combination of tropology and politics makes us wonder about some interpretations of Dante which distinguish a moral from a political level. Dante, of course, is no stranger to political interpretations of the Bible on the tropological level. In his *De Monarchia* he refutes some popular interpretations of passages which purportedly show the superiority of church over state; and, indeed, he is a little impatient not only of 'improper' meanings of biblical texts, but also of looking for mystical interpretations where

13. See the convenient diagram of literal and spiritual meanings in Edgar de Bruyne, *Etudes d'esthétique médiévale* (Brugge, 1946), II, 312–13.

14. Smalley, pp. 325–27. Miss Smalley attributes to Sts. Thomas and Albert the first use of the *Politics* as a school book, p. 324.

they do not exist and where the literal clearly suffices. Sometimes, however, there is a question of figurative language,[15] and this question leads us to reexamine the literal level.

According to Alexander of Hales, the literal level may be divided 'secundum rem' and 'secundum rei similitudinem.'[16] This second division is where Aquinas would place not only metaphor, but allegory and parable as well. But the question of prophecy is a little more complex; Peter of Poitiers, for example, disagrees with his favorite authority Bede in the latter's example of allegory: 'There shall come forth a rod out of the root of Jesse etc.; that is, the Virgin Mary shall be born of the stem of David and Christ of her.' Peter comments: 'but certain men say that this is history related metaphorically.'[17] Another passage leading to similar problems is Balaam's prophecy (Num. 24:17). Miss Smalley attributes to Stephen Langton 'the clearest, firmest and yet the subtlest treatment of the question.' Langton feels that since this is a manifest prophecy of Christ, 'no literal interpretation other than the prophecy ought to be understood. Thus should we expound the letter: A star Christ shall rise through incarnation out of Jacob the Jewish people. . . .' Miss Smalley then comments:

Langton means that part of Balaam's prophecy had its literal fulfilment under David, and that this in its turn symbolized the coming of Christ. He counts it as part of the literal sense because he believes that it should all be included in the prophet's original meaning. He sees that metaphor, symbolism, and allegory can come into the literal exposition if they were present in the prophet's mind. We know that he kept the literal sense of the prophecy distinct, since the passage is given its 'spiritual exposition' later on; allegorically the star is the Blessed Virgin, the sceptre her Son; tropologically, the star is the 'light of good works,' the sceptre 'chastisement of conscience' (p. 233).

15. De Monarchia, III, iv–ix.

16. Alexander is quoted by de Lubac, IV, 291. The literal sense for St. Thomas is not the figure of speech, but the content of the figure, Summa theol. Ia. q.1, a.10, ad.3.

17. Smalley, p. 232.

Even more complex is the interpretation of the Song of Songs. This book is unlike most of the other books of the Bible in that it does not describe actual events but is an epithalamion: it is thus *allegoria in dictis*, not *allegoria in factis*. Since it is part of the Bible, the work is divinely inspired and must therefore contain spiritual truths, but it needs particular care in interpretation. In fact, most commentators agree that it has only spiritual significance and, indeed, is the most profound spiritually of the sapiential books. The literal level is thus explained metaphorically, and the things to which the words refer are then appropriately spiritualized according to Christian belief. On the allegorical level, a double interpretation often appears: the love of Christ for both his Church and his Mother. Honorius of Autun, as a matter of fact, sees a twofold meaning on each level, based on the two kinds of literal marriage represented, respectively, by Solomon and the daughter of Pharaoh and by Mary and Joseph.[18] Eventually guidelines appear for a solution to this problem of the relation between literal and spiritual meanings, and St. Thomas gives us a clear exposition of the guidelines. To quote Miss Smalley's summary of his position: 'Human writers express their meaning by words; but God can also express his meaning by "things," that is by historical happenings. *The literal sense of Scripture, therefore, is what the human author expressed by his words; the spiritual senses are what the divine author expressed by the events which the human author related.* Since the Bible is the only book which has both a divine and a human authorship, only the Bible can have both a literal and a spiritual sense' (p. 300; italics mine).

Multiplicity of meaning also characterizes an enormous number of biblical images, as seen vividly in the *distinctiones* (in effect, dictionaries of such imagery). One such repository is the *Allegoriae in Sacram Scripturam*, which lists, for example, twenty-nine meanings for *aqua*, twenty-seven for *manus*, twenty-two for *oculus*, each meaning accompanied by its appropriate biblical source (*PL*, CXII, 849–1088). St. Bonaventure's list of twelve meanings of *sol* is outclassed by the other's nineteen; but Bonaventure with his love

18. *PL*, CLXXII, 349. For the rationale of exegesis of Songs, see St. Gregory's comments on words and things, *PL*, LXXIX, 473.

for numbers, arranges them four to each of the three spiritual levels.[19] These remarks might well call to mind the Middle English *Pearl*, where multiplicity of meaning has long been recognized but has often been restricted to the image of the pearl, which the narrator has lost. Which meanings of the image belong on which level has not always been carefully worked out. One of the most controversial meanings is that of the literal level; Sister Mary Vincent Hillman offers the very interesting suggestion that on this level the pearl is a real pearl and (since the dream maiden addresses him as 'gentle jeweler,') the narrator is a real jeweler.[20] Although certainly in what we have called the 'classical' tradition of typology, such an interpretation offers perhaps too much literalness for the literal level. Since this level can also include allegory, the pearl may be taken as an allegory for the narrator's daughter. Thus when the narrator speaks of losing a pearl, what he really means is that his daughter has died.[21]

In addition to these various kinds of ambiguity, a historical perspective presents still another problem of applying the fourfold method to literature. Up to the twelfth century, as we noted, exegesis was theology. Now the two gradually go their separate ways. Exegesis can either remain for a while rooted in the older tradition, or move in one of two directions: a greater emphasis upon the literal meaning through a revived interest in such matters as biblical languages, Jewish antiquities, the rabbinical tradition; or the exegesis could belittle the literal and develop a spiritual meaning so subjective—even eccentric—that the result is a spiritual exercise which

19. De Lubac, IV, 268.

20. *The Pearl* (Convent Station, N.J., 1961), pp. xi, 75.

21. This kind of allegory is very much in the rhetorical tradition: 'Oratio aliud verbis, aliud sententia demonstrans ("A kind of speech in which the words denote one thing, but their meaning denotes another") in the definition given in the work *Ad herennium*, which equates allegory with figurative language,' Edgar de Bruyne, *The Esthetics of the Middle Ages*, trans. Eileen B. Hennessy (New York, 1969), p. 8. (This is an English translation of the shorter version of de Bruyne's three-volume work.) See also in this connection de Lubac, IV, 136–37. For Bede's division of allegory into seven subordinate tropes, see de Bruyne, *Etudes*, I, 159; in this division, the pearl as the poet's daughter would be enigma.

has nothing to do with exegesis or with theology, properly speaking. De Lubac notes a tendency in St. Bernard towards spiritualizing the text in his commentary on Songs, as well as in Hugh of St. Victor, whose detailed description of Noah's ark seems designed primarily for the sake of its typological meaning. Thus the distinction between allegory of poets and that of theologians becomes blurred, and spiritual writers employ the former, just as they interpret pagan poetry in a threefold spiritual sense.[22] A further complicating factor in this latter tendency is the attacks on the fictional nature of poetry, which elicit defenses that match the attacks in vehemence, such as Boccaccio's, and which argue among other things for the position of the *poeta-theologus*.[23] In the old myth, Perseus becomes tropologically, the wise man who triumphs over vice and attains virtue; allegorically, the pious man who scorns worldly delight and contemplates heavenly things; and last anagogically, he becomes Christ Who conquers the Prince of this World and then ascends to heaven—a peculiar arrangement and interrelationship in view of the classical grouping of typological meaning. We can sympathize when Boccaccio prefers not to unfold all these meanings for every myth since he finds one meaning quite enough.[24]

If all these historical considerations seem to mark the fourfold tradition as capricious, we can cite still other aspects which might support such an assumption. Although the Fathers are apparently unanimous in supporting multiple interpretation, they often limit themselves to one or two. They were constantly making adaptations according to changing intellectual, moral, and spiritual needs of the time and of the audience.[25] Certain Fathers became identified with specific levels; St. Bonaventure associated the allegorical

22. For the change, see, for example, de Lubac, III, 10–11, 364, 418–35; Smalley, pp. 79, 244–45, 260, 293–94, 370. For St. Bernard, see de Lubac, II, 584–99; for Hugh, *ibid.*, III, 325–27. For interpretation of pagan poetry, *ibid.*, IV, 182–262.

23. For the concept, see E. R. Curtius, *European Literature and the Latin Middle Ages* (New York, 1953), pp. 214–27.

24. *Genealogia Deorum Gentilium*, I.iii, quoted by Charles G. Osgood, *Boccaccio on Poetry* (New York, 1956), p. xviii.

25. See Smalley, pp. 244, 255 for examples.

level with Sts. Augustine and Anselm; the tropological with Sts. Gregory and Bernard; the anagogical with pseudo-Dionysius and Richard of St. Victor; Hugh of St. Victor, however, excelled in all.[26] Another instance of apparent caprice is the fact that not all passages of Scripture are to be interpreted on all three spiritual levels: some have two levels of meaning, some only one. Moreover, several medieval commentators observed that the levels sometimes overlapped, especially allegory with either tropology or anagogy. And finally, exegetes are so concerned with understanding spiritually that they often pay no attention to such things as narrative sequence, or they paint themselves into corners by insisting on spiritualizing all aspects of the lives of Old Testament figures—of David, for example.[27] But no matter, for all passages find their unity in Jesus Christ, and the Bible as a whole is a set of theme and variations.

To salvage some sense of order out of this bewildering tradition, the modern critic would probably do best to insist on a fourfold meaning in medieval narrative which comes as close to the classical method as possible: a strong feeling for realistic event on the literal level, and a literal level strong enough to bear three interlocking spiritual meanings which derive at least indirectly from Christ's act of redemption. These meanings will probably rise simultaneously only when the narrative progression is reduced to outline; they will thus be four aspects of the overall theme which the narrative yields. Unfortunately, but inevitably, individual details will vary in the number of levels on which they operate; otherwise, the literary work will reduce either to as sterile an exercise as the codification into four levels itself, or as capricious an exercise as our comments on historical perspective seemed to indicate. In actual practice, however, the typological tradition is not sterile, nor is it all that capricious: our historical perspective suggests as well a flexible sys-

26. Quoted by de Lubac, IV, 269.

27. Aquinas discusses the number of interpretations in Quodl. 7, q.6, a.15; for overlapping of meaning, see Caplan, p. 287; for discussion of the conflict between spiritual and literal senses to David, see A. C. Charity, *Events and their Afterlife: the Dialectics of Christian Typology in the Bible and Dante* (Cambridge, Eng., 1966), p. 109.

tem, dynamic, bearing a maximum amount of Christian relevance, bursting into a riot of meanings which illuminate human experience. Indeed, from its very origins typology answered the Christian need for relevance, in its solution to the problem of what value the abrogated Old Testament contains for the New. Typology sweeps across the centuries, underscoring what existence means, basing its explanation in Christ's redemption as foreshadowed, actuated, continued, and finally completed. This act of redemption continues now, today, as exhibited in the individual soul, in the lives of saints, in the events of history, in the things of creation itself, in the divine office, in the sacraments, in the Holy Eucharist, in the sacrifice of the Mass—a continuous, constant, irreducible relevance. Thus, to paraphrase Célestin Charlier, typology has relevance 'only insofar as it stresses the recurrence of an essential theme.'[28] And if we classify this recurrence, the resulting compartments can only partially suggest the depth of meaning which the theme possesses.

Typology, then, is not properly a literary technique, nor can it be reduced to one. But it is a mode of spiritual perception and can affect literary techniques and can resemble literary modes. We should, however, carefully mark the distinction between the classical tradition with its connection to theology, and splinter traditions whether in spiritual writings or in humanistic defenses of poetry, or in actual exegesis. The consequence of observing this distinction is an accent on the cohesiveness—as opposed to arbitrariness—of event and meaning, which Dom Célestin explains so clearly:

In order for typology to exist it is not sufficient that a relation of figure to reality be discernible; this relation must also be bound by an objective link which establishes the historical preparation of the figure, just as much as the ideal prefiguration, of the reality which it stresses.

We shall give here a single example . . . : the scarlet ribbon suspended by the courtesan Rahab from the wall of besieged Jericho. The scarlet ribbon has no other connection with the blood of Christ than its color and a functional similarity which is completely external: it saved Rahab, and the blood of Christ saves the Chris-

28. 'Méthode historique et lecture spirituelle des Ecritures,' Bible et Vie Chrétienne, No. 18 (1957), p. 24, quoted and trans. McCall, p. 252.

tian. *But is this sufficient for affirming that the Holy Spirit has hidden a prefiguration of one under the other? No internal bond unites the red ribbon and the redeeming blood. One did not take rise from the other; faith in the second did not spring from contemplation of the first. It is completely different, for example, with the Paschal Lamb, or with the blood which Moses sprinkled on the people, in order to consecrate the Alliance, at the foot of Sinai; these rites efficaciously gave start, in the religious conscience of Israel, to an opening movement subject to the revelation of the sense of the Passion, on the day of the New Alliance, and they efficaciously prepared, in the history of the People of God, the objective germination of the event.*[29]

Certainly if we are going to look for poetic imitation of this classical tradition, a similar cohesiveness must be established between the literal and the spiritual meanings. In order to do so, it seems best to stress *events* on the literal level (*allegoria in factis*) rather than persons or things (*allegoria in res*).

One of the most interesting commentaries on Dante which applies the typological mode with some measure of success is that of A. C. Charity. The literal level corresponding to the historical reality of the Old Testament is Dante's life, which is deliberately stylized by a metaphorical journey to demonstrate Dante's self-conforming to the life of Christ. Thus the literal takes its significance from the Christological (allegorical) level. 'What Dante *does*, in his journey,' says Charity, 'Christ *has* done. Dante's descent into Hell, and his release from it, is a typological repetition, a "subfulfilment" of Christ's.' This is the significance of dating the journey from Good Friday, 1300, until Dante is released 'from what, at just the point at which the ascent begins, is called the *tomba* of Hell . . . on the morning of Easter Day.'[30] The significant aspect of this journey is the conversion toward, and the consequent imitation of, Christ—an almost literal rendering of the concept of dying with Christ. The journey thus becomes a type of Dante's

29. *Ibid.*, pp. 252–53.

30. The reference is to *Inferno*, XXXIV, 128. For Charity's discussion, see esp. pp. 245–58; the quotations are from pp. 245, 246.

own future, for what he gains from the journey through his dependence on Christ, is the 'other life.' In this interpretation it is the redemptive act of Christ which gives significance to the literal level at the same time that the literal sense describes events whose fullness of meaning can be said to be contained in the act of redemption. The three spiritual levels to which the literal events give rise are neatly summed up for Charity by Dante's exposition of the passage 'In exitu Israel,' which forms part of his discussion of method in the *Letter to Can Grande:* 'if we look at the allegory, it signifies our redemption through Christ; if we look at the moral sense, it signifies the turning of the soul from the sorrow and misery of sin to a state of grace; if we look at the anagogical sense, it signifies the passage of the blessed soul from the slavery of this corruption to the freedom of eternal glory.'[31] The three spiritual levels thus interlock, and all four levels stress, in Dom Célestin's phrase, 'the recurrence of an essential theme.'

Although he is thus able to establish a marked similarity between Dantean and biblical typology, Charity is nonetheless aware of differences. He contends 'that the *Divine Comedy's* use and understanding of typology has a kind of continuity, if not identity, with the use and understanding of typology in the Bible' (p. 257). Robert Hollander has recently considered the kind of relationship between the two typologies; he rejects the formulation of Joseph Mazzeo that 'Dante's literal sense is to be understood as a metaphoric approximation of the literal sense of Scripture.'[32] Instead, he prefers the solution of Charles Singleton: 'let us be content to say that Dante wrote in imitation of God's way of writing.' Perhaps the problem might be seen in better perspective if we pick up another of Singleton's insights in his discussion of the *Vita Nuova:* what Dante does is write by *analogy* with typology. This analogy can be of two kinds, which perhaps help to clarify some of the disagree-

31. Charity notes, p. 249, that Singleton makes a similar point in his essay ' "In exitu Israel de Aegypto," ' 78th Annual Report of the Dante Society (1960), pp. 3, 13. The translation of the *Letter* is Nancy Howe's, in *Essays on Dante,* ed. Mark Musa (Bloomington, 1964), p. 37.

32. *Allegory in Dante's Commedia* (Princeton, 1969), p. 62n. The reference to Singleton is on p. 23.

ment surrounding Dante's use of typology—analogy of proportion and analogy of proportionality.

In analogy of proportion, two things are analogous because they bear different relations to one and the same thing: they are alike as regards the term to which they are proportioned, different in their mode of relation to the term. Thus the *Commedia* and the Bible share the quality of typology, but differ in their relationship to that term: the two uses of typology will not coincide in all particulars. This is also described as analogy *secundum intentionem tantum et non secundum esse*—i.e., typology is predicated properly only of Scripture but is applied to Dante by 'extrinsic denomination.'[33] At the same time, God's intention in writing Scripture gives meaning to Dante's technique: the latter presupposes the former, and the former is partially included in the latter. Seeing Dante's poem as analogous by proportion orients the resulting literary analysis towards medieval theory and practice and attempts to define the work more sharply as a piece of medieval literature. It obviously offers insights which an ahistorical approach cannot bring. An ahistorical approach does, of course, emphasize the nature of the *Commedia* as literature, and we can thus set up an analogy of proper proportionality. In this kind of analogy, *typology* must have a corresponding literary equivalent, which—as critics have finally realized—for Dante is *symbolism*. Thus we can posit the proportionality, typology: Scripture:: symbolism: *Commedia*. The common concept in the two works which is realized formally and properly in each analogate is the relationship between literal and non-literal levels. But since the nature of analogy depends on similarity and difference, the critic still has the problem of distinguishing typology from symbolism. The immediate purpose of such a distinction would be to define the peculiarly literary nature of the *Commedia*. We can fairly enough sum up the two analogical perspectives by saying that analogy of proportion stresses the similarity to typology, and that of proportionality the differences.

Not all literary applications of typology will bear as close an approximation as Dante's; most adaptations will show traces of their

33. For my discussion of analogy I have relied principally on James F. Anderson, *The Bond of Being* (St. Louis, 1949).

heritage but reveal only a few points of similarity. Erich Auerbach's valuable concept of *figura* is a case in point. 'Figural interpretation,' says Auerbach, 'establishes a connection between two events or persons in such a way that the first signifies not only itself but also the second, while the second involves or fulfills the first.' This relationship marks, of course, that between the Old and New Testaments, but Auerbach extends the concept to literature, especially to Dante. The characterization of Cato of Utica, Virgil, and Beatrice in the other world 'is a fulfillment of their appearance on earth, their earthly appearance is a figure of their appearance in the other world.' So also the individual souls of the dead, whose characterization attains fulfillment. 'Their career on earth was only the figure of this fulfillment.'[34] Figural realism is thus an excellent application of the mode of typology. Another example, also from Dante, is Singleton's analysis of the *Vita Nuova*. Beatrice's actions as bringer of beatitude while alive prefigure her fulfillment as bringer of salvation after her death. The particular technique which the typological mode employs in this instance is not allegory, as Singleton explains, but analogy of proportion 'of Beatrice and *salute* through her, to Christ and *salute* through Him.'[35] Perhaps one of the chief distinctions between allegory and analogy is the relationship of tenor to vehicle. In allegory the tenor stands outside the context, yet controls the vehicle from without; in analogy, as in metaphor (which is really a kind of analogy), the vehicle is brought into the context to illumine the tenor, which is the term already in the context.[36] To distinguish analogy from metaphor, I would restrict metaphor to the comparison of objects of different categories,

34. *Mimesis*, trans. Willard Trask (New York, 1957), pp. 64, 171. See his essay ' "Figura," ' trans. R. Manheim, in *Scenes from the Drama of European Literature* (New York, 1959), pp. 11–76.

35. *An Essay on the Vita Nuova* (Cambridge, 1949), pp. 112–13, 161. For a brief discussion of the typology in this work, see Auerbach, ' "Figura," ' pp. 73–75.

36. See Wimsatt, p. 13; Harry Berger, *The Allegorical Temper* (New Haven, 1957), p. 129, includes in a note a brief but helpful bibliography on analogy. For a longer bibliography on analogy, see Supplement III in Lynch, pp. 213–15.

and analogy to comparison of objects within the same class, especially a comparison of one person to another.

A final example of the problems that can arise in literary application of the typological mode, and indeed which will require a sharper distinction among kinds of exegetical typology, is *Beowulf.* The poet draws at least an implicit analogy between Beowulf and Christ in the last section of the poem. He can thus bring to Beowulf's action of laying down his life for his people something of the emotive values of Christ's action; the fact that the technique is analogy means that the differences between the two can also increase the emotive meaning. Thus there is a kind of gentle irony in the comparison of the results of the two actions: Beowulf's death does not really save his people. If the poem did not have strong Christian sentiment elsewhere, we might conclude that the analogy to Christ is similar in function to the analogy with Siegfried earlier in the poem. But as it stands, the analogy to Christ reinforces the strong undercurrent of Christian significance in the poem as a whole, in which the life of Beowulf has some bearing on the Christian life. The poem has been interpreted as allegory, but that seems hardly satisfactory in view of the strong pagan element which remains despite the Christian coloring. The best solution seems once again to be analogy, this time analogy of proportionality, i.e., the good prince:secular life :: the good Christian:spiritual life. Thus, 'good Christian' is not the tenor which controls the actions of Beowulf, but is suggested in comparison as an outside term brought in to illuminate Beowulf, the term already in the poem. Beowulf thus retains his full identity as pagan hero while concurrently suggesting a Christian relevance. Now although *Beowulf* is thus given Christian meaning, and although the life of Christ serves as an analogy which gives partial meaning to Beowulf's actions, this interpretation does not reflect the same kind of exegetical typology as the *Commedia.* It relates, instead, to a kind of typology which merely sets up a comparison between the earthly and the heavenly. This is what I will refer to later as pseudo-historical typology.

But *typology* has still another meaning in addition to the mode of biblical exegesis. Typology in this additional sense refers to the relationship between spiritual values and the natural world—to reading the Book of Nature in addition to the Book of Scripture.

The medieval interpretation of nature found one biblical justification in Romans 1:20: 'For the invisible things of Him . . . are clearly seen, being understoood by the things that are made.' Father de Lubac characterizes this interpretation as ' "anagogique,"—nous dirions aujourd'hui: contemplative' (IV, 175). But if it is anagogy, it is, since the fall, 'anagogie manquée.' Although nature hides God, 'il demeure toujours, en lui-même, apte à le révéler. Par le détour de l'Ecriture, qui contient l'opus restaurationis, l'opus creationis retrouvera sa signification. Ce premier livre qu'était la grande fabrica mundana sera de nouveau déchiffré. Préparée maintenant par l'histoire, l'allégorie et la tropologie, l'anagogie réussira' (IV, 174). This kind of typology, then, relates to theological typology.

Nature typology may also be divided into two kinds. One has definite Platonic overtones. The sensible things of this world prompt us to contemplation and then to desire for the beauty of their Creator. 'De droit, la contemplation délectable du beau sensible doit éveiller en nous un désir incompressible de l'Infini,' writes de Bruyne.[37] Thus visible beauty is the sign of the invisible beauty of God. Now the beauty of God is manifested spiritually in souls, sensibly in things; thus the more beautiful the soul, the more divine beauty it can perceive in visible things. For St. Bonaventure, 'every creature is the image and resemblance of the Creator of its very nature,' and furthermore, 'to be the image or vestige of God cannot be anything accidental, but only a substantial property of every creature.'[38] Gilson's term for St. Bonaventure's thought applies equally well to other expressions of similar ideas—universal analogy, i.e., the analogy of being which exists between all creatures and their Creator. But when this kind of typology seeks specific meanings in visible things, we are off into an arbitrary species. Thus, for instance, when we look at a rose, and its beauty and perfection lead us to meditate on and desire the beauty and perfection of God him-

37. Etudes, II, 215; on pp. 208–18 he discusses this concept in the Victorines.

38. Etienne Gilson, The Philosophy of St. Bonaventure, trans. Illtyd Trethowan (Paterson, N.J., 1965), pp. 194–95. Bonaventure's distinction among shadow, vestige, and image is summarized on p. 467.

self, we have an example of analogy of being. If, however, when we see a red rose, we think of the martyrs, or a white rose we think of the virgins around the throne of the Lamb, we have arbitrary typology, and the literary context will determine whether the image is metaphor, symbol, or (probably) allegory. The bestiaries, for instance, are arbitrary typology, and are probably best described as allegories. Despite their insistence on the nature of beasts, the ultimate control seems rather the spiritual signification. The medieval term which describes the bestiaries is *allegoria in res*, too general a term to have much meaning in a literary context.

To sum up: we can distinguish two basic kinds of typology, exegetical and natural. Exegetical may be further divided, following G. W. H. Lampe, into historical typology, which 'consists in a recognition of historical correspondences and deals in terms of past and future,' and allegorical typology, which views Scripture 'as a single vast volume of oracles and riddles, a huge book of secret puzzles to which the reader has to find clues' and thus 'takes no account of history.'[39] But a certain arbitrariness can even creep into the first kind; this kind of typology, says Lampe, 'tends, like allegory, to disregard historical verisimilitude, the original significance of texts or the meaning of events in their proper context in history, and the intention of the ancient authors.' The correspondence which this kind of typology establishes 'is not so much a relation between the past and the future, the foreshadowing and the fulfilment, as between the earthly and the heavenly, the shadow and the reality.' His example, like Dom Célestin's, is Rahab, where 'the parallel between the type and its supposed fulfilment is plainly unreal and artificial.' This latter kind of typology I shall call pseudo-historical; we have seen a suggestion of this kind in *Beowulf*. The 'classic' tradition of typology I prefer to call theological typology, wherein events are prefigured and fulfilled, and Christ's act of redemption is the focus. The term also is intended to suggest the medieval equation of exegesis with theology. Admittedly, in my discussion in this paper, I have reduced theological typology to its 'pure' form, even while acknowledging in effect that it rarely

39. G. W. H. Lampe and K. J. Woollcombe, *Essays on Typology* (Naperville, Ill., 1957), pp. 29–34. The quotations are from pp. 30, 31, 33.

existed in such a form. The purpose of abstracting so 'pure' a form is, of course, to provide a satisfactory basis for discussion of literary application. If we follow the many variations from the 'pure' form, or if we include in addition allegorical typology and pseudo-historical typology, we will wind up with so broad a definition as to make our discussion less than meaningful. Whenever we mention typology, however, we must define more sharply to which of the three exegetical typologies we are referring. Or we may be referring to one of the two kinds of natural typology, which we have termed respectively analogy of being and arbitrary typology. Here again the distinction is important. If we observe these distinctions, we might not have more critical agreement on specific interpretations, but we might avoid some arbitrary interpretations in both medieval and early American literature.

Three
Aspects of
Seventeenth-
Century
New England
Typology

'With My
Owne Eyes':
William
Bradford's
*Of Plymouth
Plantation*

The Separatist
Background of
Roger Williams'
Argument
for Religious
Toleration

Cotton Mather's
Magnalia and
the Metaphors
of Biblical
History

There must be Contrition and Humiliation before the Lord comes to take possession. . . . This was typified in the passage of the Children of Israel towards the promised Land. They must come into, and go through a vast and roaring Wilderness, where they must be bruised with many pressures, humbled under many overbearing difficulties, before they could possess that good land which abounded with all prosperity, flowed with Milk and Honey.   Thomas Hooker, Application of Redemption, 1659

Although that which is foretold . . . was in part fulfilled when the people of God returned from Captivitie in Babylon at the end of seventie yeares: yet

we must not limit the place to that time onely. . . . Many things that literally concerned the Jewes were types and figures, signifying the like things concerning the people of God in the latter dayes. . . . And this may be added further, that this place seemes not onely to be meant of the private or personall conversion of this or that particular Christian, but also further, of the open and joynt calling of a company. Richard Mather, An Apologie of the Churches of New-England for Church-Covenant, 1643

'With My Owne Eyes': William Bradford's *Of Plymouth Plantation*

Jesper Rosenmeier
Tufts University

In the year 1650, when he had ceased recording the role of Christ's New Plymouth plantation in the great and ancient warfare between God and Satan, William Bradford took up the study of Hebrew. As a notebook for his painstaking exercises he used some pages in the manuscript of his History, copying more than a thousand Old Testament words and phrases, together with their English translations.[1] The particular words seem to have been chosen at random, but of the twenty-five phrases, almost half deal with family relationships, especially that of fathers and sons. Having translated about two hundred words (the first is 'to walk before him') Bradford explains why he was trying to learn Hebrew:

> Though I am growne aged, yet I have had a longing
> desire to see, with my owne eyes, somthing of that most
> ancient language, and holy tongue, in which the Law
> and Oracles of God were write; and in which God
> and angels spake to the holy patriarks of old
> time; and what names were given to things
> from the creation. And though I canot
> attaine to much herein, yet I am refresh-

1. The Hebrew exercises preceding the History have been published in Isidore S. Meyer, 'The Hebrew Preface to Bradford's History of the Plymouth Plantation,' *Publications of the American Jewish Society*, XXXVIII (June, 1949), 289–305.

> ed to have seen some glipse hereof;
> (as Moyses saw the land of Ca-
> nan a farr off.) My aime and
> desire is, to see how the words
> and phrases lye in the
> holy texte; and to
> discerne somewhat
> of the same,
> for my owne
> contente.[2]

As we see in the 'hourglass,' Bradford did not begin the study of Hebrew merely to learn another language or to keep active in his later
years. He was possessed by a 'longing desire' to realize as literally
as he could the most ancient holiness, the holiness manifest in creation and the first people of God; he felt compelled to return to
that glorious language in which the Spirit of God had spoken the
world into being and the angels had conversed with the holy patriarchs. Of course, Bradford believed that the Bible in any language
would speak about judgment and salvation with power and author-
it, but the Hebrew contributes a vividness lacking in other versions. Hearing God speak in his original tongue, as, for example, in
Psalm 29, when his voice divides the flames of fire and shakes the
wilderness, might bring Bradford directly back to the moment
when the voice was first heard; he would be permitted to be present
in the past.

Bradford's remarkably strong yearning for the resurrection of the
past suggests, as I hope to show, more than mere nostalgia; he tena-
ciously insisted that the holiness of the ancient moments still stood
as the perfect image for the present and future. The more carefully
and precisely the ancient moments are unearthed, the more fully,
he seems to have believed, would they mirror the divine. By learning the most ancient and holiest of tongues, Bradford hoped to see
with his 'owne eyes' something of the coming kingdom, of the time

2. Meyer, 'Preface,' p. 296. The 'hourglass' was first published in Proceedings of the Massachusetts Historical Society, XI (Boston, 1870), 402.

when the holiness first revealed in creation would again be fully visible.[3]

Yet, at the same time, we recognize that the Hebrew studies were done for Bradford's 'owne contente.' In addition to demonstrating his longing for the past and his dream of a future glory, they are a very private work and disclose his isolation from the outside world. We do not see Bradford looking into Canaan as the confident leader of a chosen people. Behind him the ranks of a nation do not close in support and anticipation; the people of Plymouth are looking toward other lands.

The effort to resurrect the literal language of some original perfection is not unique to Bradford; it can be found in the writings of

3. Peter Gay, *A Loss of Mastery* (Berkeley, 1966), pp. 3–52. I am indebted to the following: Cyclone Covey, *The American Pilgrimage: The Roots of American History, Religion and Culture* (New York, 1961), pp. 12–14; Richard S. Dunn, 'Seventeenth-Century English Historians of America,' in *Seventeenth-Century America*, ed. J. M. Smith (Chapel Hill, 1959), pp. 201–03; Norman S. Grabo, 'William Bradford: *Of Plymouth Plantation,*' in *Landmarks of American Fiction*, ed. Henning Cohen (New York, 1969), pp. 3–19; Grabo, 'The Veiled Vision: The Role of Aesthetics in Early American Intellectual History,' *William and Mary Quarterly*, XIX (October, 1962), 493–510; William Haller, *The Rise of Puritanism* (New York, 1938); David Levin, review of Mr. Gay's book, in *History and Theory*, VII (1968), 385–93; Perry Miller, *The New England Mind: The Seventeenth Century* (Cambridge, Mass., 1939); Miller, *The New England Mind: From Colony to Province* (Cambridge, Mass., 1953); Perry Miller and Thomas H. Johnson, *The Puritans* (New York, 1938), pp. 81–91; Edmund S. Morgan, 'The Historians of Early New England,' in *The Reinterpretation of Early American History*, ed. Ray Allen Billington (San Marino, California, 1966), pp. 41–63; Samuel Eliot Morison, Introduction to *Of Plymouth Plantation* (New York, 1952), pp. xxiii–xliii; Kenneth B. Murdock, *Literature and Theology in Colonial New England* (Cambridge, Mass., 1949); Murdock, 'Clio in the Wilderness,' *Church History*, XXIV (1955), 221–38, especially pp. 223–25; Cecelia Tichi, 'Spiritual Biography and the "Lords Remembrancers," ' *William and Mary Quarterly*, XXVIII (January, 1971), 64–85; Alan B. Howard, 'Art and History in Bradford's *Of Plymouth Plantation,*' *William and Mary Quarterly*, XXVIII (April, 1971), 237–66. Mr. Howard's very interesting article reached me after my own essay had gone to press.

many other Separatists, most notably in Henry Ainsworth's *Annotations on the Pentateuch, or the Five Books of Moses; the Psalms of David; and the Song of Solomon.*[4] In the *Annotations*, Ainsworth presents extended commentaries on Deut. 3:25–27, 34:1, and Num. 27:12, where Moses' view of Canaan from the top of Mt. Pisgah is described. In Deut. 3:25–27, God denies Moses' supplication to pass over Jordan 'and see the good land . . . beyond,' and orders Moses instead to 'speak no more unto me of this matter. Get thee up into the top of Pisgah, and lift up thine eyes westward, and northward, and southward, and eastward, and behold *it* with thine eyes: for thou shalt not go over this Jordan.' In Deut. 34:1, Moses obeys God's command, and goes 'up from the plains of Moab unto the mountain of Nebo, to the top of Pisgah, this *is* over against Jericho,' where God tells him that the Canaan he sees before him is the land promised to the ancient fathers, 'unto Abraham, unto Isaac, and unto Jacob.'

In his commentary on these texts, Ainsworth takes great care to draw a picture of Canaan rich in physical detail; he wants the reader to have as literal a view of Canaan as Moses had when he stood on Mt. Pisgah. On Moses' looking toward Jericho and Zoar, Ainsworth comments:

JERICHO,] In Gr. Jericho, a city within the land of Canaan, which the Israelites first conquered, by faith causing the wall to fall down. . . . CITY OF PALM-TREES,] So Jericho is called here . . . of them and other fragrant fruits there growing, as balsam and the like; the city had the name of Jericho, by interpretation 'odoriferous,' or 'fragrant.' UNTO ZOAR,] In Gr. Segor. Thus the last part which Moses viewed was nearest unto him, and the pleasantest of all the land of Canaan: for 'all the plain of Jordan, was well watered, it was as the garden of the Lord.'[5]

And interpreting the phrase 'this good mountain and Lebanon,' Ainsworth writes:

MOUNTAIN,] That *is*, mountain country: See Exod. 15:17.

---

4. Henry Ainsworth, *Annotations* . . . 2 vols. (Edinburgh, 1843).

5. *Ibid.*, II, 404–05.

LEBANON,] In Gr. Antilibanon; in Chald. the house of the sanctuary, *because the temple was built of the cedars that grew on
mount Lebanon. . . . So the temple is called Lebanon. . . . But that
seemeth not to be meant here; but rather the mount Lebanon in
the north part of the land, which was both an high and fragrant
mountain, with sweet and goodly trees growing thereon. . . . This
great desire Moses had, because of the promises which God had
made to Israel, to be accomplished in that land, the figure of our
heavenly heritage.*[6]

Living in Holland several thousand years after Moses, Ainsworth
did not expect to write a commentary on the Old Testament that
would be 'scientifically' exact. Rather, the quality he sought was
the fullness of God's revelation to Moses. The Canaan Moses sees
before him is the fulfillment of the promises given to Abraham and
his seed. If, Ainsworth believes, the reader is to see what Moses saw,
he must be transported back and stand with Moses on the high and
fragrant mountain and look at the pleasant Jordan flowing toward
Jericho and Zoar. The more directly he can see with Moses' eyes,
the more vividly and graphically the past will live. For Ainsworth,
the ancient facts are figures and types, and the more vividly the past
lives, the more effective as prophecy it may become. Made real to
our senses, Mt. Nebo, planted with sweet and goodly trees, more
fully prophesied the time when ' "John from an high mountain
was showed the holy Jerusalem," Rev. 21:10.' Moses' Canaan is 'a
figure of our heavenly inheritance, proposed to them that do the
law, but given to them that are of the faith of Christ, John 1:17.'
And God 'showeth Moses all the kingdoms and glory of Canaan,
from an high mountain, for his comfort and strengthening of his
faith, who saw the promises afar off, saluted them and died, as did
his godly forefathers, Heb. 11:9, 13.'[7] In God's denial of Moses'
request to cross into the promised land and in his death are 'fore-
showed the end and abrogation of Moses' law, when men are
come to the gospel of Christ: for, "after that faith is come, we are
no longer under the schoolmaster," Gal. 3:25.'[8] What Moses saw
—and, Ainsworth hopes, later men will see—from the top of Mt.
Pisgah is the fulfillment of the Old Testament quest for the prom-

6. *Ibid.*, p. 200.   7. *Ibid.*, p. 404.   8. *Ibid.*, p. 405.

ised land. But Moses sees something more and other: for his 'comfort and faith,' God shows him the future promised land, of which the Canaan before him is the figure and type.

The fusion of graphic detail and prophetic vision in these passages is remarkable in seventeenth-century typology. Few other exegetes bring past and future, detail and dream, so unselfconsciously and richly together. Others who interpret the history of redemption may be profoundly familiar with the meanings of the types; and in their preaching and writings they may demonstrate their skill at finding deep connections between the old and new dispensations, as well as their knowledge of the spiritual values emblemized in the ancient people and events. Yet most typologists do not endeavor to realize so sensuously the land that Moses saw. They explicate the typological meanings of Canaan, but the land itself remains distant and unresurrected. By means of his rich literalness Ainsworth brings Moses resurrected into the world of seventeenth-century Englishmen and makes him walk before them. The vividness of his exegesis has its source in Ainsworth's experience of Christ's incarnation. Like Luther, who believed that Christ was the sun who lights up the Old Testament figures and types, Ainsworth sees all of the Bible as the revelation of the same divine light. It is the presence of Christ that illuminates facts and transforms them into prophecy. Therefore, the more fully Ainsworth can share Moses' view of Canaan, the profounder, he expects, will be his description of Christ's incarnation. Ainsworth cannot rest merely knowing that Moses saw Canaan afar off; he must himself see the living land. For Ainsworth, the ancient facts are ripe with Christ.

In his commentaries on Num. 27:12 and on the two texts from Deuteronomy, Ainsworth refers repeatedly to chapter 11 of the Epistle to the Hebrews, where Paul writes about the nature of faith and its relationship to the promised lands, both Moses' Canaan and Christ's kingdom on earth. 'Faith,' Paul says, 'is the substance of things hoped for, the evidence of things not seen.' It was by believing in God's promises that the Old Testament saints were given eyes to see into the future promised land. 'By faith,' he writes, Abraham 'sojourned in the land of promise, as in a strange country . . . for he looked for a city which has foundations, whose builder and maker is God.' Abraham, Abel, Noah, and Sara all died before the promises had been fulfilled. Yet though they 'died in faith, not having received the promises, but having seen them afar off,' they were 'persuaded of them and embraced them, and confessed that they were strangers and pilgrims on earth' who desired 'a better country, that is, a heavenly: wherefore God is not ashamed to be called their God: for he hath prepared for them a city.'

The city that God had prepared for his New Testament saints differs from that prepared for Abraham and the ancients. By Christ's kingdom is not meant the land between the Jordan and the Mediterranean. Nevertheless, it was possible for Ainsworth to identify so profoundly with Moses because the life and object of faith were the same for Old and New Testament believers. Though outwardly the promised lands are very different manifestations, they are, Ainsworth thought, incarnations of the same Christ.[9] And because he found Christ present in the entire history of redemption, Ainsworth trusted that the New Testament promises of the New Jerusalem would flower into fact in the same way Abraham had faith that the Old Testament prophecies of Canaan would be fulfilled in visible form. Furthermore, the oneness of old and new believers would extend to their earthly lives. As the Old Testament faithful chose to suffer affliction rather than 'enjoy the pleasures of sin,' so Christ's chosen who have come 'unto the city of the living God, the heavenly Jerusalem' must serve him with 'reverence and godly fear' whatever their sufferings.

The country the Separatists sought was, as Paul writes, heavenly, not earthly.[10] The New Jerusalem, though in this world, would not be of it. The Separatists were indifferent to the specific, physical place they settled. As people of faith, they believed that they had received the promises, and they considered themselves to be strangers and Pilgrims on earth. The land they wanted to leave behind as they went to Holland and America was the land of spiritual darkness and corruption which knew no physical boundaries but could be found in most of Europe's nations. Their task, John Rob-

9. See Richard Reinitz, 'The Separatist Background of Roger Williams' Argument for Religious Toleration,' pp. 107–37 below.

10. See Alan Heimert, 'Puritanism, the Wilderness, and the Frontier,' New England Quarterly, XXVI (1953), 370.

inson explained in *A Justification of Separation from the Church* *of England*, was to build the temple anew:

The apostle writing unto the Galatians . . . calls the church of the *new testament, 'Jerusalem which is above, and the mother' of the* *faithful: and John in the book of the Revelation . . . opposeth unto* *Babylon spiritual, the new Jerusalem coming from God down out* *of heaven: and the tabernacle of God, where he dwelleth with men,* *making them his people, and himself their God. Now as the people* *of God in old time, were called out of Babylon civil, the place of* *their bodily bondage; and were to come to Jerusalem, and there to* *build the Lord's temple, or tabernacle, leaving Babylon to that de-* *struction, which the Lord by his servants, the prophets, had de-* *nounced against it . . . so are the people of God, now to go out of* *Babylon spiritual to Jerusalem . . . and to build up themselves as* *lively stones into a spiritual house, or temple for the Lord to dwell* *in, leaving Babylon to that destruction and desolation, yea further-* *ing the same, to which she is devoted by the Lord.*[11]

How much more significant the spiritual journey was to the Separatists than their physical circumstances Bradford expresses in the climactic passage in chapter IX of *Of Plymouth Plantation* where he contrasts his own standing on the dunes of Cape Cod with Moses standing on Mt. Pisgah. The Pilgrims, Bradford writes, could not 'as it were, goe up to the tope of Pisgah, to vew from this wildernes a more goodly cuntrie to feed their hopes; for which way soever they turned their eyes (save upward to the heavens) they could have little solace or content in respecte of any outward ob-jects. For summer being done, all things stand upon them with a wetherbeaten face; and the whole countrie, full of woods and thickets, represented a wild and savage heiw.'[12] The heavenly king-dom above that Bradford so dramatically contrasts with the savage

11. John Robinson, *A Justification of Separation from the Church of Eng-* *land* . . . , in *Works*, 3 vols. (London, 1851), II, 304. Hereafter cited as *Works*.

12. William Bradford, *History of Plymouth Plantation, 1620–47*, ed. Wor-thington C. Ford, 2 vols. (Boston, 1912), I, 156. Hereafter cited as *Of* *Plymouth*.

wilderness of New England in November is the city of eternal light, the New Jerusalem described in chapter 21 of the Book of Revelation. The Pilgrims believed that in the not-too-distant future, John's vision would become reality; a glorious society would be gathered where God would dwell so fully in all that 'no temple' would be 'therein, for the Lord God Almighty and the Lamb are the temple of it,' and 'the city' would have 'no need of the sun, neither of the moon, to shine in it: for the glory of God did lighten it, and the Lamb *is* the light thereof.' Yet until the day of the city's descent to earth, the chosen cannot do without temples. They must, as Paul wrote to the people of Corinth, come out of uncleanness, for they are the temple of the living God; 'a holy priesthood,' Peter calls them, 'lively stones,' joining together to build a spiritual house in love and affection.[13] Though each soul experiences salvation in its own unique and separate way, the central experience is the same for all, and in the new light, the wall between private and public is broken down.

The blueprints for the Separatists' spiritual house can be seen in two of John Robinson's letters, the first written at the 'parting' in 1620, the second sent in 1621 to 'the Church of God, at Plymouth, in New England.' Writing as their shepherd, Robinson, 'in love and dutie,' laid down the rules the Church must follow if it hoped to be a living temple. First, all brothers and sisters in Christ must daily 'renew . . . repentance with God,' for sins both known and unknown. In their precarious situation with a dangerous voyage before them, repentance for sins unknown became especially important. If, like the Ninevites, they repented sincerely, they might, though under judgment, avert God's wrath; if they did not, they would suffer the fate of Jonah. If he earnestly repented, a man would be pardoned; and 'great,' Robinson promised each Pilgrim, 'shall be his securitie and peace in all dangers, sweete his comforts in all distresses, with hapie deliverance from all evill, whether in life or in death.' When, after repentance, 'heavenly peace' rules in each man's heart, the next task is to make the peace live among all hearts. Robinson warned them to take special care 'that with your commone imployments you joyne commone affections truly bente

13. II Cor. 6; I Pet., 2:5.

upon the generall good, avoyding as a deadly plague of your both commone and spetiall comfort all retirednes of minde for proper advantage, and all singularly affected . . . maner of way.' It was crucial that 'every man represe in him selfe and the whol body in each person, as so many rebels against the commone good, all private respects of mens selves.' 'Be . . . I besheech you, brethern,' Robinson pleaded, 'careful that the house of God which you are, and are to be, be not shaken with unnecessarie novelties or other oppositions at the first setling thereof.'[14] In the second letter, written almost a year after the first, Robinson insistently echoes his earlier call for 'heavenly peace.' 'God forbid,' he writes, 'I should need to exhort you to peace, which is the bond of perfection, and by which all good is tied together, and without which it is scattered. Have peace with God first, by faith in his promises, good conscience kept in all things, and oft renewed by repentance: and so one with another, . . . for Christ's sake.'[15] Of all the corruptions threatening their peace, none turned out to be more destructive of their spiritual house in Plymouth than the 'deadly plague' of private affection. Late in life, as Bradford reviewed the past, it was the rebellion against the common good that he judged the cause of Plymouth's failure to fulfill its early promise. In his sly warfare against God, Satan had entered Plymouth disguised as 'necessitie' and 'insensibly by degrees'[16] destroyed the people's love for each other. It was by pleading 'necessitie' that some people had managed to break away from Marshfield in 1632; an act of encouragement to others, Bradford thought, who wanted to move 'under one pretense or other, thinking their owne conceived necessitie, and the example of others, a warrante sufficiente for them.' The result, he feared, would be New England's 'ruine.'[17]

That, even in the first years, Robinson's fear of private affection was well founded is indicated by Robert Cushman's 'A Sermon Preached at Plimmoth in New-England, December 9, 1621. . . .

14. *Of Plymouth*, I, 131–34.

15. 'Governor Bradford's Letter Book,' *Collections of the Massachusetts Historical Society*, 1st ser., III (Boston, 1794), 45.

16. *Of Plymouth*, I, 76.   17. *Ibid.*, II, 153.

Wherein Is Shewed the danger of self loue, and the sweetnesse of true friendship.'[18] The Plymouth community already is plagued by self-love; the people are succumbing to temptation. Taking his text from I Cor. 10:24, 'Let no man seek his own, but every man, another's wealth,' Cushman called his audience 'belly-gods' who sought riches, ease, 'new doctrines and deuices,' outward honor, and their own wills. Instead of seeking 'their owne bellies,' Cushman told them to concede their need of each other, for 'it is here yet but the first dayes, and (as it were), the dawning of this new world.' It was time 'to looke to present necessities . . . to open the doores, the chests, and vessels, and say, brother, neighbour, friend, what want yee?'[19] If each gave to all, Cushman promised them that they would be translated from 'this wandering wildernesse vnto that ioyfull and heauenly *Canaan*.'[20]

The harder the Separatists strove to bring their new world into being, and the more they suffered for its sake, the intenser grew their speculation about the time when they might expect the promises to be fulfilled in the incorruptible inheritance. Increasingly they became convinced that the inheritance would not be passed to them in England or on the Continent. Three years after the beginning of the Thirty Years Wars, Cushman wrote of the terrible judgment God was about to let loose on 'his people in the Christian countries of *Europe* (for their coldnesse, carnality, wanton abuse of the Gospel, contention, etc.), either by Turkish slavery, or by Popish tyrannie,'[21] and Robinson not only expected Babylon in Europe to be destroyed but considered it his obligation to further its destruction. Of course, this profound sense of impending disaster was general among English Puritans. For example, in 1629, John Winthrop stated in his *Reasons to be considered for iustifieinge the undertakers of the intended Plantation in New England, & for incouraginge such whose hartes God shall move to ioyne wth them in it*[22] that the 'churches of Europe are brought to desolation, & our sinnes, for which the Lord beginnes allreaddy to frowne

18. London, 1622. The following quotation is on pp. 5–8.

19. *Ibid.*, p. 15.   20. *Ibid.*, p. 20.   21. *Ibid.*, 'The Epistle Dedicatorie.

22. In Robert C. Winthrop, *Life and Letters of John Winthrop*, 2 vols. (Boston, 1869). The quotation is from Vol. I, p. 309.

upon us & to cutte us short, doe threatne evill times to be comminge upon us.' In this 'generall calamity,' God had provided New
England as a place of 'refuge,' where the church could be served by
spreading the gospel among the Indians, by raising a 'Bulworke'
against the Jesuits who were busy building Antichrist's kingdom,
and by helping 'on the comminge of the fullnesse of the Gentiles.'

As the day of darkness descended on Europe, the light of the
heavenly kingdom began to dawn in the American wilderness. As
more and more true Christians came to New England, 'a light,'
Cushman wrote, would 'rise up in the dark.' He could not 'thinke
but that there is some judgement not farre off, and that God will
shortly, euen of stones, rayse up children vnto Abraham.'[23] Likewise, Robinson, in his farewell sermon to the Pilgrims, told them
of a great glory awaiting them on the other side of the ocean. Surveying the state of the Protestant Churches in Europe, Robinson
could not but 'bewail' their 'condition.' He acknowledged that
Luther and Calvin had been 'precious shining lights in their times,'
but clearly God had still much grace to reveal. Robinson, Edward
Winslow wrote in Hypocrisie Unmasked, told the Church 'he was
very confident the Lord had more truth and light yet to break forth
out of his holy word,' for it was 'not possible the Christian world
should come so lately out of such Antichristian darkness, and that
full perfection of knowledge should break forth at once.'[24] The moment of 'full perfection' would, of course, be the millennium, and
no Separatist preacher dared predict the precise year of Christ's
coming; but for many years, Robinson had been stating his belief
in a glorious harvest of souls to take place about the year 1700.
Thus, in A Justification, he writes, ten years before the Pilgrims left
Holland: 'And the many that are already gathered by the mercy of
God into the kingdom of his Son Jesus, and the nearness of many
more through the whole land, for the regions are white unto the
harvest, do promise within less than a hundred years, if our sins and

23. Cushman, 'The Epistle Dedicatorie.'

24. Edward Winslow, Hypocrisie Unmasked (London, 1646), quoted in
Chronicles of the Pilgrim Fathers . . . , ed. Alexander Young (Boston,
1844), pp. 397–98.

theirs make not us and them unworthy of this mercy, a very plenteous harvest.' For this great harvest—Robinson envisaged it as another reformation—the Separatists were to act as forerunners, as sowers seeding the fields with future Luthers and Calvins in the same way 'John Huss and Jerome of Prague finished their testimony in Bohemia and at Constance, a hundred years before Luther; and Wickliffe in England well nigh as long before them, and yet neither the one nor the other with the like success unto Luther.' 'It must be . . . considered,' Robinson wrote, 'that religion is not always sown and reaped in one age: "one soweth and another reapeth!" '[25]

Throughout his life, Bradford shared Robinson's belief in the Separatists as sowers of the imminent reformation. Thus in chapter IV of *Of Plymouth Plantation* he gives as one of the four major reasons for the Pilgrims' decision to move to New England their 'great hope . . . for the propagating, and advancing the gospell of the Kingdom of Christ in the remote parts of the world; yea though they should be but even as stepping-stones, unto others for the performing of so great a work.'[26] It was not simply a desire to save the souls of the Indians that made the advancing of the Gospel crucial for the Pilgrims; equally important, perhaps more so, was their conviction that the Indians must be converted if the marriage of Jew and Gentile that heralded the coming of Christ's Kingdom were to be consummated.[27] Later, in the annal for 1629, Bradford expresses his hope that the arrival of more members from Leyden signifies 'the beginning of a larger harvest unto the Lord, in the increase of his churches and people in these parts, to the admiration of many, and allmost wonder of the world.'[28] As the seventeenth century progressed, Bradford began to wonder if the fields of the Lord had not ripened much earlier than Robinson had foretold. In 1648, he had 'Ancient Men' of the *First Dialogue* tell 'Young

25. Robinson, Works, II, 66.   26. Of Plymouth, I, 55.

27. See Sacvan Bercovitch, 'The Historiography of Johnson's Wonder-Working Providence,' Essex Institute Historical Collections, CIV (1968), 138–61.

28. Of Plymouth, II, 63.

Men,' that it seemed 'as if' Robinson 'had prophesied of these times'[29]—of 1648 rather than of 1700. Four years later, when he composed the *Third Dialogue*, he was less certain that these were the promised times, but he did not relinquish his faith in being part of a great cycle of redemption. 'In the beginning of the Protestant reformation, "Ancient-Men" ask "Young-Men," how could they so clearly see in the dawning, as we may now in the meridian, if we will but open our eyes?'[30]

No passage more convincingly demonstrates the fierceness of Bradford's millennial expectations than the long 'A late observation, as it were by the way, worthy to be noted,' that Bradford adds to *Of Plymouth Plantation* in 1646. 'A late observation' opens with Bradford's acknowledgment that the English Puritans' victory over spiritual Babylon has caught him by surprise. 'Full little did I thinke,' he writes, 'that the downfall of the Bishops, with their courts, cannons, and ceremonies, &c. had been so neare when I first began these scribled writings (which was aboute the year 1630, and so peeced up at times of leasure afterward) or that I should have lived, to have seene, or heard of the same; but it is the lords doing, and ought to be marvelous in our eyes!' As Bradford celebrates the destruction of the Anglican bishops, 'Babell,' he strings together texts from the Old and New Testaments proclaiming the triumph of God's saints over the satanic forces of Babylon. Like the Jews conquering the promised land from the giant Anakims, and like David, newly crowned king of Israel, routing the Jebusites from Jerusalem, the Puritans have slain the forces of evil and taken possession of their heavenly Jerusalem. Addressing the saints at Plymouth, Bradford asks them:

Doe you not now see the fruits of your labours, O all yee servants of the lord? that have suffered for his truth, and have been faithfull witneses of the same, and yee little handfull amongst the rest, the least amongest the thousands of Israll? You have not only had a seede time, but many of you have seene the joyfull Harvest.

29. William Bradford, *A Dialogue . . . Anno Domini 1648*, in Young, *Chronicles . . . Pilgrim Fathers*, p. 423.

30. William Bradford, *A Dialogue or 3d Conference*, in *Proceedings of the Massachusetts Historical Society*, XI (Boston, 1870), 448.

Should you not then rejoyse? yea, and again rejoyce, and say Hal-
lelu-iah, salvation, and glorie, and honour, and power, be to the lord
our God; for true, and righteous are his Judgements. Rev. 19:1, 2.

As he continues, Bradford's fervor rises to a pitch, and he reaches
for the text from Revelation where John sees the heavens open and
Christ on a white horse leading the heavenly hosts to the glorious
victory that ushers in the reign of peace for a thousand years. 'Who
hath done it?' Bradford asks rhetorically, 'who, even he that siteth
on the white horse, who is caled faithfull, and true, and judgeth,
and fighteth righteously. . . . Whose garments are dipte in blood,
and his name was caled the word of God. . . . For he shall rule them
with a rode of Iron; for it is he that treadeth the winepress of the
feircenes, and wrath of god almighty! And he hath upon his gar-
mente, and upon his thigh, a name writen, The King of Kings, and
Lord of Lords. . . . HALLELU-IAH. Anno Dom: 1646.'[31] The
long-awaited moment had finally arrived. For decades, the Separatists had identified the Anglican episcopacy with the antitypical
Babylon that must be destroyed if the heavenly city were to be
built. The more the bishops persecuted them by imprisonment,
exile, and death, the deeper the Separatists' conviction grew, and
when the longed-for downfall finally did happen, Bradford could
see its momentous significance only by relating it to John's vision
of Christ's descent.

Bradford's joy at the bishops' downfall is deep and genuine; it is
also shrill, almost desperate. God has poured his blessing on England; New England is not the chosen place. What role than for the
Church at Plymouth, that 'little handfull amongst the rest,' who
had been among the sowers and now were witnessing the 'joyefull
Harvest' in God's English fields? Twenty-five years earlier they had
crossed into the wilderness, confident that, as Robinson had promised them, 'the Lord had more truth and light to break out of his
holy word.' But now, in 1646, Bradford had to admit that the light
had broken out first in the very land they had left behind. Still,
Bradford by no means thought all was lost for Plymouth. The New
England churches remained within the universal Israel, the true

31. *Of Plymouth,* I, 14–16.

church. What he and his people must do was to accept God's judgment, repent, and reform.

The textual evidence suggests that Bradford responded to the downfall of the bishops' Babel by writing most, if not all of Book Two of Of Plymouth Plantation. Just as, in 1630, the planting of true churches elsewhere in America had been one reason for his writing Book One, so in 1645–46, events in England prompted him to make a formal history of the notes he had been keeping for fifteen years. In these two periods, one beginning in 1630, the other probably in 1645–46, Bradford's feelings of joy at the spreading light and his fear of God's judgment on Plymouth grew so acute that he felt compelled to picture the glorious past, so that the younger generation might see and emulate their ancestors. About the date of composition for Book One there is no question. Bradford himself said that he began it in 1630. Probably it did not take long to write; it fills only fifty-two of two hundred and seventy pages in the manuscript, and, in contrast to Book Two with its twenty-six separate annals, Book One stands a sustained and continuous narrative divided into eleven chapters. With regard to composition of Book Two, we can say with great certainty that Bradford wrote all the post-1631 annals, about one-third of the history, after 1639. In the 1631 annal, Bradford includes a passage about Isaac Allerton taking an 'oath . . . concerning this ship, the Whit-Angell, before the Governor and Deputie, the 7 of September, 1639.'[32] However, more crucial for a precise dating of the writing of Of Plymouth Plantation is a passage in the annal for 1621 where Bradford tells of the first marriage in Plymouth, which, 'according to the laudable custome of the Low-cuntries, in which they had lived, was thought most requisite to be performed by the magistrate, as being a civill thing . . . and most consonate to the scriptures, Ruth ·4· and no wher found in the gospell to be layed on the ministers as a part of their office. . . . And this practiss hath continued amongst, not only them, but hath been followed by all the famous churches of Christ in these parts to this time, Anno: 1646.'[33] There is nothing in the manuscript that indicates the date

32. Ibid., II, 128.   33. Ibid., I, 218–19.

'Anno: 1646' was not written at the same time as the rest of the passage. On the contrary, the color of the ink, the uniform hand-writing, even the evident flaw in the pen, all indicate strongly that the larger part of the 1621 annal and all the subsequent history were written twenty-five years after the events had taken place. In other words, very likely, all of *Of Plymouth Plantation* is a work of retrospection. The writing of Book Two took about four years. The last annal, that of 1646, was finished in 1650; Bradford comments on Edward Winslow's trip to England, that he 'was detained longer than was expected . . . and so he hath now been absente this '4' years.'[34]

Identifying the likely dates for the composition of *Of Plymouth Plantation* makes it possible for us to draw two general conclusions about Bradford's decision to turn historian. First, that Bradford wrote his History in the two relatively short periods points to his unspoken assumption that history written is less vital than history lived. Second, in the exultant, anxious moments when Christ's kingdom seemed to be advancing elsewhere in the world his need to write his notes into formal history became pressing. His note-taking indicates that from the beginning he may not have been entirely satisfied with the way Plymouth was acting its role in the history of redemption, but his dissatisfaction did not become suffi-ciently strong to urge him to write formally until 1630 and 1645. For the first decade and for the years between 1630 and 1645, Bradford judged the life of the Plymouth Church to be, in some measure at least, the living fulfillment of the ancient promises. Like many of his contemporaries, Bradford believed history would be fulfilled, not in another book, another written word, but in a new state of being. History, he thought, was not something that just happened *to* him and his fellow Separatists; it lived *in* and *through* them. Of course, they did not regard themselves as the ultimate antitypes; but they did firmly believe that their lives were divine synecdoches, minute but vital parts in the great arch of grace spanning from Abraham to the New Jerusalem. As long as they could be reasonably confident that they stood under God's special providence, that they were growing in brotherly affection

34. *Ibid.*, II, 393–94.

and evolving toward the future glory, what need to record past events? As long as Christ the Word lived within as love and affection, what more would history offer? Surely mere words could not equal a living body as an expression of power. To be history transcended writing history.

The Pilgrims believed God had chosen them to be his synecdoches in history because their religious experience had convinced them they could be no other. In their present life, they had, they felt, tasted and seen the life of the future. Describing the setting up of the first Separatist Churches, Bradford writes that God had touched the people's 'harts . . . with heavenly zeale for his trueth,'[35] by which he meant that they had experienced a new life within them; out of death, of void and nothingness, another man had emerged. Not Adam, but Christ now lived within them. This divine touch altered not only the way they felt about the world but the way they acted in the world. To be one with the Spirit made the body into a temple of God. The flesh became the means for testifying or making manifest the new man within. And what was true of the individual was true also of the community; in its outward life, its body, a society of faithful declared that God dwelled in its midst. Further, in both individual and community, the religious experience created an assurance of redemption as a never-ending process. The new birth within had been so momentous that what had sprung to life must, it seemed, continue to grow until its ultimate union with the divine, a union consummated in silence, in, as Bradford wrote, quoting Zechariah, the stillness of flesh before the Lord.[36]

In 1630 and 1645 when the living stones of Plymouth seemed to be hardening into dead walls, when private interests were threatening the common good, and God was signifying his displeasure by choosing other men and places to receive his blessings, the time had come to hold up a mirror of past glory wherein the people might see their ancestors' former holiness. In his mirror, Bradford hoped, the ancient virtues would be so literally and brightly reflected that they would act as an irresistible model for imitation. Consequently, Bradford fashioned *Of Plymouth Plantation* to

35. *Ibid.*, I, 20.   36. Zechariah 2:12.

make the strongest possible impression on the younger generation. Undoubtedly, he wanted to demonstrate to the whole world what great deeds Christ had performed in New England but, more immediately, he wanted to assist the children at home as they carried on their warfare against Satan. Throughout *Of Plymouth Plantation*, certain episodes are related and others ignored; some letters are quoted fully and some not at all. Bradford wrote biographies of his personal heroes while neglecting other important figures. Clearly he weighed which episode, letter, or biography would make the greatest impact on his spiritual heirs. As historian, Bradford's aim is not to portray the past with the fullest possible objectivity but to resurrect a bygone holiness; a holiness that, he knows and never loses sight of, must be resurrected by and in his audience.[37]

Sometimes Bradford's exhortation is explicit, at other times implicit, but it is always present. For example, in the passage from chapter IX in Book One, 'But hear I cannot but stay and make a pause . . . ,' Bradford emphasizes the first planters' sole reliance on 'the spirite of God and his grace' to make their children 'rightly say: *our faithers were English men which came over this great ocean, and were ready to perish in this willdernes, but they cried unto the Lord, and he heard their voyce, and looked on their adversitie, etc. Let them therefore praise the Lord, because he is good, and his mercies endure for ever. . . . Let them confess before the Lord his loving kindnes, and his wonderfull works before the sons of men.'*[38] If, in the most desperate circumstances, your fathers had such a faith in the Lord, what, Bradford seems to be asking the young, ' "may and ought" you not believe who have received so many more outward evidences of his grace?' 'What great work of the spirit is not in store for you if you return to trusting in the Lord as they did?'

37. I am indebted to Professor John Demos' discussion of the parent-child relationship in Plymouth. See John Demos, *A Little Commonwealth: Family Life in Plymouth Colony* (New York, 1970); see also Professor William Scheick's perceptive essay, 'Anonymity and Art in *The Life and Death of That Reverend Man of God, Mr. Richard Mather*,' *American Literature*, XLII (January, 1971), 457–67.

38. *Of Plymouth*, I, 155–58.

Again, in chapter IV, Bradford's purpose is more complex than simply to give the reasons for 'removall.' Indirectly, he is inviting the young in New England to measure their actions against their fathers' unselfish devotion to the common good. Were they, he wondered, those 'others' who would advance the great work of redemption in the wilderness? At a time when they were moving away from Plymouth,[39] Bradford wanted them to measure their 'necessity' against the hardships the older generation had endured to preserve the sacred bond of their fellowship. Was it worth tearing it asunder for a little more land? Did they want to leave Plymouth, as their elders had left Holland, 'not out of any new fangled-nes, or other shuch like giddie humor, by which men are oftentimes transported to their great hurt, and danger. But for sundrie weightie and solid reasons'?[40] From his description of their fathers' heated debate about moving, did the young not see how deeply people could disagree without destroying the covenant? Had they considered the cost, the 'great hurt'?

Bradford's exhortations are stated more directly in the brief comments accompanying many of the letters he inserted throughout *Of Plymouth Plantation.* For example, in chapter VI, having quoted letters and documents extensively, Bradford concludes by explaining that he has 'bene the larger in these things, and so shall crave leave in some like passages following, (thoug in other things I shal labour to be more contracte,) that their children may see with what difficulties their fathers wrastled in going throug these things in their first beginnings, and how God brought them along notwithstanding all their weaknesses and infirmities. As allso that some use may be made hereof in after times by others in shuch like waightie imployments.'[41] Bradford quoted so many letters because, he said, he wanted to show no prejudice. He would relate some events more fully than others, but he desired rather 'to manefest

---

39. See Samuel Eliot Morison, *The Story of the 'Old Colony' of New Plymouth* [1620–1692] (New York, 1956), pp. 138–40; George D. Langdon, *Pilgrim Colony: A History of New Plymouth, 1620–91* (New Haven, 1966), pp. 38–57; and Darrett B. Rutman, *Husbandmen of Plymouth; Farms and Villages in the Old Colony 1620–1692* (Boston, 1967), pp. 3–27.

40. *Of Plymouth,* I, 52.   41. *Ibid.,* I, 120.

things' in other people's own 'words and apprehentions, then in my owne, as much as may be, without tediousness.'[42] However, Bradford's impartiality is not the same as disinterest. He would let people speak their own pieces; and in their deceiving or loving words, they would show more clearly than Bradford could on whose side they had fought in the great war between God and Satan. Tedious it might be to quote letters full of details about obscure financial matters, but the minutest of details was supremely important for the faith or the betrayal it manifested. As Bradford would later turn to the literal language of creation to see for himself the ancient holiness, so he inserted the literal facts of Plymouth's past in order that the young might see the naked truth with their own eyes. Letters were the means whereby the truth could be literally drawn out of the past to live again in the present; letters, Bradford agreed, 'were the better parte of histories.'[43]

If letters were the most important way Bradford chose to bring the past into the present in *Of Plymouth Plantation*, the second most important way to realize the original state was biography. In letters, a man's nature could speak for itself, but in biography, the historian could inject his own views and create a memorial, a paean and an exhortation. In biography, the virtues of the dead had not died but spoke to their children. Bradford wrote two major biographies in *Of Plymouth Plantation*, one of Robinson in chapter III of Book One and one of Brewster in the 1643 annal. In his picture of Robinson, Bradford emphasized the Leyden pastor's love of his flock and his devotion to the common good. He was, Bradford writes, in 'every way . . . a commone father unto them,' and when he died, it was as hard for the Pilgrims to find another leader as it had been for 'ye Taborits to find another Ziska.'[44] The biography of Brewster is very different. Where in 1630 Bradford is content to stress Robinson's devotion to the fellowship, his attitude fifteen years later is much more violent and apocalyptic. He portrays Brewster as a man of great faith and courage who patiently suffered poverty, persecution, exile, and other tribulations. As elder of the Church, Brewster was careful 'to preserve good order . . . and puritie . . . , and to suppress any error or contention that might begine

42. *Ibid.*, p. 317.   43. *Ibid.*, p. 106.   44. *Ibid.*, p. 43.

to rise up amongst them.'[45] His most 'singuler good gift' was in prayer, in 'ripping up the hart and conscience before God.'[46] As evidence of God's special blessing and 'marvelous providence' on Brewster, Bradford singles out his long life. Exposed more than ordinary men to dangers that could easily have killed him, Brewster lived to be almost eighty—a clear testimony that he and his fellow believers were 'upheld' by God in the same manner the Old Testament patriarchs Daniel and Jacob were preserved by special providence. 'Daniell,' Bradford writes, 'could be better liking with pulse then others were with the kings dainties,' and 'Jacob though he wente from one nation to another people, and passed thorow famine, fears, and many afflictions, yet he lived till old age, and dyed sweetly and rested in the Lord, as infinite others of Gods servants have done, and still shall doe.'[47]

These parallels between the old and modern heroes are interesting examples of Bradford's use of the Old Testament, but even more remarkable is the framework of threat and damnation within which the whole biography is set. After a brief description of Brewster's dying moments, Bradford asks if he 'was the worse for any former sufferings? What doe I say, worse? Nay, sure he was the better, and they now added to his honour.'[48] And Bradford, then, in the manner of 'A late observation' quotes several Bible texts that, on one hand, promise the just that their sufferings will be rewarded in the imminent kingdom, and, on the other, warn the wicked that they 'shall rott (with their marble monuments).'[49] In other words, in the beginning of the biography, Bradford implicitly asks the reader where he wants to be: in the field of the saints ripening for the harvest, or rotting with the wicked? This implicit question is renewed in the end when he quotes two texts from Job and Psalms where the destruction of 'bloody and deceitfull men,' and the cutting off 'ye branch of ye wicked'[50] are threatened. This attitude, at once promising the greatest of delights and threatening the ultimate rejection, can be found throughout Of Plymouth Plantation; but it emerges sharply in the later annals, indicating Bradford's increasing uneasiness with the spiritual state of

45. Ibid., II, 350.   46. Ibid., pp. 350–51.   47. Ibid., pp. 351–53.

48. Ibid., p. 343.   49. Ibid.   50. Ibid., p. 353.

Plymouth. It also demonstrates the tenacity with which he clung to his belief in the promises. Though events might have gone counter to his expectations for the future, he could not possibly give up his faith in the New Jerusalem. Like Ainsworth, having had a profound experience of fulfillment within himself, Bradford could not conceive of the promises as false or irrelevant. On the contrary, the further Plymouth seemed to fall from grace, the more Bradford felt the need to assert the validity of the promises. And the more adamant his insistence, the more violent his threat of destruction, the fiercer his call for repentance and sacrifice.

How profoundly Bradford and the Pilgrims conceived their lives in terms of this double attitude is seen in Robinson's *New Essays; or, Observations Divine and Moral*, especially chapter III, 'Of God's Promises,' chapter XXVIII, 'Of Afflictions,' and chapter XIX, 'Of Examples.' Following conventional covenant theology, Robinson defines 'the promises of God' as 'a kind of middle thing between [God's] purpose, and performance of good unto them, whom he loveth.' Because of his love, God has revealed the promises as signs of his willingness to be 'a debtor' to man, 'though not by receiving from us, yet by promising unto us; promise being as we say, due debt.' In order that God's love may 'satisfy itself in a gracious purpose of good towards us in his heart, and actual performance of it accordingly, in due time,' God makes the promise

known unto us beforehand, both for our present comfort in the knowledge thereof, and for the ground of our hope and expectation of the good things promised, and accordingly to be received at his hands, in their time: he having by his promise bound over unto us both his love, and truth, and other attributes for performance. And herein, the Lord provides very graciously for his poor servants, who are ofttimes brought into that distressed state both outward and inward, as they have very little else, save the promises of God, wherewith to comfort themselves. Which yet are sufficient, if we improve them, as we ought.[51]

Most significantly, Robinson links afflictions with the promises and interprets sufferings as prophetic of the New Jerusalem. A man,

51. Robinson, *Works*, I, 8.

Robinson thinks, first experiences the suffering as punishment for sin, but, as he begins to mourn and repent, he perceives that God has both dealt justly with him in punishing his sin and led him to a new realization of mercy. 'It is most necessary,' Robinson writes, 'for all his people ever to hold this general conclusion; that in all their afflictions the justice and mercy of God meet together; and that he begins in justice, and will end in mercy.'[52] The believer comes to see that God does not sanctify crosses to men, but men to crosses 'in giving us grace to make a right use of them,' and right use is 'to thank God, that makes afflictions bittersweet, by turning deserved curses into fatherly corrections to us.'[53] As the repentant heart's experience of affliction changes from justice to mercy, the sufferings become harbingers of the New Jerusalem, prophecies peculiarly fitted to typify the second coming. Robinson writes in a crucially important passage:

God hath, in a peculiar manner, entailed afflictions to the sincere profession of the gospel, above that of the law before Christ. The law was given by Moses, whose ministry began with killing the Egyptian, that oppressed the Israelite; and was prosecuted with leading the people out of Egypt, through the sea, and wilderness, with great might, and a strong hand; and lastly was finished with bloody victory over Sihon, and Og the kings of Canaan. But Christ's dispensation was all of another kind: his birth mean; his life sorrowful; and his death shameful. And albeit the love of God towards his people be always the same in itself, yet is the manifestation thereof very diverse. Before Christ's coming in the flesh, in whom the grace of God appeared, God showed his love more fully in earthly blessings, and peace; and more sparingly in spiritual, and heavenly: but now, on the other side, he dealeth forth temporal blessings more sparingly; and spiritual with a fuller hand. It is not improbably gathered that, after the destruction of the dragon, and beast, and recalling of the Jews after their long divorce from the Lord, and the blessings of both kinds shall meet together, and the Church enjoy, for a time, a very graceful state upon the earth both in regard of spiritual, and bodily good things.[54]

52. Ibid., p. 140.   53. Ibid., p. 143.   54. Ibid., pp. 140–41.

The afflictions, the 'crosses of Christ' that are prophetic of the 'very graceful state' are threefold. The first cross is persecution for Christ's sake; and the Pilgrims knew persecution directly and fully. The second cross is the evil men inflict when the faithful speak out 'Christ's truth.' The last cross is the sufferings that occur 'in the course of godliness, though human, and as they do all other men; as bodily sickness, death of friends, crosses, losses by sea, and land, and the like.'[55] When these afflictions are suffered for Christ's sake —but only then—do they prefigure his kingdom. In such times, the repentant believer can rest assured that God will provide all the strength necessary to meet and overcome the trial. And if he makes the cross heavier, he will increase the strength and bring about 'full deliverance in due time. "He will redeem Israel from all his trouble." '[56]

In light of Robinson's writings on justice and mercy mixed in the afflictions, *Of Plymouth Plantation* becomes a deeply and deliberately prophetic book. The union of justice and mercy is present in little providences (the salvation of a man fallen overboard), and in great events (the journey of the entire company toward the heavenly Canaan); whether minor or major, the Pilgrims' sufferings foreshadow their 'deliverance in due time.' Bradford did not include so many remarkable and special providences simply to record the many times he had witnessed the hand of God intervening on behalf of the saints or to eulogize the steadfastness of the first planters; above all, he wanted to portray the affliction so that the promise of the New Jerusalem would be set clearly before the next generation. For example, in chapter II, when the Pilgrims leave England to go to Holland, Bradford, having struck the motif of the search for another country, shapes the voyage in imitation of Christ's crucifixion and resurrection. Like Christ, the Pilgrims were 'often times betrayed,'[57] persecuted, and imprisoned: clearly an example of affliction suffered for Christ's sake. Because of persecution, the men became separated from their wives and children and almost lost their lives in a terrible storm. However, at the point when they had given up all hope of reaching land and had resigned themselves to death, 'the ship rose againe.' Bradford writes,

55. *Ibid.*, p. 142.   56. *Ibid.*, p. 144.   57. *Of Plymouth*, I, 30.

If modestie would suffer me, I might declare with what fervente prayres they cried unto the lord in this great distres, (espetialy some of them) even without any great distraction when the water rane into their mouthes and ears: and the mariners cried out we sinke, we sinke; they cried (if not with mirakelous, yet with a great hight or degree of devine faith) yet Lord thou canst save; yet Lord thou canst save. . . . Upon which the ship did not only recover, but shortly after the violence of the storme begane to abate; and the lord filed their afflicted minds with .shuch comforts as every one cannot understand. And in the end brought them to their desired Haven, wher the people came flockeing admiring their deliverance, the storme having ben so longe and sore, in which much hurt had been don.[58]

For Bradford, the deliverance from the terrors of the storm is a remarkable instance of God's special providence whereby he saves men and gives them a life of faith more vivid than they had ever known before. But more than that, the deliverance is a prophecy of the time when the church, the ship of God's chosen, voyaging toward the promised land, has weathered the storms of history and reached its final 'haven.' It promises that those who are persecuted, imprisoned, separated, and exiled, all shall be delivered and united as the Pilgrims were after 'these first conflicts, and sharp beginings' when 'all gat over at length, some at one time, and some at an other, and some in one place, and some in an other, And mete togeather againe according to their desires, with no small rejoycing.'[59] On the other shore, the people who have gone before stand waiting.

In this passage, as throughout Book One, Bradford's tone is quietly, even joyously triumphant. Writing ten years after the crossing, he knew that the outcome of all his and the other Pilgrims' sufferings had been a most magnificent and merciful deliverance. From the setting up of the first Separatist Churches in England to the raising of the first house 'for common use' in Plymouth in the very season that Israel had begun the building of the temple in Jerusa-

---

58. *Ibid.*, p. 33.

59. *Ibid.*, p. 35; Levin, in *History and Theory*, VII (1968), 389.

lem thousands of years before, the Pilgrims' lives had been an example of the way God brought his chosen peoples out of death into new life. This certitude that all of their early history was analogous to Christ's Passion is reflected in the structure of Book One. The eleven chapters—and they are chapters, not annals—tell of remarkable providences that reenact Christ's death and resurrection, but each providential event is not an isolated episode; it is one further stage in the larger and continuous movement toward the building of the new temple. Book Two, on the other hand, is very different. Where each chapter in Book One deals with the events of more than one year, the twenty-five annals in Book Two describe what happened in each of the years between 1620 and 1646.[60] The annals are filled with extraordinary scenes from the history of Plymouth's salvation; but they do not stand as parts of a great and coherent whole, as actions in an evolving drama. The years are shining but isolated moments, beads of revelation that remain unstrung. In Book One, Bradford's primary concern is with action; in Book Two his preoccupation is with time. The difference between the two books is the distance between the voice of 1630 calmly and confidently exhorting the reader to pause and consider the people in the wilderness, and the voice of 1646 leaping to its recitation of the verses from the Book of Revelation.

However, the fact that the tone of Book One is joyous and triumphant does not mean that Bradford felt only joy and triumph about Plymouth when he began to write. The confidence of his first narrative draws its strength from being a relation of past actions; the present is not directly dealt with. Indeed, much that was happening in New England in 1630 seemed to Bradford to necessitate repentance. Most important, the people were forsaking the common good. And what did God mean to signify to Plymouth by planting so many new churches in the Bay? And what did he mean to signify by the first murder, when John Billington killed John Newcomen? Bradford may have been pleased to see so many pure and primitive churches being planted in the wilderness. So, at least, he appears to be when, in the 1630 annal, he lauds the Plymouth Church for having been that 'one small candle' whose 'light here

60. The events for 1639 and 1640 are combined into one annal.

kindled hath shone to many, yea in some sort to our whole nation; let the glorious name of Jehova have all the praise.'[61] Proud he may have been, but also, we sense, sad and wistful. Writing in retrospect fifteen years later, Bradford seems regretful and apprehensive about the consequences that the settling of Boston had had and would have on Plymouth.

Still, the situation in 1630 was a far cry from that of 1646. In 1646, the longed-for reformation was taking place three thousand miles away, in the very place the Pilgrims so deliberately and at such great cost had left behind. As Bradford confronted these events and their meaning, it seemed that God had told the people in New England that they must look inward and acknowledge their spiritual failures. And repent quickly, for though they had 'full little' expected the joyful harvest to begin so soon, it was now very clear that God was reaping all around them. The enormous tension Bradford must have felt in the late 1640's and 1650's shows itself in the way he uses the afflictions in the annals. As in Book One, he continues to see events as analogous to Christ's death and resurrection. Whether it be a terrible drought that is broken by 'sweete and gentle showers,' resulting in a 'fruitfull and liberall harvest,'[62] or famines eased by providential arrivals of relief ships or by rich catches from the sea, Bradford aims to demonstrate the myriad ways God lets life sprout out of death.

To looke humanly on the state of things as they presented them selves at this time [he writes in the 1626 annal], it is a marvell it did not wholy discourage them, and sinck them. But they gathered up their spirits, and the Lord so helped them, whose worke they had in hand, as now when they were at lowest they begane to rise againe, and being striped (in a maner) of all humane helps and hopes, he brought things aboute other wise, in his devine providence, as they were not only upheld and sustained, but their proceedings both honoured and imitated by others; as by the sequel will more appeare, if the Lord spare me life and time to declare the same.[63]

Clearly the basic pattern remains the same throughout *Of Plymouth Plantation*; what is greatly diminished is the delighted assur-

---

61. *Of Plymouth*, I, 117.   62. *Ibid.*, p. 325.   63. *Ibid.*, pp. 446–47.

ance that in bringing them into the wilderness, God is bringing them home to himself. The presence of mercy, of 'good in the later end,' is strenuously asserted; but the deliverance does not seem vividly or joyously experienced. Instead, the dominant tone becomes a mixed one of damnation and reward. The union of justice and mercy within the same experience no longer holds, and Bradford confronts Plymouth with an increasingly absolute and cataclysmic choice.

The more events did not conform to his expectations, to his knowledge of the end God has in mind in history, the deeper grew Bradford's sense of sinfulness, both personal and communal. The less liberty, order, and beauty that emerged from his sufferings, the more punished he felt, the greater failure he judged himself to be. In his pain, he responded with an angry but tightly controlled demonstration of the betrayal perpetuated on Plymouth by all those men, especially the merchant-adventurers and agents, who had put their own interests above the common good. It was not God's promises that had failed, but men who had not carried his promises along toward their fulfillment. Thus, commenting on Thomas Weston, who deserted the Pilgrims though he had promised to stand by them forever, Bradford paraphrases Psalm 146: 'Put not your trust in princes (much less in merchants) not in the sone of man, for there is no help in them.'[64] Not only does Bradford thus bring Weston under God's judgment, but in a moment of outrage, he drops his mask of objectivity and passes his own sentence on the betrayer. 'See,' he cries indignantly, 'how his promise is fulfild.'[65]

In most of the annals, Bradford, writing retrospectively, seems intent on showing what might have been if a deeper devotion of all to all had prevailed. In the 1628 annal, for example, he describes what looks like a promising turn of events. Isaac Allerton, Brewster's son-in-law and agent for the Plantation, had paid off a large part of the debt owed to the English merchants and had begun to make arrangements for the people from Leyden to come across. Having drawn this picture of promise, Bradford, in the next three annals, records how the promise failed through Allerton's rashness, deceit, and greed, and how, by 1631, Plymouth, instead of being

64. *Ibid.*, p. 258.   65. *Ibid.*, p. 263.

free, was five thousand pounds in debt. So it was with Ashley, who put private over public interests—Ashley, who walked naked among the Indians, slept with their women, learned their language, and sold them weapons. Allerton got his just reward; he was ostracized, moved to Connecticut, and died bankrupt. Ashley met his deserved end by falling overboard on a return trip from Russia, where he had been trading for beaver.[66] In these cases, Bradford's way of anticipating the future day of righteousness when God will call men to stand before him is to put down every penny and every beaverpelt that people have used to further their own ends rather than those of God's plantation at Plymouth. He will gather all the naked facts and make the judgment certain.

In his use of afflictions, Bradford, we have seen, concentrates on the relationship between present suffering and future freedom, between crucifixion and resurrection. However, he believes that Christ's Passion is more than the key to the future; it is also the experience through which to view the past. Of course, the Separatists accepted the traditional typological view of the Old Testament as prophetic of Christ and his Church. Thus Robinson writes that 'the whole priesthood of Aaron, under which the law was established . . . was a type of Christ's priesthood, though the high priests in a special manner, and their sacrifices . . . , and being a part of the law, which was a shadow or first draught . . . whereof the gospel is the lively portraiture . . . it must needs be ceremonial, and so a type.'[67] Yet, for Robinson and Bradford, it was more important to see the Old Testament figures as people who in their afflictions knew death and rebirth. Abraham's willingness to sacrifice Isaac may well be prophetic of Christ's sacrifice, but the experience precedes the prophecy. As a living reality, Christ, Bradford believed, was present to Abraham. It was this belief, similar to Ainsworth's faith in Christ's presence in both Old and New Canaans, that made it possible for the Separatists to identify closely with the holy patriarchs. Brewster's life reenacts Jacob's and Daniel's; the Pilgrims' wanderings retrace Israel's exile and search for the promised land. Arrived in New England, Bradford stands as Moses stood on Mt. Pisgah, and the downfall of the bishops brings to life once more

66. *Ibid.*, II, 107–08.   67. Robinson, *Works*, II, 183.

the defeat of Jebusites and Anakims. The Old Testament events and people are, as Bradford calls them, 'examples.'[68] Yet they are more than exemplary, more than static emblems of virtue, courage, longevity, or faith. Between Israel and Plymouth exists more than a parallel, more than an analogy; for when God's chosen peoples go in search of Canaans, the ancient lives are reenacted. The past lives again in the present. 'We are,' Robinson maintained, 'the sons and daughters of Abraham by faith.'[69] The later reenactments differ from the first drama only in fullness; the light breaking out of the Word in 1620 shines more clearly than the light breaking in on Abraham or Moses.

This sense of being one more, perhaps the final, reenactment of the primitive state extends to the Separatists' view of their Church and its place in the history of redemption.[70] 'As we do believe by the Word of God,' Robinson wrote, 'that the things we teach are not new, but old truths renewed; so are we no less fully persuaded that the church constitution in which we are set, is cast in the Apostolic and primitive mould, and not one day nor hour younger, in the nature or form of it, than the first church of the New Testament.'[71] 'In essence,' the church 'is one and the same . . . from the beginning to the end of the world.'[72] In fact, Robinson believed the ideal Separatist Church to be not an hour younger than the moment when 'the Lord created a church of angels in heaven, which were all good and holy without mixture, till some by sin fell from their first and original estate.'[73] In his writings about a church forever old, forever new, Robinson establishes a view of the history of redemption in which the moments that become crucial are other than those traditionally regarded as the apexes of the covenant of grace. Robinson accepts—almost offhandedly—the usual division of sacred history into four periods, 'the first whereof is from the beginning of the world, till the giving of the law: the second from the law, till Christ's coming: the third from Christ, till the end of the

68. Of Plymouth, II, 352.   69. Robinson, Works, II, 207.

70. For a later development of this concept in Puritan thought, see Mason I. Lowance, Jr., 'Cotton Mather's Magnalia and the Metaphors of Biblical History,' pp. 139 ff. below.

71. Robinson, Works, II, 43.   72. Ibid., p. 298.   73. Ibid., p. 119.

history of the New Testament: the fourth, and last from that time, hitherto.'[74] But for Robinson, as for Bradford, the turning points have been the moments of separation when the primitive church once more has emerged out of darkness into light. Such moments are the first gathering of the angels in heaven, the church of Adam and Eve, Israel in her exodus out of Egypt, her leaving Babylon, and the establishment of the Apostolic Church. Yet another time was, as Bradford describes it in the opening sentence of *Of Plymouth Plantation*, 'the first breakinge out of the light of the gospell, in our Honourable Nation of England.'[75] For Robinson and Bradford, those circles of light were related to each other, not as static repetitions but as interweaving cycles of ever-growing redemption. Robinson's vision was of a world with churches on every hilltop. 'Men,' he wrote, 'are not to come out of Babylon, and there to stand still, and remember the Lord afar off, but must resort to the place where he hath put his name, for which they need not go either to Jerusalem, or to Rome, or beyond the seas; they may find Sion the Lord's mountain prepared for them on the top of every hill.'[76]

Given the intensity and scope of his endeavor, it is most remarkable that Bradford abruptly stopped writing his History in 1650 with the annal for 1646. He adds the dates 1647 and 1648, but no further divine events and remarkable providences are recorded. Since his purpose as late as 1654 remained the same as in 1630, why did he shift to other forms? Why did history seem less and less an adequate means of expression? His later writings consist of three dialogues, one now lost; several poems; letters; the Hebrew exercises; and a list of 'the names of those which came over first, in the year · 1620 · and were by the blessing of God the first beginers and (in a sort) the foundation of all the Plantations and Colonies in New England; and their families.'[77] This shift to other modes was begun already in 1648 while Bradford was working intensely on the annals; but though the forms differ, Bradford's purpose and attitudes seem essentially not to have changed since he first began *Of Plym-*

74. *Ibid.*, p. 424.   75. *Of Plymouth*, I, 3.   76. Robinson, *Works*, II, 134.
77. *Of Plymouth*, II, 397.

outh Plantation. He still wants the children to return to an imitation of the fathers. As in the History, he depicts a prior glorious state, its subsequent loss, assertion of God's continued mercy if men will repent, and threat of damnation if they do not. Thus, in the first Dialogue, Bradford relates the noble lives of the first Separatists, men like Barrow, Jacob, Brown, Smith, Ainsworth, Robinson, and Clifton who were 'precious in the eyes of the Lord, and also in the eyes of such as knew them, whose virtues we with such as you as are their children do follow and imitate.'[78] Again, in the third Dialogue, 'Ancient-Men,' having proven the superiority of Congregationalism over the Catholic, Anglican, and Presbyterian Churches, tell 'Young-Men' that 'we have the rather noted these thinges, that you may see the worth of these things and not necligently loose what your fathers haue obtained with so much hardshipe.' The young are exhorted to 'stand fast in the libertie . . . wherwith Christ hath made vs free,' to obey rulers, and to help 'propagate' the truth to 'generations to come, till the coming of the Lord.'[79]

His increasing concern for his children's future caused Bradford to change from history to dialogue. He must, he felt, make the generations confront each other more immediately than in the muted way of Of Plymouth Plantation. Face to face with 'Ancient-Men,' 'Young-Men' could hear the truth more directly and become more deeply convinced of the righteousness of the past. Though he exhorts, threatens, and promises, he nevertheless portrays the relationship between fathers and sons as remarkably harmonious in the Dialogues. The severe discord and disappointments in Plymouth are vague echoes as the ancients describe the saints in the light and the glory of primitive churches. In fact, in his desire for harmony between the generations, Bradford makes it appear as if the young are imploring the old to instruct them about the past rather than the old men feeling the necessity to teach the young. Thus, the third Dialogue does not open with the old summoning the young but with 'Young-Men' asking 'Ancient-Men' 'to pardon our bouldnes, in that we have importuned you to giue vs meeting once

78. A Dialogue, . . . 1648, in Young, Chronicles . . . Pilgrim Fathers, p. 456.

79. A Dialogue, or 3d Conference, pp. 463–64.

more in this kind, for our instruction & establishmente in the truth.' They have been, they say, troubled and confused by the claims of so many churches to be the one true church, and 'humbly craue,' their elders' 'best judgment and advice.'[80] Throughout the *Dialogue*, they express repeatedly their gratitude for answers to disturbing questions; and when they leave, they are apparently much relieved to know who are the true church. As they leave, 'Ancient-Men' remain on the stage, serene and confident, ever ready to lend stability to their troubled children's lives.

The shift in the narrator's identity from the 'I' of the History relating the lives of 'they' to the 'Ancient-Men' and 'Young-Men' of the dialogues demonstrates how, in certain profound ways, Bradford's relationship to his material changed in his later years. When he began to write Book Two, he expected to show, as he had in Book One, how magnificently the Holy Spirit had manifested himself in the actions of the Plymouth saints in the preceding fifteen years. Once more he would lay bare the incarnations, the moments of light standing out against the darkness. In his desire to let the truth shine as dispassionately as possible, to have nothing interfere between the reader and the text, Bradford tells *Of Plymouth Plantation* as the story of 'they'; not once does he refer to the people at Plymouth as 'we,' although he himself was one of them. As historian, Bradford often explains what he is doing and why, but Bradford the historian never permits Bradford the governor to say 'I.' Always he describes his own acts as those of 'the governor of Plymouth.'

The effect is to create in the reader a strange, almost weird, sense that the Pilgrims were somehow more than ordinary men. Indeed, there was a world of difference between seeing themselves as merely a small group of men and women living somewhere in New England, and, on the other hand, as God's living synecdoches appointed to move through the wilderness toward the heavenly Jerusalem. By referring to his brothers and sisters in Christ as 'they,' Bradford removes them from the life of other men; they are children of some unearthly father, citizens inhabiting a new and different world. As 'they,' the Pilgrims were made impersonal actors, moving through history as expressions of a will and majesty

80. *Ibid.*, p. 407.

far greater and other than their own. That Bradford's use of 'they' is deliberate is evident when we compare *Of Plymouth Plantation* with *Mourt's Relation*, the journal published in 1622. Throughout *Mourt's Relation*, Bradford and Winslow write of themselves as 'we,' thereby involving the reader in a very different way from the way Bradford does in the History. *Mourt's Relation* tells what happens to men when they face natural hardships: harsh weather, little food, and hostile enemies. In *Of Plymouth Plantation*, the same circumstances are put in a very different context and infused with other meanings.

In the later writings, this belief in the union of actor and act, form and essence, seems to disintegrate. In the dialogues, the dramatist-narrator does not describe 'their' pilgrimage. Instead 'Ancient-Men' speak directly of 'we,' 'us,' and 'you.' To gain the face-to-face meeting of the generations, Bradford, the writer of the dialogues, breaks into that other world where for decades he had observed the Pilgrims—including his own other and newborn self —moving toward the New Jerusalem, and removes them from their sacred and secret journey. In *Of Plymouth Plantation*, the characters are energetic actors in a dynamic drama; in the dialogues, they stand like immovable statues, only their disembodied voices alive. The actors are outside, no longer one with the act.

In the poems, 'A Word to Plymouth,' 'A Word to Boston,' 'A word to New England,' and 'Some observations of God's merciful dealing with us in this wilderness, and his gracious protection over us these many years. Blessed be his name,' the disintegration goes much further. Bradford's mask of 'Ancient-Men' in the dialogues was an attempt to preserve the sense of two worlds; 'Young-Men,' he hoped, would see 'Ancient-Men' as inhabitants of the world of faith. But in the poems, Bradford speaks without mask. As 'I,' he addresses his 'dear friends, (and children whom I love),' and expresses the hope that his 'few lines' will 'move' them to 'cleave to God' so that the fate which befell Israel 'when the elders and Joshua were dead'[81] would not be New England's. Fearful that a

---

81. William Bradford, 'Some observations of God's merciful dealing with us in this wilderness, and his gracious protection over us these many years. Blessed be his name,' *Proceedings of the Massachusetts Historical Society*, XI (Boston, 1870), 477.

great and terrible 'change'[82] is in store for the land that has lost 'its former glory,' he calls on the people to 'repent, amend, and turn to God / That we may prevent his sharp rod, / Time yet thou hast improve it well, / That God's presence may with you dwell.'[83]

Sometime during his last years, Bradford returned to Book One of *Of Plymouth Plantation* and, on a reverse page, wrote a passage that more even than the poems discloses his sense of loss and failure. In 1630, he had quoted a letter of Robinson's and Brewster's in which the two ancients confidently assured Sir Edwin Sandys that their Leyden saints were 'knite togeather as a body in a most stricte and sacred bond and covenante of the Lord, of the violation wherof we make great conscience and by vertue wherof we doe hould our selves straitly tied to all care of each others good, and of the whole by every one and so mutually.'[84] In his note of twenty-five years later, Bradford spoke his pain directly:

O sacred bond, whilst inviollably preserved! how sweete and precious were the fruits that flowed from the same! but when this fidelity decayed, then their ruine approached. O that these anciente members had not dyed, or been dissipated, (if it had been the will of God) or els that this holy care, and constant faithfullnes had still lived, and remained with those that survived, and were in times afterwards added unto them. But (alass) that subtill serpente hath slylie wound in him selfe under faire pretences of necessitie and the like, to untwiste these sacred bonds and tyes, and as it were insensibly by degrees to dissolve, or in a great measure to weaken, the same. I have been happy, in my first times, to see, and with much comforte to injoye, the blessed fruits of this sweete communion, but it is now a parte of my miserie in old age, to find and feele the decay and wante thereof (in a great measure) and with greefe and sorrow of hart to lamente and bewaile the same. And for others warning and admonnition, and my owne humiliation doe I hear note the same.[85]

82. *Ibid.*, p. 473.

83. William Bradford, 'A word to New England,' *Collections of the Massachusetts Historical Society*, 3rd ser., VII (Boston, 1838), 28.

84. *Of Plymouth*, I, 76.   85. *Ibid.*

Mercy no longer seemed to grow out of afflictions. In retrospect, 'the blessed fruits' of Bradford's 'sweete communion' had been greatest in his 'first times.' Disappointed in his expectations for his community as a whole, Bradford, in his 'longing desire,' withdrew into a private conversation with the past. Too strong to be relinquished, his dream led him to learn Hebrew in anticipation of the day when resurrected to new and literal life, he would converse with first planters and walk once more before his Lord.

The Separatist Background of Roger Williams' Argument for Religious Toleration

Richard Reinitz
Hobart and William
Smith Colleges

In much of Christian writing, typology has been used to infuse the Old Testament with Christian meaning and to link the dispensations.[1] For the New England Puritans it served further to place their venture within the framework of the history of mankind and the eschatological future. It also helped individual Puritans to understand their relationship to Christ. It was a means of connecting the present with the past and the future, the unique with the universal, the human with the divine. Most students of early American

1. In the course of my work on the history of the typological argument for religious toleration, I have accumulated a number of debts. My doctoral dissertation, 'Symbolism and Freedom: The Use of Biblical Typology as an Argument for Religious Toleration in Seventeenth Century England and America' (University of Rochester, 1967), was directed by Loren Baritz, who provided much assistance. Sections four and five of this article are based on material from the dissertation. Two of my colleagues, Nancy Struever and Francis J. M. O'Laughlin, generously offered guidance through the earlier periods. For valuable specific advice, I am also indebted to Norman O. Brown, C. Norman Kraus, Mason Lowance, Jr., Darrett B. Rutman, Daniel Walkowitz and Perez Zagorin. I want particularly to thank Sacvan Bercovitch, who provided bibliographic counsel as well as much-needed editorial help. Of course, none of these shares any responsibility for the article.

The National Endowment for the Humanities supported my research for a summer under its younger scholars program, and the Hobart and William Smith Colleges Faculty Research Committee has assisted with some of the incidental expenses of scholarship.

typology have focused upon these historiographic, eschatological, and Christological functions.[2] But typology served to indicate distinctions as well as to establish connections. Much of the Old Testament is not in itself clearly relevant to the New. Typology made it possible to understand how precepts and models without any literal significance for Christians, except as history, came to be in the Bible at all. One of its most important disconnective functions can be found in Roger Williams' argument for religious toleration.

Typology was used by Williams to support the major arguments in his polemical writings. It helped him justify his absolute separatism as well as his views on church polity and matters of public worship.[3] It provided him with arguments against any suggestion that New England was a new Israel.[4] Most important, it sustained his advocacy of an absolute separation of church and state and the complete toleration of religious diversity. Biblical support for the power of the state in religious affairs had always been drawn from the example of the Old Testament magistrates, and Williams found in typology an instrument for undermining the relevance of that example for Christian rulers. He argued that the laws provid-

2. Among the works on early American typology (mostly focused on its relationship to historiography and eschatology), I have benefited particularly from the following: Sacvan Bercovitch, 'Typology in Puritan New England: The Williams-Cotton Controversy Reassessed,' *AQ*, XIX (1967), 166–91; Thomas M. Davis, 'The Traditions of Puritan Typology,' unpub. doct. diss. (University of Missouri, 1968); Mason I. Lowance, Jr., 'Typology and the New England Way: Cotton Mather and the Exegesis of Biblical Types,' *EAL*, IV (1969), 15–37; Perry Miller, *Roger Williams: His Contribution to the American Tradition* (Indianapolis, 1953); Jonathan Edwards, *Images and Shadows of Divine Things*, ed. Perry Miller (New Haven, 1948); and Jesper Rosenmeier, 'The Teacher and the Witness: John Cotton and Roger Williams,' *William and Mary Quarterly*, 3rd ser., XXV (1968), 408–31. For a discussion of studies of Puritan uses of typology, see Michael McGiffert, 'American Puritan Studies in the 1960's,' *William and Mary Quarterly*, 3rd ser., XXVII (1970), 36–67.

3. See *The Complete Writings of Roger Williams*, ed. Perry Miller (New York, 1959), I, 347, 348, 351, 360, 373, 392.

4. *Ibid.*, I, 360, III, 251, 270, 353, 416. For a discussion of Williams' use of typology to justify separatism and as an attack on the idea of American exceptionalism, see Reinitz, 'Symbolism and Freedom,' pp. 176–94, 239–56.

ing civil punishments for religious infractions and the right of the Jewish monarchs to enforce them had been functions of Israel's typical uniqueness, and therefore could not serve as precedents for any modern rulers: 'the Sword of Civill justice' under which the church had been ruled in Israel 'cannot according to its utmost reach and capacitie (now under Christ, when all Nations are merely civill, without any such typicall holy respect upon them, as was upon Israel a National Church) I say, cannot extend to spirituall and Soul-causes.'[5] As no modern nation could claim to be the antitype of material Israel—since, for Williams, the physical types of the Old Testament required spiritual antitypes under the New— so, too, the physical power which had reformed religion among the Jews could represent only a church power, not a civil one, under Christianity:

Those former types of the Land, of the People, of their Worships, were types and figures of a spirituall Land, spirituall People, and spirituall Worship under Christ. Therefore consequently, their Saviors, Redeemers, Deliverers, Judges, Kings, must also have their spirituall Antitypes, and so consequently not civill but spirituall Governors and Rulers; lest the very essential nature of Types, Figures and Shadows be overthrone.[6]

5. The Complete Writings of Roger Williams, III, 160.

6. Ibid., III, 353. Miller's book on Williams is essential for understanding the latter's use of typology, although Miller was not the first to recognize its presence in Williams' writings. He was preceded by A. S. P. Woodhouse, Puritanism and Liberty (London, 1936), p. 67; and Arthur Barker, Milton and the Puritan Dilemma (Toronto, 1942), p. 92. Miller erred when he argued that Williams was unusual among Puritans because he used typology and when he suggested that typology was the root of Williams' belief in religious toleration (Roger Williams, pp. 32, 240). Sacvan Bercovitch, Jesper Rosenmeier, and others have proven that the debate between Williams and Cotton took place within an intellectual context in which typology was accepted, although there were disagreements about how it should be used. In a very perceptive review of Miller's edition of The Complete Writings of Roger Williams, Darrett B. Rutman was among the first to point out Miller's exaggeration of the causal role of typology in Williams' thought (William and Mary Quarterly, 3rd ser., XXI, 1964, 300–04). On this point, see also Edmund S. Morgan, 'Miller's Williams,' New England Quarterly,

How did Williams come to make this argument against state power in religion? My concern here is with the answer to only a part of that question. I have argued elsewhere that the reasons for Williams' peculiar use of typology are to be found in a prior commitment to religious liberty, which in turn was based upon a peculiar conception of the nature of the conscience. He could not have arrived at such a commitment by the use of typology alone.[7] But even if typology was not the source of Williams' belief in toleration, it was certainly an important tool for him. What was the source of his peculiar use of this common method of exegesis?

There are five possible routes to Williams' typological argument for toleration. He could have taken it whole from an earlier writer (Sebastian Castellio, for example). There appears to have been a development toward such an application of typology among separatist predecessors of Williams; and, as a man very much within that tradition, Williams could have simply expanded that development. Similarly, Williams had some relationship to the Baptists, who also moved toward such an argument. Sacvan Bercovitch has demonstrated how well the figurative denial of the Old Testament precedent fits into the broader pattern of spiritualized typology. Williams could have adopted that older method to his own ends.[8] Finally, he may have simply reversed the prevailing reliance by his New England opponents on the figurative parallel of their venture with ancient Israel.[9]

All of these sources seem plausible, and they are obviously not mutually exclusive. My purpose here, however, is not to make causal claims, but to explore the separatist background to Williams' application of typology, with some brief consideration of a

---

XXXVIII (1965), 513–23; and his brilliant book, Roger Williams: The Church and the State (New York, 1967), pp. 90–94. For writings on Roger Williams prior to 1963, see Leroy Moore, 'Roger Williams and the Historians,' Church History, XXXII (Dec. 1963), 432–49.

7. Reinitz, 'Symbolism and Freedom,' pp. 202–12, 275–84, 298–326.

8. Bercovitch, 'Typology in Puritan New England.'

9. C. Norman Kraus, 'Anabaptist Influence on English Separatism as seen in Robert Browne,' Mennonite Quarterly Review, XXXIV (1960), 18, n. 36; and Kraus to Richard Reinitz, Goshen, Indiana, Sept. 4, 1967.

few more remote writers who used similar arguments. Though some separatists were influenced by their predecessors in the development of this argument, it is quite possible that an influence from outside was determinate at any point in this chain of development because mature typological arguments for toleration had appeared earlier.

There is another danger of distortion in my approach. I shall focus largely upon the disjunctive functions of typology, paying much less attention to its connective role. In fact, the beauty of the method lies in the way in which it makes it possible to find Christian meaning in Jewish history and ritual and at the same time to establish the fundamental differences between Judaism and Christianity.[10] This tension is the heart of the uniqueness of typology. My approach here of necessity obscures the fact that the typological relationship indicated not only continuity or discontinuity, but both at once.

Prior to the seventeenth century, when a Christian church or sect did not have control over the state, it might tend to deny the religious authority of the civil government. In order to make this point effectively the precedent offered by the Old Testament monarchs had to be countered in some way.[11] In the third century, before the conversion of the Roman Empire, St. Cyprian, Bishop of Carthage, maintained, without using typology, that religious violations had been punished physically under the Old Testament but under the New they were to be corrected by spiritual means.[12] In the same

10. R. A. Markus, 'Presuppositions of the Typological Approach to Scripture,' Church Quarterly Review, XLVIII (1957), 442–51; Reinitz, 'Symbolism and Freedom,' p. 5.

11. Joseph LeCler, Toleration and the Reformation, trans. T. L. Westow (London and New York, 1960), I, 31. LeCler relates shifting attitudes toward toleration to changing degrees of reliance on the Old Testament and the New. I am deeply indebted to this very learned work. It contains much valuable information about the history of the typological argument for toleration.

12. St. Cyprian, 'The Epistles of St. Cyprian,' Epistle LXI, 4, in The Ante-Nicene Fathers, ed. Alexander Roberts and James Donaldson (New York, 1925), V, 358. See also LeCler, Toleration, I, 37.

period Origen used a similar argument.[13] Such formulations were used much later by left-wing Protestants when, after the ecclesiastical unity of the Middle Ages, the Reformation produced a new diversity of religion in Europe. The radical, individualistic spiritualist Sebastian Frank (1499–1542)[14] and the pacifistic Dutch

13. Origen, Contra Celsum, trans. Henry Chadwick (Cambridge, England, 1953), bk. VII, pp. 18–22, 409–13. See also LeCler, Toleration, I, 33–38. In the late fifth century, Pope St. Gelasius denied the validity of the Old Testament as a literal precedent for state power in religion. Ibid., I, 50. During the middle ages, the most important use of the typology of the Old Testament monarchs was in arguments over the relative authority of civil and ecclesiastical rulers. For various aspects of this, see Walter Ullman, Medieval Papalism: The Political Theories of the Medieval Canonists (London, 1949), pp. 147–52; and Ernst H. Kantorowicz, The King's Two Bodies: A Study in Mediaeval Political Theology (Princeton, 1957), pp. 46, 47, 53, 36, 88, 89, 140, 160, 162. The 'York' Tractates of The Norman Anonymous of 1100 A.D. represented an extreme anti-papal position. It argued that the Old Testament 'priest prefigured that Christ would pass to the limit of death. . . . The King however, prefigured that He would reign in eternity. . . . Each is Christ and God in the spirit and in his office each is a figure or image of Christ and God: the priest of the sacerdotal and the king of the regal. The priest is of the lower office and nature—that is the human; the King is of the higher, the divine' (pp. 3, 4). I am indebted to Professor Francis J. O'Laughlin for the use of his privately prepared translation of part of this tract. On The Norman Anonymous, see George Huntston Williams, The Norman Anonymous of 1100 A.D., Harvard Theological Studies, XVIII (Cambridge, Mass., 1951), particularly pp. 131, 132. For various magisterial reformation attitudes toward the relationship between the Testaments in regard to the problem of toleration, see 1) Luther, 'Temporal Authority: to What Extent it Should be Obeyed' (1532), Luther's Works, gen. ed. Helmut T. Lehmann (Philadelphia, 1967), VL, 97; 'Commentary on Psalm 101' (1534), Ibid., XIII, 189; and LeCler, Toleration, I, 151, 160–63; 2) LeCler, Toleration, I, 313, on Zwingli; and 3) Calvin, Institutes of the Christian Religion, ed. John T. McNeil, The Library of Christian Classics, XX (Philadelphia, 1960), bk. II, chap. XI, 3–4; and LeCler, Toleration, I, 333.

14. Frank, 'A Letter to John Campanus' (1531), Spiritual and Anabaptist Writers, ed. George Huntston Williams, The Library of Christian Classics, XXV (Philadelphia, 1957), 151. On Frank, see LeCler, Toleration, I, 166–76; and George Huntston Williams, The Radical Reformation (Philadelphia, 1962), pp. 357–465. Caspar Schenckfeld (1489–1561), another spiritualist, was influenced by Frank and also argued against the Old Testament

Anabaptist Dietrich Phillips (1504–68),[15] among others, attacked the use of the Old Testament to justify the enforcement of religious uniformity by Christian magistrates.

A major event in the history of the conflict between the radical and magisterial reformers was the burning of Michael Servetus for heresy in Geneva in 1653. This incident was directly responsible for the appearance in the following year of an important tolerationist tract, *Concerning Heretics*. Although at the time this work was published under a pseudonym, it is now generally attributed to an Italian Protestant, Sebastian Castellio (1509/1515–63).[16] In this work we can find clear statements of the typological argument for toleration.

Much of the book is composed of selections from other writers. Castellio was particularly effective in turning the words of his enemies against them. In 1528, John Brenz, a prominent Lutheran leader in Wurtemberg, published a tract urging gentler treatment of anabaptists.[17] By 1554, Brenz had changed his mind, but Castellio quoted his earlier work, which contained a typological attack on the use of the Old Testament monarchs as precedents for the persecution of heresy by modern rulers.[18] Brenz argued that 'the two laws of Moses, which are adduced to prove that heretics should be

---

rulers as precedents for the religious powers of Christian magistrates. See LeCler, *Toleration*, I, 179.

15. Phillips, 'The Church of God' (ca. 1560), in *Spiritual and Anabaptist Writers*, p. 253. On Phillips, see Williams, *Radical Reformation*, pp. 489–90. Menno Simons (1483–1559), founder of the Mennonite sect, also argued against the Old Testament precedent for religious persecution (see LeCler, *Toleration*, I, 209–13), as did another Netherlander, the Catholic spiritualist Dirck Coornhert (1522–90). See *ibid.*, II, 273–86 and Williams, *Radical Reformation*, pp. 774–75.

16. On Castellio, see LeCler, *Toleration*, I, 336–47, 350–60; II, 74–77; Williams, *Radical Reformation*, pp. 627–30. On the circumstances of the writing of *De haereticis*, see Roland Bainton, *Concerning Heretics* (New York, 1935), pp. 3–11.

17. LeCler, *Toleration*, I, 244.

18. On Brenz's change of attitude see *ibid.*, I, 250–53; and Bainton, *Concerning Heretics*, pp. 50–58.

put to death by the civil sword' are not to be used by Christians because

Christianity is fundamentally different from Judaism. Among the Jews there were physical promises, physical blessings, a physical land, a physical kingdom, and priesthood: there was also a physical slaughter of enemies. These were but types of the truth to be manifested in Christianity. And the physical blessing of the Jews corresponds to the spiritual blessing of Christians, and the physical kingdom to the spiritual kingdom. The physical extermination of the Canaanites, Jebusites, and false teachers foreshadowed the spiritual extermination of the enemies of the Christian, that is, his sins and also false teachers.[19]

Under the pseudonym of Basil Montfort, Castellio[20] himself presented this argument in *Concerning Heretics.*

Why did Peter not use the sword as he would have liked to have done . . . , and as Moses and Phineas formerly did? Is it not because the sword of the Old Testament is but a figure of the sword of the Spirit of God, which is to be used in the New Testament? . . . Shall we confuse the symbol with the thing symbolized and treat the sword, poison, and words as the same things?[21]

Jacob Acontius (ca. 1500–67), also an Italian religious refugee, wrote an important tolerationist tract *Strategems of Satan*, published in 1565.[22] Although Acontius knew Castellio's work, his own religious position was rather different.[23] But he, too, utilized typol-

19. *Ibid.*, p. 159.

20. Bainton is convinced that Montfort was Castellio. *Ibid.*, pp. 5–10.

21. *Ibid.*, p. 233. Castellio used the typological argument for toleration in other works in addition to *Concerning Heretics.* See LeCler, *Toleration*, I, 353; II, 76.

22. *Ibid.*, I, 369–76. There is an extended discussion of Acontius in W. K. Jordan, *The Development of Religious Toleration in England* (Cambridge, Mass., 1932–40), I, 303–65.

23. LeCler, *Toleration*, I, 376; Jacob Acontius, *Strategems of Satan*, trans. Charles D. O'Malley, Occasional Papers of the Sutro Branch, California State Library, English Series No. 5 (San Francisco, 1940), pp. iv, v.

ogy in arguing for toleration. Acontius acknowledged that under the Old Testament there was a law requiring that those who lead men away from the true God were to be killed.

But some there are, who think that law was in force only till the coming of Christ, and that it has no place in the new covenant— the surmise being based on the fact that the people of Israel were a type of the Christian people and had also promises of things perceived by the senses, which had their use in this life, and had such sacrifices and all such things in fact, which nevertheless signified things invisible and belonging to eternal life. And since this is so, they infer that that bodily punishment was a type of eternal damnation, and therefore that this law, with all other things laid down for the signifying of things to come, ceased to exist at the coming of the Lord. This surmise seemed to me to be so far from absurd, that I could find no reason wherefore it should be rejected, unless the intention of the law was opposed to it.[24]

Acontius concluded that the intention of that law was not to justify the persecution of Christian heretics.[25]

What are the connections, if any, between these attacks on the Old Testament precedent for the enforcement of the religious power of the state and the development of a comparable line of argument among English separatists? There is still much mystery about the relationship between the radical reformation on the continent and the development of English separatism.[26] C. Norman Kraus argues that much of the apparent similarity between the early separatists, particularly Robert Browne, and the anabaptists was due not so much to direct influence as to similar responses to analogous situations.[27] One of the major differences he finds is the fact that Browne did not share with the anabaptists their typologi-

24. Ibid., p. 65.   25. Ibid., p. 69.

26. Franklin Hamlin Littell suggests that there are materials which might indicate in some detail the nature of that relationship, but they have not yet been fully used. The Free Church (Boston, 1957), p. 40.

27. Kraus, 'Anabaptist Influence,' 13, 14. This article contains a review of much of the literature on the possible connections between anabaptism and separatism.

cal reading of the Old Testament in regard to state-church relations,[28] and he comments that when this interpretation appeared
in Roger Williams, a later separatist, it may have come from the
anabaptists.[29]

Castellio seems to have had little influence in England, at least
until after 1610,[30] but Acontius lived there from 1559 until his
death. Still, the extent of his impact is questionable.[31] His work
was noted by William Ames,[32] but its most significant consequences seem not to have appeared until after the period with
which we are concerned. Part of *Strategems of Satan* was translated
(probably by the radical independent John Goodwin) in 1647.[33]

A few years before that, the typological argument for toleration had
been used in a pamphlet generally attributed to Goodwin.[34] There
are many possible sources for Goodwin's use of this argument in his
immediate predecessors,[35] but it is also possible that he picked it up
from Acontius.

In seeking to understand the development of this application of
typology among separatists, we cannot ignore the possibility that at
any point in the tentative chain of influence an outside factor may
have entered. It is altogether possible that any one of the figures I
am about to discuss read some earlier writer such as Acontius or

28. *Ibid.*, 18.

29. *Ibid.*, n. 36. The whole question of anabaptist influence on English separatism remains very much open. For other discussions of it see Williams,
Radical Reformation, pp. 787, 788 and Robert Friedmann, 'Conception of
the Anabaptists,' *Church History*, IX (1940), 341–65.

30. Bainton, *Concerning Heretics*, p. 114; Jordan, *Development of Religious
Toleration*, I, 159.

31. Jordan does not think it was very great. *Ibid.*, I, 370.

32. Acontius, *Strategems of Satan*, p. xiv.   33. *Ibid.*

34. *M. S. to A. S.* (London, 1644), p. 51. For the attribution of this pamphlet to Goodwin, see Jordan, *Development of Religious Toleration*, III,
380.

35. See Reinitz, 'Symbolism and Freedom,' pp. 327–41.

Castellio and derived his use of typology as an argument for toleration from him. We simply do not know at this point.[36]

The earliest development of English separatism is almost as obscure as the influence of anabaptism in England, but with the formation of a separated church by Robert Browne (1550?–1633?) and Robert Harrison in 1580, the movement became highly visible. In the short period of their activity as separatists during the first half of the 1580's (Harrison died around 1585 and Browne recanted in that year), they published a number of tracts condemning the Church of England as false and calling for all good Christians to leave it.[37] The central argument of the original Brownists was that it was wrong for Christians to wait for the state to reform the Church. It was necessary to begin at once to establish congregations which would be shaped in accordance with the New Testament and which would institute a purified worship and church polity.[38] In

36. Whatever their impact on separatism as such, the Dutch anabaptists evidently did influence the early English Baptists, some of whom came to baptist beliefs through separatism. LeCler suggests that two leading English Baptists of the early 17th century, John Smyth and Thomas Helwys, may have derived their ideas about state-church relations from the Dutch Mennonites (*Toleration*, II, 462). See also Verne Dale Morey, 'The Brownist Churches: A Study in English Separatism, 1553–1630,' unpubl. doct. diss. (Harvard University, 1954), pp. 501, 502. The Baptists are a possible source of Roger Williams' argument. John Smyth used typology disjunctively to support some beliefs common to separatists and Baptists ('Paralleles, Consures, Observations,' [1609], in *The Works of John Smyth*, ed. W. T. Whitley [Cambridge, Eng., 1915], II, 375–80). And Thomas Helwys argued against the precedent of the Old Testament monarchs as justification for the religious power of modern rulers (*A Short Declaration of the Mistery of Iniquity* [London, 1935, originally published in 1612], pp. 42–50). Williams referred to Smyth as 'a man fearing God' (*Complete Writings*, I, 343).

37. *The Writings of Robert Harrison and Robert Browne*, ed. Albert Peel and Leland H. Carlson, Elizabethan Nonconformist Texts, II (London, 1953), 1–6; Morey, 'The Brownist Churches,' pp. 97–102, 146. Williams, of course, knew of Browne and even defended the much-maligned name of 'Brownists.' *Complete Writings*, I, 384.

38. Morey, 'The Brownist Churches,' pp. 501, 502.

urging this position, both Harrison and Browne utilized typology. The ancient Jewish kings had instituted religious reform, and the Old Testament could be cited as justification for delaying until the Christian magistrates were ready to act. Referring to the defenders of the Church of England who made this argument Harrison wrote:

Yf they aleadg the Kyngs of Juda & Moses & Kings of Isreall ffor begginning of refformation in the church—we answer that yt they did in ecclesiasticall or spirituall matters they did it as they were fygures of Christ & that yt they did syvillye in fforsyng they did it by the sevyll sword for they had authority in bothe casses yt our Kings & Princes want ffor the fyguratyue maner was ended in Christe.[39]

Browne replied to those who argued that 'Moses and the kings of Juda did reforme the Church, and they were taried for, therefore we also must tarie for our Magistrates' by saying: 'Beholde nowe howe the shame of their faces doeth testifie against them, which dare against their consciences, make our Magistrates prophetes with Moses, yea high Priestes as he was and figures of Christ, as both he was and the Kings of Juda also.'[40] Browne was prepared to demonstrate the typical character of the Old Testament magistrates.

But they aske how we proue that Moses & the kings of Judah & the Judges before thē were figures of Christ. They know it true, & dare not denie it, & yet to quarel & trifle with the trueth, they must have it proved. . . . Iacob did prophesie, that one should take the spiritual kingdom & be Lord thereof, namelie Christ Iesus, and euer more one of the tribe of Iuda & house of Dauid, should foreshew the same in figure. . . . And again it is written, In steade of they fathers shal they children be, whom thou shalt make Princes throughout all the earth. And this is spoken of the posteritie of Salomon, which as figures of Christ, were Lords of the world. . . .

39. 'A Treatise of the Church and the Kingdome of Christ' (1580 or 1581), Harrison and Browne, Writings, p. 41.

40. 'A Treatise of Reformation without Tarying for Anie' (1582), Harrison and Browne, Writings, p. 163.

And againe, it is writtē, that Christ shall sit upō the throne of his father David, & vpon his kingdom. . . . Wherefore was it called the trone of Dauid & his kingdome, but because in a cōtinual course it shadowed out the kingdom of Christ till his coming. Therefore also are Dauid, Salomon, Iehoshaphat, Hezekiah, Iosiah, and others, set downe in the Scriptures as figures. Yea and the euill Kings of Iuda, though not in their wickednesse, yet in that authoritie and calling whiche they should haue rightlie used, were figures.[41]

Browne's and Harrison's efforts to discredit the precedent of the Old Testament magistrates were extremely limited. They were anxious to make it clear that they were not attacking the civil authority of the state: 'to redress things ciuile, the ciuile Magistrate must meddle, and none is to take his authority from him.'[42] Nor did they deny all religious authority to the state. Harrison even used the Old Testament to show what powers in religion a Christian magistrate should exercise:

As the kings of Juda did reforme by their ciuile power, those things which outwardly were sett up for abominations: namely, as they did break downe the altars, cutt downe the groves, burne the images with fire, slay the Preistes of Baal, and such like things: So it appertaineth to the Magistrate now, to break downe idolatrous altars, plucke downe their buildings, burne their images with fire, & to slaye those, which have revolted frō Christianitie to open idolatrie and heresie wee prayse the Lorde, who strengthned our Princes handes, to worke so farre, as was wrought therein.[43]

The general course of public reformation was accepted as the responsibility of the magistrate by Harrison. Private men are to act only in the narrowest way: 'But herein lieth the dutie of Gods people, to remove themselves from these & al other abominations, & not to ioyne hands with open wickednes, but to keepe ourselves vnspotted therof.'[44]

41. *Ibid.*, pp. 164, 165.   42. *Ibid.*, p. 167.

43. 'A Little Treatise uppon the firste verse of the 122. Psalm' (1583), Harrison and Browne, *Writings*, p. 118.

44. *Ibid.*, p. 120.

To the extent that the Old Testament provided precedents for the people to wait before reforming their own worship, Browne and Harrison used typology as a means of attacking inhibitions on the establishment of separated congregations; but they extended its disjunctive functions no further. The argument served only this essential, but narrow, separatist objective. They did not deny that the state should exercise power in religious matters on the model of the Old Testament, and they even gave the state an important role in the process of reformation. They advocated no general toleration.

This is far from Roger Williams' position, but the logic of the figurative argument which they used was, in a more restricted sphere, similar to his. In the Old Testament, men had to wait for the magistrates to reform religion. Because those kings were types of Christ in this particular function, the relationship of the people to them provided no precedent for men waiting for the magistrate in Christian times. To arrive at Williams' argument, one only needs to read more functions of the Old Testament magistrates typologically.

After the death of Harrison and the abrogation of Browne, leadership of the separatists passed into the hands of Henry Barrow and John Greenwood. They wrote much in the late 1580's and were executed for sedition in 1593.[45] Their position on the religious powers of the magistrate was essentially the same as that of Browne and Harrison,[46] but they did not use typology to justify it. They maintained that 'the trones [sic] of David' were 'a figure of the holye eldership of the church,' but they did not extend that inter-

---

45. On Barrow and Greenwood, see *The Writings of Henry Barrow 1587–1590*, ed. Leland H. Carlson, Elizabethan Nonconformist Texts, III (London, 1962), 1–46; and Jordan, *Development of Religious Toleration*, I, 277–84. Williams wrote favorably of Barrow and Greenwood as martyrs to separatist principles. *Complete Writings*, I, 380; and III, 409, 410.

46. See *The Writings of John Greenwood, 1587–1590, Together with the Joint Writings of Henry Barrow and John Greenwood, 1587–1590*, ed. Leland H. Carlson, Elizabethan Nonconformist Texts, IV (London, 1962), 125, 126 and *The Writings of Henry Barrow*, 229, for examples.

pretation to deal with the question of the Christian magistrates' religious powers.[47]

Henry Ainsworth (1571–1622 or 1623) was one of the major separatist leaders of the next generation, during the period when the movement was largely in exile in the Netherlands. He was one of the founders and original ministers of the separatist church in Amsterdam. Educated at Cambridge, Ainsworth became an extremely productive scholar and theological polemicist, as well as an active minister. At one time he lead a schism out of the Amsterdam church in reaction to Presbyterian tendencies in the parent body. His scholarship and exegetic writings (particularly his *Annotations Upon The Five Bookes of Moses; The Booke of the Psalmes; and The Song of Songs, Or Canticles*) were highly regarded among Puritans of various persuasions.[48] Ainsworth's Biblical studies were admired by both John Cotton and Roger Williams.[49]

47. *Ibid.*, 79. In a context not directly related to the problem of toleration, Greenwood and Barrow even argued that the figurative role of the Old Testament Kings did not preclude their use as models by Christian rulers. *The Writings of John Greenwood*, 251, 252.

48. William Edward Armatage Axon, 'Henry Ainsworth,' *Dictionary of National Biography* (London, 1922), pp. 161–64; W. K. Jordan, *Development of Religious Toleration*, II, 224. Some indication of Ainsworth's widespread influence may be seen in the fact that there were thirteen editions of the books which compose the *Annotations* published either singly or in various combinations between 1616 and 1639 (A. W. Pollard and G. R. Redgrave et al., *A Short Title Catalogue of Books Printed in England, Scotland, and Ireland And of English Books Printed Abroad 1475–1640* (London, 1926), p. 6. I have made use of the first edition, containing all of the parts in one binding, which was published in London in 1627. Each section of this vast work is named for the biblical book to which it refers, and is paged separately.

In footnoting, I will indicate the scriptural book, chapter, and verse to which Ainsworth's comment refers before the page number. When I have occasion to refer to the work as a whole, I will call it *Annotations*.

49. For Williams' comments see *Complete Writings*, I, 382; III, 307, 308. For Cotton's, see 'A Reply to Mr. Williams his Examination,' *ibid.*, II, 206,

The *Annotations* is the best single place in which to see the varied uses of typology by a separatist commentator.[50] The book is full of types, figures and shadows. Ainsworth viewed each of the five books of Moses as a whole as a kind of type:

In Genesis, (which history endeth with the going down of Israel into Egypt,) we have the Image of a naturall man, fallen from God into the bondage of sinne. In Exodus, is the type of our regeneration, and state renewed by Jesus Christ. In Leviticus, the shadow of our mortification, whiles we are made sacrifices unto God. In Numbers, the figure of our spiritual warfare; whereunto we are mustered and armed to fight the good fight of faith. In Deuteronomie, the doctrine of our sanctification, and preparation to enter into our heavenly Canaan, (after Moses death) by the conduct of Jesus the sonne of God.[51]

Numerous individuals in these five books were seen as prefigurations of Christ, either in their whole person, in specific things they did, or in the offices they held. Some of the Patriarchs were such shadows of Christ. In his blessing, Abraham 'figured Christ, sent of God to blesse us.' One of the most important types was David, who 'was a figure of Christ in his kingdome, and a father of his according to the flesh.'[52] Solomon also 'prefigured' Christ 'in Kingdome, wisedome, and glory.'[53] One monarch of particular significance was Melchisedek, king and priest of Salem or Jerusalem: the 'king of justice . . . and therein was a figure of Christ, he that reigneth in

---

207; and a quotation from *The Way of the Congregational Churches Cleared, ibid.*, III, 308, n. 1.

50. For a detailed analysis of Ainsworth's use of typology, see Reinitz, 'Symbolism and Freedom,' pp. 71–135.

51. Ainsworth, *Annotations*, 'Preface' (no pagination).

52. *Ibid.*, Gen. 14:19, p. 57; Ps. 2:1, p. 3. See also *ibid.*, Ps. 69:1, p. 103; 72, p. 107; Cant., 1:13, p. 15; Gen. 4:2, p. 21; 5:29, p. 28; 3:17, p. 18; and 22:4, p. 84, among many other examples.

53. *Ibid.*, Cant. 1:1, p. 4. See also *ibid.*, Ps. 72:1, p. 108. There are few references to the Kings of Israel, as opposed to the persons of David and Solomon, in these early books of the Old Testament, but Ainsworth did interpret that office typologically. See *ibid.*, Deut. 17:13, p. 67.

justice.'[54] Except for Melchisedek, the offices of magistrate and priest were generally separated, each being in its way figurative of Christ. God 'separated Aaron unto the Priesthood' and Moses 'unto the government in Israel. . . . And . . . these two offices figured the grace given by Christ unto his Elect, whom he hath made Kings and Priests.'[55]

The Tabernacle and the services connected with it were the richest of all sources of types and figures for Ainsworth. 'The chief signification' of God's promise to set his Tabernacle among the Jews 'was concerning Christ, who should dwell in the tabernacle of our flesh . . . and under this figure, eternal life in heaven was implied.'[56] The Tabernacle 'is to be applied as a type, first unto Christs person, . . . then to every Christian man . . . and Church, both particular . . . and universall.'[57] The typology of the tabernacle service was used by Ainsworth to demonstrate continuity and discontinuity between the Testaments in the same figure. The sacrificial ritual performed by the priest in the tabernacle was radically different from, as well as similar to, Christ's sacrifice. The most obvious difference was that Christ 'in performing the truth of this type, was both Priest and sacrifice.'[58] Leviticus 6 forbade the priest to eat meat from the animals whose blood had been sprinkled on the altar. This limitation on the use of the sacrifice demonstrated the inadequacy of the Levite priesthood:

And in that the legal priests, might not eate of the flesh of that sinne-offring, whose blood was carried into the holy place, but the body was all burnt without the camp: the apostle from hence saith; we have an Altar (meaning Christ) whereof they have no right to eate, which serve the Tabernacle: (so excluding from Christ, all that cleave to the rudiments of Moses. Which he prove thus,) For

54. Ibid., Gen. 14:18, p. 56.   55. Ibid., Num. 16:5, p. 100.

56. Ibid., Lev. 26:11, p. 167.

57. Ibid., Exod. 25:8, p. 100. This is a good example of the way in which typology could serve to expand the relevance of the Old Testament to several Christian ideas at the same time. Christ, every Christian, and the church are all antitypes of the same type here.

58. Ibid., Num. 19:3, p. 117.

the bodies of those beasts, whose blood is brought into the sanctu-
ary by the high Priests for sin (wherein Christs sacrifice was most
lively figured) are burnt without the campe; (so that the Priest had
no meat, or livelyhood thereby:) Wherefore Jesus also, that he might
sanctifie the people with his owne blood, suffered without the gate;
(so accomplishing the type; and showing withall, that such as
would still serve the worldly sanctuary, had no right to eate of him,
and live by him.) [59]

The main thrust of Ainsworth's typology was to infuse the Old Testament with Christian meaning. Similarities between Jewish ritual and the story of Christ served to emphasize the fundamental continuity of true religion. There was a danger, though, in this emphasis on continuity. The religion of the Jews had been in its time a true religion but was no longer valid. While it was important to Christianize the Old Testament, it was equally necessary to clarify the fundamental differences between the old dispensation and the new. It was the great paradox of typology that it could serve both purposes at once. The typological relationship was based upon resemblance, but it was a kind of resemblance which implicitly expressed an ultimate difference between type and antitype. The inadequacy of the sacrificial ceremonies of the tabernacle suggested the inability of the law to bring men to salvation, the mistake of relying upon works for justification and the damnation of all, Jew and Christian, who would seek God in empty ritual devoid of Christ himself.

The *Annotations* reveals very little about Ainsworth's attitude toward the relationship between church and state. He did not find a prefiguration of state-enforced religion in the Old Testament, but neither did he use typology as a way of denying the validity of the precedent of the religious power of the kings of Israel and Judah for modern rulers. He amplified the connection between the magistrate and the priest. The regulations for the sanctification of the people were to be enforced by both civil and religious officers. These laws 'both Moses the Magistrate, and Aaron the minister,

59. *Ibid.*, Lev. 6:30, p. 35. Ainsworth's interpretation here involves the application of Hebrews 9 and 13 to this Old Testament passage.

must speake, and teach, and see carefully practised.'[60] In some contexts the relationship between church and state in the Old Testament had Erastian implications: 'Because the expiation of the whole Church dependeth on the High Priest' on the day of atonement and because on that day 'he most solemnly figured Christ in his office and worke,' the governors and 'magistrates, looked carefully unto him, both for his puritie, and for information of him in his duty this day.'[61]

Ainsworth presented examples of the magistrate's power in religion without any attempt to apply them to Christian societies. Like Williams, he regarded the magistrates as types of Christ, but he did not draw from that fact any conclusion as to their validity or invalidity as models for the authority of Christian rulers over religion. He simply added the typological level to his historical account of the state in the Old Testament without, in this context, drawing conclusions for modern times or suggesting the nature of any interpenetration between the typological and historical levels of description. His statement of the reasons for the establishment of a government for the ancient Jews illustrates this. God gave Israel a king 'for the good of their commonwealth and Church, and for a figure of Christ to whom the kingdome of Israel did belong.'[62]

Ainsworth did have pronounced views on the power of the state in religious affairs and on the use of the Old Testament as precedent for that power, views which if he had allowed them to appear in the *Annotations* would undoubtedly have made his work less acceptable to many. His position on the religious role of the magistrate can be seen in his *Counterpoyson*, a polemical book devoted primarily to denying that the Church of England was a true church. Since that church was a false one, the arguments of those who would support the power of the English state to enforce conformity to it on the basis of the model of the Old Testament rules were invalid: 'reformation by the Kings of Judah, fit not their turnes; for Judah was a true Church, (though some corruptions had crept in, as wil easily doe into the best.)' He cited examples of the Kings of Judah reforming the church and approved of such actions

60. *Ibid.*, Lev. 11:1, p. 53.   61. *Ibid.*, Lev. 16:33, p. 96.

62. *Ibid.*, Deut. 17:15, p. 67.

as precedents for similar reformations by Christian rulers in places other than England where the churches were true. Even this approval was subject to a significant qualification: 'These examples we acknowledge all Christian princes should follow; having equal power with these kings of Judah, to abolish all idolatry within their dominions; yea and to punish all idolatry and not suffer any superstitious worship among their subjects; but to procure their conversion by the word, yet not to compel them to be members of the Church, because they cannot give them faith and repentance, which is the only dore into Christs kingdome, and can not be opened to any but by God alone.'[63] The magistrate could destroy obvious idolatry and false worship and cite the Old Testament for his authority to do so, but he could not force the church upon those who were not members.

This position was similar to that of his separatist predecessors. It satisfied the needs of those who believed that the church was an exclusive community of saints, who, unlike their nonseparating brethren, wished to deny the power of the English government to force them into the English Church, but who by no means wanted to undermine the civil peace by allowing a proliferation of sects. It met the needs of early seventeenth-century separatism, but it also could contribute to developments in religious theories of church-state relations which would parallel the logic of proliferation inherent in the principle of separation.

Ainsworth's extensive use of typology, then, did not affect his view of the religious function of the state. His typology was a way of infusing Christianity into the Old Testament and of defining the relationship between the dispensations; but since that relationship was not seen in exclusively discontinuous terms and since the weight of his figurative interpretation was on the religious rituals and not on the secular features of ancient Israel, typology in his hands was not an instrument of secularization. He did not use it

63. Ainsworth, *Counterpoyson* (n.p., 1608), pp. 229, 230, 231. This specific argument of Ainsworth's was cited by John Canne as the definitive separatist position on the relationship between church and state. *A necessitie of Separation from the Church of England Proved by the Non-conformists' Principles* (1634), ed. Charles Stovel (London, 1849), p. 223.

to undermine the use of the Old Testament kings as models for the authority of modern rulers over religion, even though in other contexts he questioned that precedent and that authority. Neither did he utilize Browne's typological denial of the Old Testament precedent for waiting for the magistrate for reform. In general, he did not move beyond Browne, Harrison, Barrow, or Greenwood in denying religious authority to the state, but he remains a central figure in our account of the separatist background of Roger Williams' argument, because, unlike any other early separatist, Ainsworth was a widely respected scholar and exegete.

John Canne (d. 1667?) was Henry Ainsworth's successor as minister to the separatist church in Amsterdam. He had a long and interesting career as a left-wing Puritan, serving at different times as minister to congregations in Holland, Bristol, London, and Hull.[64] His religious ideas underwent considerable change during his long life. At various times he inclined toward Baptist beliefs;[65] and in the 1650's, he was identified with the Fifth Monarchists.[66] In spite of the inconsistency in his religious convictions (which on the surface appear not unlike the variations in those of Roger Williams, but which in the case of Canne involved much more fundamental theological deviation in the later part of his life) in the mid-1630's, when his A necessitie of Separation appeared, he would seem to have occupied a theologically orthodox position, although he was, like Williams, on the extremist fringe of separatism.

Williams knew of Canne and had evidently read and agreed with his A necessitie of Separation.[67] In the absolute way in which they

---

64. For Canne's complex career, see William Edward Armytage Axon, 'John Canne,' The Dictionary of National Biography, III, 863–64; W. K. Jordan, Development of Religious Toleration, II, 224, 225; Geoffrey F. Nuttall, Visible Saints (Oxford, 1957), pp. 33, 36, 52, 120, 152.

65. William Haller, Liberty and Reformation in the Puritan Revolution (New York, 1963), p. 175; Jordan, Development of Religious Toleration, II, 224, 225.

66. Nuttall, Visible Saints, p. 147.

67. Roger Williams, Complete Writings, I, 381, 386, 393.

rejected the Church of England, Williams and Canne were closer to each other than either was to moderates such as John Robinson.[68]

Canne was something of a Biblicist, although not a scholar on the order of Ainsworth.[69] Most of his use of Scripture in his *A necessitie of Separation* was non-typological.[70] However, on some issues crucial to Congregationalism and separatism, Canne departed from this literalism—and specifically in arguing for his basic idea that a true church must be in its original composition composed of saints—he turned to typology:

The material temple was a type of the visible churches under the gospel; now we read that it was built from the very foundation, of costly stones . . . all prepared aforehand, hewed and perfect for the building, so that neither hammer, nor axe, nor any tool was to be heard in the house, in the building of it; . . . What in all this was signified? Surely this: such as will build a spiritual house for the Lord to dwell in, must be a holy people.[71]

In his *A necessitie of Separation*, Canne's position on the relationship between church and state was similar to that of his separatist predecessors. Although it was 'the duty of all the faithfull' to build true churches, they should do so without usurping civil authority. He did not intend 'that any private person should med-

---

68. Cyclone Covey, in his *The Gentle Radical: A Biography of Roger Williams* (New York, 1966), pp. 56–72, forcefully and properly places Williams within the separatist tradition. He particularly identifies him with Henry Ainsworth in the extremity of his hostility to communion with the Church of England, but he does not mention John Canne at all (*ibid.*, p. 64).

69. I have been unable to consult his *Reference Bible*, of which there were editions in 1647 and 1664. In any event, the value of this work for my purposes is questionable because by the time it appeared, Canne's religious position had changed from what it had been in 1634.

70. Canne's basic argument for separatism was rooted in a literal reading of II Chronicles 11:14, 16, and in a direct comparison between those Israelites who were true to their faith and those Englishmen who left the Anglican communion. See *A Necessitie of Separation*, pp. 91, 92.

71. *Ibid.*, p. 195.

dle with the affairs of the realm, but that every one in his own person do place himself about the throne of God, leaveing the abuses of the public state to be reformed by such as have a lawful calling thereto.'[72] The magistrate should refrain from interference in the establishment of true churches: 'It is certain' that such churches must be gathered 'though princes are utterly against it. . . . The primitive Christians had not the magistrates leave to serve God, yet they did whatever he commanded them.'[73] Canne denied to the magistrate any power 'of making Churches by the sword.'[74] There was for him no proper scriptural justification for rulers compelling men to join churches. He asked those who would give such a power to the state 'to tell us where they have learned to enforce and constrain men to be members of their churches; I think they will not find a precedent for it in the world, unless they take it from Mohamet's doctrine.'[75]

Canne's treatment of the problem of the precedent for state power over religion, which could be found in the Old Testament, reveals that he did not consistently favor the separation of church and state. He did deny that the power of the magistrate to establish churches could be justified 'by the practice of the Kings of Judah';[76] but he made a careful distinction between establishing churches and compelling men to join them on the one hand, and, on the other, enforcing the authority of true churches over those who had voluntarily joined them. The Old Testament could not be used to justify the application of state power to make men enter churches, but it did provide precedent for the civil authority to compel religious obedience on the part of those who were already members of a true church: 'Howsoever Judah fell fearfully into sin, yet by virtue of the Lord's couvenant with her forefathers, . . . remained still the true church of God, and was not . . . quite broken off; and therefore the magistrate compelled not the people to be members, but to perform the duties thereof, they being members truely before.'[77] Since Canne's most fundamental belief was that the Church of England was no true church, this argument could provide no justification for the English state to impose conformity on it, but it did

72. *Ibid.*, pp. 173, 174.   73. *Ibid.*, p. 174.   74. *Ibid.*, p. 221.

75. *Ibid.*, p. 225.   76. *Ibid.*, p. 223.   77. *Ibid.*, p. 221.

allow for the theoretical possibility of a state supporting a future true church. It is not clear whether Canne's willingness to allow a magistrate authority to enforce conformity among members of a proper church was due to his not having fully escaped from the precedent of the state-church of the Jews, or whether he failed to deny that precedent because he wished to preserve a degree of religious authority in the state in the expectation that such power would prove of value when truly reformed churches came to be generally established.

Canne's position in 1634 on church-state relations and the problem of the Old Testament magistrate was very similar to Ainsworth's position of two decades earlier. Like Ainsworth, he denied that the religious power of the Old Testament kings was a model for the exercise of a similar power by the kings of England without ·entirely denying the validity of the example in other contexts. He made some use of typology, though much less than Ainsworth; but neither of them applied it to this problem of the precedent of the Old Testament magistrates' authority over religion.

Ainsworth and Canne represented the extremist wing of separatism, at least in regard to the totality of their rejection of the Church of England. John Robinson, whose life span (1576?–1625) fell roughly between the life spans of Ainsworth and Canne, at one time shared that extreme hostility, but he came in the course of time to express a more moderate view (although he adhered to separatism to the end of his life). He has been one of the best known of all the separatists because he was the progenitor of the Plymouth colony.[78] Roger Williams, who for a time served the Church of Plymouth, was, of course, well aware of John Robinson.[79]

Robinson's approach to the Bible was similar to that of Henry Ainsworth. In relating the New Testament to the Old, Robinson found continuity and discontinuity, both of which he expressed in part through typology. One element of continuity was the salvation

78. Alexander Gordon, 'John Robinson,' Dictionary of National Biography, XVIII, 18–22. See Covey, The Gentle Radical, pp. 66–72, for a recent general comparison of Robinson with Roger Williams.

79. Williams, Complete Writings, I, 386; IV, 316; VI, 50.

of the Old Testament Jews, as well as modern Christians, by faith: 'for their ordinances in their institution, & right use, their Circumcision was a seal, or signe of the righteousnes of fayth: their offerings a sweet savour unto the Lord, for the forgiveness of sins, as leading to Christ by fayth: their washings applying the blood of Christ, which they figured.'[80] But though Robinson, like Ainsworth, emphasized continuity, he also denied the literal relevance of the Jewish civil law, church government and religious ceremonies to Christian requirements:

the Old Testament is nothing but that external policy instituted by Moses in the judicial and ceremonial law, for the dispensation of the typical kingdom and priesthood of Christ, shadowed out by that of Melchisedec king and priest, represented by the administrations of Moses and Aaron, and after continued in the priesthood of the Levites, and kingdom of David and his sons, till Christ, in the dispensation of those worldly and carnal ordinances. . . . Now as the judicalls, which were for the government of the congregation civilly, are dead, and do not bind any civil polity, save as they were of common equity: so are the ceremonies, . . . deadly, and may not be revived by any church save as any of them have new life given by Christ.[81]

Robinson's attitude toward religious liberty and church-state relations was ambivalent. He cautiously supported the idea of toleration:

Considering, that to tolerate is not to approve; and that Magistrates are Kings & Lords over men properly, and directly as they are their Subjects, and not [as] they are Christs; but that by accident, and as the same persons who are civilly their Subjects, are Spiritually Christs and Christians; and lastly, considering that neither God is pleased with unwilling worshipers, nor Christian societies bettered, nor the persons themselves neither, but the plain

80. *Of Religious Communion Private and Publique* (Leyden, 1614), pp. 84, 85.

81. 'A Justification of Separation' (1610) in *The Works of John Robinson,* ed. Robert Ashton (Boston, 1851), II, 207.

contrarie in all three: the saying . . . seemeth approveable, that it is
one of the three things which God hath kept in his own hands, to
urge the conscience this way, and to cause a man to professe a
Religion, by working it first in his heart.[82]

His expressions of approval for the principle of religious freedom
were hedged about with qualifications: 'Yet I do not denie all compulsion to the hearing of Gods Word, as the means to work Religion, and common to all of all sorts, good and bad; much lesse
excuse civill disobedience palliated with Religious shews and pretences; or condemne convenient restraint of publike Idolatry.'[83]

Clearly, Robinson was unsettled in his view of the relations between church and state. He was suspicious of the exercise of civil
power over religion and willing to allow some breach in the principle of uniformity (as separatism by its very nature required). Yet
he still felt some need to restrain idolatry and heresy (apparently
assuming that they would be recognized), and he wanted the state
to exercise some compulsion to the hearing of the Word. Some
kinds of Old Testament civil sanctions for religious compulsion, he
felt, particularly those which were reinstituted in the New Testament, remained valid for Christians:

the moral equity of those commandments in the Old Testament
touching the demolition and subversion of idolatrous temples, and
other like superstitious monuments, doth bind as well now as then.
Which commandments are also in effect renewed in the New
Testament.[84]

But he made a sharp distinction between the way in which the
modern state was entitled to regulate religion and the way in which
it had been done by the Jewish magistrates. Robinson conceded
that 'godly magistrates are by compulsion to repress public and
notable idolatry, as also to provide that the truth of God in his ordinance be taught, and published in their dominions,' but no king

---

82. Robinson, *Observations Divine and Morall for the Furthering of Knowledge, and Virtue* (n.p., 1625), p. 50.

83. *Ibid.*   84. Robinson, *Justification*, II, 472.

was 'to draw all the people of his nation into Covenant with the Lord, how much less before they are conveniently taught, and to confirm the same by oath, and to inflict death upon all that refuse it, or remain wicked, as the kings of Judah were to do by the people of that nation.'[85] He explicitly asserted that the religious powers of the Jewish monarchs 'will not serve for precedents' for those of modern rulers.[86]

The relationship in the Old Testament between excommunication as a spiritual punishment for religious crimes and the civil punishment for the same crimes was highly relevant to the problem of whether or not the religious power of the Jewish magistrates was a valid model for a similar power on the part of modern rulers. If (as Robinson believed) there was no such thing as excommunication in the Old Testament apart from sentences of death or banishment, those civil punishments by implication were intended not as literal models for compulsive measures to be taken by Christian governments, but as symbolic representations of spiritual sanctions, such as excommunication, by Christian churches: 'As the Lord usually conveyed spiritual both blessings, and curses unto the Jews under those which were bodily so . . . was the spiritual judgment of excommunication comprehended under this bodily judgment of death.'[87] It had been possible to represent spiritual penalties in ancient Israel with physical ones because of the singular fact that God had covenanted with the Jews as both a church and a nation. Typology played an important part in Robinson's development of this argument against the presence of excommunication in the Old Testament:

The Lord did choose the whole nation of the Jews to be his peculiar people, and took all and every one of them into covenant with himself, gave them the land of Canaan for an inheritance, as a type of the kingdom of heaven, erected a polity over them, civil and eccle-

---

85. *Ibid.*, II, 314, 315.   86. *Ibid.*, II, 315.

87. *Ibid.*, II, 199. The issue of whether or not the Old Testament church practiced excommunication was to be important in the debates between Roger Williams and John Cotton.

siastical, in the judicial and ceremonial law, called the Old Testament, making the same persons and all of them, though in divers respects the church, and the commonwealth, whereupon the church is also called the commonwealth of Israel. . . . Hence it followeth, that except a man might enjoy one type of the kingdom of heaven, as was the land of Canaan, and not another, as was the temple, or tabernacle . . . except he might be under one part of the Old Testament, or covenant of God, namely the judicial law for the commonwealth, and not under. another part of it, the ceremonial law for the church, it cannot be that any such ordinance as excommunication could be used lawfully in the Jewish Church.[88]

In short, because both citizenship and church membership in Israel were types of the same thing, the enjoyment of heaven, excommunication as distinct from civil banishment or capital punishment would separate a man from one type of heaven but not from another. Therefore excommunication never existed under the Old Testament. It was there represented by civil punishments, from which it was indistinguishable. Since such civil sanctions were equivalent to excommunication, they could not serve as precedents for similar sanctions on the part of Christian rulers when excommunication could be practiced by churches apart from any civil action.

In a book published at the end of his life, Robinson summarized his objections to the use of the model of the state church of the Old Testament to justify Christian magistrates' forcing men, under pain of civil punishment, to join the church. With John Canne, he argued that there was, in fact, a distinction between making men who were members of a church perform those duties to which they had committed themselves, and compelling men who had not adhered to the church to join it; although significantly, unlike Canne, he did not base this argument on a contrast between a true church and a false one. The power which the Jewish kings had exercised had been over church members: 'none were in truth compelled to the Israelitish Church and Religion; but being of it, whether Israelites, or Proselites, were to be cut off from the Lords people, and destroyed out of the Land for presumptuous sins, or working in-

88. Ibid., II, 197.

iquitie, or for not serving God with all their heart and might.'[89] This argument was a limited attack on the use of state power over religion insofar as it allowed for the exercise of such power over those who were church members. Although it defined the religious role of the state in the Old Testament narrowly, it implicitly acknowledged the validity of using that role as a model for modern state-church relations.

However, by this time Robinson had at hand the elements of a more inclusive, typological argument against the use of the religious powers of the Old Testament kings as precedents to justify the exercise of similar powers by Christian monarchs. 'If the order in Israel be objected' against a denial of religious authority to modern states, Robinson would answer 'that the Land was holy, as no Land now is; that one Nation separated from all other Nations to be the Lords peculiar people, as no Nation now is, the Kings types and figures of Christ, as no Kings now are.'[90] He had laid the groundwork for an absolute, typological rejection of the kings of Judah and Israel as models for the religious powers of modern rulers; Roger Williams was to develop this argument into an instrument to support the complete separation of church and state and total religious liberty.

Robinson sometimes held that those things which were ceremonial, typological, or figurative in the Old Testament did not bind Christians. He expressed the idea that the very land, people, and state of Israel, as well as its church, were unique and typical. And he did, at least once, judge this uniqueness to be such as to prohibit the use of Jewish precedents for the power of Christian states over religion; although it is not clear that he ever explicitly integrated the elements of this argument so as to conclude that it

89. Robinson, *Observations*, pp. 50, 51. I have used comments on church-state relations from both Robinson's *Justification* of 1610 and his *Observations* of 1625 on the grounds that his fundamentally ambivalent attitude did not change. In the earlier work, he was concerned more with the specific problem of state-church relations in England, and in the later more with the issue in general; but aside from a certain mellowing of his language, as well as the integration of the typological argument in the later book, the position presented in the two works was essentially the same.

90. Robinson, *Observations*, p. 50.

was because it was typical that Israel was no valid model for such state power over religion. He had grave doubts about the right of the state to exercise compulsion in religious affairs, but it was left for Williams to draw out the full implications of that argument—to deny the state all such power and to affirm complete religious freedom.

I have not argued that there is a clear pattern of influence of one separatist on another. Certain themes recurred in the use of typology by separatists, and there seems to have been some movement toward the application of its disjunctive function to the problem of state-church relations; but that I am not suggesting a simple chronological sequence should be evident from the fact that I have placed Robinson, who came closest to Williams' argument, last, in spite of the fact that Canne's work was done later. It is true that there is but a short step from the limited use of typology to justify toleration in Robinson's *Observations* to its extended application to that purpose in Williams' *Bloudy Tenent*; and this may have been the direction from which Williams' argument came. Yet as I have suggested, there were many other possible sources for it.

In this brief discussion of part of Williams' intellectual heritage, I have ignored most of the major conceptual problems involved in the use of typology to support religious freedom. Williams' reasons for seeking that kind of freedom are more significant than the argument with which he justified it.[91] There may have been factors inherent in the intellectual and ecclesiastical circumstances of the separatists that predisposed them to utilize the disjunctive function of typology. I have not dealt with the complex way in which that disjunctive function was related to the more common uses of typology as a means of connecting men to the past and the future, nor have I been concerned with the generally secularizing role which typology may have played in the development of seventeenth-century literary thought.[92] Most interesting of all, perhaps,

91. See Reinitz, 'Symbolism and Freedom,' pp. 256–84 for a discussion of some of those reasons.

92. See Victor Harris, 'Allegory to Analogy in the Interpretation of Scriptures,' *PQ*, XLV (1966), 3–6, 10–11.

is the question of whether or not symbolic methods of interpretation are inherently more liberating than literal ones. The future study of typology and toleration might well address itself to the general problem of the relationship between language and liberty.[93]

93. Norman O. Brown maintains that symbolic forms are inherently liberating because they indicate more than one possible meaning. He refers to Williams' typological argument for toleration in this context: 'Roger Williams' fight for symbolic understanding is his fight for freedom' (*Love's Body* [New York, 1966], pp. 204, 205). I believe that Perry Miller probably made the same assumption implicitly in his interpretation of Williams. Recent studies which have shown how widely typology was used by Puritans who held conflicting views on toleration would tend to discredit any general connection between typology and freedom. But the question is not really resolved. There may be a logical relationship between the disjunctive uses of typology and ideas of liberty. Brown's broader argument is made on psychological as well as literary grounds, and we have no studies of the psychological significance of biblical typology in the seventeenth century.

Cotton Mather's *Magnalia* and the Metaphors of Biblical History

Mason I. Lowance, Jr.
University of
Massachusetts

In the afternoon of November 17, 1689, Cotton Mather stood before his congregation at the North Meeting House in Boston and delivered a sermon on the Old Testament subject of Noah and the Ark. His text was Genesis, chapters 6–9, but his treatment of the Scripture reflected a tension between his desire to provide a straightforward exegesis and his temptation to offer, through analogy, an application of the Old Testament lesson to the New English Israel.

After an introductory statement, Mather approached the subject of Noah with a metaphor drawn from the New Testament consistent with the Puritan habit of mind that found resemblances and correspondences between events recorded in the Old Testament and those provided in the New. The preacher declared that

The wise men that of Old were travelling and Enquiring after the Lord Jesus Christ found Him a Babe in Swadling Cloaths and paid Respect unto Him, King of the World. As many as are, and God forbid that any should not be inquisitive after the Holy Child Jesus, may behold Him in the Swadling Cloaths, which the types of the Old Testament Enwrapped Him in.[1]

He could hardly have done otherwise. Theologians had long stressed the importance of reading the Old Testament in terms of

---

1. *Work Upon the Ark* (Boston, 1689), pp. 1–2.

its prefiguration of Christ, and the varied schemes of typological exegesis helped to determine the precise relationship between the New Testament and many episodes contained in the Old. By establishing the correspondences between the two Testaments, the exegete could show how God's revelation was progressive and continuous from one moment in history to another. Thus the historical figure Isaac became a 'type' of Christ in the Genesis episode where he is almost sacrificed by his father Abraham. This adumbration of the New Testament event is later fulfilled by the corresponding 'antitype,' which concludes or abrogates the type. It is important that Abraham and Isaac were ignorant of their roles in the prefiguration of events in Christ's experience, and the foreshadowing of the New Dispensation looks forward through the continuity of time rather than simply representing some abstraction in the allegorical fashion. The events or persons prefigured, the 'antitypes,' fulfill the earlier shadows and establish a spiritual bond between the two Testaments.

The central tenets of typological exegesis were established by the early Fathers; and St. Augustine's notion that 'in the Old Testament the New lies hid; in the New Testament, the meaning of the Old becomes clear,' puts simply the basis of Cotton Mather's exegetical plan. The fundamental assumption was that the Old Testament could not be explained as a separate document by itself; rather, it contains a series of providentially inspired, prophetic adumbrations of the ultimate revelation, the 'antitype.' However, the individual exegete's decisions regarding the exact relationship between type and antitype were crucial. During the Middle Ages, typology had been exploited by some ingenious interpreters to mean something altogether different from the historical fulfillment of a prophetic foreshadowing. Some medieval typologists emphasized allegory, or allegorical correspondences, based on the representation of a spiritual idea by a physical or imaginary counterpart. This approach was derived from the Platonic conception of a spiritual universe that exists beyond the physical world, which is merely its representation or symbol. In contrast, for some of the early Church fathers and for Mather, the 'type' was a very particular kind of symbol, historically true and eternally verifiable because it was instituted to perform a specific function in the historical scheme of things. Types were not 'bare allegories,' or emblems or imaginary fictions, even though in spirit these may also reflect ideas of Christ; rather, the types were actual, historical prefigurations of some aspect of Christ's experience. Despite attempts to 'allegorize' or 'spiritualize' the types by destroying their historical foundations, conservative exegetes had always tried to distinguish between typology and ingenious or invented devices such as tropes and allegories, which they did not believe to be instituted by God.

Conservative exegesis and liberal spiritualizing continued to influence each other throughout the latter part of the seventeenth century, so that a number of works represent a mixture of the spiritualized Old Testament narrative and an orthodox exegesis of the types within the same narrative. Moreover, by Cotton Mather's time, the scientific approach to the natural universe provided not only a wholly new epistemology, but also tempted the writers to combine their perception of God's revelation in nature with more rational explanations of the natural phenomena. Thus the role of Scripture and typology as a pattern for New England's experience in the wilderness became less a vital force in the Colonial culture and more of an abstracted myth that was nurtured by the guardians of tradition. Although conservative lines of scriptural exegesis were maintained throughout the period by such men as Samuel and Cotton Mather, John Davenport, and Thomas Shepard, the barriers between spiritualizing and typology were lowered, and it had become easier for exegetes to draw upon a variety of epistemological sources in determining the nature of God's revelation. Cotton Mather, whose life bridged the seventeenth and eighteenth centuries, attempted a reconciliation of the scriptural and natural, the typological and the allegorical, even while he continued to read history according to the instituted scheme of type and antitype. Cotton Mather's understanding of the doctrine of the types may be seen in his use of the ideas posited by his uncle Samuel in the *Figures or Types of the Old Testament Opened and Explained* (Dublin, 1683) and in his employment of scriptural analogues as metaphorical controls in the *Magnalia Christi Americana.*

The congregation before which Mather stood that day in 1689 would have been well prepared to receive a sermon on Noah in which the Ark and the Church were compared. Among the Puritans of New England, the Ark of Noah was commonly regarded to be a type of the Christian church, but Mather still felt compelled to clarify the typological method of exegesis with a terse explanation:

Those Christians, that Lived before the Incarnation of Our Lord, had a Glorious Gospel, in Shadows of Good Things to Come. A Type is in short, an Instituted Resemblance of Gospel Mysteries. The things which the Gospel gives us a naked Representation of were veiled under many Signs and Seals which God made unto his Ancient People as it were Sacraments of Good Things to Come. And not only the person of the Messiah, but His Conditions, Endowments, His Benefits, and His Ordinances, too, yea, and the Miseries, and the Enemies from which we are by Him delivered; all of these were preached in and by those Types of Old.[2]

Although he tended to exaggerate the particular aspects of Christ's life that were usually included in more conservative systems of typological exegesis, Mather's basic definition corresponds to that set forth earlier by Samuel Mather, whose *Figures or Types* had provided Puritanism with a systematic and conservative approach to the doctrine of typology. If Cotton Mather spiritualized the biblical type, or sometimes allegorized a type outside its biblical context and applied it to an issue of life in New England, he always possessed a sound understanding of scriptural typology as a basic system of linking the Old and New Testaments. His *Work Upon the Ark* explores the Ark of Noah as a type of the Congregational Church in New England, which becomes, only by way of analogy to the New Testament Church, its spiritual corollary.

Two of Cotton Mather's most important works reflect this conservatism in exegesis. The *Magnalia Christi Americana*, first published in 1702, is an ecclesiastical history of New England, complete with individual biographies of the leading persons, cast in the framework of the providentially designed 'errand into the wilderness.' It is written with a continuous emphasis on the role of New England in history, which is no more than the earthly fulfillment of God's cosmic design. The second document, the 'Biblia Ameri-

2. Mather, *Ark*, p. 2.

cana' (1700–1714?), a manuscript on deposit at the Massachusetts Historical Society, is a translation of the Bible and a ponderous biblical commentary, with numerous digressions to discuss specific matters like the typology of the Old Testament. This work is especially important in determining the nature of Mather's typology, and in showing the significance of exegetical typology to his reading of New England's history.

Mather exhibits very conservative approaches to typology in the 'Biblia Americana,' and the tightening of his exegetical method is perhaps understandable because he is attempting to explain specific correspondences between the testaments as they arise in his tedious exegesis. He is not specifically concerned with the relations between Old Israel and New England, although there are frequent echoes of the parallels he had established earlier in the *Magnalia Christi Americana*. Although Cotton Mather was not a 'spiritualizer' of the biblical types, he did indulge a penchant for allegorizing nature and he sometimes used the biblical types as illustrative examples so that parallels between Old Israel and the 'New English Israel' would appear to have been providentially instituted. In the *Magnalia*, these exegetical correspondences are occasionally used as metaphorical controls, and throughout the work, the sense of providential destiny is strong.

Mather's restatement of the 'errand' theme as late as the end of the seventeenth century is an important commentary on the development of attitudes among Puritans toward their original mission. Not only was the *Magnalia* designed to glorify the founders of New England; it was also conceived with an awareness of the mission that New England had been assigned by Providence and with a concern for her apostasy from that calling. He seems concerned to establish the analogy between New England and the Israel of old, without insisting that New England was the antitypical fulfillment of the scriptural types. While he considered New England to be a fulfillment of the promises of Scripture, he was too conscious of the contemporary decline from the Reformation ideals to view her as wholly antitypical. Although Mather's reading of contemporary history in the light of biblical exegesis represents an extension of scriptural typology into modern times, his use of the types was only illustrative and spiritual. Unlike John Cotton, who regarded New

England to be the antitype of Old Israel and who expected the imminent return of Christ, Cotton Mather established the analogy between New England and Israel without insisting so strongly that Massachusetts Bay was to be transformed into the Millennial Kingdom. Therefore, his use of the types suggests that imitation of the Israelite theocracy would have only moral or spiritual significance, so that New England could not flatter herself into believing that she had come to fulfill all the promises of Scripture.

Nevertheless, Mather's belief in the divine appointment of New England to her errand is found throughout the *Magnalia:* 'The *leader* of a *People* in a *Wilderness* had need been a *Moses,*' he declares, 'and if a *Moses* had not led the people of *Plymouth Colony,* when this worthy person was their governour, the people had never with so much unanimity and importunity still called *him* to lead them.'[3] William Bradford is only one of the many Puritan leaders for whom such biblical analogues have been established. Throughout the *Magnalia,* Mather associates Israel with New England and indicates the correspondences between their leaders. Of John Winthrop, he writes:

Accordingly when the noble design of carrying a colony of chosen people *into an* American wilderness, *was* by some eminent persons undertaken, this eminent person was, by the consent of all, chosen for the Moses, who must be the leader of so great an undertaking: and indeed nothing but a Mosaic spirit could have carried him through the temptations, to which either his farewel to his own land, or his travel in a strange land, must needs expose a gentleman of his education.*[4]

In a history that so naturally emerges from the lives of eminent persons, the leaders of Israel were natural Scripture-analogues for Mather to employ. But with such divergent contemporary figures as Bradford and Winthrop being compared to the same biblical type, the value of the comparison would have to be moral and spiritual rather than typologically precise. In the life of John Cotton, another Moses analogue is presented, and Mather even

3. Mather, *Magnalia Christi Americana,* 2 vols. (Hartford, 1820), I, 104.

4. *Ibid.,* I, 109–10.

included Woodbridge's poetical description of John Norton, Cotton's successor, who is compared to Joshua, Moses' successor:

Though Moses be, yet Joshua is not dead:
I mean renowned Norton; worthy he,
Successor to our Moses, is to be.
O happy Israel in America,
In such a Moses, such a Joshua.[5]

Rather than establish New England as a typological reincarnation of ancient Israel, Mather uses the biblical figures metaphorically and morally to organize the *Magnalia* around certain prominent themes that were common to the scriptural and the contemporary situations. For example, he declares that "The most crooked way that ever was gone, even that of *Israel's* peregrination *through* the *wilderness*, may be called a *right* way, such was the way of this little *Israel*, now going *into* a *wilderness*." and he uses the parallel between Israel and New England to accommodate and illustrate God's providential concern through the history of redemption.[6]

The lives of eminent men become Mather's most prominent means of securing New England's place in providential history. Mather transformed history into biography, concluded Peter Gay in *A Loss of Mastery*, but the objective remained constant: to prove that New England and her people stood in a particular relation to God. In the introduction to the biography of his father, Increase, Mather posits a methodology for historical writing that he had earlier followed in composing the *Magnalia*:

I know not how the Pen of an Historian can be better Employ'd, than in Reporting the Vertuous Tempers and Actions of the Men that have therein shown forth the Vertues of our Blessed REDEEMER, and been the Epistles of CHRIST unto the rest of Mankind. Nor indeed has Mankind generally found any sort of History more Useful and more Grateful, than what has been given in the Lives of Men that have been distinguished by an Excellent

---

5. Poem by Benjamin Woodbridge, culminating 'Life of John Cotton,' in *Magnalia*, I, 259.

6. *Magnalia*, I, 48. See also Peter Gay, *A Loss of Mastery* (Berkeley, 1966).

Spirit. *The Best of Books does very much Consist of such an History!*[7]

Mather is here answering John Oldmixon's attack on the *Magnalia*, but his conviction that history should be the biography of saints derives from a belief that Scripture history worked in this manner. While establishing the analogues for the life of William Phips, he could be even more explicit in revealing his method. 'So *obscure* was the *original* of that memorable person, whose *actions* I am going to relate,' he says, 'that I must, in a way of writing, like that of *Plutarch*, prepare my reader for the intended relation, by first searching the *archives* of antiquity for a *parallel*.'[8] These 'archives' included the Old Testament, Greek and Roman mythology, and a number of figures from ancient history. The sense that history has become for Mather a spiralizing process of progressive regeneration in no way violates his view that the types of Scripture were fulfilled and abrogated by Christ; rather, it complements his traditional and conservative interpretation of the biblical figures. Not only did Mather regard the history of New England to be evidence of God's continuing Providence as a leader for his New Chosen; he attempted to use the Scripture parallels metaphorically and spiritually to establish specific parallels between New England and Israel. This represented a desperate cry for a return to the original mission in an age when natural science and other modes of historical epistemology were coming into prominence, and the metaphorical control of an 'errand into the wilderness' provided the ideal setting for the writing of history by way of biography. Not only are personal analogies developed with biblical types; the wilderness itself is employed as a metaphor for the natural environment of New England throughout the work. Puritans considered the forests to be the dwelling place of Satan and frequently justified their expeditions against the Indians by ascribing to them Satanic influences. In the *Magnalia*, one senses that the wilderness is an aspect of the eternal war between Good and Evil; it provides a setting in which the

---

7. 'Introduction,' *Parentator. Memoirs of Remarkables in the Life and the Death of the Ever-Memorable Dr. Increase Mather* (Boston, 1724), p. ii.

8. *Magnalia*, I, 152.

Christian *peregrinus* may find his way back home to God. If one reads the *Magnalia* closely, one can discover the systematic linking of the wasteland and its natural elements to spiritual (and sometimes scriptural) analogues. For example, the 'wilderness having always had *serpents* in it,' is compared to the forces of evil and to the devil.[9]

Cotton Mather used his Old Testament in two distinct senses in the *Magnalia*. First, he was thoroughly aware of the abrogation of the types in Christ, and he recognized the totally distinct mission of New England in her errand into the wilderness. But his sense of history and his conception of the progressive nature of God's revelation led him to make continuous associations among the Old Testament, the ancients, and contemporary events. Since he did not affirm that New England was antitypical or a fulfillment of the Scripture types, and since he avoided suggesting that New England was a *fulfillment* of the future kingdom, his use of typology was designed to establish a system of analogues between historical periods, the one illuminating the other. Moreover, if contemporary events could be identified by reading ancient and biblical history to discover parallels, it could also be asserted that New England was moving forward toward a preordained end, known only to God. In this context, the new world, New England, and the 'errand into the wilderness' were repeated historical episodes in the larger framework of the history of redemption. His foremost objective was to show that New England was under continuous providential guidance, and the purpose of the parallels with pagan history was primarily illustrative; Mather did not consider Greek or Roman history to be guided by Providence, from which both Israel and New England received direction. Mather's adaptation of Plutarch's reading of history by way of the lives of prominent individuals and special events was not unique; however, his sense of history as a process of repetition within a teleological destination must be understood in the unique context of Puritan eschatology. The warning implicit in this magnificent Jeremiad is that only by a return to the original calling would New England enjoy release from current disaster, which was surely the reproof of a displeased Lord.

9. *Ibid.*, II, 426.

Reorientation, however, would insure the role of New England in the grander history of the work of redemption.

Typology, then, becomes the key by which moral examples from the Old Testament are accommodated to the New English Israel and to posterity. Cotton Mather's way of reading history may have utilized the types to elucidate contemporary events, but it did not destroy his scholarly sense of biblical and exegetical typology. In the *Magnalia*, we find a few allusions to typological exegesis as a system for interpreting Scripture, and sometimes the allusions help to clarify the reader's understanding of the doctrine as Mather conceived it:

In our asserting, a matter of the Old Testament, to have been typical, 'tis not needful, that we be always able to particularize any future mysteries of the New Testament therein referred unto; truths which were then of a present consideration, were sometimes represented in the types then used among the people of God, which helps to understand the case . . .[10]

In the tradition of exegesis established by the early church fathers, Mather attempts to show how the types of the Old Testament were a means of God's revelation to those people living before the Incarnation:

Although the Work of Redemption was not actually wrought by Christ, till after his incarnation, yet the virtue, efficacy and benefits thereof, were communicated unto the elect in all ages successively from the beginning of the world, in and by those promises, types and sacrifices wherein he was revealed and signified to be the seed of the Woman, which should bruise the Serpent's head, and the Lamb slain from the beginning of the world, being yesterday and to day the same, and for ever.[11]

More often, however, Mather is concerned to employ typology for moral and illustrative purposes. In the 'general introduction' to the *Magnalia*, he posits a methodology for utilizing the types in the *Magnalia* and asserts the way that he intends to relate the history

10. *Ibid.*, 228.   11. *Ibid.*, 163–64.

of Israel to that of other ancient peoples in establishing analogues for New England.

assisted by the Holy Author of that Religion, I do, with all conscience of Truth, required therein by Him, who is the Truth itself, report the wonderful displays of His infinite Power, Wisdom, Goodness, and Faithfulness, wherewith His Divine Providence hath irradiated an Indian Wilderness. . . . Certainly, it will not be ungrateful unto good men, to have innumerable Antiquities, Jewish, Chaldee, Arabian, Grecian and Roman, brought home unto us, with a sweet light reflected from them on the word, which is our light; or, to have all the typical men and things in our Book of Mysteries, accommodated with their Antitypes: or, to have many hundreds of references to our dearest Lord Messiah, discovered in the writings which testifie of Him, oftner than the most of mankind have hitherto imagined: or, to have the histories of all ages, coming in with punctual and surprising fulfillments of the divine Prophecies, as far as they have been hitherto fulfilled; and not meer conjectures, but even mathematical and incontestible demonstrations, given of expositions offered upon the Prophecies, that yet remain to be accomplished.[12]

Although Cotton Mather published no document similar to Samuel Mather's Figures or Types of the Old Testament, so that we cannot examine his typology by comparing a single work with his uncle's treatise, it is possible to discern in the Magnalia the influence of the Figures or Types and to explore further its conservative doctrine in the 'Biblia Americana.'

On February 10, 1714, Mather wrote in his Diary, 'It seems now high time for me, to come into Action, and to do what my Hand finds to do, that the, Biblia Americana, may be brought forth into the World. Lett me therefore publish a Sheet, entituled, A New Offer, to the Lovers of Religion and Learning [published in 1714], therein giving an Account of the work, and so an Opportunity for

12. Ibid., I, 23, 32. The second part of this quotation describes Mather's technique in the 'Biblia Americana,' which is discussed in the 'General Introduction' to the Magnalia as a way of making all 'learning . . . gloriously subservient unto the illustration of the sacred Scripture.'

Subscriptions towards the Encouragement of it; and not only spread Copies of that offer, thro' this Countrey, but also send them to Europe' (ii, 283). A less specific proposal for the 'Biblia Americana' had appeared in Bonifacius in 1710, and as early as 1706, Mather had written in his Diary, 'I compose (and by the Fleet now going for England, I send over to be published,) an Account of my Biblia Americana' (i, 570).[13]

The projected American Bible never materialized. The manuscript occupies six ponderous volumes and has never been organized or catalogued and indexed. But in the New Offer to the Lovers of Religion and Learning, Mather had predicted twelve divisions for the 'Biblia Americana,' including

IV. The TYPES of the Bible, accommodated with their Antitypes: And this Glorious Book of God, now appearing a Field, that yields a marvellous Mixture of Holy Profit and Pleasure, in those Paragraphs of it, which have sometimes appeared the least Fruitful with Instruction.[14]

Not only was the 'Biblia Americana' never published; it hardly achieved the impressive format outlined in the New Offer, even in manuscript.

Despite Cotton Mather's immense energies, the projected plan in the New Offer, when compared to the six-volume manuscript of the 'Biblia Americana,' would indicate that the project was too formidable for a single man to complete. Although materials are included in the 'Biblia Americana' that are foreshadowed under the titles designated by the New Offer, most appear to be digressions from the main business of interpreting the Scriptures in a most ordinary manner. Here and there Cotton Mather's genius for synthesizing wide-ranging ideas is evident; for example, in handling the many problems of the Exodus, he presents a clear summary of the

13. Thomas J. Holmes, Cotton Mather: A Bibliography of his Works, 3 vols. (Cambridge, Mass., 1940), II, 734. As the Magnalia advertisement for the 'Biblia Americana' makes clear, Mather had been working for a number of years to prepare the Bible commentary for publication.

14. A New Offer to the Lovers of Religion and Learning (n.p., n.d. [Boston, 1714?]), p. 12. From Holmes, III, 731.

ceremonies and persons to be given typological recognition in his exegesis. His position throughout the 'Biblia Americana' is extremely conservative, and his reliance on the typology of Samuel Mather is everywhere present. Moreover, he sometimes directly refers to his uncle's work by suggesting that the reader turn to the *Figures or Types* for further illumination. In his conclusion of a lengthy discussion of the typology of feasts and ceremonies, for example, he remarks: 'It is now time for mee to acknowledge, that in those *Illustrations*, the discourse of my uncle, *Samuel Mather*, on ye *Types of Ye Old Testament*, have not a little assisted mee.'[15]

Typology as a separate subject was only a facet of the overall design of the 'Biblia Americana.' Originally planned to be an exhaustive commentary on the whole body of Scripture, the six folio volumes are subdivided into many seemingly diverse parts, and they contain no table of contents or index to specify the classification of information. However, Mather's literal-minded approach to the historical episodes of the Bible is reflected in his inclusion of a variety of tables and graphs. This kind of fidelity to historical truth is central to a conservative doctrine of typology, and Mather's opinions concerning the types appear frequently enough in the 'Biblia Americana' to show his latent conservatism as a biblical exegete:

Book VII. *This First Promise was afterwards expanded in very many prophecies of the Messiah. The Prophecies are with an amazing artifice interwoven with other matter. God instructing . . . [of the?] Glorious one. The Bible is filled with the Prophecies and the most particular circumstances of the Glorious . . . Coming anew with the New Testament we find them all most punctually accomplished.*[16]

But Cotton Mather was the product of a generation that had been exposed to the rationalist philosophy of John Locke, so that he

15. 'Biblia Americana,' unpubl. MSS. (6 vols., in Massachusetts Historical Society, n.d.), II, n.p. I should like to thank Mr. Stephen T. Riley, Director of the Massachusetts Historical Society of Boston, for his kind permission to publish excerpts from Cotton Mather's manuscript of the 'Biblia Americana,' which is housed in the Historical Society.

16. 'Biblia,' II, n.p.

could hardly have read either Scripture or Nature in precisely the same manner as his uncle Samuel. For example, in a digression entitled 'The Harmony of the Gospels,' Mather provides a somewhat scientific appraisal of the Creation and its perception by man:

There is in the creation, abundance of Invisible matter and motion. The Great God could have made ye matter which is most Invisible by man, to have been seen, in all the minute and curious terms, of it. He who found the Light, and the Soul, could have made ye fibre of ye nerves, in such a delicate manner, even in this life (which probably may be done, for ye Celestial Body) as to give man a kind of Natural Microscope. But for His own Divine Substance, we can not see it. We cannot hope for the sight.[17]

Moreover, there are occasional places where the typology of Samuel Mather appears to have been allegorized, abstracted from the Old Testament context to illustrate a point of argument. In some instances, Cotton Mather has subverted the biblical types as exegetical instruments and has used them as moral or representative examples, even as Samuel Mather had allowed when a type was initially endowed with moral equity. For example, there is a discussion of Abraham, where the patriarch serves not only as a type of Christ to come but also as a Christian *peregrinus* making his way from the earthly city of Babylon to the heavenly city of Jerusalem:

To Earthly Creatures this world is their own countrey, & their Father's House. Tho' there are many places, which they know little of, yett in general, they know what ye World is, and what its enjoyments are. Here they are at home, & with their Kindred; with people disposed like themselves. Heaven is a countrey more unknown to them, than Canaan was to Abraham. It is only God that can discover the countrey unto us, & the way to it, as He led Abraham, into Canaan. Abraham's action is in the Scripture, made a Figure of a Christian's life in this world; who is but a Pilgrim and Stranger here. Thus David Expounds it, when he was King of Israel, Psal. 39:12. . . . Tho' the Patriarchs did certainly beleeve, that their posterity should inherit the earthly Canaan, yett they understood

---

17. 'The Harmony of the Gospels,' in 'Biblia,' III, n.p.

Better Things *contained in this promise, even an* Heavenly Countrey, *which they expected, as their* Inheritance.[18]

This extension of the typological symbol beyond the limits of the biblical context to represent a Christian pilgrimage was not unknown to either Samuel or Cotton Mather; John Bunyan's *Pilgrim's Progress* was popular literature throughout the late seventeenth century. Although in the preface Bunyan declares that he 'speaks by types,' his work is clearly a sustained allegory, and his narrative a fiction representing the progress of the Christian soul toward salvation. It is interesting to find this kind of extended typology in Mather's 'Biblia Americana,' where aspects of the literal and historical situation are endowed with allegorical significance, suggested in Mather's final remarks on Abraham. In all other respects, the treatment of Abraham is thoroughly historical in its presentation of the typological correspondences.

Occasionally, we find Mather's deliberate attempts to reconcile typology and the allegorizing of the Old Testament. His mystical interpretation of the Creation story approaches spiritualizing in certain parts. He declares, for example, that

The marriage between Adam and Eve was a Sacrament. (Eph. 5:32) *of the Intercourse between the Lord Jesus Christ, and his* church. *There is a* Mystical Marriage *between the Lord and His* people; *the Song of Solomon, the Forty-Fifth Psalm* (with 2 Cor. ii:2) *are lively descriptions of it. Eve was taken out of Adam, and the Lord with His Church, makes but one* (Eph. 5:30). *Adam was* Asleep *when Eve was formed out of him; and yee Lord was cast into* a deep, Dead Sleep, *for three days, by which means Hee procured* a Church *unto himself* (Tit. 2:14). *The side of Adam was opened, that Eve might be fetched out, and the* Blood of Our Lord, *which purchased His Church for Him, came out of His Opened Side.* (Joh. 19:34).[19]

In the same allegorical vein, there is a particularly illuminating allusion to the Garden of Eden, in which Mather abandons typological correspondences altogether and finds only metaphorical value in

18. 'Biblia,' II, n.p.   19. *Ibid.,* I, n.p.

the Garden, which he endows with specific allegorical significance: 'And ye Church is the *Tillage* of Our Lord Before Christ, as the *Garden* was of *Adam*. (Compare Gen. 2:15 with Cant. 4:16).'[20]

Generally, however, Mather's whole aim in the 'Biblia Americana' was to develop a conservative doctrine of scriptural exegesis through allusion to pagan mythology, typology, and commentaries by other hands. Therefore his digressions into allegorizing, while significantly different from his exegesis of Scripture typologically, must be viewed as being representative of his concern to utilize every available epistemological means for the accommodation of spiritual truth. For example, without discarding the typological significance of the Sabbath, Mather insists on the moral equity of the instituted day of rest and shows how it has meaning for the Massachusetts theocracy. In commenting on Paul's Epistle to the Hebrews, he says:

There is a state of Glorious and Wonderful Rest. Which our Blessed Jesus, which will give unto His Church in that Great Millennial Sabbath . . . every Rest mentioned in the Scripture as already obtained by the People of God, was but a Type of the Rest which Yett Remains to bee, expected and obtained. . . . It followes, then, that there must Remain a Rest, beyond all this, which Our Lord Jesus Christ, will bring his people unto, even that Rest all this was a Figure of.[21]

The problem that Thomas Shepard had devoted several hundred pages to solving was no stranger to Cotton Mather. After Christ's coming, should the Sabbath be observed despite the abrogation of all types and ceremonial institutions by the coming of the Flesh? Both Cotton and Samuel Mather show how the Sabbath as an instituted day of rest was not wholly abrogated by Christ, because it is a perpetual symbol shadowing forth the rest that is to be given the true believer at the conclusion of all history.

Mather's reading of the types should not be considered to be isolated images of Christ. The preacher makes clear that the Old Testament has a teleological role in the redemption of the world and that it is incorporated into a broader scheme of creation and restora-

20. *Ibid.*   21. *Ibid.*, IV, n.p.

tion than the literal narrative would indicate. He insists that the Law and the Gospel are dispensations by the same author, just as Samuel Mather had regarded the Old and the New Testaments to be products of a single spirit. He says that

The Law of Moses was established on many rites, to be observed nowhere but in the Land of Canaan. . . . But yett we must consider these things, as a method of providence, working toward the great end always in view, even the Generall Restoration of Mankind from the Curse of the Fall, and the opening of that Scheme of the Divine Proceedings, which was to bring a blessing upon all the Nations of the Earth. Accordingly, when Abraham received the promises, he had assurance given him, not only of Peculiar Blessings to Himself and his Offspring but also of a General Blessing to be convey'd thro' him to all Mankind.[22]

Both the Law and the Gospel, their covenants, and the typological correspondences through which they are manifested to mankind are part of a divine plan for the reorientation of mankind in the post-lapsarian condition. In a concluding paragraph treating the typological significance of the Creation, Mather asserts that

Adam in Losing, Adam in Hurting, is a figuration of our Lord Jesus Christ in Gaining, Helping, Saving. From Adam wee derive sin (Gen. 5:3) but Grace (Joh. 3:16) from Our Lord Jesus Christ. From Adam, wee derive Death; (Rom. 5:18), but Life (Joh. 3:36) from Our Lord Jesus Christ. Yea, the Confusion which is brought upon the World by Adam, shall bee one day, by our Lord Jesus Christ, repaired.[23]

Once this basic pattern of exegetical correspondences has been established, it is easier for the reader to see how the 'Biblia Americana' reflects a systematic typology in other specific instances of exegetical commentary. Mather's doctrine of the types appears prominently in his exegesis of the Old Testament and in his treatment of the Book of Hebrews in the New. Moreover, his commentary on certain passages from Galatians, provided in connection with his exegesis of Genesis, gives an impression of the kinds of

22. Ibid.   23. Ibid., I, n.p.

correspondences he sought to establish between the Testaments. In the exegesis of Galatians 4:24, he writes:

The differences and the properties of the Two Covenants are from Abraham exhibited unto us. (Gal. 4:24) In Hagar, wee see the Covenant of Works. Hagar was a Bondwoman; Thus, wee are entangled in Bondage if wee are united unto the First Covenant. Hagar had a child, by the Strength of Nature. Thus, wee are under the Old Covenant, if we go to repent, and beleeve, & Bring forth Fruit unto the Lord by any Strength of Our Own. Hagar had a Son, that was a Persecutor of Men, that know no other than the Covenant of Works, are of a Persecuting Spirit. Hagar & Her seed must bee Cast Out, and the Law as a Covenant, must bee Cast Off. An Abraham indeed may turn aside unto Hagar, for once, or so; and thus a beleever may have some Acting, as under the Covenant of Works. But, hee was with Sarah. The Covenant of Grace, wee see, in her. This Covenant has the Freedom of Sarah in it, the Divine Assurance & Influence that Sarah had.[24]

This interpretation of the relationship between the Covenants is the traditional one, first established by St. Paul in Galatians and preserved in the exegesis of more orthodox commentators. But the framework within which Cotton Mather developed his own conception of the typological correspondences was extended to incorporate some rather fanciful analogies. Like Samuel Mather, Cotton was concerned to accommodate not only the literal and figurative meaning of Scripture to his readers but also to open to them the doctrine of the types. Samuel Mather had explained Samson as a type of Christ, for example, by comparing him to the mythical Hercules; Cotton Mather provides a similar kind of exegesis when he interprets Abraham's sacrifice of Isaac. Although he would have the sacrifice typify God's willing sacrifice of his own Son, Mather allows his penchant for explaining the spiritual meaning of a literal text to carry him away from the straightforward correspondences recorded in the two Testaments. Characteristically, he begins with a thorough and detailed analysis of the biblical text itself, so that we have no doubt of the historical veracity of the story about Isaac

24. *Ibid.*

and Abraham given in Genesis 22, nor should we misunderstand the typological correspondences between Isaac and Jesus:

Amazing the History, which we have, of Isaac's obedience His Father said, My Son You Must Bee A Burnt Offering Unto the Lord. Behold, without any Replying without any repining, hee submitts unto that strange demand. This hee did, tho' hee were twenty-five years old at least. And yett, this was but a little shadow of what Our Lord Jesus did. His Father said, My Son, Become Thou a Burnt Offering that My Justice May be Satisfied, & Glorified Forever. Well, Hee complies, without any resistance, without any reluctance. His answer was, Lord, I come. (Isa. 53:7 and Joh. 10:18).[25]

Once the general correspondences have been established, however, Mather proceeds to examine the text in such detail that he digresses into a discussion of some fanciful analogies between the Old and New Testament episodes that borders, at times, on allegory. For example, when he explains the origin and purposes of the Ram in the Sacrifice, he not only indicates a mysterious prefiguration of the atonement, but specifically asserts that the Ram and Isaac together represent the dual nature of Christ, the Divine and the Human Jesus:

Q. What singular Mystery was there in ye Ram, caught & kill'd by Abraham, for a Sacrifice?

A. In the sacrifice offered by Abraham, wee must consider it was the Ram that felt the Knife. This admirably answers to the two natures of Our Lord Jesus Christ; both of which together contribute unto the Sacrifice of the New Covenant. The Divine Nature of Our Lord, suspending the Expressions of His Power & His Glory, was the Mystery of Isaac ty'd. The Humane Nature of Our Lord, crucify'd, was the mystery of the Ram slain, So Remarkable a concurrence of things, that it is ascribed entirely unto the contrivance of Almighty God, The Lord Will Provide.[26]

---

25. 'Commentary on Genesis,' in 'Biblia,' I, n.p.

26. *Ibid.* See also Samuel Mather, *Figures or Types of the Old Testament Opened and Explained* (London, 1705), ed. Mason I. Lowance, Jr. (New York: Johnson Reprint Corporation, 1969), p. 84.

This interpretation of the role of the Sacrificial Ram in the Genesis account of Isaac's sacrifice represents a departure from the typological correspondences established by Samuel Mather in the *Figures or Types*. Although the 'type' has not itself been 'spiritualized' to represent an abstraction in the Platonic manner, an aspect of the type has been endowed with allegorical significance extraneous to the usual typological adumbration. In Samuel Mather's account, there are no references to the special powers of the Ram in the Sacrifice of Isaac, and there is no attempt to indicate that the Ram and Isaac adumbrate the dual nature of Christ.

In the 1689 sermon, *Work Upon the Ark*, Cotton Mather had stated that 'Noah's Ark was a Type of the Church.' His interest in the typology of Noah and the Ark had not diminished over the years between 1689 and the completion of the 'Biblia Americana.' One of the most extensive examples of his typology is given in the exegesis of Genesis 7, 8, and 9 and it is interesting to compare his views of the types provided in the earlier sermon with his judgments about typology abstracted from this portion of the commentary in the 'Biblia Americana.'

In the *Work Upon the Ark*, Mather had indulged his penchant for allegorizing details, although he had ostensibly set out to define typology and to provide his congregation with some examples of orthodox typological correspondences taken from the Genesis account of the Ark. One example will suffice here; while explaining how the Ark became a 'type' of the Christian Church, Mather begins to record the significance of each part of the Ark, and to allegorize all the physical dimensions of the construction. He says:

As a ship is by Humane ingenuity, often made a Resemblance of the Church, so the Ark, which was a Sort of Ship, is by Divine Authority, exhibited as a Figure or Shadow of it. They compare the Pump in a Ship to Repentance, which fetches out the Corruption that endangers our souls. They compare the Sails, to our Affections, in which when the Wind of the Holy Spirit Blows, we are carried swiftly on to the Harbour of Eternal Blessedness. The Rudder, that May be Compared unto the Tongue of Man; the Compass, that May be Compared unto the Word of God. But These Comparisons are innumerable, as they that have read Navigation Spiritual-

ized by some worth[y] English Writer must needs be sensible; and
I hope ever[y] Gracious Mariner does accustome himself to such
reflections.[27]

Mather has provided his congregation with excerpts from John
Flavel's Navigation Spiritualized as a gloss for his presentation of
the typological significance of Noah's Ark. Although he would not
have us abandon the historically oriented pattern of prefiguration
and fulfillment, he does concede the value of allegorizing in the
accommodation of spiritual truth. This was, of course, an important achievement. The direct mention of Flavel's companion piece
for Husbandry Spiritualized—the model for his own Agricola, or
the Religious Husbandman—indicates how Mather had drawn
some of his own metaphors from Flavel's practice of allegorizing
Nature, and that he would attempt a synthesis of the kind of metaphorical analogies drawn by Flavel and the spiritualizers with the
more conservative emphasis on biblical typology.

In the 'Biblia Americana,' as we have already seen, Mather also
used allegorical and metaphorical comparisons to reinforce his exegesis of the typological correspondences. However, the thrust of
this massive commentary was to establish the types within the
framework of an orthodox and traditional exegesis, so that the examination of Noah and the Ark is more straightforward than the
earlier mixture of typology and spiritualizing had been. There is a
tightening of his typology into a quasi-systematic form in the
'Biblia Americana,' which can partially be explained as a late effort
by Mather to hold together a way of reading history and a method
of exegeting Scripture that had already been weakened when he
first came to know it. 'The Ark will prove a Type of Our Saviour
out of whom there is no Salvation,' he declares, and his way of ac-
commodating this doctrine is to link the Flood to Christian Baptism in a manner that utilizes ingenious allegorical correspondences.[28] As the water buoys up the Ark, so the soul of the regenerate
is buoyed up by the water of Baptism. However, the correspondences established for the Flood and Baptism within this framework

27. Ark, p. 4.

28. Mather, 'Commentary Upon Genesis 8,' in 'Biblia,' I, n.p.

are always set in a linear, historical relation to each other, and they are metaphorically associated in such a way that the antitypical significance of the latter concludes the former.

This systematizing of the typological correspondences in the 'Biblia Americana' should not be construed as a change in Cotton Mather's exegetical method late in his career. It must be remembered that the earlier *Work Upon the Ark* was written in the same period that he composed the diatribe against witchcraft, *Memorable Providences Related to Witchcraft and Possessions.* Throughout his writing, there is a sense that underneath the natural universe there lies a spiritual significance that wants explanation. However, Mather's interest in the allegorical meaning of natural events was characteristically Puritan; it does not conflict with a reading of Scripture that rejects the allegorical mode for a system of correspondences that are related through historical time. On the contrary, Mather combined the allegorical sense with the typological reading of the two testaments to render an exegesis that was clearly traditional if occasionally accommodated by the establishing of an allegorical analogy. In the earlier sermon, for example, the features of the Ark were allegorized to reinforce the typological correspondence between the Ark and the Church; in the 'Biblia Americana,' the important correspondences are maintained throughout the exegesis, while spiritualized aspects of the Genesis account receive only limited attention. The range of Mather's theological concerns was bound to lead to an exploration of alternative modes of epistemological fulfillment; however, the mainstream of his exegesis from the *Work Upon the Ark* to the *Magnalia Christi Americana* to the 'Biblia Americana' reflects a respect for the traditional correspondences of orthodox typology, with only an occasional interest in the spiritualized symbols used by writers like John Flavel. He never abandoned his strong faith in an eschatological view of history, in which his doctrine of the types was firmly rooted. All human history was to be assessed in the light of its relation to God's divine plan. As Cotton Mather himself put it, 'The *Covenant* of God lives at ye *Bottom* of *All.*'[29]

29. *Ibid.*

Edward Taylor

Poetry and
Doctrine in
Edward Taylor's
*Preparatory
Meditations,*
Series II, 1-30

'The World
Slickt Up
in Types':
Edward Taylor
as a Version
of Emerson

Edward Taylor
and the
Poetic Use
of Religious
Imagery

Moses farewell. I with a mournfull teare
    Will wash thy Marble Vault, and leave thy Shine
To follow Joshua to Jordan where
    He weares a Type, of Jesus Christ, divine.

That blazing Star in Joshua's but a Beam
    Of thy bright Sun, my Lord, fix such in mee.
My Dish clout Soul Rence Wring, and make it clean.
    Then die it in that blood that fell from thee.
    And make the Waiting men within my heart
    Attend thy sweetest praise in evry part.

Meditation 10, Second Series

Poetry and Doctrine in Edward Taylor's *Preparatory Meditations,* Series II, 1-30

Robert E. Reiter
Boston College

As one reads through Edward Taylor's *Preparatory Meditations* in Donald E. Stanford's edition of the *Poems* (New Haven, 1960), the first thirty meditations of the Second Series are quickly seen to be a striking group, as Louis Martz first pointed out (p. xxi), because most of them take an Old Testament type as their subject matter. In this essay, I propose to examine these poems and their typology in order not just to comment on Taylor's doctrinal use of typology but also to try to see how the typology functions in the structure and imagery of the poems. That is to say, since obviously Taylor's typological hermeneutic is quite traditional and orthodox, the real literary interest in the typology of these poems lies in the way Taylor as poet rather than Scripture scholar uses typology.

Edward Taylor's poems are unusual in many ways, not least of which are the circumstances of composition. None of the other devotional poets of the seventeenth century so closely dovetailed his poetry and his ministry, and none has left so carefully dated a body of poems. Although Taylor, like the other devotional poets, wrote his poems as meditations, he seems to have been the only poet-minister who wrote his poems as personal accompaniments to the sermons he preached on the days he administered the Sacrament in Westfield. To Taylor, therefore, there must have been a close connection between the sermon and the poem, a connection that is, unfortunately, mostly lost to us because few of his sermons have survived. In the Introduction to his edition of Taylor's *Chris-*

tographia (New Haven, 1962), Norman S. Grabo explains that the poems were composed after the sermons were written, that the poems were meditations upon the doctrines preached in the sermons, and that the poems are more the concluding, affective part of a traditional meditation than complete meditations in themselves (pp. xxxiv–xxxv). It would certainly improve our understanding of Taylor's poetic process if we had all the sermons; but failing that, we can legitimately assume that Taylor usually composed the same way he did in the *Christographia* series. Since the *Preparatory Meditations* thus constitute the concluding section of a large devotional exercise that begins with the sermon, we can expect to find the poems generally cast in the form of an address to God or a colloquy between the poet and God.

Like many preachers, Puritan and otherwise, Taylor often preached over a span of many weeks a connected sequence of sermons on a single large theme or doctrinal issue. Such, for example, is the series he called *Christographia*. The first thirty of the second series of *Preparatory Meditations* also form a sequence which undoubtedly reflects a course of Sacrament-day sermons on typology preached between 1693 and 1699. Considering that the first fifty-odd poems of the second series are Christological in their doctrine, one can assume that for about ten years Taylor's Sacrament-day sermons were devoted to a full exploration of Christology, beginning with the foreshadowings of Christ in the Old Testament. To judge from the evidence in the thirty meditations on types, the function of the associated sermons was to explain to the Westfield congregation how to read the Old Testament as a Christian should, that is, neither strictly literally nor allegorically, but typologically.

The thirty meditations on types deal with personal types of Christ (nos. 1–14 and 30), with Israelite rituals as types (nos. 15–27), and with one thing (Noah's Ark, no. 29) as a type. Taylor, therefore, deals with almost the entire range of Old Testament typology, omitting in this sequence, however, the typology of events such as the Exodus and the Covenant, though they are the subjects of later poems in the Second Series (e.g., nos. 58–61). Meditations 8, 19, and 28 lie, so far as I can presently determine, outside the series on types; though if we had the accompanying sermons, their tenuous connection with the rest of the series would probably become more apparent. The poems on the personal types of Christ (i.e., Old Testament persons who in one way or another foreshadowed Christ) open with a general introductory meditation (no. 1) and conclude with a summary meditation (no. 14).

Meditation 1, on Col. 2:17—'Which are shaddows of things to come and the body is Christs'—is a poem that deals with typology in general and not with any specific type of Christ. As is true of so many of these poems, the connection between the announced text and the completed poem seems loose because the poem grew out of the doctrine developed in the sermon that was preached on the text. To judge from the poem, the sermon probably developed a general exposition of the idea of typology, emphasizing the superiority of Christ to all types.

The poem is simply structured in a three-part form that Taylor nearly always uses: (1) a confessional or personal introduction; (2) development of a type; (3) a prayerful, affective conclusion. The first stanza is a confession of sin and of lack of zeal. Stanzas 2, 3, and 4 make up the second part of the poem, the only part in which typology figures. The second stanza makes the transition from the confession of sin to the doctrine of type and antitype by developing a conceit of cleaning. 'The Excellency in Created Shells' is not sufficient to clean the stains on the poet's 'leather Coate' (i.e., the sins and coolness of stanza 1). This train of thought then leads to Taylor's saying that the 'Excellency in Created Shells' is 'but a Shade to that' which can really remove his 'Stains.' The image that Taylor is building up in this conceit is one of light and dark expressed as 'Excellency' and 'Stains.' Then he develops in the last lines of the second stanza an analogy between (1) the relationship between the cleansing of his coat's stains by shells and the cleansing of his soul by Christ and (2) the relationship between type and antitype.

From this analogy the meditation on typology proceeds, emphasizing Christ's superiority to the types in terms of glory, which in stanza 4 is associated with light. The third and fourth stanzas I take to be the core of the poem, very likely reflecting the doctrine Taylor preached on that Sacrament-day in 1693. The doctrine is orthodox, but the poetic use of typology is somewhat unusual in that the focus is essentially on the antitype. When we remember, however, that the function of a sermon is to explain and exhort and that the poem grew out of the sermon, then the focus of the poem becomes more understandable. And lest Taylor's congregation lose sight of the true importance and superiority of the New Testament, wherein are the antitypes, he necessarily emphasized the fulfill-ment of types. We do not know exactly how he did this in the sermons that Meditations 1–30 accompany, but beginning with the first of his poetic meditations on types, he uses images of greater and lesser glory and greater and lesser light to focus proper atten-tion on the antitype.

The last two stanzas are directly addressed to the Lord and deal with Taylor's spiritual condition, which had been expressed in the images of stanza 1. The image of the 'beams / Of Holiness' of lines 31 and 32 is, at least in part, derived from the image of glory and light in stanzas 3 and 4. The blood image of lines 33 and 34 prob-ably refers to the blood of the Eucharistic celebration on Sacra-ment-day. Like most other poems in this series, this Meditation closes with a reference to Taylor's poetry or singing, which, in the context of the poems, results from the accomplishment of the affec-tive acts of the concluding parts of the meditation.

Without the sermon that originally accompanied Meditation 2, it is difficult to see exactly how this poem forms part of a sequence on types. That there was Christological doctrine preached in the sermon is evident from the fierce tone and the denunciation of old heresies in the second and third stanzas. One does not usually find 'Sabellians' and 'Arrians too and those / Socinians calld' in lyric devotional poetry. The general emphasis of this poem is perhaps contained in line 36: 'The First Born's Antitype: in whom they're shrin'de.' Since the 'First Born' is Christ, according to both the text (Col. 1:15) and the development of the poem, then in the line quoted above 'Born's' is not a possessive but a contraction of 'Born is'; otherwise the 'First Born' would have to be Adam, which is not the customary usage of the term. Syntactic problems such as this plagued Taylor and continue to plague his readers.

The third meditation in the sequence is on Rom. 5:14, the typol-ogist's *locus classicus*, for only there in the New Testament is the Greek word (*typos*) anglicized as 'type' used in the sense that we have become accustomed to. With this poem, one of the better meditations in the sequence, Taylor begins his considerations of the more significant Old Testament persons who were types of Christ. It is also, at least in the first stanza, one of the few meditations that seems to reflect the natural world at the time of composition (October 15, 1693). Apples are in season then (line 5), and marigolds can still flower in October in Massachusetts; though the dew (line 3) often freezes lightly, making the hoar frost of line 4.

The light of the sun/Son, in the pun beloved of seventeenth-century poets, unifies the poem. To Taylor the light becomes also an image for the Old Testament types:

When Lord, mine Eye doth spie thy Grace to beame
　Thy Mediatoriall glory in the shine
Out Spouted so from Adams typick streame
　And Emblemiz'd in Noahs pollisht shrine
Thine theirs outshines so far it makes their glory
In brightest Colours, seem a smoaky story.

Adam, the first of the types, is the fount from which 'Mediatoriall glory' spouts out in a 'typick streame.' Although Taylor associates light and glory with the types, he insists that the light and the glory of the antitype is far greater. This image of the differences in the light and glory of type and antitype becomes, in the subsequent meditations on types, Taylor's favorite image of typology. Light is a large image, often used by the poets and having many and varied meanings and overtones. In the devotional poets, it is usually associated in some way with the Divine. Milton makes the identification of God and light brilliantly at the end of Book II and the opening of Book III of *Paradise Lost*. Taylor's association of light with types likely proceeds from many sources. Certainly, the New Testament image of Christ as the light of the world is one source, for if Christ is light, then those who prefigured him must also be lights, though lesser. Since types were also often called shadows and since shadows necessarily imply light, Taylor might very well have derived his controlling image of light and types from a contemplation of shadows. The importance of Taylor's large image of light and types lies, I believe, in the poetic possibilities it offered him. He had, of course, a clear understanding of the doctrinal aspects of typology, but straight doctrine rarely makes for good poetry, as the second and third stanzas of Meditation 2 show. Henceforth, however, his light image gave him something he could rely on when composing his meditations. By finding an image capable of development, Taylor was able to make poetry out of orthodox typology. One might almost say that Taylor's perception of the Old Testament types is conditioned by this image. It was to him, I suspect, intellectually comforting and spiritually profitable to have such an image always at his command for writing his poems.

With the fourth Meditation, Taylor's purpose in the sequence becomes clear. He is proceeding through the books of Genesis, Exodus, Judges, and Kings, looking for the principal types of Christ. Meditation 4 is on Abraham. The remaining poems in the sequence treat Isaac (no. 5), Jacob (no. 6), Joseph (no. 7), Moses (no. 9), Joshua (no. 10), Samson (no. 11), David (no. 12), and Solomon (no. 13). Meditation 8 is not part of this sequence. Most of the ten poems in the sequence are structured like Meditation 1. In traditional meditative practice, Taylor found a convenient and fruitful scaffolding for his poems and stuck with it. Meditation 7, on Psalm 105:17, is an example of the way Taylor makes the light image work for him. The poem is in seven stanzas. The first stanza is introductory, the second through the sixth detail the typological relationship between Joseph and Christ, and the seventh concludes the poem with a prayer. The introductory stanzas of Taylor's Meditations usually state the poet's poor spiritual condition under various metaphors. In Meditation 7 Taylor says he is 'All Dull, my Lord, my Spirits flat, and dead.' The key word is 'Dull,' which can be taken as signifying spiritual apathy, 'flat, and dead / All water sockt and sapless to the skin.' Thus 'Dull' as a metaphor would usually end, but Taylor keeps the literal meaning of dull in the back of his mind as the poem develops.

With the first lines of the second stanza we meet Taylor's image of light and types: 'Is Josephs glorious shine a Type of thee? / How bright art thou?' Here, the type, because it is light, has a 'shine.' Joseph's coat of many colors, which Taylor never directly mentions, fits in with the light and shine of the type. The central part of this poem simply versifies the obvious (to the typologist) actions wherein Joseph resembled Christ. The light image does not recur until the sixth stanza, where it is used to sum up the comparison:

Josephs bright shine th'Eleven Tribes must preach.
And thine Apostles now Eleven, thine.
They beare his presents to his Friends: thine reach
  Thine unto thine, thus now behold a shine.
  How hast thou pensild out, my Lord, most bright
  Thy glorious Image here, on Josephs Light.

This stanza makes it clear that Joseph's light, or shine, is ultimately due to his being a type of Christ, from whom the light really comes. Therefore, by gazing on Joseph, Taylor has indeed been gazing on the Lord's 'glorious Image here.' The doctrine of typology and the poetic image of light thus perfectly reinforce each other.

The light image, moreover, gives substance to Taylor's prayer in the last stanza as well as connecting it back to the first stanza's image of dullness:

This I bewaile in me under this shine
  To see so dull a Colour in my Skin.
Lord, lay thy brightsome Colours on me thine.

Although one expects the first word of the last stanza to be 'thus' instead of 'this,' the latter does make sense if it refers to 'To see so dull a Colour in my Skin.' Taylor's prayer, 'lay thy brightsome Colours on me,' thus is part of the large image of light and color that controls the poem. Joseph's many-colored coat is, assuredly, at least in the background here. According to modern taste, the prayer unifies the poem by being couched in the controlling image. Unfortunately, Taylor's final three lines,

Scoure thou my pipes then play thy tunes therein.
I will not hang my Harp in Willows by.
While thy sweet praise, my Tunes doth glorify.

though pious and appropriate to a poet-preacher, destroy the neatness and imagistic unity that had earlier been achieved. This is not uncharacteristic of the poet on his errand into the wilderness and writing for himself alone.

Other meditations in this sequence, for example, numbers 6, 9, 10, 11, and 12, are similar to number 7 in handling the light image. It is usually found in the first and last stanzas loosely, and the types meditated upon are associated with light. It would seem that the pattern set in Meditation 6 and fully developed in number 7 adequately served Taylor's poetic. The light image, as what might be called a poetic hermeneutic, was satisfying and effective to Taylor as poet and as preacher.

Following the poems on the personal types there are three poems (Meditations 14, 15, and 16) on the traditional offices (roles) of Christ as prophet, priest, and king. Meditation 14, the subject matter of which is the wisdom of Christ, considers the prophetic, kingly, and sacerdotal types as ways of getting at this wisdom. The sixth stanza deals with all three typic roles in Taylor's favorite light image:

How Glorious art thou, Lord? Cloathd with the Glory
  Of Prophets, Priests, and Kings? Nay all Types come
To lay their Glory on thee. (Brightsome Story).
  Their Rayes attend thee, as Sun Beams the Sun.
  And shall my Ulcer'd Soule have such reliefe?
  Such glorious Cure? Lord strengthen my beliefe.

In effect, Meditation 14 is both a summary of the preceding poems on the personal types and an introduction to the poems that follow on Christ as Nazarite (no. 15) and as king (no. 16), in which the treatment of types is conventional and uninteresting. There follows an extended sequence on various aspects of Israelite worship that were taken as types. One cannot but be amazed at Taylor's poetic (not to say his homiletic) confidence in undertaking to write poems on this most intractable of Old Testament subjects. It seems to me that the dependence of the poems on the sermons is most evident in these ten poems (Meditations 17–27), for no one but a preacher who was resolutely committed to plowing through the Old Testament types and who was also committed to composing poems on the doctrines he preached could possibly have accomplished both the sermons and the poems. It took great perseverance on Taylor's part to finish the job.

Meditations 19 and 28 do not fit into the sequence on ritual typology. Meditation 29, on Noah and his Ark, and Meditation 30, on Jonah, are not, strictly speaking, on ritual types either. Noah's Ark is a type of baptism according to I Peter 3:21, the verse that follows the announced text, though Taylor really does not treat that aspect of the typology. The text for Meditation 30 (Matt. 12:40) is a *locus classicus* of typology, for it is a saying of Jesus, who thus himself makes the connection between the acts of an Old Testament person and his own acts. Curiously enough, however, Taylor concentrates in this poem not so much on the Resurrection, which is what one would expect, but on the Atonement.

The poems of the sequence on ritual types follow the same general structure as those on the personal types: a confession of sin or fault, an exploration of the type, and an affective conclusion. The large image associating light and glory with the types plays a far smaller role now than it did in the earlier typological poems. As if to compensate for the objectifying power of that image, which gave Taylor a control over his subject matter, the poems on the ritual types seem to dwell more on the spiritual condition of the poet. One of the better poems of the sequence, Meditation 26 on Hebrews 9:13, 14, shows how Taylor makes a respectable poem out of his rather difficult subject.

The Epistle to the Hebrews (especially chapters 8 through 10) goes further than any other part of the New Testament in making connections between the ritual laws and actions of Israelite Temple worship (as codified in the Pentateuch) and the actions of Jesus in the Gospels. It is, therefore, the part of the New Testament generally used by Christian exegetes to assimilate Jewish ritual to Christian salvation history by means of a typological interpretation sketched in Hebrews itself. Taylor stands squarely within the central Christian tradition of interpreting Israelite ritual via the Epistle to the Hebrews. In the ninth chapter of Hebrews, its author argues that if the blood rituals of the Old Law had the power to purify men outwardly, then the blood of Christ, who is both high priest and sacrificial victim of the New Law, has even greater power—power to cleanse consciences and sin. This argument is concluded in verses 13 and 14, which Taylor chose as the text for his sermon and accompanying meditation.

Taylor opens Meditation 26 with a stanza about his own spiritual condition:

Unclean, Unclean: My Lord, Undone, all vile
Yea all Defild: What shall thy Servant doe?

Unfit for thee: not fit for holy Soile,
  Nor for Communion of Saints below.
  A bag of botches, Lump of Loathsomeness:
  Defild by Touch, by Issue: Leproust flesh.

The central image of uncleanliness is particularly appropriate because it can refer either to the ritual uncleanliness of the Old Law,
or, in a more generalized application, to his consciousness of sin.
The latter, of course, is the more important sense; but before he
really deals with it, Taylor takes two-and-a-half stanzas to consider
the necessity of being 'Pure, Cleane, and bright, Whiter than whit-
est Snow / Better refin'd than most refined Gold' before entering
Church fellowship and ultimately heaven. But he is not clean, and
thus cannot enter 'Thy Churches.' The poem turns at lines 15–18
as he questions:

Shall I defile them, tumbled thus in mire?
  Or they mee cleanse before I current pass?
  If thus they do, Where is the Niter bright
  And Sope they offer mee to wash me White?

In the next stanza Taylor answers these questions:

The Brisk Red heifer's Ashes, when calcin'd,
  Mixt all in running Water, is too Weake
To wash away my Filth: the Dooves assign'd
  Burnt, and Sin Offerings neer do the feate
  But as they Emblemize the Fountain Spring
  Thy Blood, my Lord, set ope to wash off Sin.

The Old Law sacrifices, the blood of bulls and doves, are of themselves 'too Weake / To wash away my Filth.' Only insofar as the
bulls and doves 'Emblemize . . . Thy Blood' is there any power of
cleansing in them. Thus the questions of the third stanza are answered here by recourse to typology. But the typology is not so obvious as in many of Taylor's poems. It is, indeed, understated, but
is the key to the whole poem, for it provided Taylor with both a
theologically exact answer to his questions and a poetically logical
structure for the answers because the typology involved centers on
blood. The complete decorum of the typology of blood becomes

beautifully apparent in the last two stanzas when we remember that the poems were composed before entering upon Sacrament-day worship and that the blood of Christ is integral to that worship. The last stanza shows Taylor in his roles as individual, private Christian, as leader of the congregation at Westfield, and as poet, all purified by what has happened in the poem:

Oh! wash mee, Lord, in this Choice Fountain, White
   That I may enter, and not sully here
Thy Church, whose floore is pav'de with Graces bright
   And hold Church fellowship with Saints most cleare.
   My Voice all sweet, with their melodious layes
   Shall make sweet Musick blossom'd with thy praise.

It was not often, unfortunately, that Taylor was thus inspired by his subject matter and his own condition to write so compactly in his typological poems. The typology does not need to be detailed, because Taylor did not here write a poem about a type; rather, the typology offers him an insight into the relationship existing among himself, the Old Testament, and the New Testament that is similar, I suggest, to what Hopkins called (in a different context) inscape. The insight here is subsumed under the figure of blood, which is not only the typological core of the poem but also the agent of cleansing and worship, the situation and images around which the poem is built. When Taylor writes thus, he is not just piously versifying his sermon's doctrine, he is truly making a poem out of typology.

To most readers, the poems in Taylor's sequence on ritual types are probably not very attractive. Though the rather wild imagery of the second stanza of Meditation 18 has often been noted, it is not at all typical of these poems. Most of them are straightforward, competent attempts at reducing some rather esoteric and generally unappealing typology to a personal application, which inevitably comes in the last stanza or two. The meditative structure afforded Taylor much help in versifying his doctrine, but only rarely (e.g., Meditations 24 and 26) does the typology really make rather than just decorate the poem. However, Taylor did achieve a decent level of competence in these poems on what must be the most intractable and 'unpoetic' of Biblical subjects.

Despite the poetically inhibiting but nonetheless self-imposed discipline of writing almost thirty consecutive poems on very similar theme, Edward Taylor's achievement in his whole typological sequences is considerable. Taylor is one poet who has clearly wrestled with biblical typology as a subject matter for a substantial body of verse. That he sometimes lost the match ought not to be held against him. In the best poems of the sequence, the meditative structure that he had chosen is reinforced by a controlling image derived from the typology that forms the subject matter. In the poems on the personal types of Christ, this image is the large one of light, which offers many variations to the poet. Taylor is less often successful in the poems on ritual types; perhaps because he found no large image to rely on, or because the light image, which does figure in Meditations 20, 21, 23, 24, and 27, simply worked better for men than for rituals. When he is successful in the ritual types poems, the controlling image grows directly and polysemantically out of the type, as does the blood in Meditation 26 and the delightfully elaborate conceit of tents in Meditation 24. When the typology offered him an image that would make sense in personal, New Testament, and Old Testament applications, he had the poetic instinct and talent to seize upon it and develop it into a good poem. Thus we can say that when, as especially with light, the image central to the typology was also one that was congruent with the personal, meditative structure of the poem, Edward Taylor was able to achieve the very difficult: making a successful poem out of typology.

'The World Slickt Up in Types': Edward Taylor as a Version of Emerson

Karl Keller
San Diego
State College

In many ways, Edward Taylor is a fairly conventional typologist. In his meditative poems and his extant sermons, Christ is the antitype to the usual prophetic parallels in the traditional Christian imagery constructing the Puritan view of human history. Because he is rigidly orthodox, Taylor rarely goes outside the catalog of canonized types. For the most part, he is a conventional lover of Christ, with the old list of trick types to bolster his faith.

Taylor is unique among New England typologists in the obvious delight he takes in playing with the conventions, stretching them wittily until they are personally relevant and extending them until his theology yields him an esthetic theory. In his handling of conventional types, we have a view of literature and life that for the Puritan period was esthetically forward-looking. Though typology as a poetic mode was by his own time old-fashioned, even archaic, Taylor used the mode's stock-in-trade of conceits, puns, jumps in logic, and meiotic talk about man and hyperbolic talk about God to express the joy with which he contemplated the hard matters of his faith and to make room for individuality within the closed system of thought that typology represented. These assisted him in probing the nature of reality. It was plainly a thing of beauty to him to find the world so neatly arranged, so comfortably convincing, so much a part of a divine scheme. As a game, there is delight and excitement in his vision of the continuity of human with divine experience—all made possible by his uses of typology.

Samuel Willard wrote in his *Compleat Body of Divinity* (1726)
that 'Types and figures must be allowed to the Scriptures . . . to
move the affections.'[1] Though, as Taylor admitted, typology was on
the surface 'a poore, weake, beggarly, Inefficacious and foolish
thing' and sometimes little more than 'a Charm' or 'dark draughts
and resemblances,' Taylor himself was moved by what he called
'Typicall Worship.'

*The truth of the Promises of the Types, and Ceremonies of the
Law, is of Such Concern that all Religion, Faith, and Obedience
ever since the Fall of our First Parents lieth on it. If it faile, all this
is groundless, and falls down.*[2]

Taylor was intrigued with the significance that the person of Christ
gave his own life and the life of the world. He was moved, he said,
to a firm conviction of the 'Sweet harmony' between man and God
and to an insight into 'a wonderfull Wisdom' running through the
analogical correspondences among all created things.[3] Though he
recognized that 'Grace excells all Metaphors' ('The varnish laid
upon it doth but darken, and not decorate it: its own Colours are
too glorious to be made more glorious, by any Colour of Secular
glory'), yet he believed that through the game of types he could divine the Divine: 'There are Some things [most notably "Adams
Sons"] whose Excellency is flourisht over with Metaphors.'[4] Taylor
knew it was a language game but also felt that one wins Christian
conviction by playing it imaginatively. It was such conviction that
he was after.

The humor with which Taylor conceits conventional types is
definitely a sign of the delight he found in spiritual matters. Calvinism was to him, after all, delightful; life a divine comedy; judgment sweet; and eternity blissful. How could he be grim for long
about such things? His witty use of types in his private Meditations

---

1. (Boston, 1726), p. 33.

2. *Edward Taylor's Christographia*, ed. Norman S. Grabo (New Haven, 1962), p. 280.

3. *Ibid.*, pp. 122–24. This is the view of typology taken in his Sermon IV, February 15, 1701/02.

4. *Ibid.*, p. 253. Sermon VIII, November 8, 1702.

(and there are no types in all of his other poetry) is a private chuckle at how logic and language have again surprised him with the truth of his convictions.

Taylor's joy over the truth that his types reveal to him causes him to handle the usual catalog of 'personal' and 'real' types of Christ wittily.[5] The Tree of Life in the Garden of Eden is baroqued by Taylor, for example, into a cross that is a golden tree on which Christ's limbs are 'richly hung' (I.29).[6] The broken covenant of the Fall of Man is extended as both the broken body of Christ and the broken bread of the Sacrament of the Lord's Supper (II.104). The Flood becomes the 'mighty Tide' of Christ's overwhelming blood, the veins of the earth and the veins of Christ both flowing freely into the blood stream of the elect (I.1). Noah's ark, decked out as a rich storehouse, is rebuilt into the wood of Christ's cross, which is a 'living Tree / Where life lies treasurde up for all in thee' (I.33). Jacob, as a young stud, seeks a spouse and sires twelve sons; and similarly, Christ in his marriage to the Church 'stud[s]' the Church elaborately with twelve apostles (II.6). Joseph in Egypt prepares against famine, and the crucified Christ 'layes in' the Bread of Life for all (II.7). David's stock/stalk (along with root, stem [of Jesse], branch, bough, and all) becomes Christ's cross-beam for holding up the temple of the sky (I.30). Samson, rising from his bed of sin to tear down the doors of the palace in anger, becomes Christ rising from the sinful world to take 'Deaths Doore . . . off o'th'hooks'—all for love! (II.11). The Tabernacle becomes the body of Christ; it is a structure made of '[in]Carnation leafes,' a cross of pine boughs, staples for crucifying nails, and repentance for rent (II.24). Circumcision becomes Christ's blood that washes

5. These are Samuel Mather's categories of types in his sermons, The Figures or Types of the Old Testament (London, 1673), a work which Taylor might have known through his friend Increase Mather, a brother of Samuel. By 'personal' type, Mather means those individuals 'chosen and singled out by [God] from all the world' to prefigure Christ; by 'real' type, those 'occasional' props of Old Testament episodes like Noah's ark or the burning bush or manna, as well as the more 'perpetual' items like the Law of Moses, Solomon's temple, the Priesthood.

6. All references in the text are to the first and second series and to the numbered Meditations in The Poems of Edward Taylor, ed. Donald E. Stanford (New Haven, 1960).

away the filth of the world (II.70). Solomon's garden is made over into the Church with its 'Plants of Grace,' aromatic spirits, and grapes bleeding on the altar (II.83). The Red Sea is metamorphosed into the red blood of Christ, with the Church out paddling canoes 'Along this blood red Sea': 'Here's Covenant blood, indeed' (II.78).

Such wit as all of these conceits show is not mere play with types, but serious delight in the relationships that language gives to reality. The factors of metaphor are to Taylor the facts of reality. As both Puritan and poet, Taylor seems, like Emerson, to have apprehended words as signs of spiritual facts; his typological puns show this as much as the love acrostics and funeral anagrams that he wrote. Taylor interprets 'The Word was made flesh' to refer to the promises, prophecies, and types of the Old Testament, taking 'Word' fairly literally as meaning 'words.' To have faith in language in the way that types require is to Taylor to have faith in Christ.

Though Taylor was not free to choose his types ('It is not safe to make any thing a Type merely upon our own fancies and imaginations,' wrote Samuel Mather; 'it is Gods Prerogative to make Types'[7]), yet he was free to play with them, binding type to antitype with the apt extravagance of extended punning. The Rose of Sharon of the Canticles, a favorite type of Taylor's, becomes, for example, both flower and risen Christ through a play on the word 'rose' (I.4). The flower, like the crucified Christ, has 'Blushes of Beauty bright, Pure White, and Red.' The dew on the flower is 'Sweats of Glory' on the suffering Christ, and the 'Rosy bed' is the bed of the crucified Christ. In the seventeenth century, the syrup of roses was used as a purgative, allowing a metaphorical connection with Christ's blood as a purgative for the souls of men: 'Rosy Oyle' can 'Consumptive Souls restore . . . When Dayly usd.' God is a 'Chymist' and can mix oil, syrup, sugar, and rose water together and come up with the sacramental bread. To make this new bread out of old roses, as in the crucifixion and resurrection,

> this Brave Flower must Pluckt, stampt, squeezed bee,
> And boyld up in its Blood, its Spirits sheed,
>   To make a Physick sweet, sure, safe for mee.

7. Mather, pp. 58–59.

Man is thereby saved from the sickness of his mortality by Christ the Risen/Rosy One. The thorns of the Rose of Sharon, then, become Christ's crown of thorns and crown of victory. In the poem that follows I.4, 'The Reflexion,' the sun that makes the roses bloom is the Son that gives the light of salvation to man, and the rose's thorns are knives for cutting the meat/bread at the Lord's Supper. Again, all of this play with correspondences serves to shore up Taylor's faith. Puns were apparently epistemology enough for his theology.

To justify the ordinance of the Sacrament of the Lord's Supper— his long-range intent in the two series of the *Preparatory Meditations*—he often turns a type-antitype correspondence into a series of puns. For instance, Isaiah's Dyed-Robes type has its antitype in the bloody crucifixion of Christ (I.12), with Taylor punning to show his delight in the fulfillment of prophecy. The robes are 'Died,' and Christ died. The robes are made of wool from Bozrah sheep, and Christ was slaughtered like a lamb. Dyed robes made one look 'Glorious' and 'Divine,' and Christ, shedding his blood, became 'Glorious' and 'Divine.' Christ, like a lover, then comes 'in Pinckted Robes . . . forth to Wooe.' The pinckted robes are the pierced flesh of Christ, and the pink is the red and the white, the blood and the flesh, of the sacramental wine and bread, which is given in love to those who have been wooed, the elect.

Likewise, the Sacrifice-of-Isaac type has an antitype in the crucifixion of Christ (II.5), when Taylor catches the ram's blood in the 'Altars Drippen pan' to become his sacramental wine and takes the 'Roast Mutton' of the burnt offering for the flesh/bread. The idea of sacrifice is made delightful when it is thus punned into the 'Choice Angell Mess' of the Lord's Supper.

In a poem on the text 'Thy love is better than Wine' (II.98), to give another example, Taylor takes the Vine-in-the-Garden type (a version of the Tree-of-Life type) and sees the antitype in Christ as a vine that produces grapes for the sacramental wine:

A Vine, my Lord, a noble Vine indeed
  Whose juyce makes brisk my heart to sing thy Wine.
. . . .
The Choicest Vine, the royallst grape that rose,

Or ere in Cana'ns Vinyard did take Root,
Did Emblemize thy selfe the True Vine. . . .

The language provides Taylor a number of faith-promoting puns in this example: Christ risen and the rising vines; the crucified Christ and the crushed grapes; the blood as spirit, the wine as spirits, and the sacramental wine as something spiritual; the heart of Christ, the wine as a cordial, and the sacrament warming 'the gracious heart'— all together making the phonic pun vine/wine a historical and spiritual reality:

This Wine thy Love bleeds from thy grape, how sweet?
To spiritualize the life in every part.

This concept of language as a scheme of almost endlessly interwoven puns was for Taylor, no doubt, evidence of divine order in the world.

By contrast, the typologists closest to Taylor in his own time were much more serious about such matters. In 1697, his friend Samuel Sewall, a classmate at Harvard and fellow participant in judicial affairs of the Massachusetts colony, wrote his *Phaenomena Quaedam Apocalyptica*, a deadly serious attempt to document what he doggedly believed to be a 'synchronisme' between the Old Jerusalem of the Jews, the Christian Kingdom of God, and the New Zion in America. His use of types is earnestly epical: America is the final Garden of Eden, and the returned Christ the last Adam. This new nationalism was a serious matter to Sewall, a justification of America as fulfillment of prophecy, and no language game at all. There was no room for levity in the pride that prophetic types made possible.

In 1686, another friend of Taylor's, Increase Mather, who was both friendly literary critic and advisor in theological matters to Taylor, wrote a book also requiring a typology as elaborate as Sewall's, *The Mystery of Christ Opened and Applied*, and it too is humorless. Mather was much more of a literalist than Taylor about scriptural similes. The 'special providences' in both history and Nature were to be taken wholly seriously. His regard for types was intellectual and scientific rather than imaginative and witty.

But Taylor had an important reason for the wit with which he stretched the conventional schemes of typology: it made room for him personally in an otherwise impersonal cosmology. Therefore, to the Tree of Life, Taylor grafts himself, though only a withered twig. For the broken body/bread, he develops an appetite, though sick with sin. His dull face needs the color of Joseph's coat and of Christ's blood in his cheeks. He is an animal locked up in the ark, trash in the House of Israel, a poor pin to hang coats on in Solomon's temple, a bandage soaking up the blood of both circumcision and crucifixion, and scores of other meiotic artifacts worked wittily into the conventional types.

Taylor was of a breed of Puritans who were at home among Old Testament prophecies and yet tied to a New Testament cosmology. Typology offered the Puritans a comfortable way of combining their role in human history with their role in a divine cosmology, and Taylor is an important writer in this regard—not in combining types and antitypes but in seeing the involvement of the individual in this scheme. Other typologists of the time handle the correspondences rather remotely, as if Old Testament foreshadowing is answered fully by Christ, the Church, or New England Puritanism. But Taylor includes himself (the individual) in that scheme. He wants to see himself as part of the scheme of salvation and not merely an onlooker of Judeo-Christian history.

Taylor accomplishes this self-inclusion by writing about Christ as a fulfillment of Old Testament foreshadowings in such a way that he is involved unobtrusively but noticeably in the relationship. Christ as Lily-of-the-Valley antitype needs a garden to grow in, and Taylor is prepared to offer himself as part of the antitype in the form of humility/humus/dirt:

My Blessed Lord, art thou a Lilly Flower?
Oh! that my Soul thy Garden were, that so
Thy bowing Head root in my Heart, and poure
Might of its Seeds, that they therein might grow.
Be thou my Lilly, make thou me thy knot:
Be thou my Flowers, I'le be thy Flower Pot. I.5

Christ as First-Born-of-Every-Creature antitype is 'Gods onely Son begot,' who, because of the unity of the Trinity, is also a Father in need of a son; and Taylor is ready to be his lowly 'Babe' with the

'Birth Right' of grace (II.2). Christ as Solomon-the-Bridegroom antitype lacks a bride; and Taylor though vile, waits to be enravished:

O let thy lovely streams of Love distill
  Upon myselfe and spoute their spirits pure
Into my Viall, and my Vessell fill
  With liveliness, from dulness me secure.
  And I will answer all this Love of thine
  When with it thou hast made me all Divine.   II.32

As these examples show, Taylor is for the most part attracted to types into which he can slip himself without in any way changing the nature of the original type-antitype relationship, thereby sneaking himself into the plan of salvation by means of the vehicle of language. The Canticle types were attractive to Taylor for this reason; they invite inclusion of the typologist as part of the antitype (lover and beloved) and, through metaphor, encourage the illusion of oneness with Christ (through the metaphors of marriage). Other types and texts were equally attractive because they invited Taylor to append himself to the spiritual realities that Christ made possible.

Taylor slips several times and calls Christ the type rather than the antitype (II.11, 17, 18, 20, 23), perhaps because he desires intensely to see himself as antitype to Christ. Just as life is 'spiritualized' when Christ is seen as providing an antitype to the 'Naturall' world of types, so, too, Taylor feels that his own life is 'spirituallized' when, through the sacrament, it is united with Christ. Conceiving of types as conceits which can be imaginatively extended, Taylor finds room for himself in the scheme:

Shall not that Wisdom horded in thee (which
  Prophetick Types enucleate) forth shine
With light enough a Saving Light to fix
  On my Poore Taper?   II.14

What Taylor is saying by thus personalizing his types is that a man's business is to hope for a part in the cosmic drama, to hope for the recognition of his personality, however trite and thin and absurd his conceited types show it to be, and, amid the immanence of alienation and indifference, to hope for consideration of his ex-

istence. By contrast, Increase Mather seems content in his writings
to construct types in which there is no personality, no individuality,
no self; all are dissolved in the love of Christ. But Taylor finds a
place in the typologist's scheme for the *lover* of Christ. Where
Mather writes about doctrine, Taylor writes about himself and his
place in the plan of salvation. Similarly, the concern in Sewall's
types is for place, not persons. In the 'cognations' which he sees between Old Testament types and New Testament antitypes, Sewall
finds room for New England as further antitype. But where types
have for Sewall historical and political meaning, for Taylor they
have personal meaning.

This desire to proclaim his worth amid fears of worthlessness and
to involve his personality in the nature of things without commit-
ting the sin of spiritual pride, is still a long way to Emersonian in-
dividualism, but it is beyond Calvin. Though of little consequence,
Taylor wishes to announce his existence. It is not that in personalizing his types Taylor was breaking the mold of a way of thinking
that in New England sustained Calvinism past the period of its so-
cial viability; but that in giving to the mold the shape and colors of
his own personality—showing his God how imaginative he can be,
how ingenious and yet faithful he is, how much of a sincere offering
of himself he can make—he was showing how his desire for identity
was stronger in him than the self-denial that necessity/reality insists on. Though a long way from Emerson, he is, in his consciousness of self and his recognition of the fantastic variety of correspondences of self with Nature, a first, small version of Emerson.

Taylor's witty use and personalized extension of types follow
necessarily from his concept of Christ in the role of antitype to the
world, a concept that in its own way was almost as far-reaching as
Jonathan Edwards' ideas on the esthetic significance of divine and
supernatural light. For his attempt to account for the movement of
Puritan naturalism from Edwards to Emerson, Perry Miller would
have found in Taylor's Christology evidence of a transcendental-
ized thaw of Puritan esthetics.[8]

In a sermon on the text 'Full of truth,' December 27, 1702,
Taylor discusses at length the theological and esthetic implications

8. 'From Edwards to Emerson,' in *Errand into the Wilderness* (New York,
1964), pp. 184–203.

of a typology in which the role of Christ as antitype is primary.[9] To Taylor, 'Truth is in Christ' in a number of ways: through prophecies ('He is foretold without any express obligation upon it'), through covenants ('God doth . . . put in bond to do the thing Promised'), and through types. It is mainly when considered typologically that Taylor's Christ is 'full of truth':

As he is foretold in the Type, God doth as it were pensill out in fair Colours and [ingrave] and portray Christ and his Natures and Properties in him. And as these are given out, they flow from the very fountain of Truth: but yet their truth appeareth not while that which is foretold is not apparent[;] but to some, (viz, as believe them not) they are lookt on as fictitions, and fancies: to others, as dubious, and doubtfull: and to all not as visibly true. . . . Christs coming made them True. Their Truth lieth in him. He is the truth of them.

Taylor's attempt to celebrate Christ appears to demand the logic of typology. Man is commanded to be obedient to God, Taylor reasons, but the obedience intended in the *moral* law was reserved to be performed by Christ. The law was broken by all persons, but it exacts obedience and satisfaction which they never can give. So mankind is constrained 'to make their recourse unto Christ to obtain true obedience unto the law performed by him for them.' As a result, Christ is 'the Truth of the Obedience to the Law, and full of this Truth also which it could not be, if wee could attain obedience to it of our own, or if the Truth of Obedience was not in Christ.' Therefore, as man and Nature are shown to have a relationship to Christ, they take on importance, for, through him, they have obedience to the law. 'Christs coming made them True. Their Truth lieth in him. He is the truth of them.'

This goes beyond the logic of simple metaphor, in which the factors of an analogy have importance independent of each other and, combined, modify the meaning of each other. In any system of typology, the type does not really exist until there is an antitype. It is the antitype (Christ) that gives life to the type (Nature and human history):

9. *Christographia*, pp. 267–96. Sermon IX.

If these Promises, and Types should never be fulfilld; they would be false, and assert untruth. Hence in respect unto their being true, there must be the fulfilling of them. . . . They derive their Truth from him in whom they are fulfilld, and therefore their truth is all Stored up in him. He is their truth. . . . Now then seing the truth of these things lies in their fulfilling, and their fulfilling lies in Christ, its plain that their truth is in Christ, and hence Christ is full of truth.

Taylor says much the same thing in Meditation 50 (first series):

Thou givst thy Truth to them: thus true they bee.
They bring their Witness out for thee. Hereby
Their Truth appeares emboxt indeed in thee,
And thou the true Messiah shin'st thereby.
Hence Thou, and They make One another true
And They, and Thou each others Glory Shew.

Thus it is not that Christ is divine because he fulfills prophecy but that, because of relationships with the divinity of Christ, whether real or metaphorical, Nature has existence and human history has significance.

They are not untrue before they are fulfilld: nor are they true before they are accomplished. The accomplishment of them is necessary in order to their truth. . . . They derive their Truth from him in whom they are fulfilld, and therefore their truth is all Stored up in him. He is their truth.

Just as a type does not have any significance until matched with its antitype, so to Taylor an object or an individual does not have inherent reality but has reality only in its coherence with the reality of Christ.

The truth of the Promises of the Types, and Ceremonies of the Law, is of Such Concern that all Religion, Faith, and Obedience ever since the Fall of our First Parents lieth on it. If it faile, all this is groundless, and falls down. . . . All this comes upon Christ, who is the glory of them all and no more, if compared to his glory than the light of a Candle to the Shining Sun. . . . To use the type is to say, the Shadow is better than the Substance, and to denie that the

*thing typified is come. It is therefore to blow out the light of
Christs truth. . . . When the light is Come, the Shadows fly away.
And seeing he is the truth of all types, which were erected onely to
typify him[,] when he is come their typicall relation to him ceaseth,
and when the nature Ceaseth, and is destroyed the thing is dead,
and not for use.*

All types meet in Taylor's Christ, which means that solely because of him is there any reality at all.

*Hell, Earth, and Heaven with their Whole Troops come
    Contrary Windes, Grace, and Disgrace, Soure, Sweet,
Wealth, Want, Health, Sickness, to Conclude in Sum
    All Providences Works in this good meet?
    Who, who can do't, but thou, my Lord? and thou
    Dost do this thing. Yea thou performst it now.   I.35*

It would appear that, in his love of the things of the world, Taylor
wishes to see them as having purpose, and to him they have significance as types of Christ. Perhaps this helps to explain the profusion
of strained comparisons of worldly things with Christ in his Meditations. Christ is the unifier of all disparities, the atoner (i.e., the
at-one-er) of Nature and man.

In this system of correspondences between Nature and Christ, it
is not far from Taylor's attempt at seeing divine purpose in Nature
to the deification of Nature by nineteenth-century writers. Just as
in Taylor the relevance of the things of Nature and human history
to the person of Christ makes those things spiritual, so in Emerson
the correspondence of Nature and man to Over-Soul gives them a
spiritual life. Emerson simply moved the emphasis from the insti-
tutional Christ to the Holy Spirit:

*Ever the Rock of Ages melts
    Into the mineral air,
To be the quarry whence to build
    Thought and its mansions fair.*

With Taylor, that which is related to Christ by metaphor is holy,
and with Emerson, that which is part of the whole/Nature/Over-

Soul is holy.[10] This identification of the spiritual scheme of reality accounts for the delight Taylor takes in documenting the typological correspondences and accounts for the inclusion of himself in a universal scheme.

Like the theoreticians of typology, from the Jewish philosophers of Alexandria through Aquinas and Calvin to William Ames and Samuel Mather, Taylor believed that reality has a symbolic structure in which nothing has meaning in itself but in which everything refers beyond itself—in Taylor's case, to Christ. It then follows that, if Christ were a cheat, there would be no meaning anywhere in all the Creation! To Taylor, although the Creation has a 'Naturall' existence, it is not 'spirituallized' unless it stands in some relationship to Christ. Because of the typological arrangement of reality, its value and meaning are absolutely dependent on him. As with Edwards' view of the meaning of the Creation through dependence on God, Taylor makes it dependent on Christ.[11] If the Creation is fallen and yet we sense it to be real, to have value, to be beautiful, there must be something which saves it from the Fall and gives it its reality, its worth, its beauty. To Taylor, 'Christ is the man in Whom their truth is found.' Through correspondence with Christ, that which is fallen gains life.

All Humane royalty hereby Divin'de.
The First Born's Antitype: in whom they're shrin'de. II.2

10. See my 'From Christianity to Transcendentalism: A Note on Emerson's Use of the Conceit,' *American Literature*, XXXIX (1967), 94–98. Emerson's lines are a rejected quatrain written about 1830 when he was undergoing a change in thinking from Christianity to Transcendentalism. It is found in *Complete Works of Ralph Waldo Emerson*, ed. Edward W. Emerson (Boston, 1904–05), IX, 355.

11. The theological necessity of types proved to Taylor the evil of those arch-enemies of Puritanism, the Catholics and Quakers. To Taylor, Catholicism had built ceremonies around Old Testament types without regard to their reference point in Christ, so the 'Morall Signification' is missing and the divinity of Christ denied. The Quakers' idea of God as direct emanation of light, to Taylor's way of thinking, denied the centrality of Christ in human history and made 'all the promises and types as mere lies.'

Therefore, to deny Christ is to deny all of reality, for in him it has its significance as reality. Through types Christ 'reconcil[es] the world to God.' Nature and human history are in this way included in the divine plan; without the typological arrangement of reality, they are totally excluded. Because of the metaphorical miracle of typology, Taylor, through love of Christ, could love the world and commit no heresy. No wonder he turned to the writing of poetry; his system of types made it possible for him to maintain his faith both in the world and in spite of the world.

Taylor's metaphors of light in his Meditations, like Edwards' in his *Dissertation Concerning the End for Which God Created the World*, are theologically important to his typological concept of the source of the Creation. The light from the sun—that is, the Son as source, as Father—shines through the various media of Nature and human history (the types) and falls full on the Son (the antitype), who as sun himself has light that streams forth on worthy objects (the types) (I.67a). In this, Taylor thinks very much as Edwards was to do—that man and Nature are given importance as media of the light, God, but themselves have no light until it is focused in the only object that can reflect the light back, Christ. Then the various media (the types) become what Taylor calls 'shines.' They appear and exist as part of the nature of things when the light passes through them (as types) from Father to Son and when it is reflected from the Son back to them. Taylor himself hopes to be a 'Reflexion' of that light. This is the process of God/Christ giving glory to himself and thereby sustaining the Creation *as means*. Things are the media of God's/Christ's glory, therefore glorious. As both medium and reflection, the physical world, therefore, becomes important to the divine purpose in a way not so clear in Puritan thinking before Taylor. To a Puritan, only a system of types could accomplish this view of the world. While Taylor probably did not sense the relief that this view would offer modern esthetics the way Edwards did, he nonetheless was among the first to give voice to it.

Nature and human history, though participating in the Fall, thereby take on importance, and Puritanism has at last started on its way to nineteenth-century Transcendentalism, where, in the hands of Emerson, the Over-Soul takes the place of the institutionalized Christ as the touchstone of reality. Types are simply secularized. Faith and imagination become interchangeable terms of man's ability to unify the spiritual and the physical. And Man Believing/Man Thinking gains his individuality by first recognizing his relationship with that Nature which God is using as medium of his own glory. Furthermore, Taylor's typologizing is esthetic as well as theological in that only an act of imagination can relate the past and the secular to the person of Christ. Thus, faith lies *in* the imagination; and the man of imagination, because of his ability to relate all things to Christ by means of typological relationships, is already a man of faith.

Because he saw his concept of Christ-vitalized Nature as giving new life to his faith, Taylor must have taken the typological fancies of New England's leaders from John Winthrop to Sewall and Cotton Mather as secular and presumptuous, for their way of interpreting events in New England as fulfillment of Scripture largely left Christ out. Both Taylor's and theirs were attempts at spiritualizing the phenomena of one's own life, but only Taylor's typology keeps Christ at the center of things. 'The glory of all Types,' he exclaimed, 'doth meet in thee' (II.1). Taylor is like them in one way: just as covenant Puritans in New England personalized their types by seeing themselves as antitypes of Biblical promises, so Taylor personalized the process by seeing himself as participating in Christ's antitype through the Sacrament of the Lord's Supper. But Taylor would not have passed over Christ as Samuel Sewall does in proclaiming that 'The New Jerusalem [in America] is that which the Old and New Testament do ring of,'[12] and would not have felt with Cotton Mather that New England participates in Christ because of the parallels between New England heroes and biblical figures.[13] Nor would he have been the literalist that Increase Mather was, to see types as evidence of Christ's divinity rather than seeing them as a way of ordering reality in which the light of Christ gives meaning to all else.

12. *Phaenomena Quaedam Apocalyptica ad Aspectum Novi Orbis Configurata. Or, Some Few Lines Toward a Description of the New Heaven As It Makes to Those Who Stand Upon the New Earth* (Boston, 1697), p. 28.

13. *Magnalia Christi Americana* (London, 1702), pp. 259ff.

Taylor's is the more fideistic approach of giving Christ primacy over national- and self-interest, and, in a way, the more Emersonian approach of seeing a divinity unifying Nature and giving it its meaning. However, so obsessed were the settlers with the biblical parallels of the history they felt they were making that Taylor's attempts, in sermon and verse, to keep Christ central (rather than themselves) were futile. The 'special providences' of types that Sewall, the Mathers, and others were basing much of their faith on (and their politics) must have been to Taylor self-centered, not Christ-centered. His purpose in writing with and about his types the way he did was perhaps to prevent or change that. But his was only one voice crying in the wilderness of an extremely self-conscious and self-celebratory early nation.

While Taylor may at first seem a conventional typologist who inherited a tradition from the Middle Ages just as he inherited his theology from that source, he is, in his handling of his typology, as Edwards was to be, closer to Emerson than to Calvin in his esthetics.[14] 'Slickt up in Types,' the world takes on glory to him, has a place for him in its order, and gives the specific realities of his life a spiritual dimension.

14. There are three discussions of Taylor as typologist. An introduction to his interest in typology is in Stephen A. Fender, 'Edward Taylor and the Sources of American Puritan Wit,' unpubl. diss. (University of Manchester, 1962–63), pp. 46–59. The two others are by Ursula Brumm—'Edward Taylor's Meditations on the Lord's Supper,' *American Thought and Religious Typology*, trans. J. Hoaglund (New Brunswick, 1970), pp. 56–85; and 'The "Tree of Life" in Edward Taylor's Meditations,' *EAL*, III (1968), 72–87. Professor Brumm seems overzealous, however, in reading all of Taylor's uses of the Bible as types, and cursory in seeing his poetry as merely limited to the barest conventions of the tradition. Though not mentioned in Charles Feidelson's 'An American Tradition' in *Symbolism in American Literature* (Chicago, 1953), Taylor fits nicely into his thesis about the evolution of Puritan typology into the symbolisms of Emerson and Melville. H. H. Waggoner seems to have been the first to recognize in Taylor a version of Emerson (*American Poets: From the Puritans to the Present* [New York, 1968], pp. 16–24), though it is to Waggoner his concreteness and ingenuity that smack of Emerson, not the uses of metaphor to unify. See also William R. Epperson, 'The Meditative Structure of Edward Taylor's "Preparatory Meditations,"' unpubl. diss. (Kansas, 1965), pp. 97–127.

Edward Taylor
and the
Poetic Use
of Religious
Imagery

Ursula Brumm
Berlin Free
University

A few decades ago, religious typology was discovered as being a force in Puritan thinking and writing, and it has since been given attention by a considerable number of scholars. What seemed at first merely a quaint or even bizarre mode of thought which had to be studied in order to understand the Puritan mind, has, in the process, become interesting, even strangely attractive, to modern scholars. This is evident in the recent research on Edward Taylor which pays increasing attention to his use of typology.[1] No doubt, the interest has been aroused because his work cannot be fully understood without a certain knowledge of this ancient method of biblical exegesis. This involvement in Taylor's poetry poses a number of questions both for typology and Taylor, in particular with respect to typology's position and function within a literary work of art and thus of the meaning of typology both for the Puritan and the modern reader.[2]

1. While in a general way the use of typology by Taylor had been noted before, recent essays have concentrated on this issue. Cf., for instance, Thomas M. Davis, 'Edward Taylor and the Traditions of Puritan Typology,' EAL, IV (1969), 27–47; Ursula Brumm, 'The "Tree of Life" in Edward Taylor's Meditations,' EAL, III (1968), 72–87; and 'Edward Taylor's Meditations on the Lord's Supper,' in American Thought and Religious Typology, trans. J. Hoaglund (New Brunswick, 1970), 56–85. All references to Taylor's poems are to Donald E. Stanford's The Poems of Edward Taylor (New Haven, 1960).

2. From the point of view of theological orthodoxy and in reference to some

The problem is a very complex one. On its most basic level, it involves the difficult relationship of belief and art, a question which critics have discussed time and again in an effort to determine to what extent a strong religious belief which informs a work of art excludes non-believers from its appreciation. Within this context, Taylor is an extreme case, in that for him the theological, even dogmatic, meaning is the primary concern, and he neglects esthetic niceties to bring out a fine point of dogma. For these and related reasons, some scholars have assigned Taylor a minor place in the hierarchy of American poetry.

But the general estimation of Taylor, expressed in a considerable amount of criticism, is high and has grown, since the spectacular discovery of his works in the late thirties. Obviously, a great number of scholars and general readers who are not Puritans are captivated by his poetry. One has to assume that this interest is not simply antiquarian in nature, nor directed toward a quaintness in Puritan belief, as it is, for instance, in the case of Wigglesworth, but that the modern reader responds in some way to the intensity of Taylor's poetry, expressed as it is in the bold metaphysical juxtaposition of thought and image.

Within both Taylor's thought and imagery, typology figures largely. In some meditations, indeed, it becomes so dominant that the poetry could be taken for instruction in this form of biblical exegesis which links specific Old Testament events and personalities to their fulfillment in Christ.

Christ's Antitype Isaac his Type up spires
  In many things, but Chiefly this because
This Isaac, and the Ram caught in the briars
  One Sacrifice, fore shew by typick laws
  Christs Person, all Divine, joynd whereto's made
  Unperson'd Manhood, on the Altar's laid.
  (*Med. II, 5; Poems,* p. 88)

However, this is rather the exception than the rule. Taylor gives us a clue to a more general application in Med. II, 1:

---

medieval writers, this problem has been discussed by Stephen Manning, 'Scriptural Exegesis and the Literary Critic,' pp. 47 ff. above.

The glory of the world slickt up in types
In all Choise things chosen to typify,
His glory upon whom the worke doth light,
To thine's a Shaddow, or a butterfly. Poems, p. 83

If, thus, typological parallels link the best in all creation to the Godhead, what is their role in Taylor's poetry?

In the investigation of this question, we should remember that Taylor is not an isolated case; the English metaphysical poets also made use of typology. Rosemund Tuve, for example, has shown that a full understanding of George Herbert's poetry is impossible without proper attention to his typological thought.[3] Herbert's case is indeed relevant: his use of typology, although often more disguised or more integrated esthetically, is comparable to Taylor's and can perhaps help us to a fuller exploration of the problem. Obviously, we face a double problem of understanding: we have to understand typology in the sense in which Taylor and his contemporaries conceived it, and at the same time we have to evaluate its meaning in a more general, perhaps 'timeless' esthetic context.

In this investigation, the whole of Taylor's work is relevant. However, since each of his meditations is a closely knit whole of meaning and imagery, a tight system of cross references, here the problem of esthetic relevance can be tested only within one such poetic unit. Thus, one meditation closely examined serves as a test case. I would like to open the debate by concentrating on a meditation which is not one of his outspokenly typological poems, but which nevertheless makes extensive, if somewhat disguised use, of typological thought: Meditation 10 of the First Series. My answers will not cover the whole question of typology's use or misuse in poetry, but will show how typology functions within a specific meditation, and thus indicate its esthetic adaptability in the hands of Edward Taylor.

10. Meditation. John. 6:55. My Blood is Drinke indeed.
Stupendious Love! All Saints Astonishment!
Bright Angells are black Motes in this Suns Light.
Heav'ns Canopy the Paintice to Gods tent

3. *A Reading of George Herbert* (Chicago, 1952), *passim.*

Can't Cover't neither with its breadth, nor height.
Its Glory doth all Glory else out run,
Beams of bright Glory to't are motes i'th'sun. Poems, p. 20

God's glory—very likely an abstract, perhaps even an empty, term to the modern reader—is at the very center of Taylor's attention. It is introduced as a major theme after an intricate play with the consecutive use of the letters A, B, and C, and is thrice repeated, as if to cover the divine Trinity. To praise God's glory is the intense desire which Taylor expresses in every single meditation; this is also the duty of every believer and is his highest aspiration.

God's glory is the summary term for the self-revealed character and being of God;[4] to comprehend something of it is not only an act of supreme understanding but, at the same time, a proof of grace. For grace is an essential part of God's glory, a result of his love for man. But human beings can, at best, only perceive the outward splendor of the supreme excellence of God. The ability to shine is therefore an important quality of God's glory; it sends out 'beams' which strike the human eye. That is why Taylor exults in images of light and brightness.

God's glory is also the frame for the supreme drama of the human life, the drama of redemption. While God is complete *sufficientia* and perfection, sinful man is insufficient in every way. This accounts for the immense distance between glorious Godhead and miserable man which Taylor dramatizes by contrasting man's miserable and filthy nature and God's glory.[5] The great tension within this contrast necessitates the drama of redemption which the Puritan continuously reenacts in his mind. Christ, Son of God and God-Man, makes this redemption possible by his death. Thus a link is provided which bridges the immeasurable distance between Godhead and man: the typological parallel. Out of 'stupendious love,' Christ sacrificed himself for sinful man to provide grace and thus enable those who are predestined to accept it to perceive the glory of God.

---

4. Cf. 'God's Glory,' in *A Dictionary of the Bible*, ed. James Hastings (New York, 1923), II, 184.

5. On Taylor's use of scatological imagery, cf. Karl Keller, 'The Rev. Mr. Edward Taylor's Bawdry,' *NEQ*, XLIII (1970), 382–406.

After this prelude, which introduces the overarching theme, stanzas 2 to 5 make up the second part of the poem, which, according to the theory of meditation, should undertake the analysis of the meditation theme. In these stanzas, the drama of redemption experienced by man as the recipient of grace is re-created in its essential meaning. The poet speaks of himself as a representative of sinful humanity:

My Soule had Caught an Ague, and like Hell
  Her thirst did burn: she to each spring did fly,
But this bright blazing Love did spring a Well
  Of Aqua-Vitae in the Deity,
  Which on the top of Heav'ns high Hill out burst
  And down came running thence t'allay my thirst.

The generic condition of man after the Fall is sickness, but he can be cured from the sickness of his sin by *aqua vitae,* the 'water of life,' which is provided by God's love. In his poem, 'The Agonie,' George Herbert deals with the same theme: man's sinfulness which is redeemed through Christ's suffering and love. This theme is summed up in the final couplet of the poem:

Love is that liquour sweet and most divine,
Which my God feels as bloud; but I, as wine.[6] (ll. 17–18)

While the blood–wine correspondence of the last line is an obvious reference to Christ's sacrifice and its celebration in the sacrament of the Lord's Supper, 'that liquour' of the preceding line remains unidentified and isolated in the context of Herbert's poem. It is, of course, the liquor *aqua vitae,* the 'Liquour brew'd,' which Taylor puts into the center of his meditation and explores in its entire meaning and extension: the water of life is indeed the dominant image of Med. I, 10, which discusses Christ's redemption as a life-saving drink for sick humanity.

6. Herbert, 'The Agonie,' in *Works,* ed. F. E. Hutchinson (Oxford, 1953); all references to Herbert's poems are to this edition. The use of *aqua vitae* in Taylor's meditations, noted below, has been traced by Kathy Siebel and Thomas M. Davis, 'Edward Taylor and the Cleansing of *Aqua Vitae,*' *EAL,* IV (1969), 102–09. However, the authors do not see the image in its typological context.

Aqua vitae is the symbolic as well as the typological nexus of the poem. In its most basic meaning of water as life, it has an archetypal ubiquity, revered and held sacred by most primitive people and often even represented by divinities. In the numinous conception of a 'water of life' which heals, rejuvenates, and restores to life, or gives immortality, it found its way into myth and folk tale.[7] This ancient conception was taken as a name for a liquor which, in Taylor's time, was a most popular remedy, used internally as a stimulant and externally for the sterilization of wounds. Early emigrants to America were advised to take at least a gallon of aqua vitae with them in order to be well-equipped for life in the wilderness.[8]

Water has a special importance in the Bible, from the river in the garden of Eden in Gen. 2:10 to the water of life in the last chapter of Revelation (22:17). In the arid territory of the Orient, water was particularly precious—to have or to find water was a matter of life or death. In the Old Testament, therefore, water appears with its purifying, redeeming, and life-giving qualities. Water has a special relation to God, as is testified by the river Jordan, which is connected with a covenant and with baptism, or by Jesaia's 'wells of salvation.' Moses is told by God several times where to find water for the people of Israel:

And from thence they went to Beer, that is the well where of the LORD spake unto Moses Gather the people together, and I will give them water. (Num. 21:16)

'Beer,' the Hebrew word for spring or well, is one of Taylor's favorite puns;[9] it is an image with a typological dimension, for the quotation given is one of the texts which qualify Moses as a type of

7. Cf. 'Water of Life,' in Mary Huse Eastman, Index to Fairy Tales, Myths and Legends, 2nd ed., 3 vols. (Boston, 1926–52), and Grimm's Märchen, Nrs. 97 and 121, 'Das Wasser des Lebens' and 'Der Königssohn, der sich vor nichts fürchtet.'

8. George Francis Dow, Every Day Life in the Massachusetts Bay Colony (reissued, New York, 1967), p. 3.

9. E.g., in the seventh stanza of Med. I, 10, or in the fourth of II, 60 B. This 'beer' pun has often been mistaken for one of Taylor's homely images, as by Donald E. Stanford in the note to II, 60 B, in Poems, p. 189.

Christ: he saved the children of Israel from death, as Christ redeems humanity.

This brings us back to the interaction of symbol and type to which 'real types' lend themselves more easily than 'personal types.'[10] As a pictorial equivalent of Christ, a cipher which represents his acts and capacities as redeemer, the 'water of life' is a symbol as well as a type of Christ; it draws its cogency and persuasion from ancient and enduring experience of mankind as well as from Old Testament types in which this primordial experience was dramatized into sacred history. Taylor, in Med. I, 10, uses the conception of 'water of life' as the generic term for all the liquids which stand for Christ as savior: as aqua vitae, it is the medicine against the sickness of human depravity; it is the 'Drinke indeed' of John 6:55, the sacrificial blood which contains grace, 'a well . . . in the Deity,' 'blessed Nectar,' the 'Red Wine' of the Lord's Supper, the 'chiefest grape to bleed into my cup.'

It is evident from this list that Taylor combines a number of different biblical images and events in an effort to reveal in them the one fundamental meaning of God's glory and grace. The motto of Med. I, 10, 'My Blood is Drinke indeed,' is taken from the address Jesus made after he had fed the five thousand and walked on the sea:

Whoso eateth my flesh, and drinketh my blood, hath eternal life; and I will raise him up at the last day.
For my flesh is meat indeed, and my blood is drink indeed.
He that eateth my flesh, and drinketh my blood, dwelleth in me, and I in him.   John 6:54–56

Before, Jesus had spoken of himself as the 'bread of life' after the type of 'manna'; now, Taylor concludes, when he asks his believers to drink his blood, he sees himself in the type of the 'water of life.' In order to bolster this interpretation, Taylor, in the second stanza, quotes the significant words 'spring' and 'well' from John 4:14, where Jesus speaks of himself as the source of life-giving water to the woman of Samaria:

But whosoever drinketh of the water that I shall give him shall

10. On that question, see Brumm, American Thought and Religious Typology, pp. 42ff. and 67ff.

*never thirst; but the water that I shall give him shall be in him a
well of water springing up into everlasting life.*

(The 'Beer bowle' pun of the seventh stanza takes up the 'spring'
and 'well' reference of the second.)

On this basis, the image of the 'water of life' as *aqua vitae* assumes its dominant role in the second part of the meditation. That
Taylor understands it in its typological construction is revealed in
Med. II, 60[B], where its main typological source is identified: it is
the story of Moses drawing water from the rock in Horeb (Ex.
17:6), a type which was often elaborated and which had been made
popular through pictorial interpretation in the *Biblia Pauperum*
and other devotional books. The typological quality was already
established by St. Paul in I Corinthians 10:1–4, from which the
motto of Med. II, 60[B] is drawn:

*Moreover, brethren, I would not that ye should be ignorant, how
that all our fathers were under the cloud, and all passed through
the sea;
And were all baptized unto Moses in the cloud and in the sea;
And did all eat the same spiritual meat;
And did all drink the same spiritual drink: for they drank of that
spiritual Rock that followed them: and that Rock was Christ.*

These words make the supreme attraction of this type clear: not
only is this water the prefiguration of Christ but it is the drink of
those whom God has elected as his chosen people, including the
faithful and, hopefully, also the poet, in its typological promise:

*Christ is this Horebs Rock, the streames that slide
    A River is of Aqua Vitae Deare
Yet costs us nothing, gushing from his side.
    Celestiall Wine our Sinsunk souls to cheare.
    This Rock and Water, Sacramentall Cup
    Are made, Lords Supper Wine for us to sup.*
    (Med. II, 60[B]; Poems, p. 182)

In stanzas 4 and 5 of Med. I, 10, Taylor has dramatized his interpretation of *aqua vitae* differently:

This Liquour brew'd, thy sparkling Art Divine
Lord, in thy Chrystall Vessells did up tun,
(Thine Ordinances,) which all Earth o're shine
Set in thy rich Wine Cellars out to run.
Lord, make thy Butlar draw, and fill with speed
My Beaker full: for this is drink indeed.

Whole Buts of this blesst Nectar shining stand
Lockt up with Saph'rine Taps, whose splendid Flame
Too bright do shine for brightest Angells hands
To touch, my Lord. Do thou untap the same.
Oh! make thy Chrystall Buts of Red Wine bleed
Into my Chrystall Glass this Drink-Indeed.

This is a splendid and entertaining picture, executed in glowing colors. God is a rich and mighty Lord who keeps 'This Liquour brew'd,' the 'Red Wine,' in his 'rich Wine Cellars.' He employs a 'Butlar,' who, at his order, distributes to the elect the red wine which is stored in 'Chrystall [Christ-all] Vessells' or Buts with 'Saph'rine Taps.' At first glance, the butler who fills 'with speed' the 'Beaker full' could be taken as a playful addition which Taylor's imagination made to the picture. Actually, the butler is another type which Taylor integrated into this high drama of the distribution of grace. Again, it is a type which was made familiar beyond the class of theologians by medieval and later illustrations.[11] It derives from the story of Joseph, who is asked to interpret the dream of the Pharaoh's butler:

And the chief butler told his dream to Joseph, and said to him, In my dream, behold, a vine was before me; And in the vine were three branches: and it was as though it budded, and her blossoms shot forth; and the clusters thereof brought forth ripe grapes: And Pharaoh's cup was in my hand: and I took the grapes, and pressed them into Pharaoh's cup, and I gave the cup into Pharaoh's hand.   Gen. 40:9–11

The images of this text—the vine and its branches, the clusters of grapes, and the wine pressed from them into a cup—called for a

11. A Reading of George Herbert, p. 121.

typological interpretation and easily associated this Old Testament story to Christ, 'the true vine' (John 15:1–5), and to the wine in the sacrament of the Lord's Supper. Taylor takes up the imagery of Pharaoh's dream in the two last lines of stanzas 4, 5, and 6, respectively, and most directly at the end of stanza 6:

Thou makest Glory's Chiefest Grape to bleed
Into my cup: And this is Drink-Indeed.

Pharaoh's butler and his dream belonged to the vine, grape, and wine-press themes which pervade the Bible; they provide a rich store of images which, with the help of typology, were used to illustrate, explain, enlarge, and reinforce the significance of the Lord's Supper. While their archetypal and religious, as well as their pastoral, qualities have a direct appeal to the imagination, the modern reader may be shocked by the main image of the third stanza, which gives Christ's 'Humane Veans' as 'Golden Pipes' which pour drink to the faithful:

But how it came, amazeth all Communion.
Gods onely Son doth hug Humanity,
Into his very person. By which Union
His Humane Veans its golden gutters ly.
And rather than my Soule should dy by thirst,
These Golden Pipes, to give me drink, did burst.

Again, a typological conception is involved; it derives from a cryptic saying from Zechariah (4:11–12) which links two olive branches with 'two golden pipes' that 'empty the golden oil out of themselves.' Herbert, in 'Whitsunday,' speaks of 'those pipes of gold, which brought / That cordiall water to our ground'; Taylor, more drastic, 'bursts' these 'Golden Pipes' which conduct the saving liquid to mankind. One might take this as evidence for Taylor's rustic temperament, his delight in stark effects. More likely, this line has to be seen in the context of Taylor's mystic inclinations. On other evidence, Karl Keller has spoken of Taylor's 'serious delight in the relationships that language gives to reality.'[12] Stanza 3 documents a peculiar technique practiced in various forms by

12. 'The World Slickt Up in Types,' pp. 175 ff. above.

Taylor; it is an exercise in sound related to meaning. In explaining 'Theanthropy,' the God-Man nature of Christ as a necessary condition of his sacrifice, Taylor gives phonetic structure to the dogma of the two natures of Christ. While u (Humanity, Humane) stands for the human side, o (God) expresses the divine part: 'God's onely Son doth hug Humanity.' 'Golden gutters' indicate the same pattern of divine and human participation in Christ. Logically, the two vowels combine in 'Communion' and 'Union,' as they are inextricably locked in the ever-present metaphysical pun of son/sun.[13] The sound pattern of the 'Golden Pipes' which 'burst' follows the descent from the godly to the human realm.

The gravity of the doctrine discussed warns us not to take this as a playful exercise of wit. It is, rather, the result of something very serious: of the belief in the divine logos, in God or the word, applied to the problem of Theanthropy.[14] As in his search for typological connections, Taylor here, too, tried to establish correspondences between the human and the divine sphere. His frequent argument about language, his despair, repeated in almost every meditation, at the inadequacy of human language, springs from his conviction in an ideal correspondence between the name and the thing. That sinful man is unable to achieve this correspondence in regard to God is the crucial point in every meditation, as in the last two stanzas of Med. I, 10:

> How shall I praise thee then? My blottings Jar
>   And wrack my Rhymes to pieces in thy praise.
> Thou breath'st thy Vean still in my Pottinger
>   To lay my thirst, and fainting spirits raise.
> Thou makest Glory's Chiefest Grape to bleed
> Into my cup: And this is Drink-Indeed.
>
> Nay, though I make no pay for this Red Wine,
>   And scarce do say I thank-ye-for't; strange thing!
> Yet were thy silver skies my Beer bowle fine

13. Cf. 'Stupendious Love' as 'Sun' in the first stanza.

14. Rosalie L. Colie, Paradoxia Epidemica. The Renaissance Tradition of Paradox (Princeton, 1960), pp. 190ff., deals with Herbert's attitude to this problem.

I finde my Lord, would fill it to the brim.
Then make my life, Lord, to thy praise proceed
For thy rich blood, which is my Drink-Indeed.

The third part of the meditation—traditionally obliged to exercise the capacities of the will—returns to the overruling concern with God's glory which the poet knows he can only praise, after he has received grace, the 'Drink-Indeed' of Christ's blood. There seems to be a subtle reciprocality between the exercise of exploring, understanding, and explaining God's grace as it was undertaken in the second part of the meditation—and this was already a form of praise—and the praise of the glory that depends on the condition of grace which is delivered, in the third part. Here, praise is also an expression of gratitude for the grace received.

If to praise God's glory is thus the ultimate justification of Taylor's meditations, the proper way to do so is to find authentic illustrations for it. Typology in this regard is simply the most authentic way to trace God's intentions from their original prophetic indications to their culmination and fulfillment in Christ's sacrifice. As used by Taylor, it is primarily an effort to find the true acts and metaphors of grace in the holy history of the Old and New Testament: the water of life, the grape vine, the cluster of grapes, wine, manna, the bread and the tree of life. As he tries to understand these promises of salvation in their subtle relationship and interaction, Taylor is still within the theological context. But between type and antitype, and between various types in their meaning as vessels of grace, he inevitably discovers a rich structure of symbolic relations of which he makes abundant and exuberant use as every line of his meditations documents. Since Christ is always taken up in his supreme function as a source of grace, this quality can, with the help of typology, be presented by a string of symbols: he is a well of living water, 'The liquor brew'd' by 'Art Divine,' *aqua vitae*, a bunch of grapes pressed for man's sake, and the red wine which bleeds into my cup. In other words, typology provides Taylor with a number of biblical images which serve to illustrate the one all-inclusive theme of God's glory.

While Taylor works with these images strictly within orthodox Calvinist doctrine, in his argument there is a wider significance. In a sense, this argument itself is a specific symbol of something more general. It stands for a profound human desire which transcends dogmatic specifications: the deliverance from human weakness, sin, and corruption, as well as for the salvation of the soul. The same is true for the attempt to understand or conceive of the divine order. As these desires reach out from human insufficiency to a metaphysical realm, they parallel the typological construction which links the human actions in the Old and New Testaments to Christ's divinity. What makes these constructions so applicable is that they establish a link as well as a differentiation. Within a similarity in appearance there is a distinction in essence. Thus they provide a sophisticated technique in the interpretation of correspondences between the human and a higher order, which is a basic concern of poetry. In this perspective, typology is a specific vehicle for man's effort to determine his precarious situation *vis-à-vis* a higher power.

As some of its major elements, typology takes up images which have deep and abiding significance to the imagination—water, bread, tree, grape and wine. At their specific place in the Bible they receive a typological meaning, while in a general sense, they are symbols of life. In either form, the images draw their power from mankind's elemental experiences, which, in turn, are reinforced through their significance in the drama of Christian redemption. For all their metaphysical significance, these symbols have a wide range of application. By his wit, as well as by his intensity of thought and feeling, Taylor again and again draws them into New England reality. Thus a liquor, *aqua vitae*, can be used as a kind of conceit—actually a typological pun—for Christ.

In a different way, some of the exemplary persons and events of the Old Testament have widened their typological interpretation to a larger symbolic significance. It may be helpful at this point to refer once more to Herbert, who, in his 'The Bunch of Grapes,' combines the typological imagery we have been talking about with that of the historic-mythic events of the Exodus from Egypt. 'The Bunch of Grapes' is, as its typological title indicates, also a poem about grace and the possibility of salvation, and it takes much of its argument from typology:

The Bunch of Grapes.
Joy, I did lock thee up: but some bad man
   Hath let thee out again:

And now, me thinks, I am where I began
  Sev'n yeares ago: one vogue and vein,
  One aire of thoughts usurps my brain.
I did towards Canaan draw; but now I am
Brought back to the Red sea, the sea of shame.   ll. 1–7

Bolder and somewhat more secular than Taylor, Herbert inserts himself into the typological parallels. The dangers and troubles of the children of Israel have their correspondence in Herbert's own and every Christian's spiritual pilgrimage, which thus receives a magnificent symbolic equivalent.

For as the Jews of old by Gods command
  Travell'd, and saw no town;
So now each Christian hath his journeys spann'd:
  Their storie pennes and sets us down.
  A single deed is small renown.
Gods works are wide, and let in future times;
His ancient justice overflows our crimes.   ll. 8–14

Then have we too our guardian fires and clouds;
  Our Scripture-dew drops fast:
We have our sands and serpents, tents and shrowds;
  Alas! our murmurings come not last.
  But where's the cluster? where's the taste
Of mine inheritance? Lord, if I must borrow,
Let me as well take up their joy, as sorrow.   ll. 15–21

In that the model history of the Old Testament prefigures the individual struggle toward salvation, it also illustrates and explains what otherwise would remain abstract and inexplicable. In other words, it serves as a symbol for a highly complex spiritual development. Again, what is biblical and specific is made to serve a larger meaning: the typological image becomes symbolic to a larger public.

For Herbert, the Exodus-like troubles are his Christian heritage; the long and arduous wanderings to Canaan are his own difficult way to salvation. In this application, Herbert is one step more removed from strict typology than is Taylor. Of course, Taylor too saw himself as the recipient of aqua vitae, but only through Christ's doings, while Herbert directly links the guardian fires and clouds, the manna and serpents, to his own life as a Christian. At the same time, his trust in the sacraments is greater than Taylor's:

But can he want the grape, who hath the wine? l. 22

As the children of Israel in a much elaborated type found the branch with the cluster of grapes and 'bare it between two on a staff' (Num. 13:23), so the poet 'hath the wine,' and with the sacrament the promise of salvation.

I have their fruit and more.
Blessed be God, who prosper'd Noahs vine,
*   And made it bring forth grapes good store.*
*   But much more him I must adore.*
Who of the Laws sowre juice sweet wine did make,
Ev'n God himself being pressed for my sake. ll. 23–28

Both Herbert's 'The Bunch of Grapes' and Taylor's Med. I, 10 offer a rich amount of biblical material which only by careful interpretation can one understand in its intended meaning. Being thus structured by biblical quotations and references, these meditations are not unlike some modern poems which also rely on a pattern of highly cryptic references. In both cases, this structure operates also as a challenge; for the labor of discovery is a method of participation and satisfaction. It is therefore not so much in his difficulty and obscurity that Taylor is of another time, but in the strictness of his theological concern. Much more than Herbert, Taylor is limited to one theme which he presents in numerous variations: God's glory and man's redemption through grace.

Med. I, 10 can be taken as representative for Taylor's 'Preparatory Meditations' in that it is an exercise on his one and all-inclusive theme of God's glory. Each and every meditation is a new and different attempt to investigate this theme in all its grandeur and immensity. Despite this variety, there is in all meditations a general pattern which remains the same, because it is inherent in the theme of God's glory: the contrast between God's perfection and man's depravity which is transcended by grace. Within this overall structure, typology fulfills an almost indispensable function. By definition, those scriptural incidents are typological that refer to Christ's redemptive power; in other words, they constitute a roster of symbolic equivalents of grace. To understand and explore grace as the supreme quality of God's glory, Taylor makes use of this rich lore of authentic explanations by selecting appropriate elements and combining them into new poetic units. Thus, typological imagery, used to visualize the redeeming power of Christ's sacrifice, appears as a structuring element in Taylor's meditations. Typology, in affording proof, illustration, and illumination for the theme of grace, also provides archetypal images which are able to serve as symbols of life and salvation: they are 'Drink-Indeed' for the imagination.

The Eighteenth
Century
and Beyond

'Images or
Shadows of
Divine Things'
in the Thought
of Jonathan
Edwards

The book of Scripture is the interpreter of the book of nature two ways, viz., by declaring to us those spiritual mysteries that are indeed signified and typified in the constitution of the natural world; and secondly, in actually making application of the signs and types in the book of nature as representations of those spiritual mysteries in many instances.   Jonathan Edwards, Image 156

It is easily seen that there is nothing lucky or capricious in these analogies, but that they are constant, and pervade nature. . . . Throw a stone into the stream, and the circles that propagate themselves are the beautiful type of all influence. Ralph Waldo Emerson, Nature

He is a type of New England's hereditary spirit; and his shadowy march . . . must ever be the pledge, that New England's sons will vindicate their ancestry.   Nathaniel Hawthorne, "The Gray Champion"

'Images or
Shadows of
Divine Things'
in the Thought
of Jonathan
Edwards

Mason I. Lowance, Jr.
University of
Massachusetts

When Samuel Mather announced that 'a type is some outward or
sensible thing ordained of God under the Old Testament to represent and hold forth something of Christ in the New,' he was summarizing a conservative doctrine of typological exegesis that had
persisted since the employment of the science by the early Church
fathers.[1] Mather's declaration corroborates Augustine's notion that
'in the Old Testament the New lies hid; in the New Testament, the
meaning of the Old becomes clear.' The basis of this assumption is
that the Old Testament is not a complete document in itself, but
contains a series of prophetic adumbrations of Christ, the 'antitype.' The historical events, personages, and ceremonies of the Old
Testament were regarded, under this scheme, to be providentially
inspired prefigurations of the fulfilling revelation. The notion that
these events exist in a historical, linear relation to each other is significant because during the Middle Ages, typology had been exploited by some exegetes to mean something altogether different.
The allegory, or allegorical correspondence, had always stood as an
alternative mode of interpreting the Old Testament figures, and
during the late middle ages particularly, the allegorical method of

1. Samuel Mather, *Figures or Types of the Old Testament, Opened and Explained*, 2nd edn. (London, 1705), p. 52, reprinted in *Series in American
Studies* (New York: Johnson Reprint Corporation, 1969), with introduction and notes by Mason Lowance, Jr.

interpreting Scripture subsumed the typological. Allegory is essentially based on the Platonic conception of a spiritual universe that lies beyond the physical world, which is its representation or symbol only. In contrast, the type is a particular kind of symbol, historically true and eternally verifiable because it was instituted to perform a specific function in God's grand design.

Of course, there have been many shades of gray between these two extremes. Some exegetes would regard as types only those Old Testament events and figures that are specifically instituted in the New Testament; others would be more liberal in their judgments, allowing such figures as Jacob's Ladder to adumbrate Christ's union of heaven and earth. Some would go so far as to include the red cord of Rahab, the prostitute of Jericho, as a type of the saving blood of Jesus. (Both red elements were seen as instruments of salvation.) From the beginning, there have been schools among the typologists that reflect conservative, or traditional and orthodox, exegesis, and these place great emphasis on the historical veracity of the type and the specific correspondence between type and antitype within the bounds of Scripture. More liberal typologists sometimes employ Platonic, unhistorical symbols, and these exegetes are called spiritualizers or allegorizers.

For the literal-minded Puritan, the conservative exegesis had a particular appeal. For Jonathan Edwards, however—a Calvinist and a mystic—typology as a key to the mysteries of the Universe was not so simple a matter. Conservative and liberal modes of exegesis were continuously at war during the late seventeenth and early eighteenth centuries, so that a number of Edwards' contemporaries were inclined toward a mixture of the spiritualized Old Testament narrative and an orthodox exegesis of the types. Moreover, scientific interest in the natural universe provided not only a radically new approach to epistemological problems, but also tempted theologians to combine their perceptions of nature with their reading of Scripture. Some conservative theologians, like Cotton Mather, while thoroughly grounded in the conservative orthodoxy, experimented with new forms of perception and accepted new methods of understanding nature even while they continued to read Scripture according to the instituted scheme of type and antitype.

Jonathan Edwards is a particularly interesting figure to consider in the context of this epistemological change because he sought to know God through a wide variety of sources during his lifetime. In comprehending and interpreting Scripture, Edwards was essentially a conservative; his display of scholarly textual criticism in *A History of the Work of Redemption* combines with his intense Calvinism to render a document of orthodox and traditional conviction. The *History* first appeared as a series of sermons preached in 1739, and it was left in manuscript by Edwards at the time of his death, not being published until 1774. It gives the most complete summary of Edwards' orthodox and conservative approach to the eternal work of the Holy Spirit and contains a particularly illuminating section on the typology of Scripture, by which the author understands the work of the Spirit to be the same in both testaments. But Edwards' interest in human psychology and his continuous probing of philosophical theories of knowledge resulted in a varied use of the biblical types. If he endorsed and explained the conservative doctrine of typology in *A History of the Work of Redemption*, he transformed the types in his *Images or Shadows of Divine Things*, so that nature became an alternative source of revelation. In the 'Miscellanies,' Edwards presents the types in the two distinct senses he employs them elsewhere: on the one hand, he asserts their value as historical figures within the instituted scheme of type and antitype; on the other, he suggests their significance as allegorical *figurae*.

This essay is addressed toward an understanding of these three documents. However, it should be stated that one's views of Edwards' typology should not determine the theologian's position in the spectrum of exegesis and doctrine generally. In the essential matters of Puritan theology and Calvinist doctrine, Edwards moved from the liberalism of Stoddardeanism toward the conservatism of his own final position. When it came to man's sinfulness and God's restorative Grace, Edwards endorsed the extremely traditional positions of Reformation Calvinism. But in his epistemological documents, the concern with God's accommodation of the divine idea through a natural revelation is strong, so that a number of documents may be viewed as supportive of his liberal typology even though they are not directly involved with the positing of a doctrine. *A Faithful Narrative of the Surprising Work of God* (1737), *The Distinguishing Marks of a Work of the Spirit of God* (1741), and *Some Thoughts Concerning the Present Revival of Religion in New England* (1742) treat separate aspects of revivalism during the

Great Awakening, and each provides a defense of the work of the Holy Spirit in contemporary New England. And the epistemology of the Great Awakening, as Edwards understood it, is best summarized in his A *Treatise Concerning Religious Affections*, in which the 'new sense of things'—by which the transformed member of the elect comprehends God's revelation through nature as well as Scripture—is fully explained and exhaustively argued. These documents, and the numerous allusions throughout Edwards' writing that also reflect the influence of John Locke, are of vital interest in assessing Edwards' position in the development of American thought; and they provide some assistance in establishing Edwards' place in the debate between liberal and conservative typologists.

Edwards' orthodox typology is everywhere present in the *History*. The 'Doctrine' of the first sermon states clearly what he means by redemption:

I would show how I would be understood when I use the word redemption. And here it may be observed, that the work of redemption is sometimes understood in a more limited sense, for the purchase of salvation; for so the word strictly signifies, a purchase of deliverance; . . . It was begun with Christ's incarnation, and carried on through Christ's life, and finished with his death, or the time of his remaining under the power of death, which ended in his resurrection. . . . But then sometimes the work of redemption is taken more largely, including all that God works or accomplishes tending to this end; not only the purchasing of redemption, but also all God's works that were properly preparatory to the purchase, or as applying the purchase and accomplishing the success of it; so that the whole dispensation, as it includes the preparation and the purchase, and the application and success of Christ's redemption, is here called the work of redemption . . . in one word, all that is wrought in execution of the eternal covenant of redemption; this is what I call the work of redemption in the doctrine; for it is all but one work, one design. The various dispensations or works that belong to it, are but the several parts of one scheme.[2]

2. *A History of the Work of Redemption*, reprinted from the Worcester Edition (New York, 1845), p. 299.

The continuous scheme of redemption that Edwards observed in human history is nevertheless centered specifically in Christ's eternal power. The unique design may have a variety of aspects or manifestations, both before and after Christ's historical presence on earth; however, the continuity of history provides a linear setting within which the great work is developed. 'It is but one design that is formed, to which all the offices of Christ do directly tend, and in which all the persons of the Trinity do conspire, and all the various dispensations that belong to it are united; and the several wheels are one machine, to answer one end, and produce one effect.'[3]

Edwards goes on to develop a tightly wrought, well-reasoned argument for commencing the history of the work of redemption with the fall of man. The historical period from the time of the fall to the incarnation constitutes 'Period I' of the *History*, and the justification for its inclusion in the scheme is presented in terms of its typological significance. 'The church was under various dispensations of Providence, and in very various circumstances, before Christ came,' Edwards declares, 'but all these dispensations were to prepare the way for his coming.'[4] By adopting a traditional division of the period into six units, Edwards isolates the major providential dispensations before the incarnation, then delivers judgment on the relative significance of each. The examples of typological adumbration and fulfillment are legion, and the governing force throughout the document is God's intentional preparation of the world for the coming of the antitype. Ultimately, the dispensations are all one.

Thus we see how the light of the gospel, which began to dawn immediately after the fall, and gradually grew and increased through all the ages of the Old Testament, as we observed as we went along, is now come to the light of perfect day, and the brightness of the sun shining forth in his unveiled glory.

And Christ and his redemption are also the great subject of the history of the Old Testament from the beginning all along; and even the history of the creation is brought in as an introduction to

3. *Ibid.*, pp. 299–300.

4. *Ibid.*, p. 306.

the history of redemption that immediately follows it. The whole book, both Old Testament and New, is filled up with the gospel; only with this difference, that the Old Testament contains the gospel under a vail, but the New contains it unvailed, so that we may see the glory of the Lord with open face.[5]

In clarifying the relation of the two dispensations under the law, Edwards follows earlier models and distinguishes 'moral' from 'typical':

. . . the next thing observable in this period was God's giving the typical law, those precepts that did not properly belong to the moral law. Not only those laws which are commonly called ceremonial, which prescribe the ceremonies and circumstances of the Jewish worship, and their ecclesiastical state; but also those that were political, for regulating the Jewish commonwealth, commonly called judicial laws, were many of them typical. The giving of this typical law was another great thing that God did in this period, tending to build up the glorious structure of redemption. . . . Thus the gospel was abundantly held forth to that nation; so that there is scarcely any doctrine of it but is particularly taught and exhibited by some observance of this law; though it was in shadows, and under a vail, as Moses put a vail on his face when it shone.[6]

Like Thomas Shepard and Samuel Mather before him, Edwards has here distinguished the 'ceremonial and typical' law of Israel, which was abrogated and fulfilled in the incarnation, from the 'moral' law dispensed eternally, having a perpetual historical value. By making this distinction, he has succeeded in establishing a typology of adumbration and fulfillment without violating the significance of Scripture for generations succeeding the Old Testament period but preceding the millennium. This kind of conservative and traditional approach to exegesis and typology characterizes *A History of the Work of Redemption*, and the linear, historical setting accorded the types in this document is rarely manipulated toward

5. *Ibid.*, pp. 275, 191.

6. Jonathan Edwards, *A History of the Work of Redemption*, American Tract Society (New York, 1841), pp. 85–86.

an allegorical interpretation. The eschatological presence of Christ is everywhere apparent, and while Edwards never loses sight of eschatology in his other writings, he does sometimes move in the direction of 'allegorizing' or 'spiritualizing' the manifold works of Creation. The historiography implied here—that since the Fall, mankind has been involved in the revelation of one immutable and completed act—is another subject closely related to the typological interpretation of those events; however, it sheds light on Edwards' doctrine of the types only in a peripheral way.

Standing between *A History of the Work of Redemption* and *Images or Shadows of Divine Things* in a spectrum of conservative-to-liberal typological exegesis are Edwards' 'Miscellaneous Notebooks,' particularly the entries numbered 119, 479, and 1069.[7] Number 1069, otherwise known as 'Types of the Messiah,' suggests a number of variations on the more conservative doctrine posited in the *History*. The first two entries in the 'Miscellanies' entitled 'Types,' and the only two of this kind before Number 1069, use the term loosely for images or representations of spiritual things, not unlike the use of the term in *Images or Shadows*. Like medieval allegorizing of the biblical types, the definitions delivered in these two Miscellanies hint at the prospect of spiritual revelation represented in the 'types' of the natural universe. Both entries are brief, and may be presented in full:

119. TYPES. *The things of the ceremonial law are not the only things, whereby God designedly shadowed forth spiritual things; but with an eye to such a representation were all the transactions of the life of Christ ordered. And very much of the wisdom of God in the creation appears, in his so ordering things natural, that they livelily represent things divine and spiritual, [such as] sun, fountain, vine; as also, much of the wisdom of God in his Providence, in that the state of mankind is so ordered, that there are innumerable*

7. Edwards' 'Miscellany 1069' exists in manuscript in the Beinecke Library of Yale University. It is being edited as part of the Miscellaneous Notebooks of Jonathan Edwards for the Yale Edition of Edwards' Collected Works. A less adequate edition of this particular entry may be found under the title, 'Types of the Messiah,' in Vol. IX (Supplement) of the London Edition of Edwards' *Works* (London, 1847).

things in human affairs that are lively pictures of the things of the gospel, such as shield, tower, and marriage, family [italics my own].

479. WORK OF REDEMPTION. TYPES. *Things even before the fall were types of things pertaining to the gospel redemption. The old creation, I believe, was a type of the new. God's causing light to shine out of darkness, is a type of his causing such spiritual light and glory by Jesus Christ to succeed, and to arise out of, the dreadful darkness of sin and misery. His bringing the world into such beautiful form out of a chaos without form and void, typifies his bringing the spiritual world to such divine excellency and beauty after the confusion, deformity, and ruin of sin.*[8]

The habit of mind by which men could discern the activity of God in the natural universe was neither unique nor new; the Puritan penchant for discovering remarkable providences in natural events and their belief that behind everything physical lay some spiritual truth is present in the tradition of Puritan symbolism from the beginning. However, this tradition is clearly a different avenue from the attitude toward typological exegesis as a means of reading history providentially. Edwards has thus brought together these two distinct provinces in his above definitions; for all Puritans, the wisdom of God appeared in the lively representation of the ordered natural universe. However, more conservative exegetes were careful to indicate how the *biblical* types had been abrogated and fulfilled in the incarnation. Like the medieval allegorizers before him, Edwards here seems to be moving toward an interpretation of the spiritualized natural universe, which contains analogues of the scriptural types. Moreover, he suggests that the types of the Old Testament operate analogously to Platonic symbols in their revelation of Christ.

'Miscellany 1069' opens with a statement that is misleading. One would almost assume that Edwards will proceed to an exegesis of the types according to the historical scheme of adumbration and fulfillment:

---

8. I am indebted to Professor Thomas A. Shafer of the McCormick Theological Seminary, Chicago, for transcribing these entries from the manuscripts in the Beinecke Library.

We find by the Old Testament, that it has ever been God's manner, from the beginning of the world, to exhibit and reveal future things by symbolical representations, which were no other than types of the future things revealed. Thus, when future things were made known in visions, the things that were seen were not the future things themselves, but some other things that were made use of as shadows, symbols, or types of the things.[9]

So far, so good; Edwards has simply introduced the idea that types are indeed symbols or shadows of 'good things to come.' But he moves away from this initial position rather quickly, offering as examples of the types a number of allegorical figures in the Old Testament that could only relate to New Testament matters in a Platonic fashion. 'We find that God was often pleased to bring to pass extraordinary and miraculous appearances and events, to typify future things,' Edwards says, in a passage that corroborates the conservative notion that history is an instituted process of continuous revelation. But he immediately follows with an example which violates the historical principle: 'Thus God's making Eve of Adam's rib, was to typify the near relation and strict union of husband and wife, from one to the other . . .'[10] Yet throughout the 'Types of the Messiah,' Edwards asserts the prefigurative role of the Old Testament in its typological adumbration of Christ, the antitype:

Now since it was, as has been observed, God's manner of old, in the times of the Old Testament, from generation to generation, and even from the beginning of the world to the end of the Old Testament history, to represent divine things by outward signs, types, and symbolical representations, and especially thus to typify and prefigure future events, that he revealed by his Spirit, and foretold by the prophets, it is very unlikely, that the Messiah, and things appertaining to his kingdom and salvation, should not be thus abundantly prefigured and typified under the Old Testament, . . .[11]

Throughout 'Miscellany 1069,' Edwards seems inclined to rely on the linear and historical analogy between the testaments, and his

9. Jonathan Edwards, 'Types of the Messiah,' or Miscellany 1069, The Works of President Edwards (Edinburgh, 1847), IX, 401.

10. Ibid., 404.   11. Ibid., 408.

examples are largely drawn from historical events and a few outstanding 'personal types,' like David. However, as the narrative pro-
gresses, it becomes evident that Edwards is also concerned to indicate the close proximity between the 'typological' revelation and
'allegorical' representation.

*It is an argument that many of the historical events of the Old Tes-
tament are types of the great events appertaining to the Messiah's
coming and kingdom, that the Spirit of God took occasion from
the former to speak of the latter. He either takes occasion to speak
and foretel the Messiah, and the great events appertaining to his
salvation, upon occasion of the coming to pass of these ancient
events, or on his speaking of these events, celebrating or promising
them, he takes occasion to speak of these latter and greater events,
joining what is declared of the one with what he reveals of the other
in the same discourse; which is an argument that one has relation to
the other, and is the image of the other.*[12]

Finally, in the summarizing argument (as printed by Dwight) of
this highly organized and logical piece, Edwards states clearly that
he intends to regard the types in an allegorical as well as historical
sense:

*The principles of human nature render TYPES a fit method of in-
struction. It tends to enlighten and illustrate, and to convey instruction with impression, conviction, and pleasure, and to help the
memory. These things are confirmed by man's natural delight in
the imaginative arts, in painting, poetry, fables, metaphorical language, and dramatic performances. This disposition appears early
in children.*

*This may be observed concerning types in general, that not only
the things of the Old Testament are typical; for this is but one part
of the typical world; the system of created beings may be divided
into two parts, the typical world, and the antitypical world. The inferior and carnal, ie, the more external and transitory part of the
universe, that part of it which is inchoative, imperfect, and subservient, is typical of the superior, more spiritual, perfect, and*

12. *Ibid.*, 419.

*durable part of it, which is the end, and, as it were, the substance
and consummation, of the other. Thus the material and natural
world is typical of the moral, spiritual, and intelligent world, or the
city of God. . . . And those things belonging to the city of God,
which belong to its more imperfect, carnal, inchoative, transient,
and preparatory state, are typical of those things which belong to its
more spiritual, perfect, and durable state; as things belonging to the
state of the church under the Old Testament were typical of things
belonging to the church and kingdom of God under the New
Testament.*[13]

In a single statement, Edwards here indicates that, while typology applies on the one hand to the historical scheme established
between the two testaments, it also embraces the correspondences
between external representations and the spiritual ideas they
shadow forth. By indicating how Christ's life itself radiates a typological significance, or how the Christian ordinances are symbolic
of deeper spiritual principles, he consciously applies the nomenclature of orthodox typology to the allegorical correspondence,
however proximal, and thus opens the floodgates for the interpretation of the universe in terms of 'types' (the symbol) and 'antitypes'
(the idea behind the symbol). The methodology becomes clear in
reading the miscellaneous notebook that Perry Miller edited in
1948 and titled *Images or Shadows of Divine Things*. The work is
a revealing account of impressions Edwards received from the natural universe and a record of his attempt to utilize the framework
of typological exegesis as a means of interpreting these impressions.
The nomenclature of orthodox typology is employed throughout,
but the intention of the 'exegete' is clearly to expand the boundaries of scriptural typology.

Miller's edition includes a lengthy introduction, which has become almost as famous during the last twenty years as Edwards'
own work. This close association has been advantageous in that it
has directed many students of Puritanism to Edwards' important
work through their discipleship to Miller. This has been unfortu-

13. *Ibid.*, 494. Dwight prints this material at the end of the treatise. Edwards indicated, however, that it should be 'put near the beginning.' See
Miscellany 1069, Beinecke Library, p. 73.

nate because the introduction itself attempts to set the record straight about Edwards' use of the types by positing a number of definitions of typology that cannot account for *all* typological usages. Thus the reader of the introduction is provided a view of typology that is not altogether adequate for assessing the transitions in Edwards' exegesis that occur in the accompanying *Images or Shadows*.

Miller shows that Edwards wanted to employ biblical typology to counteract the contemporary tendency for reading nature 'tropologically,' as many medieval exegetes had done. He blames the Puritan rhetoricians for a confusion between the trope and the type, noting that 'it did not occur to them that the line between the trope and the type needed any further demarcation, or that as long as the rules of the plain style held sway there was any possibility of simple metaphors being so abused that to the greatest intellect among their descendants, the pious tropes would appear as much a nuisance to true piety as the scholastic types had seemed to the reformers.'[14] The distinction here is between the 'tropological' or 'allegorical' reading of the natural universe, which the Puritans certainly did make under the rubric for comprehending 'remarkable Providences' (the special dispensations of God through occurrences that violated the usual laws of nature), and the 'typological' exegesis of Scripture and history according to the instituted scheme of prefigurative 'type' and fulfilling 'antitype.' However, Miller's central assertion is that Edwards employed the typological system *to reverse* regrettable tendencies toward the tropological among contemporary writers, including Cotton Mather, whose *Agricola* was seen to reflect the consummate influences of that well-known spiritualizer, John Flavel.[15] This is an inaccurate representation of both Edwards and Cotton Mather. In the first place, while the ministers who signed the Preface to Mather's *Agricola* do indicate that he has been experimenting with the process of accommodation through the 'language of Husbandry,' the treatise itself leaves no doubt that

14. Perry Miller, 'Introduction to Jonathan Edwards,' in *Images or Shadows of Divine Things*, ed. Miller (New Haven, 1948), p. 9.

15. See Mason Lowance, Jr., 'Introduction to Cotton Mather,' in *Agricola, or the Religious Husbandman* (New York, forthcoming), pp. iii–xiv.

Mather was unable to depart from his orthodox patterns of exegesis for the 'heavenly use of earthly things.' The emphasis of the sermons suggests that Mather was more concerned with restating the traditional Puritan doctrine of salvation than with the Flavel process of spiritualizing the natural universe. But the most serious problem arises out of Miller's assessment of Edwards' response to this 'spiritualizing,' which he sees as an attempt to employ typology as a correctional vehicle.

Miller sees Edwards as the leader of a 'Puritan revolt against Puritanism.'[16] While Edwards' modifications of Covenant theology are well known, his reassertion of Calvinism is hardly present in the very liberal document, Images or Shadows; yet Miller goes on to argue that Edwards resurrected the Puritan 'types' to turn rhetoricians away from the excesses of tropology that had infected contemporary theology. 'If Edwards was to purify the art of speech in New England,' Miller says, 'he had not only to chastise the tropes but to clarify the types.'[17] Edwards thus becomes the restorer of epistemology to the straight and narrow pathway of man's response to God's direct revelation, and in the sense that Edwards indicated how God is revealed in the natural as well as the scriptural universes, Miller is certainly right. Edwards had indeed attempted to secure his new Lockean epistemology, his 'new sense of things,' by according it the status already established for typological exegesis by the theologians who preceded him. Miller says that 'the beauty of a type was exactly that, if it existed at all, it needed only to be seen, not argued. His psychological thesis led him to typology, just as it gave him a program for the correction of New England rhetoric.'[18] And this is just where the Edwardsean epistemology ceased to corroborate the older, orthodox typology.

Miller indicates these distinctions himself. But the value he assigns Edwards' typology in the introduction to Images or Shadows would credit Edwards with a more conservative typology than he presents.

16. Miller, 'Introduction to Jonathan Edwards,' p. 11.

17. Ibid., p. 24.

18. Ibid., p. 26.

In nature, said Edwards, the agreement between the animal and the divine idea would be exactly the same kind of agreement as between the types of the Old Testament and their antitype. 'There is an harmony between the methods of God's Providence in the natural and religious world.' Here was the central perception about which Edwards strove to organize God's creation: the Bible is only one among several manifestations of the typical system; the pattern of the cosmos is infinite representation, and thereby intelligible.[19]

This transformation of the typological system is a more serious matter than Miller would make it. Edwards establishes a system of analogy in Images or Shadows through which natural objects have spiritual counterparts in the allegorical fashion. But Miller seems to regard this to be no more than an 'extension of typology,' which has its foundation and basis in the continuity of the Old and New Testaments.

Edwards' typology here is in all respects a very different order of perception from the epistemology that is based on biblical exegesis and scriptural typology. In the 'naturalistic' scheme of Images or Shadows, there is little room for the linear and historical relation between the type and its antitype, so that what Edwards succeeds in achieving is a method of reading nature that should supplement the revelation of God's will in Scripture. The language employed to convey this idea is misleading, since he has used 'type' and 'anti-type' elsewhere to mean the historical and prefigurative pattern by which God's progressive revelation is established in human time. Throughout his introduction, Miller has declared that 'to attack the evils of the local scholasticism,' Edwards deliberately 'invoked the types to rebuke the tropes.'[20] He makes extremely clear distinctions between 'types' and 'tropes,' but everywhere he allows the word 'type' to mean the symbolic representation of a spiritual idea. Miller is perfectly aware that Edwards has used the exegetical types in this sense, and he even alludes to the transformation in Images or Shadows from an orthodox to a spiritualized typology: 'Had Edwards, even with Locke to assist him, done no more than create a new typology, he might deserve mention . . .'[21] Yet he nowhere

19. Ibid., p. 27.   20. Ibid., p. 24.   21. Ibid., pp. 26–27.

draws the distinction between Edwards' employment of the allegorical images that he labels 'types' and the orthodox historical typology of A History of the Work of Redemption. Rather than being a resurrection of biblical typology as a means of chastising the tropology of late seventeenth-century theologians, Edwards' new epistemology in Images or Shadows is analogous to the medieval habit of mind by which the physical universe was believed to represent the spiritual in a Platonic or allegorical fashion. More closely related to the Puritan habit of discovering 'remarkable Providences' in the natural universe than to the conservative doctrines of typological exegesis, Edwards' typology here is more like the epistemology of his empiricist contemporaries than that of his Puritan predecessors. As in Image 142, 'The silk-worm is a remarkeable type of Christ,' the analogy between the natural image and the spiritual attributes of Christ dominates the conception. And the patterns of thought developed in the collection of Images clearly argue for a new kind of typology based on the empirical psychology of John Locke.

Although there are two hundred and twelve seemingly unrelated entries comprising Images or Shadows, one can discern several underlying motifs throughout the work. Only occasionally does Edwards use an earthly image to prefigure an event of the future, although there is a controlling sense of eschatology even in the most extreme cases of his allegorizing of nature. But even where a linear and historical perspective is suggested or implied, Edwards is still not using scriptural typology as the more conservative exegetes had understood it, although his eschatological sense does represent a more conservative position than the altogether Platonic scheme through which natural objects became symbols for spiritual truths. For Edwards, there is an indissoluble continuity between revelation in Scripture and revelation through nature:

Image 156. The Book of Scripture is the interpreter of the Book of Nature in two ways, viz., by declaring to us those spiritual mysteries that are indeed signified and typified in the constitution of the natural world; and secondly, in actually making application of the signs and types in the Book of Nature as representations of those spiritual mysteries in many instances . . .

Image 169: IMAGES of Divine Things: There are some types of divine things, both in Scripture and also in the works of nature and constitution of the world, that are much more lively than others. . . . God has ordered things in this respect much as He has in the natural world. . . . There is a like difference and variety in the light held forth by types as there is in the light of the stars of the night. Some are very bright, some you can scarcely determine whether there be a star there or no, and the like different degrees, as there is the light of twilight, signifying the approaching sun.[22]

In Image 168, Edwards comes very close to revealing a possible source for his 'new sense of things,' when he asserts that a natural activity, 'viz., husbandry,' can instruct man by representing to him spiritual truth:

Image 168: There are most representations of divine things that are most in view or that we are chiefly concerned in: as in the sun, his light and other influences and benefits; in the other heavenly bodies; in our own bodies; in our state, our families and commonwealths, and in this business that mankind do principally follow, viz., husbandry.[23]

This clear echo of John Flavel's process of analogy is reinforced by Edwards' many statements affirming the value of Platonic correspondences in the typological scheme. In Image 45, he says

That natural things were ordered for types of spiritual things seems evident by these texts: John 1.9, This was the true light, which lighteth every man, that cometh into the world; and John 15.1, I am the true vine. Things are thus said to be true in Scripture in contradistinction to what is typical: The type is only the representation or shadow of the thing, but the antitype is the very substance and is the true thing. Thus, heaven is said to be the true holy of holies, in opposition to the holy of holies in the tabernacle and temple, Heb. 9:24. . . . So the spiritual Gospel tabernacle is said to be the true tabernacle, in opposition to the legal, typical tabernacle, which was literally a tabernacle.[24]

22. *Images or Shadows*, p. 109.   23. *Ibid.*, p. 119.   24. *Ibid.*, p. 56.

The problem here is not that linear and historical typological correspondences have been abandoned, but that the interpretation given
the type-antitype relationship is Platonic and allegorical when the
orthodox pattern was apparent. Edwards' understanding of typology as an exegetical science cannot be questioned, since he elsewhere demonstrates his comprehension of the traditional scheme.
But his transformation of these conservative patterns into a looser,
more flexible system of analogies is clearly the design of *Images or
Shadows*.

The medieval understanding of the Book of Nature is never far
away; Edwards' typology of nature is significantly medieval rather
than Puritan. Although he nowhere attempts an elaborate reading
of Nature according to multiple levels of meaning, as the medieval
exegetes had done, Edwards adopted an approach to nature
whereby the natural universe came to have an allegorical significance within a typological frame of reference.

The justification for such a reconciliation between nature and
scriptural typology is not found in *Images or Shadows* because this
document is more a series of meditations or reflections than a philosophical treatise. In the 'Miscellanies,' however, there is a passage
that seems to corroborate the method that emerges in *Images or
Shadows*, showing exactly how the typology of Scripture operates
according to the principle of analogy which Edwards finds prominent in nature. It merits being quoted in full:

*Indeed, the whole outward creation, which is but shadows of His
being, is so made as to represent spiritual things. It might be demonstrated by the wonderful agreement in thousands of things,
much of the same kind as between the types of the Old Testament
and their antitypes; and by there being spiritual things so often and
continually compared with them in the word of God. And it is
agreeable to God's wisdom that it should be so, that the inferior
and shadowy parts of His works should be made to represent those
things that . . . are more real and excellent, spiritual and divine, to
represent the things that . . . immediately concern himself, and the
highest parts of His work. Spiritual things are the crown and glory,
the head and soul, the very end, the alpha and omega of all other*

works. So what therefore can be more agreeable to wisdom than
that they should be so made as to shadow them forth. And we know
that this is according to God's method, which His wisdom has
chosen in other matters. Thus the inferior dispensation of the Gos-
pel was all to shadow forth the highest and most excellent which
was its end; thus almost everything that was said or done, that we
have recorded in Scripture from Adam to Christ, was typical of
Gospel things. Persons were typical persons; their actions were
typical actions; the cities were typical cities; the nations of the Jews
and other nations were typical nations; their land was typical land;
God's Providences towards them were typical Providences; their
worship was typical worship . . . and indeed the world was a typical
world. And this is God's manner to make inferior things shadows of
the superior and most excellent; outward things shadows of spir-
itual; and all other things shadows of those things that are the end
of all things, and the crown of all things. Thus God glorifies Him-
self and instructs the minds that He has made.[25]

Here the didactic function of the natural world is clear; the analogies which the medieval exegetes had perceived under the tropology of the fourfold method have been transformed into an epistemology of correspondences called 'type' and 'antitype.' Of course
there are enormous differences in the method and intent; however,
even Edwards' sense that the spiritual seals the corporeal in an
immutable and timeless act cannot refute the sense that his 'types'
here are symbolical representations of spiritual ideas. By examining
several of the images that relate to a single topic, this methodology
becomes apparent.

A characteristic motif is that series of typological correspondences given in Edwards' treatment of marriage as a sacrament symbolizing a higher type of union than that of two persons. Image 5
commences this sequence, where Edwards records that 'marriage
signifies the spiritual union and communion of Christ and the
Church, and especially the glorification of the church in the perfection of this union and communion forever.'[26] Image 9, the second part of the 'marriage group,' is more specific: 'Again, as to mar-

25. 'Miscellany No. 362.' 26. Edwards, *Images or Shadows*, p. 44.

riage, we are expressly taught that there is a designed type of the union between Christ and the Church.'[27] In Image 12, however, Edwards enlarges on the scripturally instituted typology of marriage to assert that the system of typological 'representation,' as he conceives it, should be extended to many other things, including the natural system of the universe:

We are told that marriage is a great mystery, as representing the relation between Christ and the Church. (Eph. 5.32.) By mystery can be meant nothing but a type of what is spiritual. And if God designed this for a type of what is spiritual, why not many other things in the constitution and ordinary state of human society and the world of mankind?[28]

One response to this inquiry might be that typology as a science of exegesis applies to divinely instituted relationships between persons or things or events, one of which adumbrates and prefigures the other, by which the former is abrogated. To extend typology beyond these limits is to accord any outward and external representation of an inward idea the value of 'type' and 'antitype.' Edwards clearly understands these limits, not only from what he has posited elsewhere about typology, but also from occasional references in Images or Shadows:

Image 56: There is a great mystery, i.e., a mysterious typical representation which refers ultimately to the union between Christ and the Church. God had respect to Adam and Eve as a type of Christ and the church when He took Eve out of Adam and gave that institution mentioned in Genesis.[29]

This awareness of the instituted nature of typology combined with Edwards' application of the orthodox scheme in A History of the Work of Redemption balances the impressions we are provided by the epistemology that underlies most of the examples in Images or Shadows. For example, in Image 13, Edwards is once again attempting a reconciliation between the nomenclature of typology and the psychology of Locke:

27. Ibid., p. 45.   28. Ibid.   29. Ibid., pp. 60–61.

Thus I believe the grass and other vegetables growing and flourish-
ing, looking green and pleasant as it were, ripening, blossoming, and
bearing fruit from the influences of the heavens, the rain and wind
and light and heat of the sun, to be on purpose to represent the dependence of our spiritual wellfare upon God's gracious influence
and the effusions of His Holy Spirit. I am sure there are none of the
types of the Old Testament are more lively images of spiritual
things. We find spiritual things very often compared to them in
Scripture.[30]

Again, in Image 8, the bare outline of a system of analogies is presented as a methodology for reading the Book of Nature:

Again it is apparent and allowed that there is a great and remarkeable analogy in God's works. There is a wonderfull resemblance in
the effects which God produces, and consentaneity in His manner
of working in one thing and another throughout all nature. It is
very observable in the visible world; therefore it is allowed that God
does purposely make and order one thing to be in agreeableness and
harmony with another. And if so, why should not we suppose that
He makes the inferiour in imitation of the superior, the material of
the spiritual, on purpose to have a resemblance and shadow of
them? We see that even in the material world, God makes one part
of it strangely to agree with another, and why is it not reasonable to
suppose He makes the whole as a shadow of the spiritual world.[31]

The problem is not that Edwards has adopted a Platonic or allegorical view of the universe, but that he has established his cosmology in Platonism and then has adopted the nomenclature of
scriptural typology in expounding the doctrine. For example, in
Image 59, where the idea of analogy is repeated, Edwards employs
the terminology he has used in describing typology elsewhere to describe the process of analogy:

If there be such an admirable analogy observed by the creatour in
His works through the whole system of the natural world, so that
one thing seems to be made in imitation of another, and especially
the less perfect to be made in imitation of the more perfect, so that

30. Ibid., p. 45.   31. Ibid., p. 44.

the less perfect is as it were a figure or image of the more perfect, so beasts are made in imitation of men, plants are a kind of types of animals, minerals are in many things in imitation of plants. Why is *it not rational to suppose that the corporeal and visible world should be designedly made and constituted in analogy to the more spiritual, noble, and real world?*[32]

Moreover, the transformation of nomenclature is but a small part of Edwards' new epistemology; he clearly sees the natural universe as a 'mappe and shaddow' of God's eternal will, and comprehends its 'typology' accordingly. Examples abound. In Image 64, he declares that 'hills and mountains are types of heaven, and often made use of as such in Scripture.' But immediately, he transforms the 'type' so that it has no more than allegorical significance in a scheme of interpretation which derives from his reading of nature through ingenious comparisons. There is an echo of Bunyan in lines like these, which refer to the 'typology' of the mountains and hills:

These are difficultly ascended. To ascend them, one must go against the natural tendency of the flesh; this must be contradicted in all the ascent, in every step of it, and the ascent is attended with labour, sweat, and hardship. There are commonly many hideous rocks in the way. It is a great deal easier descending into valleys. This is a representation of the difficulty, labour, and self-denial of the way to heaven, and how agreeable it is, to the inclination of the flesh, to descend the hill . . .[33]

Thus the purely representational value of the natural universe is prominently stressed. 'Hills and mountains,' Edwards says, 'as they represent Heaven, so they represent eminence in general, or any excellence and high attainment.'[34] And the phraseology of *Pilgrim's Progress* is echoed in a line found in Image 67: 'This may encourage Christians constantly and steadfastly to climb the Christian Hill.'[35]

This kind of allegorizing is incorporated into a more specific transformation of the Biblical scheme. We are prepared for Edwards' comparisons and parallels between the history of Rome and

32. *Ibid.,* p. 65.   33. *Ibid.,* p. 67.   34. *Ibid.,* p. 68.   35. *Ibid.*

Greece and the history of Christianity by Cotton Mather's similar citations in the *Magnalia Christi Americana*. But Edwards has taken the analogy one step further than Mather; he has made the Roman Empire a 'type' of Christ's kingdom on earth. This extension of exegetical typology appears in several of the images, but it is strongly voiced in Image 81:

> *The Roman triumph was a remarkeable type of Christ's ascension. The general of the Roman armies was sent forth from Rome, that glorious city and metropolis of the world, by the supream Roman authority into remote parts of the enemies' country, to fight with the enemies of the Roman state. As Christ, the captain of the Lord's hosts, was sent forth from heaven, the head city of the universe, by the supream authority of heaven, the country of heaven's enemies, to conflict with those enemies. And on obtaining some very signal and great victory he returned in triumph to the city whence he came out, entered the city in a very glorious manner. So Christ, having gone through the terrible conflict and obtained a compleat and glorious victory, returned again to heaven, the city whence he came, in a glorious triumphant manner.*[36]

Edwards' transformed typology is again illustrated in his Images that treat the sacrament. Essentially, Edwards perceives the institution of the sacrament symbolizing Christ's sacrifice repeated through the natural world, as he records in Image 68:

> *As wheat is prepared to be our food, to refresh and nourish and strengthen us, by being threshed and then ground to powder and then baked in the oven, whereby it becomes a type of our spiritual food, even Christ the bread which comes down from heaven, which becomes our food by his sufferings, so the juice of the grape is a type of the blood of Christ as it is prepared to be our refreshing drink, to exhilarate our spirits and make us glad, by being pressed out in a winepress.*[37]

Although Edwards clearly understands the value of the sacrament as a divinely instituted rehearsal of Christ's sacrifice, he is inclined to read into the institution allegorical significance so that other activities of nature reflect Christ's body and blood.

36. *Ibid.*, pp. 79–80.   37. *Ibid.*, pp. 68–69.

The most ingenious series of Images is that in which Christ is compared to the Sun. This renaissance commonplace was used extensively by Milton in *Paradise Lost* and *Paradise Regained*, and Edwards' treatment of Christ reflected in the glory of the Sun may be found throughout the seventeenth century. However, from the early Images in which he asserts only the basic tenets of the analogy between Christ and the Sun, to his lengthy diatribes on this familiar correspondence in his 'Notes on the Scriptures,' Edwards provides a consistent attempt to reconcile the linear and historical dimensions of exegetical typology to the unhistorical correspondences of allegorizing. In Image 40, for example, he asserts: 'The gradual vanishing of shades when the sun approaches is a type of the gradual vanishing of Jewish ordinance as the Gospel dispensation was introduced.'[38] This familiar analogy is reinforced by his comparison of the Law and the Gospel to darkness and light in the 'Miscellanies, Number 638.' The clarity with which Edwards perceives the relationship between the biblical 'type' and the 'antitype,' and the manner in which he has drawn this comparison through a sustained analogy taken from nature, indicate once again that Edwards allegorized the natural universe even while retaining a sense of the differences between typology and allegory.

There is an harmony between the methods of God's Providences in the natural and religious world, in this as well as many other things: that, as when day succeeds the night, and the one comes on, and the other gradually ceases, those lesser lights that served to give light in the absence of the sun gradually vanish as the sun approaches; one star vanishes after another as daylight increases, the lesser stars first and the greater ones afterwards, and the same star gradually vanishes till at length it wholly disappears, and all these lesser lights are extinguished and the sun appears in his full glory above the horizon. So when the day of the Gospel dawned, the ceremonies of the Old Testament and ordinances of the Law of Moses, that were appointed only to give light in the absence of the sun of righteousness, or until Christ should appear, and shone only with a borrowed and reflected light, like the planets, were gradually abolished one after another, and the same ordinance gradually

38. *Ibid.*, p. 52.

ceased, and those ordinances that were principall (one of which was the Jewish Sabbath) continued longest. There were a multitude of those ceremonies, which was a sign of their imperfection; but all together did but imperfectly supply the place of the sun of righteousness. But when the sun of righteousness is come, there is no need of any of them....[39]

As Milton had observed in his 'On the Morning of Christ's Nativity,'

The Sun himself withheld his wonted speed,
And hid his head for shame,
As his inferiour flame
The new-enlightened world no more should need:
He saw a greater Sun appear
Than his bright throne or burning axletree could
bear. ('The Hymn,' VII)

If Edwards had left his reconciliation of nature and scriptural typology at this level, he would have done little more than draw a splendid comparison between typological adumbration and abrogation and the natural phenomenon of light and darkness. But he went much further. In Image 50, Edwards declares that 'The rising and setting of the sun is a type of the death and resurrection of Christ.' Although his ensuing argument attempts to prove that there is more than a simple analogy between the sun rising and the coming of Christ (e.g., an instituted resemblance), Edwards here has clearly abandoned the historical scheme of adumbration and fulfillment. As the medieval exegete had done before him, Edwards turns to the vast Book of Nature for a faithful image of the spiritual realm. There is not merely an historical record of providential guidance of the chosen of God; rather the minutest details of the natural creation are provided for the edification of the regenerate individual.

If we look on these shadows of divine things as the voice of God purposely by them teaching us these and those spiritual and divine

---

39. Jonathan Edwards, 'Miscellany, No. 638,' quoted by Miller, Images or Shadows, pp. 52–53, n.

things, to show of what excellent advantage it will be, how agreeably and clearly it will tend to convey instruction to our minds, and to impress things on the mind and to affect the mind, by that we may, as it were, have God speaking to us. Wherever we are, and whatever we are about, we may see divine things excellently represented and held forth. And it will abundantly tend to confirm the Scriptures, for there is an excellent agreement between these things and the holy Scripture.[40]

This manifesto provides a summarizing doctrine to which all of Edwards' Images may be related. The seeming inconsistency in his attempt to retain the orthodox typological correspondences ('Miscellany 638') and his obvious departures into Platonic allegorizing beg the question of his place in the epistemological spectrum.

One of the most interesting examples of Edwards' transformation of scriptural typology into a 'natural typology' appears in his 'Notes on the Scriptures, Number 271,' where he writes: 'The Gospel light granted to the Old Testament Church in its different successive ages was very much like the light of the moon in the several parts of the revolution it performs, which ends in its conjunction with the sun.'[41] Although Edwards seems to draw only an analogy between the natural object and the scriptural pattern of revelation, he has used the moon image elsewhere, i.e., in 'Notes on the Scriptures, No. 315,' to present a purely sensory and naturalistic interpretation. In this context, the above passage is endowed with the significance of Edwards' continuous efforts to reconcile Scripture-types with the typology of nature as he personally conceived it. Although in many cases the orthodox Scripture-type would be a natural object, this was not a necessary prerequisite for the instituting of the biblical types, and it is in this particular aspect that Edwards' typology departs markedly from the more conservative exegesis. He was more willing than either Cotton or Samuel Mather to extend to nature the characteristics of revelation that he found in the scriptural pattern of type and antitype. Cotton Mather had halfheartedly spiritualized the natural activity of the

40. *Images or Shadows*, pp. 69–70.

41. Quoted by Miller, *Images or Shadows*, pp. 69–70.

husbandman in the manner of John Flavel, but he did not employ the nomenclature of scriptural typology in his 'exegesis' of the natural text. Rather, he allowed the analogy between the activity of the husbandman and the spiritual pursuits of the converted Christian to explain each other by developing a series of ingenious parallels between the natural world and the scriptural example. Never did he violate the integrity of the continuity of scriptural types and antitypes, although he did endow with typical value some rather fanciful analogies in the 'Biblia Americana.'

Edwards' typology of nature represented a new departure in the epistemology of divine revelation. That he provided a conservative force against liberalism in Covenant theology, and particularly against the excesses of Stoddardeanism, does not alter his influence in typology toward a broadening of the avenues by which man might perceive the will of God. The extremes to which he was willing to carry this 'new sense of things' is given in detail in A Treatise Concerning Religious Affections, which grew out of Edwards' experience during the Great Awakening of the early 1740's, indicating not only how God's will may be revealed through the natural universe to the mind of the alert regenerate, but also how a personal and saving knowledge of Christ might be obtained through an experience of the physical senses, out of which the Grace of God might be dispensed to the members of his Elect. Although the Religious Affections was only one of several documents Edwards published during the period of revival interest in New England, it is the most important statement of his emerging faith in the experimental piety of sensationalism. Moreover, it is itself a thorough and detailed argument, so that it needs little reference to the context out of which it was developed. Through the Religious Affections, we are able to understand how Edwards came to regard signs and symbols of the natural universe to be 'typical' of the supernatural, and how this modified Lockean epistemology— by which man perceived God through the external senses and through his revelation in nature—prepared the way for the romantic psychology of Emerson and the transcendentalists.

The epistemology of the Religious Affections was no accident; the 'new sense of things' had been emerging throughout Edwards' career, and isolated fragments from his other writings reveal his penchant for an epistemology based on natural revelation. He had made it clear from the beginning that revelation of the will of God in the natural universe and the corresponding dispensation of Grace was to be perceived only by the regenerate man. 'My affections seemed to be lively and easily moved,' he records in his 'Personal Narrative,' 'and I am ready to think, many are deceived with such affections, and such a kind of delight as I then had in religion, and mistake it for grace.'[42] The receiving of Grace through natural sources was for Edwards a privilege allowed only to God's Elect; and it was even then only an inspiration to the natural affections out of which an experience of Grace ensued. The 'new sense of things' that awaited the regenerate understanding is curiously illustrated by contrasting the reaction to a thunderstorm found in Edwards' 'Personal Narrative' with a characteristic response to thunder provided by Cotton Mather in the *Magnalia Christi Americana*. Mather's approach to the natural phenomenon must be understood in the context of Puritan 'providences,' by which God intervened in the activity of the universe he governs to speak to his creatures on special occasions. Mather begins by assessing the thunder from a quasi-empirical point of view:

First, it is to be premised, as herein implied and confessed that the thunder is the work of the Glorious God. It is true, that the thunder is a natural production, and by the common laws of matter and motion it is produced; there is in it a concourse of divers weighty clouds, clashing and breaking one against another, from whence arises a mighty sound, which grows yet more mighty by its resonancies. The subtle and sulphurous vapors among these clouds take fire in this combustion, and lightnings are thence darted forth; which, when they are somewhat grosser, are fulminated with an irresistible violence upon our territories.[43]

This, he explains, is the 'Cartesian account,' which is comparable to the literal understanding of a Scripture narrative. It is not long before Mather turns to God as the author of all being by whom the natural universe is ultimately controlled:

42. *Major Writers of America*, ed. Perry Miller (New York, 1962), I, 136.

43. *Magnalia Christi Americana* (Hartford, 1853), II, 366.

But still, who is the author of those laws, according whereunto things are thus moved into thunder? yes, who is the first mover of them? Christians, 'tis our glorious God.

. . . Well, and whose workmanship is it all? 'Ah! Lord, thou hast created all these things; and for thy pleasure, they are and were created.' . . . Hence, the thunder is ascribed unto our God all the Bible over; in the scripture of truth, 'tis called the 'thunder of God,' oftener than I can presently quote unto you. And hence, we find the thunder even now and then, executing the purpose of God.[44]

Once Mather has established this 'doctrine' from his reading of the 'thunder text' in the Book of Nature, he proceeds to develop seven applications of the doctrine, showing how the voice of God is present in each thunderstorm in seven different ways. One example will illustrate his methodology:

One voice of the Glorious God in the thunder is, 'that he is a Glorious God, who makes the thunder.' There is the marvellous glory of God seen in it, when he 'thunders marvellously.' Thus do these inferior and meteorous 'heavens declare the glory of God.' . . . If nothing be too hard for the thunder, we may think surely nothing is too hard for the Lord! The arm that can wield thunderbolts is a very mighty arm.[45]

Mather's 'uses' of the thunderstorm are clearly more important than the natural phenomenon itself, which is only an example of God's majesty. He has begun with nature only to make nature the servant of truth that he has already found revealed in the Scriptures. Thus natural phenomena act as corroborative evidence for scriptural revelation; the objective investigation of nature from an exclusively empirical approach was never quite accomplished as long as theological scientists like Cotton Mather were striving to force nature to conform to the truths they had already received from their reading of the Bible.

For Jonathan Edwards, however, the revealed truth of nature might sometimes have equal value to scriptural revelation, and his own assessment of a thunderstorm indicates the prominence of

44. Ibid.   45. Ibid., 367.

nature in disclosing the 'sweetness' of God's majesty to the regenerate mind. The 'new sense of things' made available new worlds of understanding for the Elect:

Not long after I first began to experience these things, I gave an account to my father of some things that had passed in my mind. I was pretty much affected by the discourse we had together; and when the discourse was ended, I walked abroad alone, in a solitary place in my father's pasture, for contemplation. And as I was walking there, and looking up on the sky and clouds, there came into my mind so sweet a sense of the glorious majesty and grace of God, that I know not how to express. I seemed to see them both in a sweet conjunction; majesty and meekness joined together; it was a sweet, and gentle, and holy majesty; and also a majestic meekness; an awful sweetness; a high, and great, and holy gentleness.[46]

This 'sweetness' culminates in Edwards' experience of God's glory as derived from his initial perception of that glory in the phenomena of nature. Even the thunderstorm provides an avenue for communion with the Divine mind:

After this my sense of divine things gradually increased, and became more and more lively, and had more of that inward sweetness. The appearance of every thing was altered; there seemed to be, as it were, a calm, sweet cast, or appearance of divine glory, in almost every thing. . . . And scarce any thing, among all the works of Nature, was so sweet to me as thunder and lightning; formerly, nothing had been so terrible to me. Before, I used to be uncommonly terrified with thunder, and to be struck with terror when I saw a thunder storm rising; but now, on the contrary, it rejoiced me. I felt God, so to speak, at the first appearance of a thunder storm; and used to take the opportunity, at such times, to fix myself in order to view the clouds, and see the lightnings play, and hear the majestic and awful voice of God's thunder, which oftentimes was exceedingly entertaining, leading me to sweet contemplations of my great and glorious God.[47]

46. 'Personal Narrative,' Major Writers of America, ed. Miller, I, 137–38.

47. Ibid.

The transformation of the natural phenomenon into an object for mystical contemplation and meditation characterizes Edwards' method in *Images or Shadows*, where natural objects are endowed with allegorical significance leading to spiritual truth. Where Cotton Mather had turned to nature and the thunderstorm to find evidence for his belief in the power and majesty of the Governor of the universe, Edwards has turned to nature for a direct apprehension of God's glory and majesty, through which he arrives at a sense of tranquility and an experience of the restorative power of Grace. The 'sweetness' and 'peace' he feels is much more than simply the esthetic satisfaction one derives from a momentary appreciation of nature's charm. Rather, Edwards' 'sweetness' is based on his apprehension of God's restorative power, made available to his regenerate perception through the 'new sense of things.'

The distinction between the regenerate and the natural understanding is crucial. If, for Emerson, the symbolism of nature was available for anyone who had been transcendentally redeemed, for Edwards, nature's revelation was possible only for an elect and regenerate sensibility. In *Religious Affections*, Edwards has made the importance of this distinction quite clear; the regenerate and the natural man are two wholly different creatures.

There is such a thing, if the scriptures are of any use to teach us anything, as a spiritual, supernatural understanding of divine things, that is peculiar to the saints, and which those who are not saints have nothing of. 'Tis certainly a kind of understanding, apprehending or discerning of divine things, that natural men have nothing of, which the Apostle speaks of, 'But the natural man receiveth not the things of the Spirit of God; for they are foolishness unto him; neither can he know them, because they are spiritually discerned.' (*I Cor.* 2:14). . . . And that there is such a thing as an understanding of divine things, which in its nature and kind is wholly different from all knowledge that natural men have, is evident from this, that there is an understanding of divine things, which the Scripture calls spiritual understanding; 'We do not cease to pray for you, and to desire that you may be filled with the knowledge of His will, in all wisdom, and spiritual understanding;' (*Col.* 1:9). It has already been shown, that that which is spiritual, in the ordinary use of the word in the New Testament, is entirely different in nature and kind, from all which natural men are, or can be the subjects of.[48]

For Edwards, the 'natural man' corresponds to the post-lapsarian Old Testament man who has not received the Grace of Christ. Just as the types were revealed to the chosen of God as a partial dispensation of 'good things to come,' the Grace of God is revealed in nature only to those whom God has similarly chosen:

From hence it may be surely inferred, wherein spiritual understanding consists. For if there be in the saints a kind of apprehension or perception, which is in its nature, perfectly diverse from all that natural nature; it must consist in their having a certain kind of ideas or sensations of mind, which are simply diverse from all that is or can be in the minds of natural men. And that is the same thing as to say, that it consists in the sensations of the new spiritual sense, which the souls of men have not . . .[49]

That the 'natural things' could provide a direct sense of the beauty of the Divine Excellency and the 'nature of divine things' is central to Edwards' epistemology. For John Flavel and Cotton Mather, the knowledge of God had ranged from an interpretation of scriptural types and their analogues in the contemporary world to an apprehension of the moral or spiritual truth represented in natural activity. That these moral truths were simply a way of corroborating scriptural revelation for Cotton Mather is proved by his frequent allusions to the Bible throughout *Agricola*. But for Edwards, nature has become an organic vehicle for the transmission of God's restorative power. The typology of Scripture was still true for those who learned of God through a reading of the Old and New Testaments; Christ was very much alive for Edwards in the figures of Moses and Aaron, Samson and David. However, an essential as-

48. Jonathan Edwards, *A Treatise Concerning Religious Affections*, ed. John E. Smith (New Haven, 1959), pp. 270–71. For an interesting discussion of Edwards' idea of beauty and the philosophical foundations for his psychology, see Roland Delattre, *Beauty and Sensibility in the Thought of Jonathan Edwards* (New Haven and London, 1968).

49. *Ibid.*, p. 271.

pect of the total Christian experience was the personal awareness of God's overwhelming majesty and man's awful depravity in sin, both of which were apparent to the regenerate sensibility. Not only could conversion be induced by natural circumstances; the regenerate being was provided a 'new sense of things' by which he continued to enjoy a special revelation of God's majesty in the natural universe. 'By this is seen the excellency of the word of God,' Edwards declares; 'Take away all the moral beauty and sweetness in the Word, and the Bible is left wholly a dead letter, a dry, lifeless, tasteless thing.'[50] If the Scripture types were to persevere, they must be accommodated in the light of natural revelation—not the cold, non-moral dry light of rationalist empiricism, or the equally barren scholasticism of exegetical orthodoxy, but through the enlightened right reason of the regenerate man, chosen by God to enjoy the ·sweetness of the universe through his new sense of its true meaning.

From what has been said, therefore, we come necessarily to this conclusion, concerning that wherein spiritual understanding consists; viz., that there consists in a sense of the heart, of the supreme beauty and sweetness of the holiness or moral perfection of divine things, together with all that discerning and knowledge of things of religion that depends upon, and flows from such a sense. . . . Spiritual understanding consists in this sense, or taste, of the moral beauty of divine things; so that no knowledge can be called spiritual, any further than it arises from this, and has this in it.[51]

Ultimately, the purposes behind the new epistemology were the same as they had been for the Puritan who understood nothing more than a few providences and the revealed truth of Scripture; Christ was the ultimate antitype for the Old Testament figures, and similarly, Christ stood at the center of the doctrine of moral perfection. Understanding of the natural world depended crucially on one's regeneration in Christ and on the gaining of a new spiritual sense, which, in turn, would lead to a renewed strength of perception out of which would arise increased spiritual knowledge.

Edwards avoided a seeming tautology by firmly rooting his typology of the senses in nature. The 'new sense of things' emphasized

50. *Ibid.*, p. 274.　51. *Ibid.*, pp. 272–73.

the natural things just as strongly as it espoused the new power of vision. The changing processes of the natural universe became a source of revelation for those who possessed this vision, and through a knowledge of Christ obtained by natural revelation one's ability to interpret the mysteries of the universe improved. This graduated movement, from natural 'type' to spiritual truth, is Platonic in design, but it is also parallel to the process of revelation followed in mysticism and it shows why Edwards has been variously labeled a Christian mystic and a religious pantheist.

The typology Edwards provided in *A History of the Work of Redemption* is conservative indeed when compared to the possibilities he outlines in *Images or Shadows* and examines in *Religious Affections*. He has taken great care to caution his readers against the dangers of Antinomianism and a spiritual personalism that would nullify the concept of God's transcendent majesty and power. But his new approach to the historic problem of man's knowledge of God had led him away from traditional methods of reading Christ in all the Scriptures and further from the Puritan habit of extending the biblical types to contemporary history. Regardless of his efforts to turn New England and his little Northampton congregation to a more fundamental and orthodox Calvinism, Edwards had argued a typology based on figures instituted in nature as well as types instituted in Scripture. Because of this strong penchant in Edwards' epistemology, he may be regarded as a precursor of certain attitudes among the nineteenth-century transcendentalists, notably Emerson. The trace of mysticism in Edwards' epistemology constitutes the primary correspondence between his writing and the American Renaissance.

The early efforts to reconcile scriptural truth to natural revelation were later modified by Edwards' repeated insistence that the natural universe was not only a 'type' of Christ and the Kingdom of God but might also actually be a direct reflection of Christ himself. In this final step, Edwards' sense of Christian mysticism develops, and through his transformed typology he most nearly approximates the total immersion in 'Nature [as] a symbol of spirit' so prominent in the writings of Emerson. For Edwards, there was still the necessity of viewing nature in the context of God's merciful revelation to fallen and sinful man, whose regenerate faculties were provided

with new and supernatural powers through which he might appre-
hend the Eternal Being. In Emerson's 'typology,' however, nature
becomes more than the announced 'symbol of spirit'; nature herself
is spirit, and a knowledge of her was available to *anyone* of uncor-
rupted, sensitive perception, because all men, while not equally
endowed with mystical insight, were emancipated from the Puritan
distinction between the regenerate and unregenerate in Emerson's
sinless universe.

In Part III, 'Beauty,' of the 1836 essay, *Nature*, Emerson seems
to echo Edwards' doctrine of Divine Excellence and the Calvinist's
view that natural beauty was a direct reflection of God's spiritual
perfection. He writes:

> . . . *this beauty of Nature which is seen and felt as beauty, is the*
> *least part. The shows of day, the dewy morning, the rainbow,*
> *mountains, orchards in blossom, stars, moonlight, shadows in still*
> *water, become shows merely, and mock us with their unreality. . . .*
> *The presence of a higher, namely, of the spiritual element is essen-*
> *tial to its perfection.*[52]

It is no surprise, therefore, when later in the same essay we find
Emerson adopting the nomenclature of Edwards' transformed typology and theory of analogy when he describes a natural phenomenon:

> *It is easily seen that there is nothing lucky or capricious in these*
> *analogies, but that they are constant, and pervade nature. These*
> *are not the dreams of a few poets, here and there, but man is an*
> *analogist, and studies relations in all objects. He is placed in the*
> *centre of beings, and a ray of relation passes from every other being*
> *to him. And neither can man be understood without these objects,*
> *nor these objects without man. All the facts in natural history taken*
> *by themselves, have no value, but are barren, like a single sex. But*
> *marry it to human history, and it is full of life. . . . Throw a stone*
> *into the stream, and the circles that propagate themselves are the*
> *beautiful type of all influence.*[53]

52. Ralph Waldo Emerson, 'Nature,' *MWA*, I, 493.

53. *Ibid.*, 495.

For Emerson, the 'type' was no more than a word picture or repre-sentation of a spiritual truth in the garments of nature. 'Every nat-ural fact is a symbol of some spiritual fact,' Emerson says, and 'every appearance in nature corresponds to some state of the mind, and that state of the mind can only be described by presenting that natural appearance as its picture.'[54] The scriptural foundations of typology are now wholly abandoned for a new epistemology based on a Platonic conception of reality.

'Types' were no longer needed as prefigurations of 'antitypes.' Rather, the type and antitype were present together in the eternal mystical moment that transcended all time in a 'sweet' and beauti-ful experience of union. The historical continuity so necessary to the biblical scheme of typical adumbration and antitypical abroga-tion was replaced by a Platonic symbolism that rejected all sense of past or future. Edwards' scheme of using the natural types as a means of discovering spiritual antitypes provided the allegorical foundation in the nomenclature of typological exegesis, so that Emerson and the transcendentalists were not the first to distort the traditional conceptions by endowing the terms with new meaning.

The types had come full circle. In reaction against the Platonic typology of the medieval exegetes, the Reformation typologists had reasserted the linear and historical conceptions of the early church; and these, in turn, had been espoused by the Puritans who read their own history as the antitypical fulfillment of the Scripture types. But their double vision, their assumption that in nature and in the providences they would find evidence to corroborate the truths revealed in Scripture, led them to a reliance on nature as a source of revelation that would supersede Scripture in the nine-teenth-century epistemology of Emerson and the transcendental-ists. The biblical types, which for the Puritans had been endowed with special meaning by God alone, gradually came to be the prov-ince of a few isolated conservative exegetes, while Edwards' fol-lowers employed the Lockean epistemology to endow nature with allegorical significance outside the biblical context. If Edwards had attempted to hold in balance a reading of Scripture through type and antitype, he had also released a psychological force in New

54. *Ibid.*

England that would soon destroy altogether the reading of Scripture as a primary source of spiritual revelation. God was not dead; but for the transcendentalist, the Word was lifeless until it could be demonstrated that some correspondence existed between the truths of Scripture and the spiritual ideas revealed in the natural universe.

Thus Edwards' transformation of the Puritan types was a significant attempt to reconcile natural epistemology and scriptural exegesis. He wound up borrowing the nomenclature of typology while endowing the natural world with spiritual significance. But the habit of mind by which Emerson saw in nature a symbol of spirit is clearly present in the epistemology of Edwards, and this epistemology must be kept distinct from the Puritan reading of history and Scripture in terms of type and antitype. Edwards, after all, had rejected Puritanism's federal theology by which the New England colonies bound themselves spiritually and historically to the Israel of old. And his primary aim in *Images or Shadows of Divine Things* was to provide a record of his own awareness of God's revealed truth in the natural universe. And the 'typology' of nature set forth in this collection becomes far more than an extension or rehabilitation of the biblical types; it is an original epistemology by which Edwards and his successors learned to read the vast and complex Book of Nature.

Annotated
Bibliography

Typology
and Early
American
Literature

If the years spent in teaching boys the Greek and Roman mythology were spent in teaching them Jewish antiquities and the connection between the types and prophecies of the Old Testament with the events of the New, don't you think we should have less infidelity and of course less immorality and bad government in the world?

Benjamin Rush to John
Adams, 21 July 1789

Annotated Bibliography

Preface

Sacvan Bercovitch

Columbia University

The organization is chronological, by period, with a selection of relevant modern commentaries appended to each section. Particular issues and influences are suggested in my annotations: e.g., the anti-Jewish polemics, the debates over levels of interpretation, the use of gnostic or cabbalistic theories, the impact of the Crusades, the question of 'correlative typology' in the Restoration (and earlier), the relevance of specific sects and movements within Protestantism (German Pietism, for example, or Cocceian 'federalism'), the variant literary applications by Catholics and Protestants during the Renaissance, and the traditions behind certain books of Scripture, such as Canticles and Psalms. In order to highlight these and other issues, I have grouped various works together in parentheses.

After some debate, I decided to restrict myself by and large to the typology of the two Testaments: e.g., to exclude many predominantly millenarian works, and, except in a few outstanding cases, to omit entirely the figural renderings of pagan myths. Both of these subjects certainly merit study as legitimate genres of typology, but each would necessitate a separate bibliography (see for example: Jean Daniélou, *The Theology of Jewish Christianity* [1958], trans. John A. Baker [London, 1964]; J. P. Martin, *The Last Judgment in Protestant Theology from Orthodoxy to Ritschl* [Edinburgh, 1963]; Harold Henry Rowley, *The Relevance of Apocalyptic: A Study of Jewish and Christian Apocalypses from Daniel to the Revelation* [New York, 1964]; and Peter Toon, ed., *Puritans, the Millennium and the Future of Israel: Puritan Eschatology 1600 to 1660* [London, 1970]). I have excluded, too, and for a similar reason, all bibliographies on theological works related to typology. Students of the subject should of course consult these, in addition to the standard encyclopaedias and dictionaries.

1. The Bible

a. Sources and Modes of Exegesis

The Greek *typus* appears in the New Testament in several ways: as 'print' or 'imprint' (e.g., John 20:25), as 'image' (e.g., Acts 7:43), as 'form' (e.g., Rom. 6:17), as 'pattern' (e.g., Titus 2:7), and as 'example' (or 'ensample'), a recurrent term—e.g., Phil. 3:17, I Thes. 1:7, II Thes. 3:9, I Tim. 4:12, I Pet. 5:3—which became important in Christian hagiography and, as such, extended to the *imitatio Christi* (cf. Col. 1:15). In its hermeneutic meaning, *typus/figura* appears, for example, in Heb. 9:24; explicitly or implicitly it may also be discerned in the following passages (among others): Mat. 12:39–42, 17:2–5; Luke 4:25–27, 11:29–31, 17:26–30, 24:27; John 3:14, 6:31–35; Rom. 3:25, 5:14, 9:12–13; I Cor. 5:7, 11:25–29, 15:20–23; Gal. 4:22–5:1, 6:13–16; Col. 2:17; Heb. 5:5–10; and I Pet. 3:20–21.

A general typological approach pervades the First Epistle of St. Peter, the Epistle to the Corinthians (especially chapter 10) and the Epistle to the Hebrews (e.g., chapters 5, 6, 8, 10, and 11), as well as the apocryphal Epistle of Barnabas. It may be seen to underlie the Gospels of St. Matthew and St. Luke, and in a broad sense the 'acted parables' of Jesus—such as the entry into Jerusalem (e.g., Mark 11:8–11)—and certain 'exemplary' events in his life, such as the flight into Egypt (e.g., Matt. 2:13–15). The many Gospel references to Jesus as the Suffering Servant and the apocalyptic Son of Man have often been linked typologically to Old Testament prophecies, especially those in Deutero-Isaiah 40–55 and Daniel 7, thus providing an important connection between typology and millenarianism. The connection extends, of course, to the passages in the Book of Revelation concerning Babylon, the Remnant, the Dragon, and related figurae: e.g., cf. Rev. 14:8 and 18:2 with Isa. 21:9 and Jer. 51:8; Rev. 12:17 with Mic. 2:12 and Zech. 8:6, 12; and Rev. 20:2 with Ps. 91:13. In this sense typology may be said to include: (a) the Old Testament types (e.g., Adam as a type of Christ, or Elijah as the type of John the Baptist [see Mark 9:13]); (b) types within the New Testament itself (e.g., the raising of Lazarus prefigures the Resurrection); (c) the Old and New Testament types of things still to come.

The role of Christ as antitype in these diverse connections lends itself to various applications—related to though distinguishable from christology and soteriology—particularly, perhaps, in the context of Reformation thought. Two of these applications may be singled out as having direct bearing upon American Puritan thought: developmental typology and correlative typology. The former relates Old Testament figures not only to the Incarnation but (in a form of sensus plenior) to the Second Coming. Thus typical objects, institutions and events (e.g., Noah's Ark and the flood, the wilderness trials and the Sabbath, the Babylonian captivity and the Promised Land) come to prefigure end-time events as well as aspects of the story of Christ. This historiographic view is complemented by the static biographical parallelism offered by correlative typology, in which the focus is not primarily upon Christ but upon certain Old Testament heroes (Moses, Nehemiah, Job, etc.) as they become, through Christ, 'redivivus' in contemporary heroes. As John Cotton put it (Treatise of Faith, [London, 1713], p. 16), 'We are not the same person with Christ and therefore we have a life not the very self-same with his,

but conformable to his, and fashioned after his Image'; like 'the Image of a Seal in the Wax,' we are 'the same in proportion, not the same in number, and it must needs be so, because the Fathers before Christ had as truly the same spiritual Life of Christ as we. The Life of his Divine Nature neither of us have . . . [but the] proportion and resemblance of his life before his Coming [they had] as we have after His Coming.'

It should be noted that both of these uses of typology rely in different ways on covenant theology, especially as this develops through Cocceius and the federalist school. Thus typology may be seen as a link between the concept of a recurrent national covenant and the concept of an unchanging covenant of grace manifest in succeeding stages of the history of redemption. It should be noted, too, that the New Englanders always retained the traditional figural mode of joining the Old and New Testaments by spiritual-literal exegesis, either theoretically or, practically, by applying the conjunction to the itinerarum mentis, the atemporal soul-journey of the saint —sometimes to urge the 'good works' that follow upon regeneration (i.e., the day-by-day duties commonly associated, in communal terms, with the national covenant). Characteristically, this conjunction entailed parallel events, such as the wilderness trial of Christ and of the Israelites, or else events, persons, objects, and institutions that seemed similar by implication: e.g., Christ's blood (esp. John 1:7 and Rom. 3:25), the blood of Abel (Gen. 4:10), and the blood of the Hebrews' 'sin-offering' (Lev. 5:9; cf. Ex. 29:16, Num. 18:17, and Ezek. 43:18); baptism and the Red Sea crossing; Jonah in the whale, Joseph in the pit, and Christ's harrowing of hell.

Finally, the student of early New England should be aware that the traditions of typology, as the colonists inherited them, extended the method of implicit or 'innate' association in a wide variety of ways: through *color*, as in the connection between the wine/blood of the Eucharist and the harlot Rahab's 'scarlet thread' (Josh. 2:18); through *numbers*, as in the connection between the twelve disciples and the twelve tribes of Israel; through *names*, notably Joshua/Jesus, but including also Cabbala-inspired relationships *via* numerical values, puns, anagrams, etc.; and through *words* that were thought to be philologically related, especially through the providential correspondence of the *linguae sanctae* (Greek, Hebrew, and Latin; see John 19:20), such as Adonai/Adonis, Jehova/Phoebus/sun-Son, and Janus/Noachus (Noah)/Jajin (Hebrew 'wine'). The latter correspondences obviously entail still another area of exegesis: the typology of pagan myths, which (as I mentioned above) I have reluctantly excluded from this bibliography. I should like nonetheless to urge further investigation—beginning, for example, with the studies already done on Hercules as a type of Samson (e.g., Marcel Simon, *Hercule et le Christianisme*, Paris, 1955), or with the Renaissance translations of certain classics. Following is a very brief list of pertinent philological (or philologically oriented) Renaissance works which would be helpful in an investigation of this kind: Johann Benedictus, *Biblia Sacra Veritas* (Paris, 1654); Johann Buxtorf, *De Abbreviaturis Hebraicis* (Basel, 1613) and *Synagoga Judaica* (Basel, 1661); John Dove, *The Conversion of Salomon* (London, 1613); John Eliot, *Communion of Churches* (Cambridge, Eng., 1665); Benjamin Holloway, *Originals* (Oxford, 1751); Samuel

Koenig, *Etymologicon Hellens Hebraeum* (Frankfurt, 1722); Edward Marbury, *Commentarie* (London, 1650); Michael Neander, *Sanctae Linguae Hebraeae Eromata* (Basel, 1657); Sancte Pagnino, *Thesaurus Linguae Sanctae* (Leiden, 1575); Thomas Playfere, *The Felicitie of the Faithful* (Cambridge, Eng., 1621); Johann Reuchlin, *De Rudimentis Hebraicis* (Pforzheim, 1506); John Robotham, *An Exposition on . . . Canticles* (London, 1651); and Andrew Willet, *Hexapla* (London, 1620).

b. Modern Criticism

Most commentaries on the scriptural texts noted in Section I(a) discuss typology, as do most Christian glosses on the Bible through the seventeenth century: e.g., see the facsimile of the Authorized Version (1611), ed. Alfred W. Pollard (Oxford, 1911). The following works are representative of the shifting viewpoints from the eighteenth century to the present.

Abbott, T. K. *The Epistles to the Ephesians and Colossians*. Edinburgh, 1897 (see also M. W. Jacobus, 'The Citation Eph. 5.14 as Affecting the Paulinity of the Epistle,' *Theologische Studien, B. Weiss Festschrift*, Göttingen, 1897).

Alexander, William. *The Witness of the Psalms to Christ and Christianity*. London, 1877.

Blasche, Johann C. *Commentar über den Brief an die Hebräer*. Leipzig, 1781.

Bleek, Friedrich. *Der Brief an die Hebräer*. Berlin, 1828 (see also Johannes H. Ebrard, *Der Brief an die Hebräer*, Königsberg, 1850).

Bonar, Andrew A. *A Commentary on the Book of Leviticus*. London, 1846 (see also his *Christ and the Church in the Book of Psalms*, London, 1859).

Brown, William. *Isaiah's Testimony for Jesus.* London, 1864 (cf. Joseph A. Alexander, *Prophecies of Isaiah*, Edinburgh, 1865).

Burnet, William. *An Essay on Scripture Prophecy.* N.p. [New York?], 1724.

Buzy, Denis. 'Les Symboles de Daniel,' *Revue Biblique*, XV (1918), 403–31 (cf. Robert B. Y. Scott, *The Relevance of the Prophets*, New York, 1944).

Cerfaux, Lucien. *The Church in the Theology of St. Paul* (1942), trans. Geoffrey Webb and Adrian Walker. New York, 1959.

Coppens, Joseph. *De Messiaanse verwachting in het Psalmboek.* Brussels, 1955.

Delitzsch, Franz Julius. *Psalms*, trans. David Eaton. 3 vols. London, 1887–89 (see also his *Brief an die Römer*, Leipzig, 1870).

Driver, S. R. 'Notes on Three Passages in St. Paul's Epistles,' *The Expositor*, IX, 3rd ser. (1889), 15–23.

Dunn, Lewis R. *The Gospel in the Book of Numbers.* New York, 1889.

Ellis, E. Earle. *Paul's Use of the Old Testament.* Edinburgh, 1957.

Farrer, Austin. *St. Matthew and St. Mark.* Westminster, 1954.

Fisher, B. 'Le Christ dans les Psaumes,' *La Maison-Dieu*, XXVII (1951), 86–113.

Goulder, Michael Douglas. *Type and History in Acts.* London, 1964.

Hanson, Richard P. C. 'Moses in the Typology of St. Paul,' *Theology*, XLVIII (1945), 174–77 (see further Peter Blaser, 'St. Paul's Use of the Old Testament,' *Theological Quarterly*, CXXXIII [1952], 152–69).

Hoskyns, Edwyn Clement. *The Fourth Gospel*, ed. Francis Noel Davey. London, 1940.

Huyghe, Carolus. *Commentarius in Epistolam ad Hebraeos.* N.p., 1901 (see also Ernest F. Scott, *The Epistle to the Hebrews*, Edinburgh, 1922).

Jukes, Andrew. *The Types of Genesis Briefly Considered As Revealing the Development of Human Nature.* London, 1858.

Kennedy, James. *Christ in the Song. An Explanation of All the Figurative Descriptions of Christ in the Song of Solomon.* Boston, 1890.

Kühl, E. *Der Brief des Paulus an die Römer.* Leipzig, 1913 (see also W. Sanday and A. C. Headlam, *The Epistle to the Romans*, Edinburgh, 1895).

Kurtz, Johann Heinrich. *Der Brief an die Hebräer erklärt.* Mitau, 1869.

Lightfoot, Joseph B. *The Epistle to the Colossians and to Philemon.* London, 1875.

Lowman, Moses. *A Paraphrase and Notes on the Revelation of St. John.* London, 1737.

Macknight, James. *A New Literal Translation from the Original Greek of All the Apostolic Epistles, with a commentary and notes.* London, 1809.

Manson, William. *The Epistle to the Hebrews.* London, 1951 (cf. J. Van Der Ploeg 'L'Exégèse de l'Ancien Testament dans l'Epître aux Hébreux,' *Revue Biblique*, LIV [1947], 187–228).

Michaelis, Johann David. *Erklärung des Briefes an die Hebräer.* Frankfurt, 1780.

Mowinckel, Sigmund O. P. *Psalmenstudien.* 2 vols. N.p., 1921–22.

O'Rourke, John J. 'The Fulfillment Texts in Matthew,' *Catholic Biblical Quarterly*, XXIV (1962), 394–403.

Prigent, Pierre. *Les Testimonia dans le Christianisme primitif. L'épître de Barnabe, I–XVI et ses sources.* Paris, 1961.

Rad, Gerhard von. *Genesis: A Commentary*, trans. John H. Marks. Philadelphia, 1961 (cf. George A. F. Knight, *A Christian Theology of the Old Testament*, Richmond, Va., 1959).

Rendall, G. H. *The Epistle of James and Judaic Christianity.* Cambridge, Eng., 1927.

Sahlin, Harald. *Zur Typologie des Johannesevangeliums.* (Uppsala Universitets Arsskrift, no. 4) Uppsala, 1950 (see also H. Ludin-Jansen, 'Typologien i Johannesevangeliet,' *Norsk Teologisk Tidskrift*, XLIX [1948], 144–58).

Selwyn, Edward Gordon. *The First Epistle of St. Peter.* London, 1947.

Simpson, Albert B. *Divine Emblems in Genesis and Exodus.* New York, n.p. [189–].

Sowers, Sidney G. *The Hermeneutics of Philo and Hebrews: A Comparison of the Old Testament in Philo Judaeus and the Epistle to the Hebrews.* Zurich, 1965 (Basel Studies of Theology, No. 1).

Stier, Ewald Rudolph. *Erklärung von siebzig ausgewählten Psalmen.* Halle, 1834.

Stinespring, William Franklin. 'Eschatology in Chronicles,' *Journal of Biblical Literature*, LXXX (1961), 209–19.

Stuart, A. Moses. *Commentary on the Epistle to the Romans.* Andover, Mass., 1832.

Tholuck, August. *Kommentar zum Briefe an die Hebräer.* Hamburg, 1850.

Townsend, George. *The New Testament.* 2 vols. London, 1825.

Walter, Nehemiah. *Discourses on . . . Isaiah.* Boston, 1755.

Westcott, Brooke F. *The Gospel according to St. John.* London, 1850 (see also his *Epistle to the Hebrews*, London, 1920 [3rd edn.]).

Windisch, Hans. *Der Barnabasbrief Erklärt.* Tübingen, 1920 (cf. N. A. Dahl, 'La Terre où Coule le Lait et le Miel selon Barnabé VI, 8–19,' in *Aux Sources de la Tradition Chrétienne*, ed. J.-J. von Allmen, Neuchâtel, 1950).

Wolfe, J. Robert. *The Messiah as Predicted in the Pentateuch and Psalms.* London, 1855.

Young, Edward J. *The Messianic Prophecies of Daniel.* Delft, 1954 (cf. Hubert Cunliffe-Jones, *The Book of Jeremiah*, New York, 1960).

c. Modern Attacks on Typology

The following list is limited to polemics specifically directed against figural exegesis, from the eighteenth century to the present. A thorough study of the subject would have to deal with the much broader issues of historical and scientific criticism of the Bible—as this develops through the works (for example) of Leibnitz, Shaftesbury, and Spinoza —and with certain sectarian polemics, notably the works of the Arminians, such as Grotius (Hugo de Groot), *De Veritate Religionis Christianae* (Paris, 1627; numerous editions and translations: e.g., by C. Barksdale [London, 1658] and S. Patrick [London, 1680; 6th edn.]), and Clericus (Jean Le Clerc), *Opera Philosophica* (Amsterdam, 1704; again, many editions and translations: e.g., J. Churchill [London, 1697]). Restricted as it is, however, I believe that the bibliography below will prove of special value to the student of the history of typology.

Adler, Herman N. *A Course of Sermons of the Biblical Passages Adduced by Christian Theologians in Support of . . . their Faith*. London, 1869 (first part of title, in Hebrew characters, is *Naphtali Elohim*; Jewish polemic; more recent, and far more sophisticated, versions of this argument—direct and indirect—are found in David Daube, *The New Testament and Rabbinic Judaism*, London, 1956, and *The Exodus Pattern in the Bible*, London, 1963; in Samuel Sodwel, *Philo's Place in Judaism*, Cincinnati, 1956; and in R. Loewe, 'The Jewish Midrashim and Patristic and Scholastic Exegesis of the Bible,' *Studia Patristica*, vol. I, ed. Kurt Aland and F. L. Cross, Boston, 1957; cf. Ian T. Ramsey, *Religious Language*, London, 1957).

Ammon, Christopher F. von. *Ueber die Aehnlichkeit des Innern Wortes einiger Neuer Mystiker mit dem Moral Worte der Kantischen Schriftauslegung*. Göttingen, 1796 (Kantian critique).

Baumgärtel, Friedrich. *Verheissung. Zur Frage des evangelischen Verständnisses des Alten Testaments*. Gütersloh, 1952 (important contemporary study; see also his 'Erwägungen zur Darstellung der Theologie des Alten Testaments,' *Theologische Literaturzeitung*, LXXVI [1951], cols. 257–72, and his essays in *Evangelische Theologie*, XIII [1953], 413–21, and XIV [1954], 298–313).

Berriman, William. *The Gradual Revelation of the Gospel from the Time of Man's Apostacy*. 2 vols. London, 1733 (Boyle Lectures for 1730–32).

Bultmann, Rudolph K. *Glauben und Versuchen*. 2 vols. Tübingen, 1952.

———— *History and Eschatology*. Edinburgh, 1957 (also published in New York under the title, *The Presence of Eternity*; major work by a major theologian; cf. his 'The Significance of Jewish Old Testament Tradition for the Christian West,' *Essays Philosophical and Theological*, London, 1955, and Joseph Bonsirven, *Exégèse Rabbinique et Exégèse Paulinienne*, Paris, 1938).

———— 'Ursprung und Sinn der Typologie als Hermeneutischer Methode,' *Theologische Literaturzeitung*, LXXV (1950), 205–12.

Cross, Leslie B. 'Flight from Reason in the Interpretation of the Bible,' *Modern Churchman*, XXIX (1949), 193–206 (cf. S. Vernon McCasland, 'The Unity of the Scriptures,' *Journal of Biblical Literature*, LXXIII [1954], 1–10).

Dopke, Johann C. C. *Hermeneutik der Neutestamentlichen Schriftsteller*. Leipzig, 1829.

Guillet, Jacques. *Thèmes Bibliques: Etudes sur l'Expression et le Développement de la Révélation*. Paris, 1951.

Holden, George. *Dissertation on the Fall of Man, in which the Literal Sense of the Mosaic Account . . . is Asserted and Vindicated*. London, 1823.

Huysman, J. B. *Het Geheim van het Oude Boek*. Heemstede, 1941 (scientific-historical approach).

McKenzie, John L. *The Two-Edged Sword*. Milwaukee, 1956 (see also his 'Problems of Hermeneutics in Roman Catholic Exegesis,' *Journal of Biblical Literature*, LXXVII (1958), 197–204; and cf. H. Grass, 'Grundsätze Kotholischer Bibelauslesung,' *Theologische Literaturzeitung*, LXXVII [1952], cols. 487–94).

Muenscher, Joseph. 'Types and the Typical Interpretation of Scripture,' *The American Biblical Repository*, 2nd ser., V (1841), 92–113 (valuable survey).

Parker, Theodore. *A Discourse on the Transient and Permanent in Christianity*. Boston, 1841 (sermon which brought Parker into prominence as leader of 'the new theology').

Prat, Fernand. *The Theology of St. Paul* (1908–12), trans. J. L. Stoddard. London, 1945 (cf. Hans Wilhelm Hertzberg, *Werdende Kirche im Alten Testament*, München, 1950).

Rau, Johann W. *Freimütige Untersuchung über die Typologie*. Erlangen, 1784.

Ruler, Arnold A. van. *Die Christliche Kirche und das Alte Testament* (1940), trans. H. Keller (from the Dutch). München, 1955.

Semler, Johann S. *Versuch einer freiern theologischen Lehrart*. Halle, 1777 (Spinozaist approach).

South, Robert. *Sermons Preached upon Several Occasions*. 6 vols. London, 1737 (Anglican Rationalist; see for example in vol. III the 1694 sermon on *Christianity Mysterious, and the Wisdom of God in Making it So*).

Stowe, Calvin Ellis. *Introduction to the Criticism and Interpretation of the Bible*. 2 vols. Cincinnati, 1835 (popularized vindication of the historical approach; cf. Thomas Paine's deistic attack, 'Examination of Prophecies,' in *Life and Writings*, ed. Daniel E. Wheeler, New York, 1908, and Elhanan Winchester's reply, in *Ten Letters Addressed to Mr. Paine*, Boston, 1794).

2. Church Fathers

Most of the works in Section 2 (a), (b), and (c) and in Section 3 (a) are found in the *Patrologiae cursus completus* . . . , ed. Jacques-Paul Migne; series graecae (161 vols.; to 1439), Paris, 1857–66; series latine (221 vols.; to 1216), Paris, 1844–55. Many of them have been often edited and translated; as a rule, the titles given below are those commonly used in the English translations: e.g., the Loeb Classical Library, the Library of the Fathers, and the Ante-Nicene Christian Library. I have retained the original title only where it has become so familiar that translation would obscure rather than clarify the content. Virtually all of the works were known to the colonial orthodoxy.

a. Early Commentators (Second and Third Centuries)

Arnobius (late 3rd C). *The Case Against the Pagans* (opposes *historia* to *allegoria*).

Clement of Alexandria (2nd C). *Stromata* (influenced by Philo and the Gnostics; first attempt towards a scheme of the Scriptural senses).

Clement of Rome (2nd C?). *First Epistle* (non-canonical, but marks the transition from historical to allegorical typology).

Irenaeus (2nd C). *Against Heresies* (cf. the synopsis by Hippolytus Romanus in early 3rd C; central source for the development of typology).

Justin Martyr (2nd C). *Dialogue with Trypho* (anti-Jewish polemic; see also the third-century polemics of St. Cyprian).

Lactantius, Lucius Caelius Firmianus, of Africa (late 3rd C). *Sacred Teachings* (development of term 'figura' both allegorically and in the Christian sense of fulfillment and foreshadowing).

Melito of Sardis (2nd C). *Homily on the Passions* (important statement of historic-prophetic typology).

Origen of Alexandria (3rd C). *Against Celsus* (major anti-Jewish polemic which remained influential throughout the Middle Ages and into the Reformation).

—— *On First Principles* (first attempt at a complete system of dogmatics; frequently cited by Augustine).

—— *Treatise on Prayer* (influenced by Philo and in turn influenced the whole course of Christian exegesis through Jerome; Puritans translated major portions of his works).

Tertullian (3rd C). *Against Marcion* (anti-gnostic polemic).

—— *Homily on Baptism* (one of the first uses of the term 'figura' in its Christian sense).

b. The Schools of Antioch and Alexandria

This great fourth-century controversy in effect clarified the main issues and directions in typological exegesis. The Alexandrians built upon the allegorical tradition of Philo, Clement, and Origen: see Harry A. Wolfson, *Philo*, 2 vols. (Cambridge, Mass., 1962); Thomas Camelot, *Foi et Gnose: Introduction à l'étude de la connaissance mystique chez Clément d'Alexandrie* (Paris, 1945); and Jean Daniélou, *Origène* (Paris, 1948). The Antiochenes insisted upon a literal-historical view of Scripture; they had little influence upon the tradition in the West until Junilius' sixth-century Latin translations: see Junilius' *Instituta Regularia*, and Heinrich Kihn's works on *Die Bedeutung der antiochischen Schule* (Berlin, 1866) and *Theodor von Mopsuestia und Junilius Afri-*

canus als Exegeten (Freiburg, 1880).

1. ANTIOCH

St. John Chrysostom. *Commentary on I Corinthians* (last major exponent of the school; attempted to establish general principles of typological exegesis).

Diodorus of Tarsus. *Commentary on the Psalms* (first important name of the school; see also Basil of Caesarea, *On the Hexameron*).

Eusebius of Caesarea. *Ecclesiastical History* (exodus typology related both to Christ's life and to current events; major influence).

Theodore of Mopsuestia. *Commentary on Galatians* (extremely important exegete, despite his condemnation as a heretic after his death).

Theodoret. *Commentary on Exodus* (see also the *Commentary on the Pauline Epistles* by Ambrosiaster, or Pseudo Ambrose, and *Homilies on the Psalms* by Asterius the Sophist; Cotton Mather considered Theodoret to be 'the best expositor of the bible among the fathers').

2. ALEXANDRIA

St. Ambrose. *Enarrations on the Psalms* (considerable influence on Augustine and thus on medieval exegesis; cf. his *Of Isaac and the Soul* and *Of Paradise*; see further Asterius of Amase, *Homilies on the Psalms*).

Cyril of Alexandria. *Exposition on Revelations*.

—— *On Isaiah* (major patristic exegete; see also Didymus the Blind, *Commentary on Zechariah*).

St. Gregory of Nyssa. *Commentary on Canticles*.

———— *Great Catechetical Oration* (parries Gnostic interpretations with original allegorisms in an extravagant fusion of allegory and historical typology; see also Methodius of Philippi and Olympus, *Banquet of the Twelve Virgins;* and cf. St. Basil the Great, *Homilies and Sermons*).

St. Hilary of Poitiers. *Treatise on the Mysteries* (typology of the Hexateuch).

St. Zeno of Verona. *On Job* (compendium of typological parallels between Job and Christ).

c. The Great Patristic Systematizers

St. Augustine (late 4th–early 5th C). *Against Faustus the Manichaean* (see also *The City of God*, especially Books XV–XVII; these works, and the others by Augustine listed below, are indispensable for a study of typology).

———— *Enchiridion on Faith, Hope and Charity* (see also the *First Catechetical Instructions*, Book III).

———— *On Christian Doctrine* (central formulation of the nature and scope of figural application which influenced similar discussions in Hugo of St. Victor's *Didascalicon,* Dante's *Convivio,* Boccaccio's *Genealogia deorum,* and Petrarch's *Familiari,* X).

St. Bede the Venerable (8th C). *On the Tabernacle and its Vessels.*

———— *The Hexameron* (cf. his *Meditations on the Passion of Christ*).

Cassian, John (5th C). *Correspondences* (*Collationes;* final codification of the fourfold pattern).

St. Eucher of Lyons (5th C). *Rules for Spiritual Understanding* (textbook of figural and ethical interpretations during the Middle Ages).

St. Gregory of Tours (6th C). *Legend of the Seven Sleepers* (figural application of profane-pagan material; some medieval descendants of this line of approach include Bernard Silvestris on Vergil's *Aeneid* and a host of interpreters on Ovid's *Metamorphosis:* e.g., Arnulf of Orléans, Giovanni del Vergilio, and Berchorius).

Gregory the Great (6th C). *Morals on the Book of Job* (allegorical and anagogical senses brought together in one 'typical' sense; see also Garnerius' lexical index).

Isidore of Seville (late 6th–early 7th C). *Some Interpretations* [*Allegoriae*] *on the Holy Scriptures* (threefold division; see also his *Books of Sentences* and his *Inquiries into the Old Testament, on the Book of Joshua* for the influential typology of Rahab).

St. Jerome (Hieronymus) (late 4th–early 5th C). *Commentary on Ezekiel* (influenced by Origen, though later turned against him).

———— *Epistle 129, to Dardanus.*

Maximus the Confessor (late 6th–early 7th C). *Commentary on Dionysus the Areopagite.*

Orosius, Paulus (5th C). *Seven Books of Histories Against the Pagans* (student of Augustine who tried to link the exegetical methods of Eusebius and Augustine; described Rome as the new chosen land).

d. Twentieth-Century Criticism Related to the Typology of the Church Fathers

Adam, Karl. *Die Kirchenbegriff Tertullians.* Paderborn, 1907 (see also his *Die geistige Ent-wicklung des heiligen Augus-tinus*, Augsburg, 1931).

Aland, Kurt, and F. L. Cross, eds. *Studia Patristica*, vol. I. Berlin, 1957 (vol. LXIII of *Texte und Untersuchungen zur der Alt-christlichen Literatur*; papers presented to the Second International Conference on Patristic Studies held at Oxford, 1955; see papers by Bonn Abramowski on Theodoret, by Jean Daniélou on the Feast of the Tabernacles and on Origen, by A. Kerrigan on St. Cyril of Alexandria, by L. Leloir on David and Christ, and by J. Pépin on allegory).

d'Alès, A. *Autour de Lucien d'An-tioch*. Bayrouth, 1938.

Altenauer, Berthold. *Patrology*, tr. Hilda C. Graef. Edinburgh, 1958 (see also his study of St. Augustine in *Historische Jahr-buch*, LXX [1951], 15–41).

Armendarez, Luis M. *El Nuevo Moises Dinamica Christocentrica en la Tipologia de Cirilo Ale-jandrino*. Madrid, 1962 (Estudios Oriensis, 3rd ser.).

Bardy, Gustave. *La Théologie de l'Eglise de Saint Clément de Rome à Saint Irenée*. Paris, 1945 (see also his 'Melchisedech dans la tradition patristique,' *Revue Biblique*, XXXIV [1926], 416–22, and XXXV [1927], 24–34; and see further E. Fabri, 'El bautismo de Jésus y el Reposo del Espiritu en la teologia de Ireneo,' *Ciencia y Fé*, XII [1956], 38–63, and F. Froidevaux, 'Sur Trois Textes de Saint-Irenée,' *Re-cherches de Science Religieuse*, XLIV [1956], 408–22).

Berkhof, H. E. *Die Theologie des Eusebius von Caesarea*. Amster-dam, 1939.

Bertrand, Frédéric. *Mystique de*

Jésus chez Origène. Paris, 1951 (see also E. de Faye, *Origène. Sa Vie, Son Oeuvre, Sa Pensée*, 3 vols., Paris, 1923–28).

Boer, Willem den. *De Allegrese in het Werk van Clemens Alexan-drinus*. Leiden, 1940.

Bonwetsch, N. *Die Theologie des Methodius von Olymp*. Berlin, 1904.

Bosset, Wilhelm. *Kyrios Christos. Geschichte des Christus-glaubens von den Anfängen des Christen-tums bis Irenaeus*. 2 vols. Göt-tingen, 1913.

Bouyer, L. *L'Incarnation et l'Eglise: Corps du Christ dans saint Atha-nase*. Paris, 1943.

Burghardt, Walter J. 'On Early Christian Exegesis,' *Theological Studies*, XI (1950), 78–116.

Casey, Robert Pierce. *The Exerpta ex Theodoto of Clement of Alex-andria*. London, 1934 (cf. J. Moignt, 'Gnose de Clément d'Alexandrie dans ses rapports avec la Foi et la Philosophie,' *Recherches de Science Religi-euse*, XXXVII [1950], 195–251, 398–421, 637–64).

Congar, Yves Maria Joseph. 'Ec-clesia ab Abel,' in *Abhandlungen über Theologie und Kirche: Fest-scrift fur Karl Adam*, eds. Hein-rich Elfers and Fritz Hofmann. Düsseldorf, 1952 (cf. in this vol-ume: Albert Mitterer, 'Christus und Kirche im Lichte ihrer An-alogie zum Menschenleib'; Jo-hannes Betz, 'Der Abendmahl-skelch im Judenchristentum'; Karl Rahner, 'Zur Theologie der Busse bei Tertullian'; Heinrich Elfers, 'Neue Untersuchungen über die Kirchenordnung Hip-polyts von Rom'; and Fritz Hof-mann, 'Mariens Stellung in der Erlösungsordnung nach dem hl. Augustinus').

——— 'Marie et l'Eglise dans la Pensée Patristique,' *Revue des Sciences Philosophiques et Théologiques*, XXXVIII (1954), 3–38 (see further: Thomas Livius, *The Blessed Virgin in the Fathers of the First Six Centuries*, London, 1893; vol. II of J. B. Terrien, *La Mère de Dieu et la Mère des Hommes d'après les Pères et la Théologie*, Paris, 1902; F. M. Braun, 'La Mère de Jesus dans l'oeuvre de saint Jean,' *Revue Thomiste*, LXI [1951], 466–89; V. G. Bertelli, 'L'interpretazione mariologica del Protoevangelio negli esegeti e teologi dopo la Bulla Ineffabilis Deus di Pio IX (1854–1954),' *Marianum*, XIII [1951], 257–91; and A. M. Dubarle, 'Les fondaments bibliques du titre marial de Nouvelle Eve,' *Recherches de Science Religieuse*, XXXIX [1951], 49–64).

Crouzel, Henri. *Origène et la Philosophie*. Aubier, 1962 (vol. XLII of *Etudes Publiées sous la Direction de la Faculté de Théologie S.J. de Lyon-Fouvière*; see also his *La Théologie de l'Image de Dieu chez Origène*, Paris, 1956).

Daniélou, Jean. *From Shadows to Reality: Studies in the Typology of the Fathers*, trans. W. Hilberd. Westminster, Md., 1960 (brilliant analysis of exegetical themes of the Hexateuch from the second to the fourth centuries; see Frank Micheli's review, 'La "Typologie" biblique,' *Foi et Vie*, L [1952], 11–18, and cf. Micheli's interesting *L'Ancien Testament et l'Eglise chrétienne d'aujourd'hui*, Paris, 1957; another fine review of Daniélou's book—which appeared in 1951 as *Sacramentum Futuri*—was written by J. J. Allmen in *Verbum Caro*, no. 18 [1951], 99–101).

——— *Primitive Christian Symbols* (1961), trans. Donald Attwater. Baltimore, 1964 (see also his 'La Typologie d'Isaac dans le Christianisme Primitif,' *Biblica*, XXVIII, 1947, 363–93, and 'La Typologie Millenariste de la Semaine dans le Christianisme Primitif,' *Vergiliae Christianae*, II, 1949, 1–16; cf. Johannes Bornemann, *Die Taufe Christi durch Johannes in der dogmatischen Beurteilung der christlichen Theologen der ersten 4 Jahrhunderte*, Leipzig, 1896).

Dempsey, P. *De Principiis Exegeticis S. Bonaventurae*. Roma, 1945.

Devreese, R. *Essai sur Théodore de Mopsueste*. Rome, 1948.

Doignon, V. 'Le Salut par le Fer et le Bois chez Saint Irenée,' *Recherches de Science Religieuse*, XLIII (1955), 535–45.

Ellis, E. Earle. *Paul's Use of the Old Testament*. Edinburgh, 1957 (cf. Hans Leisegang's stimulating philosophical study of St. Paul in *Denken Formen*, Berlin, 1951).

Farges, J. *Les Idées Morales et Religieuses de Méthode d'Olympe*. Paris, 1929.

Figueroa, Gregory Francis. *The Church and the Synagogue in St. Ambrose*. Washington, D.C., 1949.

Folliet, G. 'La Typologie du Sabbat chez S. Augustin,' *Revue des Etudes Augustiniennes*, II (1956), 371–90 (see also: Y.-M. Duval, 'Saint Augustin et le Commentaire sur Jonas de Saint Jérôme,' *Revue des Etudes Augustiniennes*, XII [1966], 9–40; R. A. Markus, ' "Imago" and "Similitudo" in Augustine,' *Revue des Etudes Augustiniennes*, XI [1964], 125–43; J. Ries, 'La Bible chez S. Augustin et chez les

Manichéens,' Revue des Etudes Augustiniennes, IX [1963], 201–15; and C. van Crombrugghe, 'La Doctrine Christologique et Sotériologique de S. Augustin et ses Rapports avec le Néo-Platonisme,' Revue d'Histoire Ecclesiastique, V [1904], 237–57).

Funk, F. X., ed. Die Apostolischen Väter. Tübingen, 1901 (excerpts with introduction from various central early church writings, including the letters of Barnabas, Clement, and Polykarp, and fragments from Papias and Quadratus).

Hanson, Richard Patrick Crossland. Allegory and Event: A Study of the Sources and Significance of Origen's Interpretation of Scripture. Richmond, 1959 (relation of early Christian typology to Jewish liturgy).

Harnoch, Carl Gustav Adolf von. Der kirchengeschichtliche Ertrag der exegetischen Arbeiten des Origenes. 2 vols. Leipzig, 1918–19 (see further R. P. C. Hanson, Origen's Doctrine of Tradition, London, 1954).

Heinisch, Paul. Der Einfluss Philos auf die älteste christliche Exegese (Barnabas, Justin und Clemens von Alexandria). Münster, 1908.

Houssiau, Albert. La Christologie de Saint Irenée. Louvain, 1955.

Jordan, Hermann. Geschichte der altchristlichen Literatur. Leipzig, 1911.

Kellner, J. B. Der heilige Ambrosius, Bischof des Alten Mailand, als Erklärer des Altern Testaments. Washington, D.C., 1928.

Kelly, J. N. D. Early Christian Doctrines. New York, 1958 (well-known interpretation).

Kerrigan, Alexander. St. Cyril of Alexandria. Interpreter of the Old Testament. Rome, 1952.

Keyes, Gordon Lincoln. Christian Faith and the Interpretation of History: A Study of St. Augustine's Philosophy of History. Lincoln, 1966.

Ladner, Gerhart B. The Idea of Reform: Its Impact on Christian Thought and Action in the Age of the Fathers. Cambridge, 1959 (discussion of prophecy and typology).

Lampe, G. W. H. The Seal of the Spirit: A Study in the Doctrine of Baptism and Confirmation in the New Testament and the Fathers. London, 1951 (cf. I. Ijsebaert, Greek Baptismal Terminology: Its Origins and Early Development, Nijmegen, 1962).

Lawson, John. The Biblical Theology of Saint Irenaeus. London, 1948.

Llamas, J. 'S. Augustin y la multiplicad de sentides literales en la Sancta Escritura,' Religion y Cultura, XV (1931), 328–74.

Lubac, Henri de. Histoire et Esprit: L'Intelligence de l'Ecriture d'après Origène. Paris, 1950 (well-known and wide-ranging interpretation; see J. L. McKenzie's essay-review in Theological Studies, XII [1951], 365–81).

Malden, R. H. 'St. Ambrose as an Interpreter of Scripture,' Journal of Theological Studies, XVI (1915), 509–22 (general discussion of St. Ambrose's role in establishing various modes of spiritual—as opposed to historical—interpretation).

Maries, Louis. Etudes préliminaires à l'édition de Diodore de Tarse sur les Psaumes. Paris, 1933.

Massaux, Edouard. Influence de l'Evangile de Saint Matthieu sur la Littérature Chrétienne avant Saint Irenée. Louvain, 1950.

Milburn, Robert L. P. *Early Christian Interpretations of History.* London, 1954 (important study; see further W. Burghardt, 'On Early Christian Exegesis,' *Theological Studies*, IX [1950], 78–116).

Mondésert, Claude. *Essai sur Clément d'Alexandrie; introduction à l'étude de sa pensée religieuse à partir de l'Écriture.* Paris, 1944.

Ogara, F. 'De typica apud Chrysostomum prophetia,' *Gregorianum*, XXIV (1943), 62–77 (discussion of Antiochene and Alexandrian exegesis; see also Max L. W. Laistner, 'Antiochene Exegesis in Western Europe during the Middle Ages,' *Harvard Theological Review*, XL [1947], 19–29; and Wilhelm Bossuet, *Jüdisch-christlicher Schulbetrieb in Alexandria und Rom*, Göttingen, 1915).

Penna, Angelo. *Principi e carattere dell'esegesi di S. Gerolamo.* Rome, 1950.

Pépin, Jean. *Mythe et Allégorie.* Paris, 1958.

Plumpe, J. C. *Mater Ecclesia.* Washington, D.C., 1943.

Polman, Andries Derk Rietema. *The Word of God According to St. Augustine.* London, 1961.

Pontet, Maurice. *L'Exégèse de Saint Augustin Prédicateur.* Paris, 1947 (see also the exhaustive works by Pierre Courcelle, *Les Confessions de Saint Augustin dans la Tradition Littéraire*, Paris, 1963, and *Recherches sur les Confessions de Saint Augustin*, Paris, 1968).

Puech, Aimé. *Histoire de la Littérature Greque-Chrétienne.* 3 vols. Paris, 1928–30.

Quasten, Johannes. *Patrology.* 3 vols. Westminster, Md., 1962–

63 (see also Hans Freiherr Von Campenhausen, *The Fathers of the Greek Church*, trans. Stanley Godman, New York, 1959, and *Fathers of the Latin Church*, trans. Manfred Hoffman, Stanford, 1964).

—— 'Der gute Hirte in hellenisticher und frühchristlicher Logostheologie,' in *Heilige Ueberlieferung: Festgabe für Ildefons Herwegen*, Münster, 1938.

Rousseau, Olivier. 'La Typologie Augustinienne de l'Hexaeméron et la Théologie du Temps,' in *Festgabe Joseph Lortz*, eds. Erwin Iserloh and Peter Manns. 2 vols. Baden-Baden, 1958 (the essay appears in vol. II, entitled *Glaube und Gedichte*; see also in this volume Jean Daniélou, 'Comble du Mal et Eschatologie chez Grégoire de Nysse,' and Marie-Dominique Chenu, 'Histoire et Allégorie au Douzième Siècle'; in vol. I, entitled *Reformation: Shicksal und Auftrag*, see Otto A. Dilschneider, 'Christologische Verkündigung Heute'; see further Robert J. O'Connell, 'The Riddle of Augustine's Confessions: A Plotinian Key,' *International Philosophical Quarterly*, IV, [1964], 327–72).

Schlier, Heinrich. *Religiongeschichtliche Untersuchungen zu den Ignatiusbriefen.* Tübingen, 1929.

Steiner, M. *La Tentation de Jesus dans l'Interpretation Patristique de Saint Justin à Origène.* Paris, 1962.

Strauss, Gerhard. *Schriftgebrauch, Schriftauslegung und Schriftbeweis bei Augustin.* Tübingen, 1959.

Vaccari, Alberto. 'La Teoria esegetica della scuola antiochena,' *Scritti di Erudizione e di Filo-*

logia, I (1952), 101–42 (see further: R. M. Grant, 'The Bible of Theophilus of Antioch,' *Journal of Biblical Literature*, LXVI [1947], 173–96; J. David, 'Eclaircissements de Saint Athanase sur les Psaumes,' *Revue de l'Orient Chrétien*, XXIV [1924], 3–57; and A. Orbe, 'Teologia bautismal di Clemente Alejandrino,' *Gregorianum*, XXXVI [1955], 410–48).

Woollcombe, Kenneth John. 'The Biblical Origins and Patristic Development of Typology,' in *Essays on Typology*, Naperville, Ill., 1957 (Studies in Biblical Theology, No. 22; a clear and informed essay).

——— 'Le Sens de "Type" chez les Pères,' *La Vie Spirituelle*, LXXXIV (1951), 84–100 (special supplement).

3. Medieval Period

a. Representative Writers

Abelard, Peter (1079–1142).
Hymns and Sequences.

*Adam: drame anglo-normand de
XIIe siècle*, ed. Victor Lazarsche.
Tours, 1854.

Adam de Saint-Victor (12th C).
Liturgical Poetry, ed. Digby S.
Wrangham. 3 vols. London, 1881
(translated from the text of Leon
Gautier; see also Gautier's translation of Adam's *Oeuvres Poétiques* Paris, 1894; cf. C. E. Ham-
mond, *Liturgies Eastern and
Western, Being a Reprint of . . .
Representative Liturgies*, Oxford,
1876, and Harry Austin Wilson's
edition of the sources of the
Missal, *The Gelasian Sacramen-
tary, Liber Sacramentum Roma-
nae Ecclesia*, Oxford, 1894, as
well as his edition of the tenth-
century *Benedictional of Arch-
bishop Robert*, London, 1903,
vol. XXIV of the Henry Bradshaw Society Publications).

Adam of Dryburgh (12th C). *Interpretations [Allegoriae] of the
Holy Scripture* (exposition of the
fourfold method).

Alan of Lille (1114?–1202). *Eight
Sermons.*

Albert of Aix (Albertus Aaquensis;
12th C). *The History of Jerusalem* (see also the twelfth-century
work by John of Würzburg,
Description of the Holy Land,
and the histories of Jerusalem by
Fulcher of Chartres and Robert
the Monk).

St. Albert the Great (13th C).
Summa Theologiae.

Analecta Hymnica Medii Aevi, eds.
Clemens Blume and Guido M.
Dreves. 55 vols. Leipzig, 1886–
1922.

Anselm of Laon (11th C). *Commentary on the Song of Songs*

(cf. Alcuin's eighth-century *Compendium on the Song of Songs*).

—— *Glossa Ordinaria* (also attributed to Walafrid Strabo, 9th century).

Bach, Adolf, ed. *Das Rheinische Marienlob: Eine Deutsche Dichtung des 13. Jahrhunderts.* Leipzig, 1934 (vol. CCLXXXI of *Bibliothek des literarischen Vereins in Stuttgart Sitz Tübingen*).

Bernard of Clairvaux (1090–1153). *In Praise of the New Knight* (see also his *Sermons on the Saints* and *Sermons on the Advent of Our Lord*; and cf. Gabriel Biel's fourteenth-century *Canonis Misse Expositio*, eds. H. A. Oberman and W. J. Courtenay, 4 vols., Wiesbaden, 1963–67).

St. Bonaventure (13th C). *Breviloquium*.

—— *The Journey of the Mind to God*.

St. Bruno of Chartreux (11th C). *Commentary on the Psalms*.

D'Evelyn, Charlotte, ed. *Meditations on the Life and Passion of Christ*. E.E.T.S., o.s. 158. London, 1921 (compendium of medieval religious lyrics; see also Edward T. Weatherly's edition of fifteenth-century English sermons, *Speculum Sacerdotale*, E.E.T.S., n.s. 200, London, 1936).

Ezzo (11th C). *Gesang von den Wundern Christi* (ca. 1065), ed. K. A. Barak. Strassburg, 1879 (also in vol. XV of *Denkmäler deutscher Poesie und Prosa aus dem 8.–12. Jahrhundert*, eds. Karl Müllenhoff and W. Scherer, Ebend, 1864; other aspects of Ezzo's poetry are reprinted—and discussed—in Konrad A. Hoffmann, *Ueber den Ezzoleich*, München, 1871; Johann Kelle,

Die Quelle von Ezzos Gesang, Vienna, 1893 [vol. CXXIX, no. 1, of the Viennese Akademie der Wissenschaft]; and W. Mettin, *Die Composition des Ezzoleichs*, Halle, 1892; see further Heinrich von Meissen, *Frauenlob, Kreuzes Leich, Leiche, Sprüche, Streitgedichte und Lieder* [ca. 1318], ed. Ludwig Ettmüller, Amsterdam, 1966, and *Die Gedichte des Wilden Mannes und Wernhers vom Niederrhein*, ed. Karl Köhn, *Schriften zur Germanischen Philologie*, no. 6, Berlin, 1891).

Gerson, Jean Charlier de (1363–1429). *De Sensu Litterali Sacrae Scripturae*, in *Oeuvres Complètes*, ed. P. Glorieux, vol. III. Paris, 1962.

Greene, Richard Leighton, ed. *The Early English Carols*. Oxford, 1935 (see, for example: 'Lo, Moises bush shynynge unbrent,' 'O fayre Rachel semely in syght,' 'O strong Judith,' 'O ardent busche that did not wast,' 'O flamed busshe withoute leasure,' 'This is Gedeonys wulle-felle,' and 'Thow art eke the flees of Gedeon').

Guibert of Nogent (late 11th–early 12th C). *The Acts of God Accomplished by the Franks* (or Crusaders; Jerusalem of the Crusades is the literal fulfillment of the prophecies, which therefore no longer need be interpreted allegorically; see also the writings of Bernard of Clairvaux and Baudry of Dol—especially the latter's *History of Jerusalem*—and Guilelmus of Tyre's *History of the Deeds Accomplished Overseas*, which sums up the earlier typological views on the Crusades).

—— *Interpretations [Allegoriae] of the Entire Holy Scripture*.

Honorius of Autun (Honorius Augustodunensis, 12th C). *Exposition on Canticles* (first medieval author to give a fourfold interpretation of the Canticles).

———. *The Seal of Blessed Mary*.

Hrabanus Maurus (or Rabanus; 9th C). *De Universo* (see also his *Commentary on the Epistle to the Galatians*).

——— *Interpretations* [*Allegoriae*] *on the Holy Scripture* (false attribution, but known under his name through the Middle Ages; a dictionary of symbolic meanings which influenced several important similar medieval undertakings: by Alanus de Insulis in the twelfth century [*Distinctiones*]; in the thirteenth century by Bartholemeus Anglicus [*De propietatibus rerum*] and Berchorius [*Reportorium*, and *Reductorium morale*]; and by John Bromyard in the fifteenth century [*Summa praedicantium*]).

Hugh of St. Cher (12th C). *Marginalia* [*Postilla*] *on the Whole Bible in accordance with the Four Senses of Scripture* (important source for medieval literary works).

Hugh of St. Victor (12th C). *On the Sacraments* (see also his *Commentary on Colossians*).

——— *On Scripture and the Sacred Writers* (revived the threefold division of scriptural interpretation, whereby typical significance is characteristic of Scripture as distinguished from all other books).

John of Salisbury (12th C). *Policraticus* (important political treatise).

John the Scot (9th C). *Commentary on St. John* (twofold division into the typical and the symbolic).

Leidrad of Lyons (8th C). *On the Sacrament of Baptism*.

Leyser, Herman, ed. *Deutsche Predigten des XIII. und XIV. Jahrhunderts*. Leipzig, 1834 (see also Franz Karl Grieshaber, ed., *Deutsche Predigten des XIII. Jahrhunderts*, Stuttgart, 1844; and Karl Roth, ed., *Deutsche Predigten des XII. und XIII. Jahrhunderts*, Quedlinburg, 1839, vol. XI, Part I of *Bibliothek der Gesammten Deutschen National-Literatur von der ältesten bis auf die neuere Zeit*).

Lutz, J. and P. Perdrizet, eds. *Speculum Humanae Salvationis* (1448). 4 vols. Meininger, 1907–09 (cf. *The Miroure of Mans Salvacionne*, "Printed from a manuscript . . . of Alfred H. Huth," n.p. [London?], 1888).

Mirkus, Joannes (15th C). *A Festial: A Collection of Homilies* (1486), ed. Theodor Erbe. E.E.T.S., e.s., XCVI. London, 1905.

Mügeln, Heinrich von (fl. 1346–69). *Der Meide Kranz*, ed. W. Jahn. Leipzig, 1908 (see also the text and commentaries on Heinrich von Laufenberg's *Buch der Figuren* [1441] in Lidwina Boll, *Heinrich Laufenberg, Lieddichter des 15. Jahrhunderts*, Düsseldorf, 1934; and Edward Richard Müller, *Heinrich Laufenberg, eine Litterar-historische Untersuchung*, Berlin, 1889).

Nicolas of Lyra (14th C). *Holy Bible with Glossary* (widely used 'moralia').

St. Paschasius Radbertus of Corbie (9th C). *The Book of the Body and Blood of the Lord* (clearest among his contemporaries in insisting upon the literal sense).

——— *Commentary on Lamentations*.

Peter Lombard (Petrus Lombardus, 12th C). *Glossa Psalterii*.

Peter of Poitiers (12th C). *Histori-cal Compendium on the Gene-alogy of Christ.*

Petrus Comestor (12th C). *Histo-ria Scholastica* (major 'history of the world').

St. Pietro Damiani (11th C). *Ser-mon 57.*

Rupertus of Deutz (12th C). *On the Glory and Honor of the Son of Man according to Matthew.*

Sachs, Hans (1494–1576). *Hans Sachs* (Complete Works with bibliography), ed. Adelbert von Keller. 26 vols. Tübingen, 1870–1908 (see, for example: *Die Oppferung Isaac* [1533], *Der Ertz-patriarch Abraham . . . ein figur Jesu Christ* [1545], and *Figur des Thuren zu Babel* [n.d.]).

St. Thomas Aquinas (13th C). 'The Literal Truth of History Must be Maintained as Axio-matic,' in *Summa Theologiae* (see also *Commentary on Sen-tences*).

——— *Quaestiones quodlibetales* (detailed consideration of the different senses of Scripture).

Vogelweide, Walter von. *Leich,* ed. C. von Kraus. Berlin, 1936 (cf. the work of this famous twelfth-century poet with the contempo-raneous *Das Marienleben des Schweizers Wernher,* ed. Max Päpke, Berlin, 1920, in *Deutsche Texte des Mittelalters, Preussi-schen Akademie der Wissen-schaften,* vol. XXVII; and Wileram's translation of the twelfth-century renditions of Canticles, *Das Hohe Lied,* Wien, 1864; for later German works in this tradition, see: *Der Marner* [1231–67], ed. Philip Strauch, Strassburg, 1876, vol. XIV of *Quellen und Forschungen zur . . . Kulturgeschichte;* Konrad

von Würzburg [d. 1287], *Die Goldene Schmeide,* ed. Edward Schroeder, Göttingen, 1926; the twelfth- and thirteenth-century manuscripts, such as 'De esau et iacob,' in Friedrich Keinz, 'Mit-theilungen aus der Münchener kön. Bibliothek;' *Germania,* XXXI [1886], 57–93; the au-thoritative collection by Phillip Wackernagel, *Das Deutsche Kirchenlied von der ältesten Zeit bis zu Anfang des XVII. Jahr-hunderts,* 5 vols., Leipzig, 1864–77 [vol. 5, eds. Otto and Ernst Wackernagel]; the fifteenth-cen-tury poetry of Herman von Sachsenheim, *Jesus der Arzt,* ed. Ernest Martin, Tübingen, 1878; and, also from the fifteenth cen-tury, Muskatblüt, *Lieder* [espe-cially 'Marienlieder'], ed. E. von Groote, Cöln, 1852).

b. Twentieth-Century Criticism

Bischoff, Bernard. 'Wendepunkte in der Geschichte der lateinische Exegese im Frühmittelalter,' *Sacris Erudiri,* V (1954), 189–281 (an informed survey of the repercussions of the clash be-tween Antiochene and Alexan-drian exegesis during the Middle Ages; cf. Albert Siegmund, *Die Uberlieferung der Griechischen Christlichen Literatur in der lateinischen Kirche,* München, 1949).

Breitenlach, Edgar. *Speculum Hu-manae Salvationis: Eine typens-geschichtliche Untersuchung.* Strassburg, 1950.

Cabrol, Fernand. *Liturgical Prayer. Its History and Spirit,* trans. 'by a Benedictine of Stanbrook.' London, 1922.

Chenu, Marie D. *Introduction à l'étude de St. Thomas d'Aquin.* Montreal, 1954.

Delhaye, Philippe. 'Le Sens Littéral

et le Sens Allegorique du Micro-cosmus de Geoffroy de Saint-Victor (Paris manuscrits latins 14515 et 14881),' *Recherches de Théologie Ancienne et Médié-vale*, XIV (1949), 155–60.

Ebeling, Gerhard. 'The Hermeneu-tical Locus of the Doctrine of God in Peter Lombard and Thomas Aquinas,' *Journal of Theology and the Church*, III (1967), 70–111 (see also J. Van der Ploeg's interesting 'The Place of Holy Scripture in the Theol-ogy of St. Thomas,' *The Thom-ist*, X [1947], 398–422).

Glorieux, Palémon. *Répertoire des maitres en Théologie de Paris en XIIIe siècle*. Paris, 1933.

Gribomont, J. 'Le Lieu des Deux Testaments selon la Théologie de S. Thomas. Notes sur le Sens Spirituel et Implicite des Saintes Ecritures,' *Ephemerides Theolo-gicae Lovanienses*, XXII (1946), 70–89 (see further: C. Spicq, 'L'Ecriture et S. Thomas,' *Bulle-tin Thomiste*, VIII [1947–53], 210–21; M. D. Mailhiot, 'La Pensée de S. Thomas sur le Sens Spirituel,' *Revue Thomiste*, LIX [1959], 613–63; and P. Synave, 'La Doctrine de S. Thomas d'Aquin sur le sens Litteral des Ecritures,' *Revue Biblique* [XXXV], 1926, 40–65).

Hahn, Fritz. 'Zur Hermeneutik Gersons,' *Zeitschrift für Theolo-gie und Kirche*, LI (1954), 34–50 (see also G. H. M. Posthumus Meyjes, *Jean Gerson, Zijn Kerk-politik en Ecclesiologie*, The Hague, 1963; and cf.: Rudolf Haubst, *Die Christologie des Nikolaus Von Kues* [1401–64], Freiburg, 1956; Frank Rosenthal, 'Heinrich von Oyta and Biblical Criticism in the Fourteenth Cen-tury,' *Speculum*, XXV [1950], 178–83; and Marie D. Chenu,

La *Théologie au Douzième Siècle*, Paris, 1957).

Hopper, Vincent F. *Medieval Num-ber Symbolism*. New York, 1938.

Jacobs, Hans Haiman. 'Studien über Gerhard von Reichersberg,' *Zeitschrift für Kirchengeschichte*, L (1931), 315–77.

Kamlach, Wilhelm. *Apokalypse und Geschichtstheologie. Die Mittelalterliche Auslegung der Apokalypse vor Joachim von Fiore*. Berlin, 1935 (an interest-ing study, originally a Göttingen dissertation, published as a monograph, no. 285 of *Histo-rische Studien*; cf.: Josef Anton Endres, *Honorius Augustodunen-sis. Beitrag zur Geschichte des geistigen Lebens im 12. Jahrhun-dert*, München, 1906; Hans Lie-berschütz, *Das Allegorische Weltbild der Heiligen Hildegard von Bingen*, Leipzig, 1930; Alois Dempf, *Sacrum Imperium: Ge-schichts-und Staatsphilosophie des Mittelalters und der Politi-schen Renaissance*, München, 1929; and Marjorie Reeves' au-thoritative *The Influence of Prophecy in the Later Middle Ages: A Study in Joachinism*, Oxford, 1969).

Kantorowicz, Ernst H. *The King's Two Bodies: A Study in Medi-aeval Political Theology*. Prince-ton, 1957 (major study; see also his *Laudes Regiae: A Study in Liturgical Acclamations and Medieval Ruler Worship*. Berke-ley, 1958; and cf. his 'The Carol-ingian King in the Bible of Sao Paola Fuori la Mura,' *Late Clas-sical and Medieval Studies in Honor of A. M. Friend*, Prince-ton, 1955, and Hans Lieber-schütz's analysis of Policraticus in *Medieval Humanism in the Life and Writings of John of Salis-bury*, Nendeln, 1968).

Kehoe, Richard. 'The Spiritual Sense of Scripture,' *Blackfriars*, XXVII (1946), 246–51 (excellent summary).

Liebner, Carl Theodore Albert. *Hugo von St. Victor, und die theologischen Richtungen seiner Zeiten.* Leipzig, 1832.

Lubac, Henri de. *Corpus Mysticum: L'Eucharistie et l'Eglise au Moyen Age, étude historique.* Paris, 1944.

—— *Exégèse Médiévale: Les Quatre Sens de L'Ecriture.* 4 vols. Paris, 1959–64 (detailed and authoritative).

Maan, P. J. 'Nicolas le Gros als Exeget,' *Internazionalen Kirchlichen Zeitschrift*, LVII (1949), 96–106.

McNally, Robert E. *The Bible in the Early Middle Ages.* (Woodstock Papers, No. 4). Westminster, Md., 1959.

—— 'Medieval Exegesis,' *Theological Studies*, XXII (1961), 445–54.

Oberman, Heiko A. 'Quo Vadis? Tradition from Irenaeus to Humani Generis,' *Scottish Journal of Theology*, XVI (1963), 225–55.

Pepin, Jean. 'S. Augustin et la Fonction Propretique de l'Allégorie,' *Recherches Augustiniennes*, I (1958), 243–86.

Pfannmüller, Ludwig. *Frauenlobs Marienleich.* Strassburg, 1913 (cf. R. Röhricht, 'Die Pilgerfahrtan nach dem Heiligen Lande vor den Kreuzzügen,' *Historisches Taschenbuch*, V [1875], 321–96).

Ratzinger, J. *Die Geschichtstheologie des heiligen Bonaventura.* München, 1959.

Salmon, Pierre. *Les 'Tituli Psalmorum' des Manuscrits Latins.*

Roma, 1959 (manuscripts with commentaries from major European centers—Florence, Dublin, Madrid, London, Zurich, the Vatican—from the eighth to the twelfth centuries; the Introduction discusses the treatment of Psalms among the Church Fathers).

Schmidt, Gerhard. *Die Armenbibeln des XIV. Jahrhunderts.* Groz-Köln, 1959 (see also Richard Sensche, *Über den Stil bei dem Alemannischen Anonymen Prediger aus dem XIII Jahrhunderts.* Berlin, 1897 (cf. Antoine Linsenmayer's secular study, *Geschichte der Predigt in Deutchland von Karl dem Grossen bis zum Ausgange des Vierzehnten Jahrhunderts*, München, 1886; the philological commentaries by Jacques Trénel, *L'Ancien Testament et la Langue Française du Moyen Age* (VIIIᵉ– XVᵉ Siècle), Paris, 1904, and by Otto Behagel, *Der Heiland und die Altsächsische Genesis*, Halle, 1922).

Seiferth, Wolfgang. *Synagoge und Kirche im Mittelalter.* München, 1964.

Smalley, Beryl. *The Study of the Bible in the Middle Ages.* Oxford, 1941 (comprehensive and illuminating survey and analysis).

Spicq, Ceslaus. *Esquisse d'une Histoire de l'Exégèse Latine au Moyen Age.* Paris, 1944.

Stegmüller, Friedrich. *Reportorium Biblicum Medii Aevi.* 7 vols. Madrid, 1950–61 (esp. vols. II– V; cf. Wilhelm Preger, *Geschichte der deutschen Mystik im Mittelalter*, 3 vols., Leipzig, 1874–93).

Wilmart, André. 'Les Allégories sur l'Ecriture attribuées à Raban Maur,' *Revue Bénédictine*, XXXII (1920), 47–56.

4. Reformation and Renaissance

a. Representative Writers

The emphasis is upon Protestant works before 1660. I have tried also to represent the use of typology by Catholic poets and theologians and to demonstrate the continuing interest in the subject from 1660 to 1700 (as in the political poems, tracts, and sermons of Restoration England). Typology plays only a minor part in the travel literature of the period relating to the Holy Land, and I have accordingly excluded such works as Thomas Fuller's A *Pisgah-Sight of Palestine* (London, 1630), though many of them do make at least some use of figuralism.

Here as elsewhere, I have not listed most of the literary works treated in the literary analyses in Section 7 (e). It may be worth noting again, therefore, that the figural method is adopted by writers of varying theological convictions: e.g., the Anglican John Cleveland (*Poems*, ed. Brian Morris and Eleanor Withington, Oxford, 1967); the Puritan Andrew Marvell (*Poems and Letters*, ed. H. M. Margoliouth, 2 vols., Oxford, 1952); the mystic Thomas Traherne (*Centuries, Poems, and Thanksgivings*, ed. H. M. Margoliouth, Oxford, 1958); and the Catholic Richard Crashaw (*Poems*, ed. L. C. Martin, Oxford, 1957; for a denial of typology in Crashaw, however, see George W. Williams, *Image and Symbol in the Sacred Poetry of Richard Crashaw*, Columbia, S.C., 1963). It seems clear that a comparative study of these poets would yield very interesting results. A study of this kind might also include the satiric or parodistic uses of typology in the poetry of the period. In any case, the student should be aware that typology lent itself not only to the traditionalist modes of, say, George Herbert (e.g., *The Temple* [1633], in

Works, éd. F. E. Hutchinson, Oxford, 1953), but to profane inversions which mock the scriptural context. Thus John Wilmot, the Earl of Rochester, celebrates the carpe diem theme in 'Upon Drinking in a Bowl' (Poems, ed. Vivian de Sola Pinto, Cambridge, Mass., 1953) by figurally invoking the concepts of the covenants, the Eucharist, the Conversion of the Jews, baptism (e.g., via Bacchus-Noah, flood-Jordan, etc.), and, perhaps, the millennium. Because critics have not examined this technique sufficiently, it may be instructive to quote part of the lyric (ll. 17–24), with a selective glossary:

> But carve thereon a spreading
>   Vine
>   [cf. Rev. 14:18];
> Then add two lovely Boys
>   [cf. Matt. 18:19–20, 22:40];
> Their limbs in amorous Folds
>   intwine
>   [cf. Jer. 23:3],
> The Type of future Joys
>   [cf. Rom. 5, Heb. 9–11].
>
> Cupid and Bacchus my Saints are
>   [cf. Philemon 7; Rev. 17:6,
>   18:24],
> May Drink and Love still reign
>   [cf. Rev. 22:5]:
> With Wine I wash away my
>   Cares
>   [cf. Rev. 1:5],
> And then to Love again.

Abbott, John. Jesus Prefigured: Or a Poem of the Holy Name. Antwerp, 1607 (cf. Thomas Washbourne, Divine Poems, London, 1654).

Ainsworth, Henry. Annotations Upon the Five Bookes of Moses; The Book of the Psalmes, And the Song of Songs, Or Canticles. London, 1627 (many editions; extensive use of Jewish commentaries; important Separatist statement; cf. further the commentaries on the Pentateuch by

Augustin de Quiros, Ludguni, 1623, and William Attersol, London, 1618, on Moses).

—— Defence of the Holy Scriptures. Amsterdam, 1609.

Alabaster, William. Apparatvs in Revelationem Iesv Christi. Antwerp, 1607.

Alard, Lambert. Pathologia Sacra Novi Testamenti. Lipsiae, 1635.

Alsted, Johann Heinrich. The Beloved City, trans. William Burton, London, 1643 (typological-millenarian tract by this well-known Ramist, originally published as Diatribe de Mille Annis Apocalypticis, Frankfurt, 1627 [translated into German in 1630 and discussed at length in Thomas Hayne, Christ's Kingdom on Earth, Opened According to the Scriptures, London, 1645]; see further Alsted's Theologia Prophetica, n.p., 1622, and his Thesaurus Chronologiae, n.p., 1628; for similar works in the same tradition, see: William Alexander, Doomes-Day [1614], ed. L. E. Kaster and H. B. Charlton, Edinburgh, 1929 [vol. XXIV, n.s., of the Scottish Text Society]; Richard Bentley, Of Revelation and the Messias, London, 1696; John Brayne, Babels Fall, London, 1649, and The New Earth, London, 1653; Mary Cary, The Little Horns Doom and Downfall, London, 1651; Isaac Craven, The New Paradise of God, London, 1658; John Dell, A Voyce from the Temple, London, 1658; M. Marsin, The Near Approach of Christ's Kingdom, London, 1696; Henry More, Apocalypsis Apocalypseos, London, 1680; John Napier, A Plaine Discovery of . . . Revelation, London, 1593 [at least 23 editions by 1700]; Dorothy White, A Trumpet of the Lord of Hosts [n.p.], 1662; for the polemic against these views, see: Robert Baillie, *A Dissuasive from the Errours of the Time*, London, 1645; Joseph Hall, *The Revelation Unrevealed*, London, 1650; Thomas Hall, *A Confutation*, London, 1653; and Alexander Petrie, *Chiastriomastix, Or, The Prophecies . . . Vindicated from the misinterpretations of the Millenaries*, Amsterdam, 1644).

Altenstaig, Johannes. *Vocabularius Theologiae*. Hagenan, 1517.

Ames, William. *The Marrow of Theology* (1629; 3rd edn.), trans. John Eusden. Boston, 1968 (standard Puritan text; see Eusden's comments on typology in his valuable introduction to this volume; see also Ames' *Fresh Suit Against Human Ceremonies in God's Worship*, London, 1633).

Andrewes, Lancelot. *Sermons*, ed. G. M. Story. Oxford, 1967 (see especially Sermon 2 on the Passion [1604], Sermon 5 on the Nativitie [1610], Sermon 11 on the Nativitie [1616], and Sermon 17 on the Resurrection [1623]; other sermon collections that reveal Andrewes' typology include the edition by John Parkinson, *Ninety-Six Sermons*, Oxford, 1841–43 [where see especially *Seven Sermons on the Wonderful Combat, for God's Glory and Man's Salvation, Between Christ and Satan*, 1592], as well as T. S. Kepler's edition of *The Private Devotions*, New York, 1956, and *Sermons on the Nativity* [editor not given], Grand Rapids, Michigan, 1955).

Bacmeister, Lucas. *Explicatio Typorum V. T. Christum Adumbrantium*. Lubecae, 1604.

Ballie, Robert. *Satan the Leader . . . to All Who Resist the Redemption of Sion*. London, 1643.

Baumann, Andreas. *Exercitum Academicum*. Jenae, 1685.

Baxter, Richard. *A Paraphrase on the New Testament*. London, 1685 (see also his *Glorious Kingdom of Christ*, London, 1691).

Beard, Thomas. *Antichrist the Pope of Rome*. London, 1625.

Bellus, Thomas. *Roma Restituta*. Glascow, 1672

Bernard, Richard. *The Seaven Golden Candlesticks*. London, 1621.

Beverly, Thomas. *Pattern of the Divine Temple*. London, 1689 (see also his *Grand Apocalyptical Vision*, London, 1689, his *Prophetical History of the Reformation*, London, 1689, and his *Thousand Year Kingdom*, London, 1691).

Beza, Theodore. *Iobis . . . Illustratus*. London, 1589 (see also his *In Epistolam D. Pauli ad Galatus, notae*, Geneva, 1578).

Bishop, George. *The Burden of Babylon*. London, 1661.

Blackwood, Christopher. *Expositions and Sermons upon . . . Matthew*. London, 1659.

Blake, Thomas. *Vindiciae Faederis; Or, A Treatise of the Covenant*. London, 1653 (cf. George Downame, *The Covenant of Grace*, London, 1647).

Boehme, Jacob. *Mysterium Magnum: or An Exposition of the First Book of Moses Called Genesis* (1623), ed. C.J.B., transl. John Sparrow. London, 1965 (highly influential mystical-topological exegesis).

Bonus, Jacobus. *De Vita et Gestis Christi*. Rome, 1526 (detailed figural comparison between Christ and Hercules).

Boteler, Edward. *Jus Poli et Fori:*

or, God and the King. London, 1661.

Boyssieres, Jean de. Les Troisièmes Oeuvres Poétiques. Lyons, 1579 (see also: Guillaume Du Peyrat [or Dupeyrat], Hymne de la Trinité, Paris, 1587; and the collections of poetry by Jean Bertant [ed. A. Chenevière, Paris, 1891], Gabrielle de Coignard [Tournon, 1595], J. Dary du Perron [Paris, 1622], and Amadis Jamyn, especially his Le Second Volume des Oeuvres, Paris, 1584).

Bradshaw, William. A Preparation to . . . the Sacrament. London, 1617.

Brenius, Daniel (Daniel Van Breen). Breves in Vetus & Novum Testamentum Annotationes, in Opera Theologica, Part II, Amsterdam, 1666.

Brerewood, Edward. A Learned Treatise of the Sabaoth. Oxford, 1630.

Bridges, Francis [F. B.]. Gods Treasurie Displayed. London, 1630.

Brightman, Thomas. A Commentary on the Canticles. London, 1644 (see also his commentary on Daniel [Basel, 1614]).

—— A Revelation of the Revelation. Amsterdam, 1615 (one of the most influential of such commentaries).

Brinsley, John. The Mystical Brasen Serpent. London, 1652.

Broughton, Hugh. Concent of Scripture. London, 1591 (see also his Texts of Scripture, London, 1591, and his explications of Revelation, London, 1609, and Jeremiah, n.p., 1608; and cf.: Johann Philipson [Sleidanus], De Quatuor summis imperiis, Ludguni-Batavorum, 1631; Robert

Rollock, In Librum Danielis Prophetae Commentarius, Edinburgh, 1591; Henry Archer, The Personal Reign of Christ Upon Earth, London, 1642 [an extremist millenarian work]; and William Greenhill, Exposition of . . . Ezekiel, 5 vols., London, 1645–62; the Fifth-Monarchy tradition is represented in different ways by John Rogers, Sagrir: or Doomes-day drawing nigh, London, 1653, by John Tillinghast, Knowledge of the Times, London, 1654, and by Robert Maton, Israels Redemption, London, 1642).

Broughton, Lucas. A Letter . . . Tovching Mordochai His Age. London, 1590.

Brunsell, Samuel. Solomons Blessed Land. London, 1660.

Bullinger, Heinrich. Isaias excellentissimus Dei propheta . . . expositus. Zurich, 1567 (see also James Pilkington, A Godlie Exposition vpon certaine chapters of Nehemiah, Cambridge, 1585, and the famous Johannes Winkelmann's Commentarius in XII Prophetas Minores, Frankfort, 1603).

Bunyan, John. Divine Emblems, or, Temporal Things Spiritualized. Philadelphia, 1808 (best early edition of this widely-read work; originally published as A Book for Boys and Girls: or Country Rhimes for Children, By J. B., n.p., 1686; the title Divine Emblems appears in all editions after that of London, 1724, in which the 74 meditations of the original edition are reduced to 49, with many modifications in the text).

—— Solomon's Temple Spiritualized. London, 1688 (see also Thomas Beverly, Pattern of the Divine Temple, London, 1689).

Burroughs, Jeremiah. Sions Joy.

London, 1641 (see also his *Exposition of the prophecie of Hosea*, London, 1643).

Burton, Henry. *A Vindication of Churches Commonly Called Independent*. London, 1644 (typological dispute on toleration; cf. Thomas Edwards' anti-toleration treatise, *The Casting Down of the Last and Strongest Hold of Satan*, London, 1647).

Calamy, Edmund. *The Godly Mans Ark*. London, 1657.

Calfhill, James. *An Answer to John Martiall's Treatise of the Cross*. London, 1565 (valuable on Samson as type of Christ; see further in this connection John Donne's *Biathanatos*, ed. J. William Hebel, New York, 1930).

Calovius, Abraham. *Systema Locorum Theologicorum*. Witebergae, 1655 (Lutheran controversialist and literalist).

Calvin, Jean. *Commentary on Hebrews in Commentaries*, ed. David W. and Thomas F. Torrance. Grand Rapids, Mich., 1960 (cf. Martin Butzer [Bucer], *Metaphrasis et enarratio in epist. D. Pauli Apostoli ad Romanos*, Basilae, 1562).

—— *Institutes of the Christian Religion*, ed. John T. McNeill, trans. F. L. Battles. 8 vols. Philadelphia, 1960 (see especially Books I and II).

Canne, John. *A Necessity of Separation from the Church of England Proved by the Nonconformists Principles* (1634), ed. Charles Stead. London, 1849 (see also Canne's popular 1662 edition of the Bible, with marginalia).

—— *A Voice from the Temple*. London, 1653.

Cartwright, Thomas. *Harmonia Evangelica*. Amsterdam, 1647.

Caryl, Joseph. *An Exposition . . . upon the book of Job*. 12 vols. London, 1644–69.

—— *Heaven and Earth Embracing; or God and man approaching*. London, 1645.

Casaubon, Meric. *A Treatise Concerning Enthusiasme, as It is an Effect of Nature: but is mistaken by many for either Divine Inspiration, or Diabolicall Possession*. London, 1656 (2nd edn.; condemns the mixture of figural exegesis with mystical or 'falsely supernaturall effects'; for another important example of this attack on excessive 'inspirational' figuralism, see Henry More, *Enthusiasmus Triumphatus, or, a Discourse of the Nature . . . and Cure, of Enthusiasme*, London, 1658 [first edn., 1655], which equates 'Mystical interpretations of Scripture,' with 'Quakings, and Visions' as a 'delusion' stemming from 'Melancholy'; cf. More's *Conjectura Cabbalistica*, London, 1653).

Castellio, Sebastian. *Concerning Heretics* (1554), trans. and ed. Roland Bainton. New York, 1935 (Italian Protestant; typological argument for toleration; see also Jacobus Acontius, *Stratagematum Satanae*, Basiliae, 1565).

Cawdrey, Robert. *A Treasvrie or Storehovse of Similes*. London, 1600.

Cerisiers, René de [Ceriziers]. *Joseph, ou la providence divine*. Paris, 1642.

Chappuys, Gabriel. *Figures de la Bible*. Lyons, 1582.

Chasteuil, L. Galaup de. *Imitations des Pseaumes de la Pénitence Royalles*. Paris, 1597 (see further Pietro Aretino [Pierre l'Aretin], *Les VII Psalmes de la Pénitence de David*, trans. F. de Rosset, Paris, 1605; and Phillipe Duppless-Mornay [or Phillipe de Mornay], *Méditations Christiennes sur Quatre Pseaumes du Prophète David*, n.p., 1591).

Chytraeus, David. *Enarratio in Apocalypsin*. Vitabergae, 1575 (see also his commentaries on Numbers and Joshua [1575], on Genesis [1568], on Leviticus [1575], and on Esther and John [1589]).

Clapham, Henoch. *A Briefe of the Bible, drawne first into English Poesy, and then illustrated by apte Annotations*. Edinburgh, 1596.

Cocceius, Johannes. *Summa Doctrinae de Foedere et Testamento Dei*. Leyden, 1648 (see more generally his *Opera Anecdota*, 2 vols., Amsterdam, 1706).

—— *Summa Theologiae ex Scripturis Repetita*. Geneva, 1662 (leader of the covenant school and hence a key figure in the development of 'federalist typology'; other important names and titles in this tradition include: Johann Braun, *Doctrina Foederum*, Amsterdam, 1688, and *Oratorio de Sapientia Veterum Hebraeorum*, Groningae, 1681; François Burmann, *Synopsis Theologiae & speciatum oeconomiae foedorum Dei*, Amsterdam, 1699; Anton Driessen, *Dissertatio Philologico-Critica*, Groningae, 1774 [see also his anti-Arminian tract of 1733]; Nicolas Gürtler, *Templariorum*, Amsterdam, 1690, and *Vocum Typico-Propheticarum brevis explicatio*, n.p., 1715 [in Hebrew and Latin, 2nd edn.]; Wilhelmus Momma, *De Varia Conditione et Statu Dei sub triplici oeconomia*, 3 vols., Amsterdam, 1694 [3rd edn.; the three states are those of the Patriarchs, the Old Testament, and the New Testament]; see also, in this tradition, the works

of the Pietist George Bellersheim).

Coppin, Richard. *Saul Smitten*. London, 1653 (correlative typology; see also the political discussions by John Caryl, *Davids Prayer for Solomon*, London, 1643, Robert Harris, *Hezekiah's Recoverie*, in *Works*, London, 1635, and John Warner, *The Devilish Conspiracy*, London, 1648).

Cornwell, Francis. *A Description of the Spirituall Temple*. London, 1646 (see also William Chub, *Two fruitfull and godly Sermons . . . touching . . . God's Temple*, London, 1585, and Samuel Lee, *Orbis Miraculum, or the Temple of Solomon*, London, 1659).

Costus, Petrus. *Typvs Messiae Et Christi Domini ex Veterum Prophetarum Praesensionibus Contra Iudaeorum*. Lvgdvni, 1554.

Cowper, William. *Three Heavenly Treatises, concerning Christ*. London, 1612.

Crisp, Stephen. *A Short History of a Long Travel From Babylon to Bethel*. London, 1694 (Quaker work; see also the Quaker Thomas Green's *A Declaration to the World, of my . . . Journey out of Aegypt . . . from Pharoah*, London, 1659; and cf. Thomas Raymond [1610?–81], *Autobiography*, ed. G. Davies, London, 1917).

Crocus, Cornelius. *Comoedia Sacra, cui titulus Ioseph, ad Christianae inventis institutionem iuxta locus inventionis, veterem artem*. Argentinae, 1537.

Daneau, Lambert. *Symboli Apostoliei Explicatio*. Geneva, 1592.

Dawbeny, Henry. *Historie and Policie Re-viewed*. London, 1659.

Denison, Stephen. *The Doctrine of Both the Sacraments . . . Baptisme and the Svpper of the Lord.* London, 1621.

Dickson, David. *Treatise on the Promises.* Dublin, 1630.

Diodati, John. *Pious and Learned Annotations upon the Holy Bible.* London, 1648 (several editions; interesting regarding use of Cabbala with typology; see also Louis Cappel [Ludovicus Cappellus], *Commentarii et Notae Criticae in Vetus Testamentum,* Amsterdam, 1689, and Samuel Clarke, *The Old and New Testaments, with annotations and parallel scriptures,* London, 1690; and cf. John Downame, *The summe of sacred diuinitie,* London, 1630, and Conrad Dietericus [Dietrich], *Analysis Evangelicorum,* n.p., 1631).

Donne, John. Sermons 2, 3, and 7 in vol. II of *The Sermons,* ed. E. M. Simpson and G. R. Potter. Berkeley, 1962 (see also, in vol. IX, sermon 9 and the great Christmas sermon for 1621, as well as 'The First Anniversary' and 'A Valediction: of the Booke,' in *Poetical Works,* ed. H. J. C. Grierson, Oxford, 1929).

Durand de Saint-Pourçain, Guillaume. *Commentaria in IV Libros Sententiarum.* Lyon, 1562.

Durham, James. *Clavis Cantici; or, an exposition of the Song of Solomon.* Edinburgh, 1668 (well-known Scottish divine, whose apocalyptic *Commentarie upon the Book of Revelation* [Glasgow, 1659] was many times reprinted).

———— *Law Unsealed.* Edinburgh, 1676 (several editions; see also the second treatise in Giles Fletcher, *Israel Redux: or the Restoration of Israel,* London, 1677; see further Vavasor Powell, *Christ and Moses Excellency, Or . . . the Two Covenants of the Gospel and Law,* London, 1650; an influential rendering of this theme and others appears in the scriptural commentaries of Johann Piscator of Herborn—not to be confused with the Ramist Joannes Piscator of Wittenberg—on the Psalms [1611], on Isaiah [1612], on Ezekiel and Daniel [1614], on Numbers [1615], and on the New Testament [1621]).

Durye, John. *Clavis Apocalyptica.* London, 1651 (see also Ludovicus Alcasar, *Vestigatis arcani sensus in Apocalypsis,* Antwerp, 1614, one of the first large-scale historical interpretations of the concept of Antichrist; some other influential commentaries on the apocalypse which to some extent rely on typology, include: John Fox, *Eicasmi,* Geneva, 1596; Alfonsus Conradus, *In Apocalypsiu . . . Commentarius,* Basiliae, 1560; Samuel Hartlib, *Clavis Apocalyptica,* London, 1651; Nathaniel Holmes, *The Resurrection Revealed,* London 1653; Pierre de Launay, *Paraphrase . . . sur l'Apocalypse,* Geneva, 1651; and Pierre Jurieu, *L'Accomplissement des Prophéties de l'Eglise,* Rotterdam, 1686; the last two works are by French Protestants).

Edwards, John. *A Compleat History or Survey of all the Dispensations and Methods of Religion, from the Beginning of the World to the Consummation of all things, as represented in the Old and New Testament.* 2 vols. London, 1669.

Edwards, Thomas. *Gangraena; or a catalogue and discovery of many of the errors of this time.* 3 Parts. London, 1645–46.

Erasmus. *De Sarcienda Ecclesiae Concordia.* Basel, 1533 (trans. Raymond Himelick in *Erasmus and the Seamless Coat of Jesus.* Lafayette, Indiana, 1971; Himelick discusses Erasmus' views on typology in the Introduction).

Escalante, Ferdinand de. *Clypeus Concionatorum Verbi Dei, in quo sunt sculptae omnes visiones symbolicae et signa reala veteris Testamenti.* Hispalian, 1611 (exposition of Catholic hermeneutics).

Everard, John. *The Gospel-Treasury Opened.* London, 1657 (see also his *Rending of the Vail,* London, 1817; mystic and hermetic use of types; the approach may be seen to lead back to earlier Renaissance Christian Neoplatonism, as evidenced, for example, in Ficino's *De la Religion Chrestienne* [trans. Guy Lefèvre de la Boderie], Paris, 1578).

F., J. *God's Goodness to Israel in all ages.* London, 1700.

Faber Stapulensis, Jacobus. *Quincuplex Psalterium.* Paris, 1513 (for parallel Catholic and Protestant commentaries, cf. Victor Bythner, *Lyra Prophetica Davidis Regis,* London, 1664; Samuel Hieron, *Davids Penitentiall Psalme Opened,* Cambridge, Eng., 1617; Wolfgang Musculus, *In Davidis Psalterium Sacrosanctum Commentarii,* Basiliae, 1589; Robert Rollock, *An Exposition vpon Some Select Psalmes of David,* Edinburgh, 1600; Johann Jacob Grynaeus, *Enarratio brevis psalmi CXXXIII,* Geneva, 1579; Nick Hemmingsen's discourse on Psalm 84, *The Faith of the Church Militant,* London, 1581; James Perez of Valencia, *Centum ac quinquaginta psalmi Davidici,* Lyon, 1514; Heinrich Moller, *Enarrationes Psalmorum Davidis,* Geneva, 1591; and

Thomas Wilcocks [Wilcox], *A Right Godly and Learned Exposition upon the whole Booke of Psalms,* London, 1591 [and see also this author's *Exposition vppon the Booke of the Canticles,* London, 1585]).

Favre, Antoine. *Les Entretiens Spirituels.* Paris, 1602 (see also his *Centurie de Quatrains Moraux,* Paris, 1602).

Featley, Daniel. *Clavis Mystica: A Key Opening Divers Difficult and Mysterious Texts of Holy Scripture.* London, 1636.

Ferguson, Robert. *The Interest of Reason in Religion; with the Import and Use of Scripture Metaphors.* London, 1675.

Fessel, Daniel. *Adversariorum Sacrorum.* Wittenberg, 1650.

Flacius, Matthias Illyricus. *Clavis Scripturae Sacrae seu de sermone sacrarum literarum* (1567). Jena, 1674 (important Protestant hermeneutical dictionary).

Fleming, Robert (the Elder). *The Fulfilling of the Scriptures.* Rotterdam, 1669 (see also his *Scripture Truth,* London, 1678; and cf. Arthur Dent, *The Ruine of Rome: or an Exposition upon the wholl reuelation,* London, 1603, and the commentaries on the Prophets by Paulus Palacios de Salazar, London, 1574, and Cologna, 1583).

Fox, George. *A Declaration to the Jews . . . that the Messiah is come, according to their own Prophets.* London, 1661 (cf. his *Cause Why Adam & Eve were Driven Out of Paradice, and the Jews out of their own land of Canaan,* London, 1683).

────── *The Great Mystery of the Great Whore Unfolded . . . how that Christ hath abolished . . . the First* [Testament] *and . . .*

established the Second. London, 1680 (other Quaker works in this tradition are: Joseph Wright, A Testimony for the Son of Man, n.p., 1660; Edward Burrough, A Measure of the Times, London, 1651; and Isaac Pennington, The Axe Laid to the Root, London, 1659).

Franz, Wolfgang (1564–1628). Tractatus Theologicus de Interpretatione Sacrarum Scripturarum. Wittenberg, 1708 (influential in New England; see also his Oratorio cur Dominis noster Jesus Christus sit vocatus Immanuel, Lugduni-Batavorum, 1700 (strongly influenced by Glassius).

Gaillard, Jacques. Melchisedecus Christus Unus, rex justitiae, rex pacis. Lugduni-Batavorum, 1686 (first part of title, in Hebrew characters, is Malkhi-Tzedek Melekh Shalom).

Gatsker, Thomas. Shadows Without Substance. London, 1646.

Gaule, John. Practique Theories; or Votive Speculations upon Jesus Christs Prediction, Incarnation, Passion, and Resurrection. London, 1629.

Gerhard, Johann. Harmoniae Evangelicae. Geneva, 1628 (see also E[dward] F[isher], The Scriptures Harmony, London, 1643).

——— De Interpretatione Scripturae Sacrae. Jenae, 1610.

Gill, Alexander. Sacred Philosophy of Holy Scripture. London, 1635.

Gillespie, George. Wholesome Severity Reconciled with Christian Liberty. London, 1645 (part of the English reaction to the Williams-Cotton controversy; see also Richard Overton, The Araignement of Mr. Persecution, London, 1645).

Glassius, Solomon. Christologia [Greek characters] Mosaicae, qua verba, dicta et typi, cuibus Jesus Christus, Filius Dei in Pentateucho Mosis . . . propitur. Jena, 1649 (see also the important figural commentaries on the Pentateuch—used at most Protestant universities, including early Harvard—by Peter Martyr Vermigli, Defensio de Eucharistiae Sacramento, 7 vols., Zurich, 1565–79).

——— Philologia Sacra. 5 vols. Jena, 1623–36 (source book for later studies on typology).

Goodwin, Thomas. Moses and Aaron. Civil and Ecclesiastical Rites, vsed by the ancient Hebrews: observed, and at large opened. London, 1625 (see also Samuel Gardiner, Moses and Aaron, London, 1653; and George Seignoir, Moses and Aaron, Cambridge, Eng., 1670).

——— Christ Set Forth. London, 1634 (5th edn.; see also his Zerrubabbels Encouragement To Finish the Temple. A Sermon Preached before the Honourable House of Commons, London, 1642, one of his several millenarian sermons).

Gouge, William. A Learned . . . Commentary on the Whole Epistle to the Hebrews. London, 1655 (see also the influential work by Henry Finch, The Calling of the Jews, a figural-millenarian treatise edited and published by Gouge).

Granada, Luis de. Le Vray Chemin pour Acquerir et Parvenir à la Grace de Dieu, trans. F. de Belleforest. Paris, 1579.

Grantham, Thomas. The Seventh-day-Sabbath Ceased as Ceremony. London, 1667.

Gregory, Francis. David's Returne from his Banishment. Oxford,

1660 (one of the many celebrations of the Restoration which shows the influence of typology; see further: Junius Bocalini [pseud.], *Iö Carole*, London, 1661; Giles Fleming, *Stemma Sacrum: The Royal Progeny Delineated*, London, 1660; Robert Howard, *Poems . . . to the King*, London, 1660; Rachel Jevon, *Exultationis Carmen*, London, 1660; and Henry King, *Coronation Sermon*, London, 1661).

Groenewegen, Henricus. *Hieroglyphica, anders Emblemata Sacra*. Gravenhage, 1693.

Guevara, Antonio de. *Livre du Mort de Calvaire*, trans. F. de Belleforest. Paris, 1589 (cf. Simon Goulart, *Trente Tableaux de la Mort* [n.p.], 1602; and Jean de Sponde [1557–95], *Méditations*, ed. A. Boase, Paris, 1954).

Guild, William. *Moses Vnuailed: Or, Those Figures Which Served vnto the Patterne and Shaddow of Heauenly Things*. London, 1620 (an unsophisticated but widely read presentation of typology; more expert in his *Harmony of all the Prophets*, London, 1626).

Hall, Joseph. *Columba Noae*. London, 1623.

—— *Plain and Familiar Explication by Way of Paraphrase of All the Hard Texts of the Whole Divine Scriptures of the Old and New Testaments*. London, 1638 (see also his *Contemplations on the Historical Passages of the Old and New Testaments*, 3 vols., Edinburgh, 1770).

Harvey, Christopher. *The Synagogue; or, the Shadow of the Temple*. [N.p.], 1640.

Hayne, Thomas. *The General View of the Holy Scriptures*. London, 1640.

Heidfeldius, Joannes. *Quartum renata . . . Sphinx Theologico-Philosophica*. Frankfurt, 1604 (wide-ranging typological associations; several times reissued; influential in New England).

Helwys, Thomas. *A Short Declaration of the Mystery of Iniquity*. London, 1612 (on the concept of monarchy; see also Johann Brentz, *De administrando*, Hoganoae, 1527, and the writings of Robert Harrison and Robert Browne, recently edited by Albert Peel and Leland H. Carlson, *Elizabethan Nonconformist Texts*, Vol. II, London, 1953).

Herberger, Valerius (1562–1627). *Magnalia Dei, de Jesu, Scripturae Nucleo et Medulla*. Hamburg, 1661 (well-known theologian, influenced by Glassius, and in turn often quoted in New England; selected gatherings of his works were published as: *Herz-Postille*, ed. J. F. Bachmann, Berlin, 1853; *Paradeis- Blümlein*, ed. C. W. Otto, Halle, 1857 [mainly on Psalms]; *Evangelische Liederkunde*, ed. H. Haase, Langensalzer, 1871; and *Ausgewählte Predigten*, ed. D. Orphal, Leipzig, 1892; for other German Lutheran works influenced similarly by Glassius, see *Paradiessgärtlein* [Amsterdam, 1682] by the great Pietist Johann Arndt, translated into English—probably by A. W. Boehme—as *The Garden of Paradise*, London, 1716; other typological works by Arndt include his famous *De Vero Christianismo*, London, 1708 [often translated], and his interpretations of the Cabbala, issued in 1783; the influence of Glassius is also felt, for example, in Antonius Hulsius, *Authentia Absoluta S. textus Hebrei vindicata contra criminationes*, Rotterdam, 1662; and Johann H. Heidegger, *Exercitationes Biblicae*, Tiguri,

1700—an attack on Spinozaist 'aberrations'—and his *Corpus Theologicae Christianae*, Tiguri, 1700, as well as his five-volume scriptural commentary, Tiguri, 1699).

Herle, Charles. *Contemplations and Devotions on . . . our Blessed Saviours Death and Passion*. London, 1631.

Howgill, Francis. *The Inheritance of Jacob Discovered, After His Return Out of Aegypt*. London, 1656.

Hulsius, Heinrich. *De Vellibus Prophetarum Sacris*. Amsterdam, 1701 (important federalist theologian of the school of Cocceius; see also his *Dissertatio de Jehova Deo Rege ac Duce Militari in prisco Israele*, reprinted in vol. 24 of Blasius Ugolinus, *Thesaurus Antiquitatum*, Lugduni-Batavorum, 1744; in vol. 8 of this series there is a reprint of the Cocceian-typological tract, *Commentarius critico-typicus de Tabernaculo Mosis* by Salomon van Til; see further van Til's *Einleitung zu den Prophetischen Schrifften*, Frankfurt, 1699, his *Malachius Illustratus*, Lugduni-Batavorum, 1701 [including geographical speculations about Eden], and his *Phosphorus Propheticus*, Lugduni-Batavorum, 1700; for other Dutch works in this vein, see: P. von Limborch, *De Veritate Religionis Christianae*, Gouda, 1687; J. Batalerius, *Dissertatio de Israelitarum Conversione*, Gravenhage, 1669; J. Hoornbeek, *Tesjubat Jehuda*, Leiden, 1655; A. Essenius, *Heilzaem Bericht*, Utrecht, 1667; J. Koelman, *De Sleutel*, Amsterdam, 1669; and P. Serrarius, *Naerder Bericht*, trans. into English as *An Awakening Warning to the Wofull World*, Amsterdam, 1662).

Hutcheson, George. *Exposition upon Job*. London, 1669 (massive compendium; see also his *Brief Exposition of the XII. Smal Prophets*, London, 1655).

Jackson, Arthur. *Annotations upon Job, the Psalms . . . and the Song of Solomon*. London, 1658.

Jansen, Hendrik. *Biblische Figuren*. Amsterdam, 1687.

Keach, Benjamin. *Antichrist Stormed; or the Papish church proved to be mystery Babylon*. London, 1689 (see also Keach's work on practical theology, *Jacob's Ladder Improved*, London, 1698).

—— *Tropologia: A Key to Open Scripture Metaphors and Types*. London, 1681 (comprehensive investigation by a Baptist theologian; approved and used by the Puritans).

Kirkconnell, Watson, ed. *That Invincible Samson: The Theme of 'Samson Agonistes' in World Literature, With Translations of the Major Analogues*. Toronto, 1966 (translations of five plays about Samson from the sixteenth and seventeenth centuries, with a valuable 'Descriptive Catalogue' by the editor, treating supplementary material).

Knell, Paul. *Israel and England Paralleled*. London, 1648 (cf. William Leigh, *Queen Elizabeth, Paraleld*, London, 1612).

Knollys, Hansard. *An Exposition of the Eleventh Chapter of the Revelation*. London, 1679 (see also his *Mystical Babylon Unvailed*, London, 1679; Anabaptist who spent some time in New England).

La Ceppède, Jean de. *Les Théorèmes sur le Sacré Mystère de Nostre Rédemption* (1613,

1622), ed. J. Rousset. Geneva, 1966 (sequence of 500 sonnets, published in two parts, which has been likened to the epics of Dante and Milton, and so seems to offer itself for an interesting comparativist typological study; for other French sonnet sequences of this period that show the marked influence of typology, see: Jacques de Billy, *Sonnets Spirituels*, Paris, 1573; Marin Le Saulx, *Theanthropagamie*, London, 1577; and especially Anne de Marquets, *Sonnets Spirituels*, Paris, 1605, and Jean-Baptiste Chassignet, *Le Mespris de la Vie* [1594], ed. A. Müller, Geneva, 1953).

Lapide, Cornelius à (van de Steen). *Commentarius in Josue, Judicium, Ruth.* Antwerp, 1618.

—— *Commentaria in Quatuor Prophetas Maiores.* Paris, 1622 (Jesuit hebraist sometimes respectfully cited by the Puritans).

La Sale, Perrot de. *Tableaux Sacrez.* Frankfurt, 1594 (see also Louis Richeome, *Tableaux Sacrez des Figures Mystique . . . de l'Eucharistie.* Paris, 1601).

Lee, Samuel. *Antichristi Excidium.* London, 1664.

Leigh, Edward. *A Treatise of the Divine Promises.* London, 1633.

Lewis, John. *Melchizedichs Antitype: Or the Eternal Priesthood and All-Sufficient Sacrifice of Christ.* London, 1624 (typological argument against Catholicism).

Lightfoot, John. *A Harmony of the Gospels.* London, 1654.

Lilburne, John. *A Copie of a Letter . . . To Mr. William Prinne Esq.* London, 1645.

Lonicerus, Johann [Lonicer]. *Eine schöne und Fruchtbare Comedia,*

auss heyliger Biblischer schrifft in rheimen bracht, mit anzeygung ihrer Allegori und geistlicher bedeuttung. N.p., 1540.

Lukin, Henry. *An Introduction to the Holy Scripture, containing the several tropes, [and] figures . . . used therein.* London, 1669.

Luther, Martin. *Lectures on Genesis.*

—— *Lectures on Romans.*

—— *Lectures on the Book of Hebrews* (a good modern edition of these writings is that edited by Jaroslav J. Pelikan [vols. 1–30] and Helmut T. Lehmann [vols. 31–55] St. Louis, 1955–71).

Manton, Thomas. *Christs Temptation and Transfiguration Practically Explained and Improved.* London, 1685.

Marisius, Samuel. *Dissertatio de Antichristo.* Amsterdam, 1640 (see also: Patrick Forbes' imposing *Learned Commentarie vpon the Revelation*, Middleburg, 1614 [2nd edn.]; Conrad Graser's apocalyptical *Plaga Regia*, Tiguri, 1600; Edward Haughton, *The Rise . . . and Fall of Antichrist*, London, 1652; Theophilus Higgons, *Mystical Babylon; or Papal Rome*, London, 1624; Elias Hooker, *The Spirit of the Martyrs Revived*, London, 1683; Samuel Petto, *The Revelation Unvailed*, London, 1693; and Nathaniel Stephens, *A Plain and Easie Calculation of . . . the Name of the Beast*, London, 1656).

Marlorat, Augustin. *Esaie Prophetia, cum Catholica expositione ecclesiastica.* Paris, 1564 (see also Hugo de S. Carlo Cardinalis, *Biblia Latina cum postilla*, Basel, 1504).

Mede, Joseph. 'Discourse XLIV,' in *Works*, ed. John Worthington, London, 1677 (see further his famous *Clairs Apocalyptica* [1627], trans. Richard More as *The Key of the Revelation*, London, 1642, and his *The Mysterie of St. Paul's Conversion, or the Type of the calling of the Jews*, in *Works*).

Melancthon, Philip. *Rhetorices Elementa*. Lugduni, 1539 (see also his *Catalogue Testium Veritatis*, which was a model for Foxe's *Book of Martyrs*; many editions of all these works).

Milton, John. *Animadversions*.

——— *The Reason of Church Government* (the standard edition of the prose works is that edited by Frank A. Patterson, New York, 1931–38).

Montague, Richard. *The Acts and Monuments of the Church before Christ Incarnate*. London, 1642.

Musculus, Wolfgang. *Commentarii in Genesin*. Basel, 1554 (cf. Benedictus Parerius' four-volume commentary on Genesis, Lyons, 1596–1602).

Myriell, Thomas. *Christs Suite to his Church*. London, 1613.

Opitz, Martin von Boberfeld. *Solomon des Hebraischen Königes Hohes Lied*. Bresslau, 1627 (cf. W. W. Cannon, *The Song of Songs, edited as a dramatic poem*, Cambridge, Eng., 1913).

Owen, John. *The Advantage of the Kingdome of Christ in the Shaking of the Kingdoms of this World*. Oxford, 1651 (see also this author's *The Shaking and Translating of the Heaven and Earth*. [1649]. *To which are annexed Prophetical Extracts . . . as relate to the Revolution of France*, Edinburgh, 1794, and his *God's Work in Founding Zion*, Oxford, 1656).

——— *The Branch of the Lord, the Beauty of Sion*. Edinburgh, 1650 (see also this author's popular *Eschol: a Cluster of the Fruit of Canaan*, London, 1648, and his *Of the Divine Originall . . . of the Scriptures*, Oxford, 1659; and see further John Bond, *Eschol*, London, 1648).

——— *Exercitations concerning the Day of Sacred Rest*. London 1671 (cf. John Wallis, *Defence of the Christian Sabbath*, Oxford, 1692).

Parker, Robert. *Scholastical Discourse Against Symbolizing with Antichrist in Ceremonies*. London, 1607 (see also John Rawlet, *A Treatise of Sacramental Covenanting with Christ*, London, 1692 [5th edn.]; and cf. the Catholic position in Gregory of Rimini, *Super Primum et Secundum Sententiarum*, Venice, 1522).

Pascal, Blaise. *Pensées*, 527, 648, 672, in *Oeuvres Complètes*, ed. Louis Lafuma, Paris, 1963 (many English translations).

Pearson, John. *An Exposition of the Creed*. London, 1662.

Penington, Isaac. *Expositions . . . on Severall Scriptures*. London, 1656.

Pererius, Benedictus (Pereyra). *Primus Tomus Disputationum in Sacrum Scripturam*. Lugduni, 1662 (Jesuit scholar; well known among Protestant as well as Catholic exegetes; cf. Louis Cappel [Cappellus], *Commentarii et Notae Criticae in Vetus Testamentum*, Amsterdam, 1689).

Perkins, William. *The Arte of Prophesying*, trans. T. Tuke. London, 1607 (major Puritan text).

——— *A Cloud of Faithfull Wit-*

nesses Leading to the Heavenly Canaan. London, 1618.

Pfeiffer, August. Critica Sacra. Zuerest, 1680 (widely read).

——— Thesaurus Hermeneuticus. Lipsiae, 1698.

Pinchion, William. The Jewes Synagogue. London, 1641 (see further Michael Drayton, Moyses in a Map of his Miracles, London, 1604).

Poole, Matthew. Synopsis Criticorum Aliorumque Sacrae Scriptae Interpretum. 4 vols. London, 1669–76.

Prideaux, John. Sacred Eloquence. London, 1659.

Puschman, Adam (1532–1600). Singebuch, ed. G. Munzer, Leipzig, 1907.

Ribera, Fransiscus. De Templo. Antwerp, 1623.

Richardson, John. Choice Observations . . . upon the Old Testament. London, 1655 (cf. William Attersol, A Commentarie upon . . . Numbers, London, 1618, and Edward Topsell's treatise on Joel, Time's Lamentation, London, 1599).

Rivet, André. Erläuterte Zwölf prophetische Psalmen. Amsterdam, 1626.

Roberts, Francis. Clavis Bibliorum. London, 1648 (several editions; the 4th, 1675, is considered the best).

——— Mysterium In Medulla Bibliorum, London, 1657 (cf. Edward Polhill, The Divine Will Considered in its Eternal Degrees, London, 1673).

Robinson, John. Manumission to a Manuduction. N.p., 1615.

——— Observations Divine and Morall for the Furthering of Knowledge, and Virtue. N.p.,

1625 (leading Separatist divine; see also his Of Religious Communion Private and Publique. Leyden, 1614).

Rogers, Daniel. A Treatise of the Two Sacraments . . . Baptisme and the Supper of the Lord. London, 1633.

Rogers, Nehemiah. The Wild Vine. London, 1632.

Ross, Alexander. Mystagogus Poeticus. London, 1647 (popular figural application of classical themes, in the tradition of George Sandys' Ovid's Metamorphosis . . . Represented in Figures, Oxford, 1632, and Natale Conti's Mythologiae, Frankfurt, 1605).

Rutherford, Samuel. Survey of the Spiritual Antichrist. London, 1648.

Salmon, Joseph. A Rout, A Rout. London, 1649.

Saltmarsh, John. Sparkles of Glory. London, 1647.

Scharp, Johann. Symphonia Prophetarum. Geneva, 1625.

Settle, Elkanah. A Panegyrick on . . . Sir George Jeffries. London, 1683 (see also John Turner, Two Sermons . . . upon the Occasion of the Birth of the Princes, London, 1688, and John Guy, The Happy Accession of . . . King William and Queen Mary . . . A Pindarique Ode, London, 1699; cf. the poems reprinted in vol. II of Poems on Affairs of State: Augustan Satirical Verse, 1660–1714, ed. Elias J. Mengel, Jr., general editor, George de F. Lord, such as John Caryll's Naboth's Vineyard, London, 1679; for the larger context of this panegyric tradition, see further Mercurius Davidicus, Oxford, 1643, and Richard Chapman's Brittania Rediviva, London, 1714).

Shute, Josias. *Sarah and Hagar* . . . , ed. Edward Sparke. London, 1649.

Sibbes, Richard. *The Excellencie of the Gospell above the Law*. London, 1639.

Smith, Henry. *Jacobs Ladder, or the High Way to Heaven*. London, 1595 (see generally his *Sermons*, London, 1607).

Smith, John (of Montague Close, Southwark). *The Mysterie of Rhetorique Unvail'd wherein above 130 of the Tropes and Figures are severally derived from the Greek into English*. London, 1657 [1656].

Smyth, John. 'Paralleles, Consures, Observations' (1609), in *Works*, ed. W. T. Whitley. Cambridge, Eng., 1915.

Speed, John. *The Geneologies of Holy Scriptures*. N.p., 1611 (see also Speed's *Clowd of Witnesses*, London, n.d.).

Spencer, John. *De Legibus Hebraeorum Ritualibus*. Cambridge, Eng., 1685.

Taylor, Thomas. *Moses and Aaron, or the Types and Shadows of the Old Testament Opened, and Explained*. London, 1653 (first edition entitled *Christ Revealed, or the Old Testament explained*, London, 1635; major typological study which set precedents for other seventeenth-century studies).

—— *The Parable of the Sower and of the Seed*. London, 1621 (see also this author's *Christ's Victorie over the Dragon*, London, 1635).

Tichborne, Robert. *A Cluster of Canaans Grapes*. London, 1649.

Tilenus, Daniel. *A Defence of* . . . *the Holy Scripture*. London, 1606.

Trapp, John. *Annotations upon the Old and New Testament*. 5 vols. London, 1654–62.

Turner, John. *Discourse concerning the Messias*. London, 1685 (cf. Amandus Polanus, *In Danielem Prophetam Visionum*, Basilae, 1599, and John Napier, *Plaine Discovery of the whole Revelation of St. John*, Edinburgh, 1645).

Tyndale, William. *A Briefe Declaration*.

—— *The Obedience of a Christian Man*.

—— *A Pathway into the Holy Scripture* (covenant theology; attack on Origen; crucial early formulation of Reformation typology; see the edition of Tyndale's work ed. G. E. Duffield, Philadelphia, 1965).

Vertue, Henry. *Christ and the Church: or, Parallels*. London, 1659.

Vitringa, Campergius. *Sacrarum Observationum*. Franeker, 1689 (important treatise on Reformation typology).

Wackernagel, Philipp R. G., ed. *Das Deutsche Kirchenlied von Martin Luther bis auf Nicolaus Hermann und Ambrosius Blaurer*. Stuttgart, 1841 (see also the proto-Reformed documents collected in Heiko Augustinus Oberman, *Forerunners of the Reformation: The Shape of Late Medieval Thought Illustrated by Key Documents*, New York, 1966, such as Cornelisz Hoen's 'A Most Christian Letter').

Ward, Richard. *Theologicall Questions* . . . *upon the gospel of* . . . *St. Matthew*. London, 1640.

Weemse, John. *The Christian Synagogue*. London, 1623 (see also his three works on the laws of

Moses, London, 1632: An Explanation of the Ceremoniall Lawes of Moses, Explication of the Iudiciall Lawes of Moses, and Exposition of the Morall Law).

―――― Exercitations Divine. London, 1632.

Welles, John. The Soules Progresse to the Celestiall Canaan. London, 1639 (see also Faithful Teate, A Scripture-Map of the Wilderness of Sin, and Way to Canaan, London, 1655).

Whatley, William. Prototypes, or, the primarie . . . presidents out of the book of Genesis. London, 1640.

Whichcote, Benjamin. Select Sermons. London, 1968 (Cambridge Platonist).

Whitaker, William. An Answer to . . . William Rainolds. London, 1585.

―――― A Disputation Concerning Scripture, Against the Papists (1588), ed. William Fitzgerald. Cambridge, Eng., 1849 (formidable Reformation statement of hermeneutic principles).

White, John. A Way to the Tree of Life. London, 1647.

Wilkins, John. Ecclesiastes. London, 1646 (cf.: John Udall's Commentarie upon the Lamentations of Jeremy, London, 1599; David Pareus [Waengler], Hoseas Propheta Commentarius, Geneva, 1617; and John Owen's massive Exercitations on . . . Hebrews, 4 vols., London, 1668–84).

Willett, Andrew. Hexapla in Exodum. London, 1608 (see also his Hexapla in Genesin, London, 1605; and cf. Joshua Stegmannus, Studii Pietatis Icon, sive Christognosia, n.p., 1630, a work well known in New England).

―――― Sacrorum Emblematum Centuria Una. Cambridge, Eng., n.d. [1592?] (emblem book which employs typology and medieval allegory; see also Andrea Alciati, Emblemata cum Commentariis, Paris, 1583).

Wilson, Thomas. A Christian Dictionary. London, 1611.

Winstanley, Gerrard (1609–60?). Works, ed. George H. Sabine. Ithaca, 1941 (see especially The Law of Righteousness [1648] and An Humble Request to the Ministers . . . and to all Lawyers [1650]).

Wither, George. A Preparation to the Psalter. London, 1619 (see also his Paralellogrammation [1622] and Exercises upon the First Psalme [1620], New York, 1967 [Burt Franklin Research and Source Works Series, no. 150; reprint of the Spenser Society edition of 1882, no. 33]).

Wits, Herman (Witsius). De Œconomia feoderum Dei cum hominibus. Leovardiae, 1677 (leading Dutch theologian of the federalist school).

―――― Miscellaneorum Sacrorum. 2 vols. Leyden, 1736.

Wollebius, Joannes. Compendium Theologiae Christianae. Cambridge, Eng., 1642.

Woodhouse, A. S. P., ed. Puritanism and Liberty: Being the Army Debates 1647–49 from the Clarke Manuscripts. London, 1938 (see especially Thomas Collier, and the anonymous Ancient Bounds and Saints Apology; Woodhouse's famous 'Introduction' to this volume includes a brief discussion of typology).

Worden, Thomas. The Types Unveiled; or, the Gospel Pick't out of the Legal Ceremonies. London, 1664.

b. Twentieth-Century Criticism

Althaus, Paul. *The Theology of Martin Luther.* Philadelphia, 1966 (analysis of hermeneutic principles).

Bizer, Ernst. 'Die Entdeckung des Sakraments durch Luther,' *Evangelische Theologie,* XVII (1957), 64–90 (cf. W. Schwarz, *Principles and Problems of Biblical Translation: Some Reformation Controversies and their Background,* Cambridge, Eng., 1955, and Y. M. J. Congar, *Vraie et Fausse Reforme dans l'Eglise,* Paris, 1950).

Bornkamm, Heinrich. *Luther und das Alte Testament.* Tübingen, 1948 (well-known discussion of Luther's typology; cf. J. Boisset et al., *Le Problème Biblique dans le Protestantisme,* Paris, 1955).

De Jong, James. 'The Millennium and the Missions,' Diss. The Free University, Amsterdam, 1970 (see further S. H. Rooy, *The Theology of the Missions in the Puritan Tradition,* Grand Rapids, Mich., 1965).

Ebeling, Gerhard. *Evangelische Evangelienauslegung: Eine Untersuchung zu Luthers Hermeneutik.* Darmstadt, 1962 (see also his 'The New Hermeneutics of the Young Luther,' *Theology Today,* XXI [1964–65], 34–46; cf. the papers by Gerhard Ebeling on Psalms, by James Atkinson on the Gospel of John, by Ruben Josefson on Christology, by Wilhelm Maurer on church history, and by Jaroslav Pelikan on Genesis, in Vilmos Vajta, ed. *Lutherforschung Heute: Referate und Berichte des 1. Internationalen Lutherforschungskongresses Aarhus, 18.–23. August 1956,* Berlin, 1958; and see further the following specialized studies of Luther's hermeneutics:

Erich Vogelsang, *Die Anfänge von Luthers Christologie nach der ersten Psalmenvorlesung,* Berlin, 1929; Werner Jetter, *Die Taufe beim jungen Luther,* Tübingen, 1954; Karl August Meissinger, *Luthers Exegese in der Frühzeit,* Leipzig, 1910; Albert Brandenburg, *Gericht und Evangelium: Zur Worttheologie in Luthers Erster Psalmenvorlesung,* Paderborn, 1960; and Günter Metzger, *Gelebter Glaube: Die Formierung reformatorischen Denkens in Luthers erster Psalmenvorlesung dargestellt im Begriff des Affekts,* Göttingen, 1964; with regard to Psalms in particular, cf. Wilfrid Werbeck, *Jacobus Perez von Valencia: Untersuchungen zu seinem Psalmenkommentar,* Tübingen, 1959).

Forstman, H. Jackson. *Word and Spirit: Calvin's Doctrine of Biblical Authority.* Stanford, 1962 (documents Calvin's 'weakness for typology').

Headley, John M. *Luther's View of the Church.* New Haven, 1963.

Herntrich, Volkmar. 'Luther und das Alte Testament,' *Luther-Jahrbuch,* XX (1938), 93–124 (see also Herman Hering, 'Luthers Taufbüchlein von 1523, besonders das Typologische Gebet in demselben,' *Theologische Studien und Kritiken,* LXXI [1892], 282–91).

Hyma, Albert. *Renaissance to Reformation.* Grand Rapids, Mich., 1951 (see further Roland H. Bainton's wide-ranging and very useful *Reformation of the Sixteenth Century,* London, 1953; specific aspects of Calvinist and Pietist exegesis are discussed in Karl Reuter, *Wilhelm Amesivs,* n.p., 1940).

Iserloh, E. *Die Eucharistie in der*

Darstellung den Johannes Eck.
Münster, 1950 (see also his *Der
Kampf um die Messe in der
ersten Jahren der Auseinander-
setzung mit Luther,* Münster,
1952).

Le Cler, Joseph. *Toleration and the
Reformation* (1955), trans. T. L.
Westow. 2 vols. London, New
York, 1960 (informative on the
typological argument for toleration; see also William A.
Clebsch's detailed study, *England's Earliest Protestants: 1520–
1535,* New Haven, 1964).

López, F. López. 'La multiplicided
de los sentides literales en la
Escritura, según los autores espa-
ñoles (1550–1560),' *Archivo
Teologico Granadino,* X (1947),
325–419.

Oakley, Francis. 'Jacobean Political
Theology: The Absolute and
Ordinary Powers of the King,'
Journal of the History of Ideas,
XXIX (1968), 323–46.

Pelikan, Jaroslav. *Luther the Expositor.* St. Louis, 1959 (very
useful general work; cf. F. Hahn,
'Die Heilige Schrift als Problem
der Auslesung bei Luther,' *Evangelische Theologie,* X [1951],
407–24).

Phelan, John Leddy. *The Millennial
Kingdom of the Fransciscans in
the New World.* Berkeley, 1970
(2nd edn., revised; discusses the
typologically influenced historiography of Mendieta, Sepúl-
veda, Las Casas, Enciso, and
other early Latin-American historians).

Plotkin, Frederick S. 'Signs from
Sion: A Study of Radical Puritan
Eschatology in England, 1640–
1660.' Diss. Columbia University, 1966.

Pocock, J. G. A. 'Time, History and
Eschatology in the Thought of

Thomas Hobbes,' *The Diversity
of History,* eds. J. H. Elliott and
H. G. Koenigsberger. London,
1970.

Renaudet, Augustin. *Etudes Eras-
miennes* (1521–1529). Paris,
1939 (see also this author's earlier *Erasme: Sa Pensée Religieuse,
et son action d'après sa corre-
spondance 1518–1521,* Paris,
1926).

Schrenk, Gottlieb. *Gottesreich und
Bund im ältern Protestantismus.*
Gütersloh, 1923 (Cocceius and
typology).

Schwartz, Karl Adolph V. *Die Theologische hermeneutik des
Matthias Flacius Illyricus.* München, 1933.

Schwartz, Werner. *Principles and
Problems of Biblical Translation:
Some Reformation Controversies
and their Background.* Cambridge, Eng., 1955.

Streuver, Nancy S. *The Language of
History in the Renaissance.*
Princeton, 1970 (cf. M. van
Beck, *An Enquiry into Puritan
Vocabulary,* Groningen, 1969).

Tavard, George H. *Holy Writ or
Holy Church: The Crisis of the
Protestant Reformation.* New
York, 1959 (a Catholic's summary of the various exegetical
movements which preceded and
contributed to the Reformation;
see also J. Steinmann, 'Entretien
de Pascal et du Père Richard
Simon sur le Sens de l'Ecriture,'
Vie Intellectuelle, XIX [1949],
239–53).

Wendel, François. *Calvin: The Origins and Development of his
Religious Thought.* New York,
1950.

Williams, Arnold. *The Common
Expositor: An Account of the

Commentaries on Genesis, 1527–1633. Chapel Hill, 1948 (see also Don Cameron Allen, The Legend of Noah: Renaissance Rationalism in Art, Science, and Letters, Urbana, Ill., 1963).

Wolf, Hans H. Die Einheit des Bundes, Das Verhältnis von Altem und Neuem Testament bei Calvin. Neukirchen, 1958.

Wood, A. Shevington. Captive of the Word: Martin Luther: Doctor of Sacred Scripture. Exeter, 1969 (cf. Ian D. K. Siggins, Martin Luther's Doctrine of Christ, New Haven, 1970).

5. Colonial America

a. Representative Writers of the Seventeenth Century

Several of the works listed here were published in the eighteenth century and several were written in Europe; nonetheless, in all cases the authors are generally considered to represent Puritan New England thought.

Adams, William. *The Necessity of the Pouring out of the Spirit from on High . . . Being a general Fast.* Boston, 1679 (cf. his *Gods Eye on the Contrite,* Cambridge, Mass., 1685; and Thomas Thacher, *A Fast of Gods Chusing,* Boston, 1678).

Aspinwall, William. *Abrogation of the Jewish Sabbath.* London, 1657 (see also his millenarian tracts, *An Explication of the Seventh Chapter of Daniel,* London, 1654, and *Thunders from Heaven,* London, 1655).

Bradstreet, Anne. 'The Flesh and the Spirit,' in *Works,* ed. Adrienne Rich. Cambridge, Mass., 1967 (see also Benjamin Tompson's elegies, in *Poems,* ed. Edward J. Hall, Boston, 1924).

Bulkeley, Peter. *Gospel-Covenant.* London, 1646.

Cotton, John. *A Brief Exposition with Practical Observations upon the Whole Book of Canticles.* London, 1655 (earlier, less complete edition in 1642; see also Cotton's commentary on Ecclesiastes and his important series of sermons preached 1639–40, *An Exposition Upon the Thirteenth Chapter of the Revelation,* London, 1656).

—— *Grounds and Ends of Baptism.* London, 1647.

—— *On the Holiness of Church Members.* London, 1647 (see also his *Some Treasures Fetched out of Rubbish,* London, 1660).

—— Treatise of the Covenant of Grace. London, 1671.

Danforth, Samuel. An Exhortation To All. Boston, 1714 (see also his father's A Brief Recognition of New-England's Errand into the Wilderness, Cambridge, Mass., 1671).

Davenport, John. The Knowledge of Christ . . . Wherein the Types, Prophecies . . . and the Mediatorial Office of Christ are Opened and Applyed. London, 1653 (see also his Gods Call to His People, Cambridge, Mass., 1669).

Eliot, John. Harmony of the Gospels. Boston, 1678 (see also his Christian Commonwealth, London, 1659).

Green, Joseph. 'Commonplace Book,' in Proceedings of the Colonial Society of Massachusetts, XXXIV (1938).

Hooke, William. Discourse Concerning the Witnesses. London, 1681.

Hooker, Samuel. Righteousness Rained from Heaven. Cambridge, Mass., 1677.

Hooker, Thomas. The Application of Redemption. London, 1659 (see also his Soules Implantation, London, 1637, and cf. Samuel Willard, A Compleat Body of Divinity, Boston, 1726).

——The Saint's Dignitie and Duty. London, 1651.

Johnson, Edward. Wonder-Working Providence of Sion's Saviour in New-England: 1628–1651, ed. J. Franklin Jameson. New York, 1910 (cf. William Bradford's writings, including his Plymouth History, ed. Worthington C. Ford, 2 vols., Boston, 1912, and his 'Description and Historical Account of New England in Verse,' Collections of the Massa-

chusetts Historical Society, 1st ser., III [1794], 77–84).

Mather, Cotton. Magnalia Christi Americana. London, 1702 (see also his Eleutheria, London, 1698, Things to be Look'd for, Boston, 1691, and The Wonderful Works of God, Boston, 1690).

—— Psalterium Americanum. Boston, 1718 (the annotations to this translation of the Psalms show his debt to a host of earlier typological commentaries on the Psalms; primarily he leans on rabbinical commentaries and on Pietist works, like Johann Arndt's Der gantze Psalter Davids, Frankfurt, 1686; a full investigation of his sources, however, would include the figural—and not infrequently millenarian—renderings of the Psalms by the Church Fathers and by the following Reformation and Renaissance writers: William Ames, Amsterdam, 1635; the Catholic Robert Bellarmine, Cologne, 1611; Theodore Beza, London, 1580; William Bradshaw, London, 1621; Ionnis P. Bugenhagen, Basel, 1524, 1526; Johann J. Grynaeus, Geneva, 1579; Niels Hemmington, London, 1681; Heinrich Moller, Geneva, 1591; Bendictus A. Montanus, Antwerp, 1605; Wolfgang Musculus, Basiliae, 1589; André Rivet, Leyden, 1626; Robert Rollock, Edinburgh, 1600; Esrom R. Rudinger, Gorlitz, 1580, 1581; Samuel Smith, London, 1614; Thomas Wilcox, London, 1624; and George Wither, London, 1620; a separate study is needed on this tradition, which extends from the Bay Psalm Book through the numerous nineteenth-century American printings of Psalm translations).

—— Work Upon the Ark. Meditations Upon the Ark as a Type of the Church. Boston, 1689 (see also the unpublished six-volume 'Biblia Americana,' located in the Massachusetts Historical Society, for the broadest demonstration of Mather's application of typology; and see further *The Call of the Gospel*, Boston, 1686, Mather's first published sermon, and, for a later view, *Utilia*, Boston, 1716, especially the first sermon in that collection, *Joshua. Or, The Joyful Sound of a Saviour leading unto Rest*).

Mather, Increase. *The Day of Trouble is Near. Two Sermons*. Cambridge, Mass., 1674 (see further: *A Sermon Shewing . . . that Wonderful Revolutions . . . are near at hand*, Edinburgh, 1710; *A Sermon Wherein is shewed . . . the Church of God is . . . a Subject of Great Persecution*, Boston, 1682; *A Discourse Concerning the Danger of Apostasy*, Boston, 1679; *The Blessed Hope*, Boston, 1701; *A Dissertation*, Boston, 1708; and *A Discourse Concerning Faith and Fervency in Prayer*, Boston, 1710).

—— *The Mystery of Christ Opened and Applied*. Boston, 1686 (see also his four sermons on *Meditations on the Glory of the Lord Jesus Christ*, Boston, 1705, his *Most Glorious Throne*, Boston, 1702, and his *Diatriba da signo filii hominis, et de secundo Messiae adventu*, Amsterdam, 1682).

—— *The Order of the Gospel*. Boston, 1700 (see further: *Duty of Parents*, Boston, 1703; *Pray for the Rising Generation*, Cambridge, Mass., 1678; *Renewal of Covenant*, Boston, 1677; and *Discourse Concerning the Subject of Baptism*, Boston, 1675).

Mather, Richard. *An Apology of the Churches in New-England for church-government*. London, 1643 (cf. his *Svmme of Certain Sermons upon Genes: 15.6*, Cambridge, Mass., 1652).

Mather, Samuel. *The Figures or Types of the Old Testament*. Dublin, 1683 (central formulation of the subject, for its own times and beyond; cf. Caroline Fry Wilson's abridgement and rewriting of this work, *The Gospel of the Old Testament*, London, 1834).

—— *A Testimony from the Scripture Against Idolatry and Superstition*. N.p. [Cambridge, Mass.?], n.d. [1672?].

Mitchel, Jonathan. *Nehemiah on the Wall*. Cambridge, Mass., 1671 (see also John Higginson, *The Cause of God and of his People in New-England*, Cambridge, Mass., 1663).

Norton, John. *The Evangelical Worshipper, in Three Choice and Profitable Sermons*. Cambridge, Mass., 1664 (see also in this collection *Sion the Out-cast healed of her Wounds*).

—— *The Heart of N-England rent*. Cambridge, Mass., 1659.

Noyes, James. *The Temple Measured*. London, 1647.

Noyes, Nicholas. *New Englands Duty and Interest*. Boston, 1698.

Oakes, Urian. *New-England Pleaded With*. Cambridge, Mass., 1673.

Penn, William. *A Reply to a pretended Answer, by a Nameless Author, in which the Principles of the . . . Quakers are . . . confirmed*. London, 1695 (amplifies his comments on typology in *A Key . . . to distinguish the Religion professed by the . . . Quakers*, London, 1692).

—— Wisdom Justified of her Children. London, 1673 (see also his The Christian Quaker, London, 1669).

Saltonstall, Gordon. A Sermon Preached before the General Assembly. Boston, 1697.

Scottow, Joshua. A Narrative of . . . the Massachusetts Colony. Boston, 1694.

Sewall, Samuel. Phaenomena Quaedam Apocalyptica . . . a Description of the New Heaven As It Makes to Those Who Stand Upon the New Earth. Boston, 1697 (cf. William Aspinwall, A Brief Description of the . . . Kingdom, London, 1653; and Thomas Parker, The Visions and Prophesies of Daniel Expounded, London, 1646).

Shepard, Thomas. Theses Sabbaticae or, The Doctrine of the Sabbath. London, 1649 (key first-generation work).

Shepard, Thomas [son]. Eye-Salve. Cambridge, Mass., 1673 (see also John Oxenbridge, New-England Freemen Warned and Warned, Boston, 1673).

Stoughton, William. New-England's True Interest. Cambridge, Mass., 1670.

Taylor, Edward. Christographia, ed. Norman S. Grabo. New Haven, 1962 (see also his Treatise concerning the Lord's Supper, ed. Norman S. Grabo, East Lansing, Mich., 1966).

—— Poems, ed. Donald E. Stanford. New Haven, 1960 (most explicit typology is to be found in the Second Series of Preparatory Meditations, 1–30).

Torrey, Samuel. An Exhortation Unto Reformation, Amplified. Cambridge, Mass., 1674.

Vane, Sir Henry. An Epistle to the

Mystical Body of Christ on Earth: The Church Universal in Babylon. London, 1662.

Wheelwright, John. Writings, ed. Charles H. Bell. Boston, 1876 (see for example his answer to Winthrop, Mercurius Americanus, London, 1645).

Wigglesworth, Michael. Diary, in Proceedings of the Colonial Society of Massachusetts, XXXV (1964).

Willard, Samuel. The Fountain Opened. Boston, 1700.

Williams, Roger. The Bloody Tenant Yet More Bloody (1652; controversy with John Cotton).

—— Queries of the Highest Consideration (1644; the most recent printing of Williams' writings is New York, 1959, ed. Perry Miller and others; see vols. I and II of this edition for John Cotton's position in the controversy).

Williams, William. The Great Duty of Ministers to Advance the Kingdom of God. Boston, 1726.

Wilson, John. The Scriptures Genuine Interpreter Asserted. Cambridge, Mass., 1678 (see also his poems in Handkerchiefs from Paul, being pious and consolatory verses of Puritan Massachusetts, ed. Kenneth B. Murdock, Cambridge, Mass., 1927).

b. Representative Writers of the Eighteenth Century

Ashley, Jonathan. An Humble Attempt to Give a Clear Account from Scripture. Boston, 1753.

Austin, David. The Dawn of Day. New Haven, 1800 (see also his Downfall of Mystical Babylon, Elizabethtown, 1794; and cf. his Voice of God to the People of the United States, Elizabeth-town, 1796, and Samuel Langdon, *Observations on the Revelation of Jesus Christ to St. John*, Worcester, Mass., 1791).

—— *The Rod of Moses upon the Rock of Calvary*. Norwich, Conn., 1816 (two sermons by Austin suggest certain relationships between the symbols of the Masonic sect and typology: *The First Vibration of the Jubilee Trumpet*, Elizabethtown, N.J., 1799; and *Masonry in its Glory*, East Windsor, Conn., 1799; see also in this regard Thaddeus M. Harris, *Ignorance and Prejudice*, Boston, 1796, where Manna is rendered as a Masonic emblem).

Barnard, John. *A Proof of Jesus Christ His Being the Ancient Promised Messiah*. Boston, 1756.

Beach, John. *Three Discourses, Casuistical and Practical*. Boston, 1768.

Beckwith, George. *Adam's Losing, and Christ's Saving All Their Seed*. Boston, 1735 (see also: Joseph Buckminster, *The Blessing of Abraham*, Boston, 1770; Jonathan Townsend, *The Believing Gentile's Sure Title to the Promise Made to Abraham*, Boston, 1749; and Timothy Upham, *A Discourse . . . on the Blessing of Abraham*, Concord, 1794).

Bellamy, Joseph. *A Dialogue on the Christian Sacraments*. Boston, 1762 (see further the following titles in his Works, 3 vols. [ed. Stephen Dodge?] New York, 1811–12: *A Treatise of the Divinity of Christ* [in vol. I]; *An Essay on . . . the Gospel of Jesus Christ* [in vol. II]; and *The Law our School-master* [in vol. III]).

—— *The Millennium*. Boston, 1758 (see also Samuel Hopkins,

A Treatise on the Millennium, Newport, R.I., 1793; and cf. Samuel Sherwood, *The Church's Flight into the Wilderness*, New York, 1776).

Bolles, Joseph. *A Relation of the Opposition*. N.p., 1761 (see also his *Concerning the Christian Sabbath*, n.p., 1757; and cf. Mather Byles, Jr., *The Christian Sabbath Explained and Vindicated*, New-London, 1759).

Bromley, Thomas. *The Way to the Sabbath of Rest*. Philadelphia, 1759.

Buell, Samuel. *A Sermon Preached at East-Hampton*. New York, 1761 (see also his funeral sermons for Occam and Tallmage, New York, 1759 and 1755; and cf. Sylvanus Conant's execution sermon, *The Blood of Abel, and the Blood of Christ*, Boston, 1764).

Burr, Aaron. *The Watchman's Answer*. New York, 1757 (cf. John White's anti-Arminian and millenarian *New-England's Lamentations*, Boston, 1734, and Thomas Prince, *Extraordinary Events of the Doings of God*, Boston, 1745).

Catlin, Jacob. *The Gentiles Inheritance of the Blessing of Abraham*. Hartford, 1799.

Chaplin, Ebenezer. *The Civil State Compared to Rivers*. Boston, 1773.

Cheever, Ezekiel. *Scripture Prophecies Explained*. Boston, 1757.

Clarke, Peter. *The Scripture Grounds of the Baptism of Christian Infants*. Boston, 1735.

Colman, Benjamin. *Christ Standing for an Ensign of the People*. Boston, 1738 (general application of various 'figures of Christ'; cf. his *A Brief Dissertation on* the Three First Chapters of Genesis, Boston, 1735, and his Two Sermons Deliver'd at Hartford, New London, 1735, especially the first of these sermons, on the 'Christian Sabbath').

Coombe, Thomas. The Harmony Between the Old and New Testaments Respecting the Messiah. Philadelphia, 1774 (cf. Marston Cabot, Christ's Kingdom Entirely Spiritual, Boston, 1743, and Richard Clarke, The Prophetic Number of Daniel and John Calculated, Charlestown, 1759).

Cooper, William. The Work of Ministers, represented under the figure of sowers. Boston, 1736 (see also his The Promised Seed, Putney, Vt., 1798).

Crosley, David. Samson A Type of Christ. Newburyport, 1796 (3rd edn.).

Davies, Samuel. The Mediatorial Kingdom and Glories of Jesus Christ. Bristol, 1783 (see further The Law and the Gospel and Poor and Contrite Spirits, in Davies' Sermons on Important Occasions, 7th edn., London, 1815, vols. I and III).

——— Miscellaneous Poems, Chiefly on Divine Subjects. Williamsburg, 1751 (included in Collected Poems of Samuel Davies: 1723–61, ed. Richard B. Davis. Gainesville, 1968).

Duché, Jacob. The American Vine. Philadelphia, 1775 (cf. Bethuel Dodd, The Singular Goodness of God to America, Whitestown, 1796).

——— Human Life A Pilgrimage. Philadelphia, 1771 (see also Discourse II in Discourses on Various Subjects, London, 1790; and Observations on a Variety of Subjects, Philadelphia, 1774).

Edwards, Jonathan. History of the

Work of Redemption (1786; David Austin's ample annotations to the Swards Edition, New York, 1793, contain many references to, and citations from, contemporary authorities on typology).

——— An Humble Attempt to Promote Explicit Agreement in Extraordinary Prayer (1747).

——— Thoughts Concerning the Revival of Religion in New England (1745).

———Types of the Messiah (a convenient edition of Edwards' works is that edited by E. Hickman, 10th edn., London, 1865; this does not, of course, include Images or Shadows of Divine Things, which was first edited by Perry Miller, New Haven, 1948.)

Ellwood, Thomas. Davideis: The Life of David, King of Israel: A Sacred Poem, in Five Books. Philadelphia, 1751 (many later editions; see also Timothy Dwight's 'additions' to Isaac Watt's continually reprinted renderings of the Psalms, New York, 1817).

Emerson, John. Isaiah's Mission Considered and Applied. Brattleborough, Vt., 1797.

Evans, David. Law and Gospel. Philadelphia, 1748 (see also William Dyer, Christ's Famous Titles, Boston, 1731, and Shippie Townsend, Gospel News, Boston, 1794).

Fisher, Edward. The Marrow of Sacred Divinity. Salem, Mass., 1793.

Foxcroft, Thomas. A Seasonable Momento. Boston, 1747.

Frink, Thomas. A King Reigning in Righteousness. Boston, 1758 (see also his election sermons for 1758 and 1759; and cf. David

S. Rowland, *Divine Providence Illustrated*, Providence, 1766, and Hugh Henry Brackenridge's famous *Eulogium*, Philadelphia, 1779).

Gale, Benjamin. *A Brief Essay . . . From the Prophetick Writings of the Old and New Testament.* New-Haven, 1788.

Gleason, James. *An Exposition of the First Three Chapters on Genesis . . . The Gospel Glass, or Travel of Zion's Church in the World, Until the Opening of the Last Great and Seventh Seal.* Norwich, 1797 (see also: Abraham Cummings, *A Dissertation on the . . . Millennium*, Boston, 1796; John C. Robinson, *A Scriptural View of the . . . Monarchies of the World . . . According to the Prophecies of Isaiah, Daniel, and John*, New York, 1798; and Joshua Spalding, *Sentiments, Concerning the Coming and Kingdom of Christ*, Salem, Mass., 1796).

Hare, Francis. *The Difficulties and Discouragements which attend the Study of the Scriptures*, London, 1714.

Holly, Israel. *The New-Testament Interpretation of the Old.* New-London, 1771.

Horne, George. *A Commentary on the Book of Psalms.* Philadelphia, 1792.

James, Thomas. *A Short Treatise on the Visible Kingdom . . . Wherein it is Proven that . . . the Old and New Testament . . . [are] the Same.* Philadelphia, 1749 (cf. Jacob Green, *An Inquiry into the Constitution of the Jewish Church.* New York, 1768).

M'Corkle, Samuel Eusebius. *A Sermon On . . . the United States of America, Contrasted with . . . the Israelites.* Halifax, 1795

(a representative figural reading of the exodus from Egypt, the Red Sea crossing, the Law delivered from Sinai, the Manna in the wilderness, and the fall of Jericho; see also his *The Divine Goodness to the United States of America*, New York, 1795).

March, Edmund. *Divine Providence . . . in Fulfilling Scripture-Prophecies.* Boston, 1762 (cf. John William Gerar De Brahm, *Voice of the Everlasting Gospel*, Philadelphia, 1792).

Mather, Moses. *The Visible Church.* New York, 1759 (cf. Joseph Bellamy's rebuttal, *A Careful and Strict Examination of the External Covenant*, New Haven, 1770).

Meyers, Simon. *An Essay on the New Birth . . . and a Short Distinction between Old and New Covenant Believers. Also—Remarks on the Spiritual Temple . . . With a Happy Prospect of its Speedy . . . Return out of Captivity.* Bennington, Vt., 1795.

Newton, John. *Messiah. Fifty Expository Discourses.* Philadelphia, 1795 (vol. II of his *Letters and Sermons*).

Niles, Nathaniel. *Two Discourses on Liberty.* Newburyport, 1774.

Parsons, Jonathan. *Manna Gathered in the Morning.* Boston, 1751 (see also his *Good News from a Far Country*, New Haven, 1756).

Parsons, Joseph. *Thirty Lectures on the Principles of the Christian Religion.* London, 1761.

Prince, Thomas. *The People of New England.* Boston, 1730.

Romayne, Jeremiah. *The American Israel.* Catskill, N.Y., 1795.

Sherman, Josiah. *The History of Melchizedek.* Litchfield, 1786.

Smith, Eunice. *Practical Language Interpreted . . . Representing a Believer . . . Speaking Canaan's Language.* Dover, 1796.

Stanford, John. *Sacred Architecture; or . . . the Temple of Solomon.* New York, 1793 (see also John Tyler, *The Sanctity of the Christian Temple,* Providence, 1771).

Strong, Joseph. *The Church of Christ One, and for Substance the Same Under the New Testament, as Under the Old.* Norwich, 1783 (see also Moses Hemmenway, *A Discourse Concerning the Church,* Boston, 1792).

Tennent, Gilbert. *Irenicum Ecclesiasticum.* Philadelphia, 1749.

—— *The Substance and Scope of Both Testaments.* Philadelphia, 1749 (see also his *Espousals,* New York, 1735; and *Sermon Preach'd at Philadelphia . . . [on] A Day of Fasting and Prayer,* Philadelphia, 1748).

Tompson, Edward. *Heaven the Best Country.* Boston, 1712.

Trumbull, Benjamin. *Twelve Discourses.* Hartford, 1799.

Vaill, Joseph. *Noah's Flood.* New-London, 1796.

Walton, John. *A Vindication of the True Christian Baptism.* Boston, 1738 (cf. Ebenezer Pemberton, *Sermons on Several Subjects,* Boston, 1738).

Wilson, James. *The Utility of the Scriptures of the Old Testament.* Alexandria, Va., 1798.

Winchester, Elhanan. *The Divinity of Christ, Proved from the Old and New Testament.* Boston, 1786.

—— *Four Discourses, Entitled, The Face of Moses Unveiled by the Gospel.* Philadelphia, 1784

(see also his *Two Lectures on the Prophecies that Remain to be Fulfilled,* Norwich, 1792, and his larger *Course of Lectures on the Prophecies,* Norwich, 1794).

Zubly, John J. *The Law of Liberty.* Philadelphia, 1775 (see also Timothy Dwight's *Discourse . . . on the National Fast,* New York, 1812, and *Discourse on Some Events in the Last Century,* New Haven, 1801).

c. Twentieth-Century Criticism

Literary criticism dealing with typology in all other periods except the colonial American period appears in Section 7 (e).

Bercovitch, Sacvan. *Horologicals to Chronometricals: The Rhetoric of the Jeremiad,* Madison, 1970 (*Literary Monographs,* 3, University of Wisconsin; see further his 'The Historiography of Johnson's Wonder-Working Providence,' *Essex Institute Historical Collections,* CIV [1968], 136–61; and cf. his 'Puritan New England Rhetoric and the Jewish Problem,' *Early American Literature,* V [1970], 63–73).

—— 'New England Epic: Cotton Mather's *Magnalia Christi Americana,*' *English Literary History,* XXXIII (1966), 337–51 (see also his doctoral dissertation, Claremont Graduate School, 1965).

—— 'Typology in Puritan New England: The Williams-Cotton Controversy Reassessed,' *American Quarterly,* XIX (1967), 166–91 (see also his reviews in *Early American Literature,* III [1968], 51–54, and IV [1969], 49–52, in *Pacific Historical Review* XXXIX [1970], 229–30, and in *Renaissance Quarterly,* XXIV [1971], 103–06).

Brumm, Ursula. *American Thought*

and *Religious Typology* (1963), trans. John Hoaglund, New Brunswick, N.J., 1970 (wide-ranging, insightful, seminal study; see Mason I. Lowance's review in *William and Mary Quarterly*, 3rd ser., XXVIII [1970], 145–46).

—— 'The Figure of Christ in American Literature,' *Partisan Review*, XXIV (1957), 403–13 (see also her 'Symbolism and the Novel,' *Partisan Review*, XXV [1958], 329–42).

—— 'The "Tree of Life" in Edward Taylor's Meditations,' *Early American Literature*, III (1968), 72–87 (cf. Cecelia L. Halbert [Tichi], 'Tree of Life Imagery in the Poetry of Edward Taylor,' *American Literature*, XXXVIII [1966], 22–34).

Darrow, Dianne. 'Thomas Hooker and the Puritan Art of Preaching,' Diss. University of California (San Diego), 1968.

Davis, Thomas M. 'Edward Taylor and the Traditions of Puritan Typology,' *Early American Literature*, IV (1970), 27–47.

—— 'The Traditions of Puritan Typology,' Diss. University of Missouri, 1968.

Feidelson, Charles. *Symbolism in American Literature*. Chicago, 1959.

Fender, Stephen A. 'Edward Taylor and the Sowers of American Puritan Wit,' Diss. University of Manchester, 1963.

Gallagher, Edward J. 'An Overview of Edward Johnson's *Wonder-Working Providence*,' *Early American Literature*, III (1971), 30–49 (see also his 'Critical Study of Edward Johnson's *Wonder-Working Providence*,' Diss. University of Notre Dame, 1970).

Heimert, Alan. *Religion and the American Mind, From the Great Awakening to the Revolution.* Cambridge, Mass., 1966.

Howard, Alan Blair. 'The Web in the Loom: An Introduction to the Puritan Historians of New England,' Diss. Stanford University, 1968 (Howard also discusses typology briefly in his excellent 'Art and History in Bradford's *Of Plymouth Plantation*,' *William and Mary Quarterly*, 3rd ser., XXVIII [1971], 237–67; for a denial of the importance of typology in the histories, see Cecelia Louise Halbert [Tichi], 'The Art of the Lord's Remembrancers: A Study of New England Puritan Histories,' Diss. University of California (Davis), 1968).

Keller, Karl. 'From Christianity to Transcendentalism: A Note on Emerson's Use of the Conceit,' *American Literature*, XXIX (1967), 94–98.

Lowance, Mason I., Jr. Introduction to Samuel Mather, *The Figures or Types of the Old Testament* (London, 1705; 2nd edn.), ed. Lowance. New York, 1969 (Series in American Studies; Lowance also discusses typology at some length in his forthcoming Twayne volume, *Increase Mather: A Critical Biography*; see also his Introduction to Increase Mather, *Ichabod, or the Glory Departing* [Boston, 1701], ed. Lowance, New York, 1971 [American Literature and Culture Series]; and, also in this series, his Introduction to his edition of Cotton Mather, *Agricola, or the Religious Husbandman*, [Boston, 1727], New York, 1971).

—— 'Images and Shadows of Divine Things: Puritan Typology in New England from 1660 to

1750,' Diss. Emory University, 1967.

Ludwig, Allen I. *Graven Images: New England Stone-carving and its Symbols, 1650–1815*. Middletown, Conn., 1966.

Manierre, William R., II. 'Cotton Mather and the Biographical Parallel,' *American Quarterly*, XIII (1961), 153–60 (cf. his 'Mather and the Plain Style,' Diss., University of Michigan, 1958; see also William J. Scheick, 'Anonymity and Art in *The Life and Death of that Reverend Man of God, Mr. Richard Mather*,' *American Literature*, XLII [1971], 457–67).

Martz, Louis. Foreword to *The Poems of Edward Taylor*, ed. Donald E. Stanford. New Haven, 1960.

Middlekauff, Robert. *The Mathers: Three Generations of Puritan Intellectuals, 1596–1728*. Oxford, 1971.

Miller, Perry. Introduction to Jonathan Edwards, *Images or Shadows of Divine Things*, ed. Miller. New Haven, 1948 (first major assessment of American Puritan concern with typology, still very challenging and impressive; see also Paul Baumgartner, 'Jonathan Edwards: The Theory behind his Use of Figurative Language,' *PMLA*, LXXVIII [1963], 321–25).

—— *Roger Williams: His Contribution to the American Tradition*. New York, 1962 (see the reviews of this book by Darrett B. Rutman in *William and Mary Quarterly*, 3rd ser., XXI [1964], 200–03, and by Edmund S. Morgan in *New England Quarterly*, XXXVIII [1965], 513–25; see further Miller's 'Roger Williams: An Essay in Interpretation,' in *The Complete Writings of Roger*

Williams, vol. VII, ed. Miller [New York, 1959]).

Morgan, Edmund S. *Roger Williams: The Church and the State*. New York, 1967 (cf.: Leroy Moore, 'Religious Liberty: Roger Williams and the Revolutionary Era,' *Church History*, XXXIV [1965], 57–76; Irwin H. Polishook's introductory essay to his anthology, *Roger Williams, John Cotton, and Religious Freedom: A Controversy in Old and New England*, Englewood Cliffs, N.J., 1967; and John Garrett, *Roger Williams: Witness Beyond Christendom*, New York, 1970).

Murdock, Kenneth B. 'Clio in the Wilderness: History and Biography in Puritan New England,' *Church History*, XXIV (1955), 221–38 (highly stimulating study; see also his Introduction to Perry Miller, *Nature's Nation*, Cambridge, Mass., 1967; and cf. Joy B. Gilsdorf, 'The Puritan Apocalypse: New England Eschatology in the Seventeenth Century,' Diss. Yale University, 1964).

Reinitz, Richard. 'Symbolism and Freedom: The Use of Biblical Typology as an Argument for Religious Toleration in Seventeenth-Century England and America,' Diss. University of Rochester, 1967.

Rosenmeier, Jesper. 'The Image of Christ: The Typology of John Cotton,' Diss. Harvard University, 1965 (see also his 'New England's Perfection; The Image of Adam and the Image of Christ in the Antinomian Crisis, 1634–1638,' *William and Mary Quarterly*, 3rd ser., XXVII [1970], 435–59).

—— 'The Teacher and the Witness: John Cotton and Roger Williams,' *William and Mary*

Quarterly, 3rd ser., XXV (1968), 403–31 (see also his review of The Wall and the Garden: Selected Massachusetts Election Sermons, 1670–1775, ed. A. W. Plumstead, Minneapolis, 1968, in William and Mary Quarterly, 3rd ser., XXVI [1969], 313–15; Professor Plumstead briefly discusses the Puritans' use of typology in his commentary to this volume).

——— 'VERITAS: The Sealing of the Promise,' Harvard Library Bulletin, XVI (1968), 26–37.

Simpson, Alan. Puritanism in Old and New England. Chicago, 1955.

Stanford, Donald E. 'An Edition of the Complete Poetical Works of Edward Taylor.' Diss. Stanford University, 1953.

Strauch, Carl F. 'Typology and the American Renaissance,' Early American Literature, VI (1971), 167–78 (essay-review of Ursula Brumm's American Thought and Religious Typology; cf. Ely Stock's review of Joel Porte's The Romance in America, in Novel: A Forum on Fiction, V [1971], 84–86).

Warren, Austin. 'Edward Taylor,' in Major Writers of America, I, ed. Perry Miller, New York, 1962 (see also Thomas H. Johnson, 'Introduction,' The Poetical Works of Edward Taylor, New York, 1939).

Williams, George H. Wilderness and Paradise in Christian Thought: The Biblical Experience of the Desert in the History of Christianity and the Paradise Theme in the Theological Idea of the University. New York, 1962 (see also the comments on the Puritan concept of the wilderness in Michael H. Cowan, City of the West: Emerson, America, and Urban Metaphor, New Haven, 1967).

6. Eighteenth and Nineteenth Centuries

a. Nineteenth-Century America

The entries are limited to the nineteenth century (eighteenth-century American works are listed in Section 5 (b), above) and to representative applications of typology by theologians; it does not therefore include such writers as Melville, Hawthorne, and Emerson. Hopefully, a study of the following works would help provide a specific cultural context in examining the use of 'types' by our major authors; of interest in this area is Jerry W. Brown, *The Rise of Biblical Criticism in America, 1800–1870* (Middletown, 1969).

Baldwin, Samuel D. *Armageddon; or the . . . existence of the United States Foretold in the Bible, its . . . expansion into the millennial republic, and its dominion over the whole world.* Cincinnati, 1854.

Bales, Milton. *Types of the Holy Spirit.* New York, n.p. [18—].

Bellamy, John. *The History of All Religions.* Boston, 1820.

Brown, John. *A Brief View of the Figures . . . in Scripture.* Middlebury, Vt., 1812.

Bush, George, editor. *The Hierophant; or, Monthly Journal of Sacred Symbols and Prophecy.* New York, June, 1842—May, 1843 (12 nos.; see also Bush's commentaries on Joshua, Leviticus, Judges, Numbers, and Daniel).

Bushnell, Horace. *God in Christ. Three Discourses.* Hartford, 1849 (the 'Preliminary Discourse' enlarges on the meaning of types in nature, in language, and in terms of Lockean epistemology; see also in this connection Bushnell's 'The Reason of Faith,' in *Sermons for the New Life*, New York, 1864, 'Of Non-Intercourse' Between Worlds,' in *Moral Uses of Dark Things*, New York, 1905 [first published 1867, as Vol. II of *Literary Varieties*], and *Views of Christian Nurture*, Hartford, 1848).

Frey, Joseph S. C. F. *A Course of Lectures on the Scripture Types*. New York, 1841.

Lord, E. *The Messiah in Moses and the Prophets*. New York, 1853.

Mass, A. J. *Christ in Type and Prophecy*. New York, 1893 (interesting Jesuit commentary).

Newcomb, Harvey. *The Four Pillars*. Boston, 1842.

—— *Christianity Demonstrated . . . With An Explanation of the Types*. Boston, 1848.

Roeder, Adolf. *The Cities of the World*. Vineland, N.J., 1893 (eccentric use of types; see also his *Handbook of the Science of Correspondence*, Vineland, N.J., 1894, and *Bible Symbolism*, Orange, N.J., 1916).

Seiss, Joseph A. *Holy Types; or, The Gospel in Leviticus: A Series of Lectures*. Philadelphia, 1866.

Silver, Abiel. *Lectures on the Symbolic Character of the Sacred Scriptures*. New York, 1863.

Smith, Ethan. *A Key to the Figurative Language Found in the Sacred Scriptures*. Exeter, 1824 (cf.: Edward E. Sealye, *Bible Emblems*, New York, 1866; and Daniel Taylor, *Sentiments*, Boston, 1741, and *The Voice of the Church*, Peace Dale, R.I., 1855).

Smith, Hannah W. *Bible Readings on the Progressive Development of Truth and Experience in the Book of the Old Testament*. Boston, 1881.

Spurgeon, Charles H. *Types and Emblems*. New York, 1876.

Terry, Milton. *Biblical Hermeneutics*. New York, 1885 (wide-ranging appraisal).

Thayer, William M. *The Morning Star; or, Symbols of Christ*. Boston, 1856.

Thomson, William H. *The Great Argument; or, Jesus Christ in the Old Testament*. New York, 1884.

Winthrop, Edward. *The Premium Essay on the Characteristics and Laws of Prophetic Symbols*. New York, 1856.

b. Europe

The following (highly selective) entries include works from both the eighteenth and nineteenth centuries. As in Section VI (a), I have limited myself to representative theological expositions, without noting the use of typology by leading creative writers of the period. Several literary critics have discussed some of these writers from this perspective: see Section VII (e). See also, for example: Friedrich Gottlieb Klopstock's famous twenty-book poem, *Der Messias*, translated in America as early as 1788 by Joseph Collye; Charles Jennens' 1741 Libretto for Handel's *Messiah* (e.g., in G. F. Handel. *Messiah. An Oratorio*, ed. J. M. Coopersmith [New York, 1941]; typological patterns also underlie the librettos to a number of Handel's dramatic oratorios, such as *Samson* and *Joshua*); and Pietro A. D. B. Mastasio's *Isacco, Figura del Relentore* [Palermo, 1743], a cantata in verse by this well-known Italian composer, which went through several editions and translations (e.g., in German).

Anon., *Joseph the Type of Christ*. N.p., 1765.

Archer, William. *Rachel of Pada-narum, Type of the Church.* London, 1843.

Bähr, Karl Christian Felix. *Symbolik des Mosaischen Cultus.* 2 vols. Heidelberg, 1837.

Barker, Thomas. *The Messiah. Being the Prophecies Concerning Him Methodized, With Their Accomplishments.* London, 1780.

Bengel, Johann Albrecht. *Gnomen Novum Testamentum.* Ulmae, 1763 (enormously influential work by a leading Pietist; see, for example, Gottfried Menken, *Schriften,* Bremen, 1858).

Bennet, Benjamin. *Truth, Inspiration, and Usefulness of the Scripture.* London, 1730.

Beyschlag, Johann H. C. Willibald. *Die Paulinische Theodicee.* Berlin, 1868.

—— *New Testament Theology,* trans. Neil Buchanan. Edinburgh, 1895 (popular interpretation; several editions).

Biermann, Johan. *Moses et Christus.* Offenbach, 1706.

Blasche, Johann C. *Neue Aufklärung über die Mosaische Typologie.* Jena, 1789 (strong defender of typology in face of critical-historical approach).

Boehm, Anton Wilhelm. *The Duty of Reformation.* London, 1718 (important Pietist follower of Francke, extremely influential in England and New England; see also the Pietist Heinrich Wilhelm Ludolf's figural-chiliastic *Considerations of the Church Universal,* London, 1726).

Böhmer, Eduard. *Zur biblischen Typik.* Halis Saxonum, 1855.

Bonar, Andrew. *The First Captivity and Restoration of the Jews, Viewed in Reference to the Coming of the Messiah.* London, 1842 (see also Samuel Clarke, *A Discourse Concerning the Connection of the Prophecies,* London, 1725).

Bradbury, Thomas. *Ass; or, The Serpent.* London, 1712.

Bryant, Jacob. *A New System, or, An Analysis of Ancient Mythology.* 3 vols. London, 1774–76.

Buddaeus, Johannes Franciscus. *Isagoge Historico-Theologica.* Lipsiae, 1727.

—— *Ordinaris Theologici.* Jena, 1710 (highly significant critique of federalist typology).

Cennick, John. *The Shadows of Christ.* Dublin, 1754.

Chevallier, Temple. *On the Historical Types Contained in the Old Testament.* 2 vols. Cambridge, Eng., 1826 (Hulsean Lectures for 1826).

Clapton, Edward. *The Precious Stones of the Bible.* London, 1899.

Clarke, Adam. *A Discourse on the Nature, Design and Institution, of the Holy Eucharist.* London, 1810 (philosophical defence of typology; cf. L. Alexander, *Connection and Harmony of the Old and New Testament,* London, 1841).

Clausen, Henrik N. *Hermeneutik des Neuen Testament.* Leipzig, 1841.

Collins, Anthony. *A Discourse of the Grounds and Reasons of the Christian Religion.* London, 1737 (especially Part I).

Cremer, Bernhard. *Typologia.* Amsterdam, 1727 (school of Cocceius).

Crusius, Christian August. *Hypomnemata ad Theologiam Propheticam.* 3 vols. Lipsiae, 1764–78 (important for typology and theology in general).

Daubuz, Charles. A Perpetual Commentary on the Revelation of St. John. London, 1720 (a voluminous and widely influential work which was abridged as A Symbolical Dictionary; in which the general significance of all the prophetic symbols . . . is laid down, London, 1842).

Delitzsch, Franz J. Die Biblisch-Prophetische Theologie. Leipzig, 1845 (for English translations of this widely read Lutheran theologian, who was influenced by Crusius, see for example his Solemn Questions Addressed to Hebrews of Culture, trans. William C. Daland, New York, 1890, and Messianic Prophecies, Edinburgh, 1880).

Denzinger, Henricus. Enchiridion Symbolorum. Wirceburgi, 1856 (32nd edn., Freiburg, 1963).

Deusingius, Hermann. Moses Evangelizans. Cologne, 1719.

Dick, John. Lectures on Theology. 4 vols. Edinburgh, 1834.

Diestel, Ludwig. Geschichte des Alten Testaments in der Christlichen Kirche. Jena, 1869 (on the problem of Christian acceptance of the Old Testament).

Doederlein, Johann Christoph. Institutio Theologi Christiani. Altorfi, 1780 (expresses the ambivalent outlook on typology by many theologians of the period).

Dove, John. A Creed Founded on Truth and Common Sense. London, 1750 (amalgam of Locke and Hutchinson).

Edersheim, Alfred. Prophecy and History in relation to the Messiah. London, 1885 (see also his Jesus the Messiah, London, 1890).

English, George B. The Grounds of Christianity Examined by Comparing the New Testament with the Old. London, 1841.

Fairbairn, Patrick. The Typology of Scripture. 2 vols. Edinburgh, 1845–47 (classic nineteenth-century study).

Farrar, Frederic William. History of Interpretation. London, 1886 (popular defence of Reformation exegesis).

Francké, August Hermann. Praelectiones Hermeneuticae. Halle, 1723.

——— Christus Sacrae Scripturae Nucleus; or Christ the sum and substance of the Holy Scriptures, in the Old and New Testament, trans. 'by an ancient Doctor of physick.' London, 1732 (see also his Manuductio ad lectionem Scripturae Sacrae, London, 1706, and his introduction to the Psalms, 1734; leading Pietist of Halle who exerted a great influence on both Cotton Mather and Jonathan Edwards, and whose works in this sense present a link between late colonial Puritanism and Edwardsian revivalism).

Guers, E. Le Camp et le Tabernacle du Désert. Geneva, 1849.

Hahn, Philipp M. Erbauungsstunden über die Offenbarung Johannis. Halis Saxonum, 1795.

Haldane, Robert. The Evidence and Authority of Divine Revelation, Being a View of the Testimony of the Law and the Prophets to the Messiah, with the Subsequent Testimonies. 2 vols. Edinburgh, 1816.

Hartmann, Anton T. Die Enge Verbindung des Alten Testament mit dem Neuen. Hamburg, 1831.

Hartmann, M. Les Prophéties Messianiques. Strasbourg, 1857.

Hengstenberg, Ernst Wilhelm. *Christology of the Old Testament, and a Commentary on the Predictions of the Messiah by the Prophets.* trans. Revel Keith. 3 vols. Washington, D.C., 1836–39 (careful consideration of typology and Christology).

Herder, Johann Gottfried von. *Briefe, das Studium der Theologie Betreffend.* Weimar, 1780 (an application of typology to nature and a general defence of the method by the great German writer).

Hermkhuysen, Bernardus van. *De Wet der Schaduwen aangaande den Tabernakel . . . opgehelderd.* Amsterdam, 1733.

Hofmann, Johann Christian Konrad von. *Weissagung und Erfüllung.* 2 vols. Nördlingen, 1841–44 (spirited defence of typology by a distinguished scholar; influenced by Hegel and therefore especially interesting in terms of the historical application of the figural method).

Horne, Thomas Hartwell. *An Introduction to the Critical Study and Knowledge of the Holy Scriptures.* 4 vols. London, 1818–21 (a standard text for Scripture study in all English colleges and universities—11th edn., 1860—which refers to Keach as an authority on the subject).

Horton, Robert Forman. *Revelation and the Bible.* London, 1892.

Hutchinson, John. *Glory or Gravity.* London, 1733.

—— *The Religion of Satan.* London, 1736.

—— *The Use of Reason Recovered by the Data in Christianity.* London, 1736 (see also this author's *Moses's Principia,* London, 1724; founder of a significant school of exegesis which blended Cabbala, allegory, and typology; see also, for example, Thomas Sherlock, *The Use and Intent of Prophecy in the Several Ages of the World,* London, 1725).

Jones, William. *A Course of Lectures on the Figurative Language of the Holy Scripture.* London, 1787.

Jortin, John. *Remarks on Ecclesiastical History.* 5 vols. London, 1751–53.

Kanne, Johann Arnold. *Christus im Alten Testament.* Nürnberg, 1818 (eccentric use of types).

Kidder, Richard. *A Demonstration of the Messias.* London, 1726 (see also his *Commentary on the Five Books of Moses,* London, 1694).

Knapp, George Christian. *Lectures on Christian Theology,* trans. Leonard Woods. 2 vols. New York, 1831–33.

Krementz, Phillip. *Israel, Vorbild der Kirche.* Fribourg, 1865 (see also his *Grundlinien der Geschichtstypik der Heiligen Schrift,* Fribourg, 1875).

Lange, Joachim. *Caussa Dei et Religionis Judaeis Revelatae.* Halae Saxonum, 1726.

—— *Mysterium Christi ac Christianismi in Fasciis Typicis Antiquitatum V.T.* Halae Saxonum, 1717 (famous Pietist, influential in New England; see also his *Hermeneutica Sacra,* Halae, 1733, and *Urim ac Thummim,* n.p., 1734).

Lavington, G. *The Nature and Use of a Type.* London, 1724.

Lee, Henry. *Sophron: or Nature's Characteristics of the Truth.*

London, 1760 (types treated in the context of nature and reason).

Leland, John. A Defense of Christianity. Dublin, 1733.

Léonard, Abbé Martin-Augustin. Traité du Sens Litteral et du Sens Mystique des Saintes Ecritures. Paris, 1727.

Lowman, Moses. Argument from Prophecy. London, 1735.

—— Dissertation on the Civil Government of the Hebrews. London, 1740 (see also his Rational of the Hebrew Worship, London, 1748; important for American use of typology through his influence upon Jonathan Edwards).

MacCosh, James, and George Dickie. Typical Forms and Special Ends in Creation. Edinburgh, 1856.

MacLaurin, John. An Essay on the Prophecies Relating to the Messiah. Edinburgh, 1773.

Marsh, Herbert. The Authenticity of the Five Books of Moses considered. Cambridge, Eng., 1792.

—— Lectures on the Criticism and Interpretation of the Bible. Cambridge, Eng., 1828 (leading theologian who gave 'innate typology' its fullest formulation; the works indebted to this approach include, inter alia, John J. Conybeare's Bampton Lectures for the Year MDCCCXXIV. Being an Attempt to Trace the . . . Secondary and Spiritual Interpretation of Scripture, Oxford, 1824).

McEwen, William. Grace and Truth; or the Glory and Fulness of the Redeemer Displayed in an Attempt to Explain the Most Remarkable Types, Figures, and Allegories of the Old Testament.

Edinburgh, 1763 (some twenty editions by 1856, both in England and America).

Meyer, Johann Friedrich von. Bibeldeutungen. Frankfurt, 1812.

Michaelis, Johann David. Entwurf der Typischen Gottesgelahrtheit. Göttingen, 1763 (fails to distinguish type from allegory).

Mildert, William van. An Inquiry into the General Principles of Scripture Interpretation. Oxford, 1815.

Molette, Constant de la. Nouvelle Méthode. 2 vols. Paris, 1777.

Nares, Robert. A Connected . . . View of the Prophecies Relating to the Christian Church. London, 1805.

Neumann, Wilhelm. Geschichte der Messianischen Weissagung im Alten Testament. Bleicherode, 1865.

Newton, Thomas. Dissertation on the Prophecies. 3 vols. London, 1754–58 (well-known work; see also his notes to his editions of Milton's Paradise Lost and Paradise Regained, which went through many printings in England and America).

Olshausen, Hermann. Ein Wort über Tiefran Schriftsinn. Konigsberg, 1824 (a rather vague attempt to work out a 'new system' of typological interpretation).

Onymus, Adam Joseph. De Usu Interpretationis Allegoricae. Bamberg, 1803.

Orelli, Conrad von. Die Alttestamentliche Weissagung Von der Vollendung des Gottesreiches in ihrer Geschichtlichen Entwicklung Dargestellt. Wien, 1882.

Otterly, Robert L. Aspects of the Old Testament. London, 1898.

Outrein, Jacques d'. Proef-Stukken van Heilige Sinne Beelden verdeelt in Twee Stukken. Amsterdam, 1700 (federalist theologian; see also his Dissertatio Philologica de Melchizedeco non Henocho, Amsterdam, 1713, and A Short Scheme of Divine Truths, 'translated into English,' London, 1705).

Patrizi, Francis Xavier. Institutio de Interpretazione Librorum Bibliorum. Rome, 1876.

Pfaff, Christoph M. Introductio in Historia Theologiae Literarium. Tübingen, 1720 (see also his important Institutiones Ecclesiasticae, Tübingen, 1721, and his Akademische Reden, Frankfurt, 1759; cf. the moralistic treatise by Christian Schottegen, Jesus der wahre Messias, Leipzig, 1748).

Prideaux, Humphrey. The Old and New Testament Connected. 2 vols. London, 1716–18.

Reinhard, Frederick. Das Alte Testament in seiner hohen Bedeutung als Vorbild des Neuen. Coblence, 1863 (cf. F. X. Reithmayr, Lehrbuch der Biblischen Hermeneutik, n.p., 1874).

Rembach, Johann J. Institutiones . . . Sacrae. Jena, 1723 (school of Cocceius).

Rhenferd, Jacob. Opera Philologica, Trajecti ad Rhenum, 1722 (typology, philology, and the federal covenant).

Sanday, William. Inspiration: Eight Lectures on the Early History and Origin of the Doctrine of Biblical Inspiration. London, 1893 (especially interesting regarding Jonah typology).

Saphir, Adolph. Christ and the Scriptures. London, 1867.

Saurin, Jacques. Dissertations . . . on the Most Memorable Events

of the Old and New Testaments, trans. I. Chamberlayne. London, 1773 (influential in America and important in general for an understanding of eighteenth-century uses of typology).

Scott, Caroline L. Exposition of the Types and Antitypes of the Old and New Testament. London, 1856.

Shuckford, Samuel. Sacred and Prophane History of the World Connected. London, 1728 (cf. Jacques Basnage de Beauval, History of the Jews, London, 1708).

Taylor, Daniel T. The Reign of Christ on Earth. London, 1882.

Tholuck, F. A. G. Das Alte Testament im Neuen Testament. Hamburg, 1836.

Townley, James. Reasons of the Laws of Moses: From the "Mose Novochim" of Maimonides, With Notes. London, 1827.

Trower, Walter J. Similitudes used in Holy Scriptures. London, 1851.

Ullmann, Carl. Reformers Before the Reformation, Principally in Germany and the Netherlands, trans. Robert Menzies. Edinburgh, 1855.

Van Mildert, William. An Inquiry into the General Principles of Scripture Interpretation. Oxford, 1815 (Bampton Lectures for 1814, by the Bishop of Llandaff and Durham).

Watts, Isaac. A Short View of the Whole Scripture History. London, 1732.

——— The Holiness of Times, Places and People under the Jewish and Christian Dispensations. London, 1738 (see also Watts's enormously influential translation of the Psalms; some of his famous hymns are explicitly typological

—e.g., the twelfth hymn of Book II—and many others employ typology implicitly; cf. Ralph Erskine, *Gospel Sonnets; or, Spiritual Songs*, Edinburgh, 1726, 2nd edn.).

Weiss, Bernhard Karl Philipp. *Biblical Theology of the New Testament*, trans. from the 3rd revised edn. by R. D. Eaton. Edinburgh. 2 vols. 1882–83.

Wemyss, Thomas. *A Key to the Symbolical Language of Scripture, by which numerous passages are explained and illustrated.* Edinburgh, 1840 (Biblical Cabinet; or Hermeneutical, Exegetical, and Philological Library, XXVI; founded on Daubuz's *Symbolical Dictionary*).

Westcott, Brooke Foss. *A General Survey of the History of the Canon of the New Testament.* London, 1889.

Wette, Wilhelm M. L. de. *A Critical and Historical Introduction to the ... Old Testament*, trans. T. Parker. 2 vols. Boston, 1843 (major theologian of the period

who advocated a 'limited' typology; see also his 'Beitrag zur Characteristie des Hebraismus,' *Studien von Daub und Crenzer*, III, 1807).

——— *Erklärung des Barnabasbriefes*. Berlin, 1869.

Willis, Edward Francis. *The Worship of the Old Covenant, Considered More Especially in Relation to that of the New.* Oxford, 1880.

Woolston, Thomas. *A Discourse on the Miracles of our Saviour in view of the present controversy between Infidels and Apostates.* London, 1729 (see also his *The Moderator between an infidel and an apostate*, London, 1725).

Worden, Thomas. *The Types Unveiled.* London, 1840 (see also Johann August Ernesti, *Principles of Biblical Interpretation*, trans. Charles H. Terrot, n.p., 1832 [vols. 1 and 4 of Biblical Cabinet]; and cf. T. E. Bridgett, *History of the Holy Eucharist in Great Britain*, 2 vols., London, 1881).

7. Twentieth-Century Studies

The term *typology* has come to be used in a non-religious sense in various disciplines, including literary criticism, either loosely (as in E. D. Hirsch, Jr., *Wordsworth and Schelling: A Typological Study of Romanticism* (New Haven, 1960), and Alan Trachtenberg, 'The Form of Freedom in *Huckleberry Finn*,' *Southern Review*, VI, NS [1970], 954–71), or as part of a specific philosophic outlook, as in Eugene Seiterich, *Die Logische Struktur des Typusbegriffes* (Freiburg, 1930), and in the essays collected in *Typologia Litterarum, Festschrift Max Wehrli* (Zurich, 1969). It has also long been a technical term in such diverse fields as mathematics, psychology, linguistics, political theory and history: e.g., Theodor Schieder, 'Der Typus in der Geschichtsswissenchaft,' *Stadium Generale*, V (1952), 228–34; Otto Hintze, *Staat und Verfassung* (Leipzig, 1941); Gilbert Knaub, *Typologie Juridique de la Fraude Electoral en France* (Paris, 1970); Boris Andreevich Uspenskii, *Principles of Structural Typology* (Paris, 1968); Jeffrey Alan Gray, ed., *Pavlov's Typology* (New York, 1964); Seymour Rubenfeld, *Typological Approaches and Delinquency Control* (Washington, D.C., 1967); Hans Ulrich Meyer-Lindemann, *Typologie der Theorien des Industriestandortes* (Bremen, 1951); and Charles F. Voegelin, *Typological and Comparative Grammar* (Baltimore, 1962). It may therefore be well to reiterate here that this Bibliography pertains only the biblical typology in the strict exegetical sense of the term, although occasionally it incorporates studies in related fields (e.g., symbolism, allegory, eschatology, and christology) when these have seemed to me especially relevant, for purposes either of comparison or contrast, to certain typological discussions.

a. General Theoretical Discussions

Alfrink, Bernardus J. *Over 'typologische' Exegese van het Oude Testament*. Nijmegen, 1945 (careful eclectic study; cf. E. C. Blackman, *Biblical Interpretation*, Philadelphia, 1957, and cf. G. Fohrer, *Messiasfrage und Bibelverständius*, Tübingen, 1957).

Amsler, Samuel. 'Où en est la Typologie de l'Ancien Testament?', *Etudes Théologiques et Religieuses*, XXVII (1952), 75–81 (see further his 'Prophétie et Typologie,' *Revue de Théologie*, III [1953], 139–48).

Auvray, P., ed. *L'Ancien Testament et les Chrétiens*. Paris, 1951 (excellent essays by L. Cerfaux, T. Camelot, and J. Leclercq; of particular general interest is J. Daniélou's broad discussion of the meaning of typology; cf. also T. G. Chifflot on the 'literal sense').

Barth, Karl. *Church Dogmatics* (1932–38), I, pt. 2, trans. G. T. Thomson and Harold Knight. Edinburgh, 1963 (includes succinct, stimulating insights on the meaning of typology; see also IV, pt. 2).

Bea, A. S. J. ' "Religionswissenschaftliche" oder "theologische" Exegese?', *Biblica*, XL (1959), 322–41.

Brisson, Jean-Paul. Introduction to Hilaire de Poitiers (320–368 [?]), *Traité des Mystères*, ed. and trans. Brisson. Paris, 1967 (Sources Chrétiennes, no. 79; see also W. den Boer, 'Hermeneutic Problems in Early Christian Literature,' *Vigiliae Christianae*, I [1947], 150–67).

Brunner, Heinrich E. *The Christian Doctrine of Creation and Redemption* (*Dogmatics*, II, 1949),

trans. Olive Wyon. Philadelphia, 1952 (brief but important discussion within a more general, highly influential formulation of theological dialectics).

Cerfaux, Lucien, J. Coppens, and J. Gribomont. *Problèmes et Méthodes d'Exégèse Théologique*. Paris, 1950 (significant survey).

Cope, Gilbert E. *Symbolism in the Bible and the Church*. London, 1959 (examines the recent concern with typology and related figural analysis to other contemporary views, such as the archetypal approach).

Coppens, Joseph. *Les Harmonies des Deux Testaments: Essai sur les Divers Sens des Ecritures et sur l'Unité de la Révélation*. Paris, 1949 (vol. VI of *Cahiers de la Nouvelle Revue Théologique*; masterly discussion of the subject, with copious bibliographical notes; the latter are supplemented in another essay on the subject, *Vom Christlichen Verständnis des Alten Testaments*, Freiburg, 1952 [Folia Lovaniensia, nos. 3, 4]; see also his *Histoire Religieuse de L'Ancien Testament*, Bruges, 1948).

Cullmann, Oscar. *Christ and Time: The Primitive Christian Conception of Time and History*, trans. F. V. Filson. London, 1962 (see the critique of this important book by Jean Daniélou, 'A Dialogue With Time,' *Cross Currents*, I [1950–1951], 78–90).

—— *The Christology of the New Testament*, trans. S. C. Guthrie and C. A. M. Hall. London, 1959 (incisive commentaries on the relation of typology, Christology, and historiography).

Daniélou, Jean. 'The Problem of Symbolism,' *Thought*, XXV (1950), 432–40.

Diem, Hermann. 'Jesus, der Christus des Alten Testaments,' *Evangelische Theologie*, XIV (1954), 437–48 (see also his *Grundfragen der biblischen Hermaneutik*, München, 1950; and see further: O. Schmitz, 'Das Alte Testament im Neuen Testament,' in *Wort und Geist, Festschrift für K. Heim*, Berlin, 1934; and cf. René Beaupère, 'La Bible, Source de l'Imaginaire Chrétien,' *La Vie Spirituelle*, no. 472 [1961], 496–505, and Seraphin Zarb, 'Unité ou Multiplicité dans la Bible?', *Revue Thomiste*, XV, NS [1932], 251–300).

Edsman, C. M. 'Gammel och ny Typologish Tolkning av G.T.,' *Svensk Exegetisk Arsbok*, XII (1947), 85–109 (and see further C. Charlier, *La Lecture Chrétienne de la Bible*, Maredsous, 1951 [4th edn.]).

Eichrodt, Walther. *Theology of the Old Testament*, trans. J. A. Baker. London, 1961 (general revaluation of typology; see also his *Israel in der Weissagung des Alten Testaments*, Zurich, 1951).

Fernandez, A. 'Sentido plenior, literal, tipico, e spiritual,' *Biblia*, XXXIV (1953), 299–326 (see also A. M. Dubarle, 'Le Sens Spirituel de l'Ecriture,' *Revue des Sciences Philosophiques et Théologiques*, XXXI [1947], 41–72).

Fritsch, C. T. 'Typological Interpretation in the New Testament,' *Bibliotheca Sacra*, CIV (1947), 87–100 (see also, in the same volume of this journal [214–22], his 'Principles of Biblical Typology').

Fuchs, Ernst. *Hermeneutik*. Bad Cannstatt, 1958.

Goppelt, Leonhard. *Typos. Die Typologische Deutung des Alten Testaments im Neuen*. Gü-

tersloh, 1939 (a basic modern Protestant work on the subject).

Grelot, Pierre. *Sens Chrétien de l'Ancien Testament*. Tournai, 1962.

Harrelson, Walter J. *Interpreting the Old Testament*. New York, 1964 (cf. Emil Brunner, *Revelation and Reason: The Christian Doctrine of Faith and Knowledge*, trans. Olive Wyon, Philadelphia, 1946; and see further: Tomas Arvedson, ' "Jesu eftenfoljd" i Nya Testamentet,' *Svensk Teologisk Kvartalskrift*, VII [1931], 134–61; D. Bonhoeffer, *Christology*, trans. John Bowden, London, 1966; and H. Alt, *Christlicher Kultus*, 2 vols., Berlin, 1851).

Heaton, Eric W. *The Old Testament Prophets*. Harmondsworth, 1958.

Hermann, Rudolf. *Gotteswort und Menschenwort: Eine Untersuchung zu theologischen Grundfragen der Hermeneutik*. Berlin, 1956 (good general introduction, including a provocative discussion of allegory and typology; see also: W. A. Irwin, 'The Interpretation of the Old Testament,' *Zeitschrift für die Alttestamentliche Wissenschaft*, LXII [1950], 1–10; E. Jacob, 'L'Ancien Testament et la Prédiction Chrétienne,' *Verbum Caro*, IV [1950], 151–64; and J. Muilenburg, 'Preface to Hermeneutics,' *Journal of Biblical Literature*, LXXVII [1958], 18–26).

Jepsen, Alfred. *Wissenschaft von Alten Testament*. Berlin, 1958 (Pamphlet I in series *Aufsätze und Vorträge zur Theologie und Religionwissenschaft*, eds. E. Schott and H. Urner; see also his 'Probleme der Auslesung des Altes Testaments,' *Zeitschrift für Systematische Theologie*, XXIII [1954], 373–86).

König, Eduard. *Die Messianischen Weissagungen des Alten Testaments . . . exegetisch behandelt.* Stuttgart, 1925.

Lampe, Geoffrey W. H. 'The Reasonableness of Typology' in *Essays on Typology,* Naperville, Ill., 1957 (studies in Biblical Theology, No. 22; a strong and informed defence; cf.: D. Lys, *A la Recherche d'une Méthode pour l'Exégèse de l'Ancien Testament.* Montpelier, 1950; O. Michel, *Das Alten Testament im Neuen Testament,* Bahnauer Hefte 5, [n.d.]; A. von Ruler, *Die christliche Kirche und das Alten Testament,* München, 1955; and T. C. Vriezen, *An Outline of Old Testament Theology,* Oxford, 1955).

——— 'Typological Exegesis,' *Theology,* LVI (1953), 201–08.

Lestringent, Pierre. *Essai sur l'Unité de la Révélation Biblique.* Paris, 1944.

Lightfoot, Robert Henry. *History and Interpretation in the Gospels.* New York, 1934 (see also N. J. Hommes, *Het Testimonia boek. Studien over O.T.-citaten in het N.T.,* Amsterdam, 1935, which treats general theoretical issues relative to the Church Fathers).

Lubac, Henri de. ' "Typologie" et "allégorisme," ' *Recherches de Science Religieuse,* XXXIV (1947), 180–226 (probing examination).

Markus, Robert A. 'Presuppositions of the Typological Approach to Scripture,' *Church Quarterly Review,* CLVIII (1957), 442–51 (a provocative and eloquent analysis).

Mascall, Eric L. *Christ, the Christian and the Church.* London, 1946.

Miller, A. 'Zur Typologie des Alten Testaments,' *Benediktinische Monatschrift,* XXVII (1951), 12–19 (see also his earlier essay by the same title in *Antonianum,* XXV [1950], 425–34, and his 'Vom Sinn der Heiligen Schrift,' *Benediktinische Monatschrift,* XXX [1954], 21–35; and cf. P. de Ambroggi, 'I sensi biblici. Direttive e studi recenti,' *La Scuola Cattolica,* LXXVIII [1950], 444–56).

Mowinckel, Sigmund O. P. *The Old Testament as Word of God,* trans. R. B. Rjornard. New York, 1959 (analysis by an eminent contemporary theologian).

Musurillo, Herbert. 'Shadow and Reality: Thoughts on the Problem of Typology,' *Theological Studies,* XXII (1961), 455–60.

Nineham, Denis Eric, ed. *Studies in the Gospels: Essays in Memory of R. H. Lightfoot.* Oxford, 1955 (see especially the essays by M. M. Farrer, C. P. M. Jones, and G. W. H. Lampe.

Pannenberg, Wolfhart. *Kerygma und Dogma.* Göttingen, 1959.

Pesch, Christian. *De Inspiratione Sacrae Scripturae.* Freiburg, 1906 (see also P. Benoit, *L'Inspiration,* Paris, 1954 [3rd edn.]; and cf. Henri de Lubac, *Catholicisme,* Paris, 1947 [4th edn.]).

Pythian-Adams, William J. T. P. *The Fulness of Israel: A Study of the Meaning of Sacred History.* London, 1938 (see also this author's *The Way of At-onement,* London, 1944).

Preus, James Samuel. *From Shadow to Promise: Old Testament Interpretation from Augustine to the Young Luther.* Cambridge, Mass., 1969 (extremely helpful in distinguishing Reformation from medieval Catholic typology).

Rad, Gerhard von. *Old Testament Theology*, trans. D. M. G. Stalher. 2 vols. Edinburgh, 1962 (major work; see also his 'Verheissung,' *Evangelische Theologie*, XIII [1953], 406–13; and see further J. C. Rylaarsdam, 'The Problem of Faith and History in Biblical Interpretation,' *Journal of Biblical Literature*, LXXVII [1958], 26–32, and H. Wildberger, 'Auf dem Wege zu einer biblischen Theologie. Erwägungen zur Hermeneutik des Alten Testaments,' *Evangelische Theologie*, XIX [1959], 70–90).

Riedmatten, H. de. 'Typology in the Scriptures,' trans. K. Pond, *Blackfriars*, XXXIII (1952), 132–41 (see also his *Les Actes du Procès de Paul de Samoste*, Fribourg, 1952).

Ringgren, Helmut. *The Messiah in the Old Testament*. London, 1961.

Rowley, Harold H. *The Unity of the Bible*. Philadelphia, 1955 (see also *The Old Testament and Modern Study: A Generation of Discovery and Research. Essays by Members of the Society for Old Testament Study*, Oxford, 1951, edited by this author).

Sailer, J. 'Ueber Typen im Neuen Testament,' *Zeitschrift für Katholische Theologie*, LXIV (1947), 490–96.

Schildenberger, Johannes. 'Vollsinn und typischer Sinn im Alten Testament,' *Bibel und Liturgie*, XXIV (1956–57), 255–59.

—— 'Weissagung und Erfüllung,' *Biblia*, XXIV (1943), 107–24, 205–30.

Schulte, A. *Die messianischen Weissagungen des Alten Testaments nebst dessem Typen*. Padenborn, 1908 (see further T. Breukelmann, *Die Vorbilder des Alten Testaments in Bezie-*

hung auf das Neuen Testament zusammengestellt, Padenborn, 1908, and H. Weiss, *Die messianischen Vorbilder im Alten Testament*, Fribourg, 1901; and cf. R. Grosche's essays on 'theological' and 'christological' hermeneutics in *Catholica*, IV [1936], 164–80, and VI [1937], 116–19).

Secrist, Jacob S. *Creation, Time and Eternity*. Elgin, Ill., 1911.

Tasker, Randolph V. G. *The Old Testament in the New Testament*. London, 1946.

Torm, Frederik. *Hermeneutik des Neuen Testaments*. Göttingen, 1930 (clear discussion of type-antitype relationship).

Vischer, Wilhelm. *Das Christuszeugnis des Alten Testaments*. Berlin, 1943 (6th edn.; see further his *Die Bedeutung des Alten Testaments für das christlichen Leben*, n.p., 1947).

—— 'Das Geheimnis Israels,' *Judaica*, VI (1950), 81–132.

—— *The Witness of the Old Testament to Christ*, trans. A. B. Crabtree. London, 1949 (extensive use of types; very well known and very controversial; see the essays in *Hommage à Wilhelm Vischer*, Montpelier, 1960, especially that of Walther Zimmerli, 'La nouvelle Exode dans le Message des Deux grands Prophètes de l'Exil').

Westermann, Claus, ed. *Essays in Old Testament Hermeneutics*, trans. J. L. Mays. Richmond, Va., 1963 (contains basic contemporary appraisals of typology: see especially the essays by Walther Eichrodt, Alfred Jepsen, Wolfart Pannenberg, Gerhard von Rad, Claus Westermann, and Hans Walter Wolff; and cf. the arguments against typology by Friedrich Baumgärtel and Rudolph Bultmann).

——— Vergegenwärtigung. Berlin, 1955.

Wilkinson, John T. Principles of Biblical Interpretation. London, 1960 (critical discussion of new views on typology; see also the cogent surveys of recent works by Ludwig Köler, 'Christus im Alten und Neuen Testament,' Theologische Zeitschrift, IX [1953], 241–59, and Heinrich Gross, 'Zur Problem Verheissung und Erfüllung,' Biblische Zeitschrift, III, [1959], 3–17).

Wilpert, Paul, ed. Judentum im Mittelalter: Beiträge zum Christlich-Jüdischen Gespräch. Berlin, 1966 (vol. 4 of Miscellanea Medievalia: Veröffentlichungen des Thomas-Instituts an der Universität Köln; this volume includes valuable specialized essays concerning typology in a number of areas: e.g., Friedrich Ohly on 'Synagoge and Ecclesia,' Peter Bloch on the iconography of the Cluny Museum, Adolf Waas on 'Volk Gottes und Militia Christi,' Beatrice Hirsch-Reich on Dante, Bernhard Blumenkranz on Jewish converts in the Middle Ages, and Wolfgang Kluxen on Maimonides in the Latin Occident).

Wilson, Walter L. Dictionary of Bible Types. Grand Rapids, Mich., 1957.

Wittram, Reinhard. Das Interesse an der Geschichte. Göttingen, 1958 (especially chapter 4 on 'Vergleich, Analogie, Typus'; and see further O. Schilling, 'Der Geistige Sinn der Heiligen Schrift,' Theologie und Glaube, XLIV [1954], 241–54).

Wolff, H. W. 'Erwagungen zur Typologischen Auslegung des Alten Testaments,' Die Zeichen der Zeit, X (1956), 446–48 (see also his Jesaja 53 im Urchristentum, Berlin, 1952, and 'Der grosse Jereeltag,' Evangelische Theologie, XII [1952–53], 78–104).

Zimmerli, Walter. Das Alte Testament als Anrede. München, 1956.

b. Historical Discussions

Albright, William F. History, Archeology, and Christian Humanism. New York, 1964 (cf. Hermann Gunkel and Leopold Zscharnack, Die Religion im Geschichte und Gegenwart, 5 vols., Tübingen, 1927–31, and Norman W. Porteus, The Old Testament and Modern Study, ed. Harold Henry Rowley, Oxford, 1951).

Amsler, Samuel. L'Ancien Testament dans l'Eglise. Neuchâtel, 1960.

Barrett, Charles K. The Background of the New Testament and its Eschatology. Cambridge, Eng., 1956 (see also this author's The Holy Spirit and the Gospel Tradition, New York and London, 1947).

Blackman, Edwin C. Biblical Interpretation. Philadelphia, 1957 (see also G. Ebeling, 'Die Bedeutung der historisch-kritischen Methode für die protestantische Theologie und Kirche,' Zeitschrift für die Theologie und Kirche, XLVII [1950], 1–46).

Burney, Charles Fox. The Aramaic Origin of the Fourth Gospel. Oxford, 1922 (cf. his The Gospel in the Old Testament, Edinburgh, 1921).

Courtade, G. 'Le Sens de l'Histoire dans l'Ecriture et la Classification Usuelle des Sens Scripturäires,'

Recherches de Science Religieuse, XXXVI (1949), 136–41.

Dittmar, Wilhelm. *Vetus Testamentum in Novo.* Göttingen, 1903 (moderate use of typology in conjunction with critical-historical method; see also for this position, Edwin A. Abbott, *The Fourfold Gospel*, 3 vols., Cambridge, Eng., 1913–15; and cf. O. Schmitz, 'Das Alte Testament im Neuen Testament,' in *Wort und Geist, Festgabe Karl Heim*, Berlin, 1934).

Dodd, Charles Harold. *According to the Scriptures: The Sub-Structure of New Testament Theology.* London, 1952 (see further his "A Problem of Interpretation; *Studiarum Novi Testamenti Societas*, II [1951], 7–18).

Duff, Archibald. *History of Old Testament Criticism.* London, 1910 (cf. R. Aubert, 'Discussions Recentes autour de la Théologie de l'Histoire,' *Collectanea Mechliniensia*, NS, XXXIII [1948], 129–49).

Farrer, Austin Marsden. *St. Matthew and St. Mark.* Westminster, 1954.

Goodspeed, George S. *Israel's Messianic Hope . . . Foreshadowings of Christ in the Old Testament and Beyond.* New York, 1900.

Goppelt, Leonhard. *Jesus, Paul and Judaism: An Introduction to New Testament Theology*, trans. Edward Schroeder. New York, 1964 (cf. William David Davies, *Paul and Rabbinic Judaism: Some Rabbinic Elements in Pauline Theology*, London, 1948).

Grant, Robert M. *The Bible in the Church: A Short History of Interpretation.* New York, 1948.

——— *The Letter and the Spirit.* London, 1957 (especially Appendix II; authoritative summary).

Gründer, Karlfried. *Figur und Geschichte. Johann Georg Hamanns 'Biblische Betrachtungen' als Ansatz einer Geschichtsphilosophie.* Freiburg, 1958.

Hänel, Johannes. *Das Wort Gottes und das Alte Testament.* Berlin, 1932.

Harnoch, Carl Gustav Adolf von. 'Das Alte Testament in den Paulinischen Gemeinden,' *Sitzungsberichte der Preussischen Akademie der Wissenschaften.* Berlin, 1928.

Higgins, Angus John Broad, ed. *Studies in Memory of Thomas Walter Manson, 1893–1958.* Manchester, 1959 (see the essays by C. K. Barrett, H. Clavier, O. Cullman, A. J. B. Higgins, J. Jeremias, G. D. Kilpatrick, H. Riesenfeld, and H. G. Wood).

Hoskyns, Sir Edwyn. *The Riddle of the New Testament.* London, 1930.

Jocz, Jakob. *The Spiritual History of Israel.* London, 1961 (see also his *The Covenant*, Grand Rapids, Mich., 1969, and James Barr, *Biblical Words for Time*, Naperville, Illinois, 1962; and cf.: R. N. Flaw, *Jesus and His Church*, London, 1938; G. Johnson, *The Doctrine of the Church in the New Testament*, Cambridge, Eng., 1943; E. Lohmeyer, *Kyrios Christos*, Heidelberg, 1928; A. B. Davidson, *Old Testament Prophecy*, Edinburgh, 1903; and J. Jeremias, *Jesus als Weltvollender*, Gütersloh, 1930).

Kraeling, Emil G. H. *The Old Testament Since the Reformation.* London, 1955 (interesting on the importance of typology as a political instrument).

Lockhart, Clinton. *The Messianic Message of the Old Testament.* Des Moines, Iowa, 1905 (see also C. A. Briggs, *Messianic Prophecy*, Edinburgh, 1886, and L. Guy, *Le Millénairisme*, Paris, 1904).

Mickelsen, A. Berkeley. *Interpreting the Bible.* Grand Rapids, Mich., 1963.

Müller, Alois. *Ecclesia—Maria. Die Einheit Marias und der Kirche.* Freiburg, 1955 (2nd edn.; see further: Yves M. J. Congar, *Christ, Our Lady and the Church*, Westminster, Md., 1951; Quentin Quesnell, 'Mary in the Church,' *Thought*, XXXVI [1961], 25–39; E. Schillebeek, *Marie, Mère de la Redemption*, Paris, 1963; S. Tromp, 'Ecclesia Sponsa Virgo Mater,' *Gregorianum*, XVIII [1937], 3–29; and in particular Karl Rahner's *Our Lady and the Church*, trans. Sebastian Bullough, New York, 1961, and *Mary, Mother of the Lord*, trans. W. J. O'Hara, New York, 1962).

Ploeg, Johannes Van Der. 'Profetie en Vervulling,' *Studia Catholica*, XXVIII (1953), 81–93 (see also his *The Church and Israel*, trans. 'by a religious of the Retreat of the Sacred Heart,' London, 1956; and cf. Rudolph Otto, *The Idea of the Holy*, trans. John W. Harvey, London, 1925, and Ernst Sellin, *Der Alttestamentliche Prophetismus*, Leipzig, 1912).

Rackham, Richard B. *The Acts of the Apostles . . . Westminster Commentary*, ed. Walter Lock. London, 1901 (cf. Burton Scott Easton, *Early Christianity: The Purpose of Acts*, ed. Fred C. Grant, Greenwich, Conn., 1954 [a separate printing of *The Purpose of Acts* is in *Theology: Occasional Papers*, 1936]).

Ringgren, Helmer. *Sacrifice in the Bible.* London, 1962 (see also his

Israelite Religion, trans. David Green, London, 1966; and cf. F. Weber, *Jüdische Theologie*, Leipzig, 1897, and H. Englander, 'The Exodus in the Bible,' *Studies in Jewish Literature, Festschrift für K. Kohler*, Berlin, 1913).

Robinson, H. Wheeler. *Inspiration and Revelation in the Old Testament.* Oxford, 1946 (cf. H. H. Rowley, *The Rediscovery of the Old Testament*, Philadelphia, 1946).

Schildenberger, Johannes. *Das Geheimnis des Gotteswortes.* Heidelberg, 1950.

Schoeps, Hans Joachim, *Theologie und Geschichte des Judencristentums.* Tübingen, 1949 (cf.: S. Bonsirven, *Le Judaisme Palistinien au Temps de Jésus-Christ: La Théologie*, 2 vols., Paris, 1934–35, especially on eschatology; A. H. McNiele, *New Testament Teaching in the Light of St. Paul*, Cambridge, Eng., 1923; F. Johnson, *The Quotations of the New Testament from the Old*, London, 1896; and Oscar Cullmann, *Königsherrschaft Christi und Kirche im Neuen Testament*, Bâle, 1941).

Scott, Charles A. A. *Christianity According to St. Paul.* Cambridge, Eng., 1937.

Smart, James. *The Interpretation of Scripture.* Westminster, Md., 1961 (links typology and allegory).

Vandenbroucke, François. 'Le Psautier, Prophétie ou Prière du Christ?', *Paroisse et Liturgie.* N.p. 1918.

Vögelin, Erich. *Israel and Revelation.* Baton Rouge, 1956 (typology and historiography; first volume of a series entitled *Order and History*).

Vrooman, Hiram. *Religion Rationalized*. Minneapolis, 1911.

Waterman, Leroy. *Forerunners of Jesus*. New York, 1959 (cf. A. Chevallier, *L'Esprit du Messie dans le Bas Judaisme*, Paris, 1958, and A. Cole, *The New Temple*, London, 1950).

Wilkinson, Samuel H. *The Divine Plan of the Ages Foreshadowed in the Jewish Calendar*. London, n.d. [1911?].

Wood, James D. *The Interpretation of the Bible: A Historical Introduction*. London, 1958 (cf. Ernest G. Wright's works: *The Challenge of Israel's Faith*, Chicago, 1944; *The Old Testament Against its Environment*, London, 1950; and *God Who Acts*, London, 1952).

c. Special Topics

Alfrink, B. J. *Josue mit de Grondehst Vertaald en uitgelegd door agr. Uitgeuers*, 1952.

Anderson, Bernhard W. 'Exodus Typology in Second Isaiah,' in *Israel's Prophetic Heritage*, eds. B. W. Anderson and W. Harrelson. New York, 1962 (see also Jindrich Mánek, 'The New Exodus in the Books of Luke,' *Novum Testamentum*, II [1957], 8–23).

Audet, P. J. *La Didachè*. Paris, 1958 (see also his 'L'Hypothèse des Testimonia. Remarques autour d'un Livre Récent,' *Cahiers de la Revue Biblique*, LXX [1963], 341–405).

Barrett, Charles Kingsley. 'Pillar Apostles,' *Studia Paulina in honorem Johannes de Zwaan*, eds. K. de Zwaan and J. Pieter. Haarlem, 1953.

Bentzen, Aage. *Messias-Moses Redivivus-Menschensohn*. Zurich, 1948 (later issued as *King*

and Messiah*, London, 1955; see also J. E. van Dodewaard, 'Een proeve van spirituale exegese. Het gesprek van Moses en Elias met Jesus op de Berg der verheerlijking,' *Nederlandische Katholicke Stemmen*, XLVII [1951], 321–25, and Lansing R. Hicks, 'Messiah, Second Moses, Son of Man,' *Anglican Theological Review*, XXXIII [1951], 24–29).

Benz, Ernest. *Ecclesia Spiritualis*. Stuttgart, 1934.

Beskow, P. *Rex Gloriae: The Kingship of Christ in the Early Church*. Stockholm, 1962.

Black, Matthew. 'The Messiah in the Testament of Levi, XVIII,' *Expository Times*, LX–LXI [1948–50], 321–22 (see further his 'The Pauline Doctrine of the Second Adam,' *Scottish Journal of Theology*, VII [1954], 170–79).

Bouyer, Louis. 'Liturgie et Exégèse Spirituelle,' *La Maison-Dieu*, VII (1946), 27–40 (see also this author's *The Paschal Mystery*, trans. Sister Mary Benoit, Chicago, 1950).

Brown, Raymond E. *The Sensus Plenior of Sacred Scripture*. Baltimore, 1955 (see also his essays on the history of 'Sensus Plenior' as a theory and on recent scholarship on the subject, in *Catholic Biblical Quarterly*, XV [1953], 141–62, and XXV [1963], 262–85; and cf.: B. R. Bierberg, 'Does Sacred Scripture have a Sensus Plenior?,' *Catholic Biblical Quarterly*, X [1948], 484–95; G. Courtade, 'Les Ecritures ont-elles un sens "plénier?",' *Recherches de Science Religieuse*, XXXVII [1950], 481–97; Anthony Nemetz, 'Literalness and the Sensu Literalis,' *Speculum*, XXXIV [1959], 76–89; A. Colunga's treatments of 'sensus plenior' in

La Ciencia Tomista, LXIV
[1943], 327–46 and Estudios
Biblicos, II [1943], 423–47; J.
Leal, 'El sentido plenior de la
Sagrada Escritura,' Razón y Fe,
L [1951], 474–82; E. F. Sutcliff,
'The Plenary Sense as a Principle
of Interpretation,' Biblica,
XXXIV [1953], 333–43; J.
Schmid, 'Die alttestamentliche
Zitate bei Paulus und die Theorie
vom sensus plenior,' Biblische
Zeitschrift, NF, III [1959], 161–
73; P. L. Suarez, 'El sensus ple-
nior y la Semana Biblica Espa-
ñola,' Illustracion del Clero, XLV
[1952], 21–28; and F. M. Braun,
'Le sens plénier et les encycli-
ques,' Revue Thomiste [1951],
294–304).

Carcopino, Jérôme. Le Mystère
d'un Symbole Chrétien: L'Ascia.
Paris, 1955 (see also his Etudes
d'Histoire Chrétienne, Paris,
1953).

Cazelles, H. 'Instaurae Omnia in
Christo (Eph. 1, 10),' Biblica,
XL (1959), 342–52.

Childs, Brevard S. Myth and Reality in the Old Testament. London, 1960 (eschatology and
typology; see also his 'Prophecy
and Fulfillment,' Interpretation,
XII [1958], 259–69).

Clements, Ronald Ernest. God and
the Temple. Philadelphia, 1965
(see also his Prophecy and Covenant, Naperville, Ill., 1965).

Comblin, J. L'Exode dans l'Apocalypse. Paris, 1965 (see further
D. J. Monleon, Le Sens Mystique de l'Apocalypse, Paris 1948,
and J. Steinmann, 'L'Exode dans
l'Ancien Testament,' La Vie
Spirituelle, no. 360 [1951], 229–
40).

Cooper, David L. Messiah: His
Nature and Person. Los Angeles,
1933 (see also his Messiah: His

First Coming Scheduled, Los
Angeles, 1939).

Coppens, Joseph. 'Nouvelles Ré-
flections sur la Divers Sens des
Saintes Ecritures,' Nouvelle
Revue Théologique, LXXIV
(1952), 3–20.

———— 'Le Protevangile. Un Nouvel
Essai d'Exégèse,' Ephemerides
Theologicae Lovanienses, XXVI
(1950), 5–36 (see also his essays
in same journal: 'L'Argument des
Prophétries Messianiques selon
"Les Pensées" de Pascal,' XXVII
[1951], 53–69; 'Où en est le
Problème du Messianisme?,'
XXVII [1951], 81–92; and 'La
Prophétie de la 'Almah,' XXVIII
[1952], 648–78).

Cullman, Oscar. Salvation in His-
tory. London, 1967 (see also his
Baptism in the New Testament
[1948], trans. J. K. S. Reid,
Chicago, 1950; and see further
Harold Sahlin, 'The New Exo-
dus of Salvation According to
Saint Paul,' The Root of the
Vine, ed. Anton Fridricksen,
Westminster, Md., 1953, and
J. de Senarelens, Le Mystère de
l'Histoire: Introduction à une
Conception Christologique du
Duvenir, Genève, 1949).

Dahl, Nils A. 'Christ, Creation and
the Church,' The Background
of the New Testament and Its
Eschatology, eds. W. D. Davies
and D. Daube. Cambridge, Eng.,
1956 (series of essays presented
in honor of Charles Harold
Dodd; cf. also Dahl's Das Volk
Gottes, Oslo, 1941; and see
further A. Peter, Das Echo von
Paradieserzählung und Paradies-
mythen . . . unter besonderer
Berücksichtigung der prophetischen Endzeitschilderungen,
Wurzbourg, 1947).

Daniélou, Jean. 'The Conception
of History in the Christian Tra-

dition,' Journal of Religion, XXX (1950), 171–79 (see also his 'Christos Kyrios, Une Citation des Lamentations de Jerémie dans la Testimonia,' Mélanges Jules Lebreton, 2 vols. Paris, 1951–52 [vols. XXXIX–XL of Recherches de Science Religieuse], and his Lord of History, trans. Nigel Abercrombie, Chicago, 1958; see further Leopold Malevez, 'La Vision Chrétienne de L'Histoire dans la Théologie Catholique,' Nouvelle Revue Théologique, LXXI [1949], 244–64, and Theo Preiss, 'The Christian Philosophy of History in the New Testament,' Journal of Religion, XXX [1950], 157–70).

———— 'Le Symbolisme Eschatologique de la Fête des Tabernacles,' Irénikon, XXXI, 1958, 19–40 (see also his 'Les Psaumes dans la Liturgie de l'Ascension,' La Maison-Dieu, XXI [1950], 40–56, his 'Les Quatre-Temps de Septembre et la Fête des Tabernacles,' La Maison-Dieu, XLVI [1956], 114–36, and his 'Catéchèse Pascale et Retour au Paradis,' La Maison-Dieu, XLV [1956], 100–10; and cf. J. Comblin, 'La Liturgie de la Nouvelle Jérusalem,' Ephemerides Theologicae Lovanienses, XXIX [1953], 29–33).

Davidson, Andrew B. Old Testament Prophecy. Edinburgh, 1903.

Davies, John G. He Ascended into Heaven: A Study in the History of Doctrine. London, 1958 (ascension typology).

Delporte, L. 'Les Principles de la Typologie Biblique et les Eléments Figuratifs du Sacrifice de l'Expiation (Lev. 16) (à propos d'un ouvrage récent et d'une critique),' Ephemerides Theologicae Lovanienses, III (1926), 307–27.

Dennefeld, Ludwig. Le Messianisme. Paris, 1929.

Dix, Gregory. The Shape of the Liturgy. Glasgow, 1945.

Dölger, Franz X. J. 'Der Durchzug durch das Rote Meer als Sinnbild des Christlichen Taufe,' Antikes Christentum, II (1930), 63–69 (see also his 'Der Durchzug durch den Jordan als Sinnbild der Christlichen Taufe,' Antike Christentum, II [1930], 70–79, and Edward J. Duncan, Baptism in Demonstrations of Aphraates [Catholic University of America, Studies in Christian Antiquities], Washington, 1945; and cf. C. M. Edsman, La Baptême de Feu, Uppsala, 1940, and Emmanuel von Severus, 'Die Bedeutung der Kirchenväter für unser Liturgisches Leben,' Liturgisches Leben, V [1938], 98–110).

———— Die Sonne der Gerechtigkeit und der Schwarze. Münster, 1918 (especially interesting on baptism; see also his Sol Salutis; Gebet und Gesang im Christlicher Altertum, Münster, 1925, and his studies of the liturgy, Das Sakrament der Firmung Historisch-Dogmatisch Dargestellt, Wien, 1906, and Der Exorzismus im Altchristlichen Taufritual, Padenborn, 1909).

Downie, Hugh Kerr. Harvest Festivals: Old Testament Feasts, Types of New Testament Truths. New York, 1951.

Eichrodt, Walther. 'Vom Symbol zum Typos,' Theologische Zeitschrift, XIII (1957), 509–22 (cf. Frederick W. Dillistone, Christianity and Symbolism, Philadelphia, 1955).

Farbridge, Maurice H. Studies in Biblical and Semitic Symbolism. London, 1923.

Fitz-Simmon, Vincent A. The

Christ of Promise in Homer, Hesiod, Vergil, Ovid, Horace, etc. New York, 1909.

Fullerton, Kemper. *Prophecy and Authority.* New York, 1919.

Gaebelein, Arno C. *As It Was—So It Shall Be . . . A Study of the First Age and Our Present Age.* New York, 1937.

Gessmann, Hugo. *Der Messias.* Göttingen, 1929.

Hamilton, Frank. *The Bible and the Millennium.* Ventnor, N.J. n.d. [194–] (see also his *Evidences that Jesus is the Messiah,* Ventnor, N.J. n.d. [194–]).

Harrisville, Roy. *The Concept of Newness in the New Testament.* Augsburg, 1960.

Hebert, Arthur G. *Throne of David.* London, 1941 (see also this author's *The Authority of the Old Testament,* London, 1947).

——— *When Israel Came Out of Egypt.* Richmond, 1961.

Hooker, Morna D. *Jesus and the Servant.* London, 1959.

Hühn, Eugen. *Die alttestamentlichen Citate und Reminiscenzen im Neuen Testament.* Tübingen, 1900.

Hummel, Horace D. 'The Old Testament Basis of Typological Interpretation,' *Biblical Research,* IX (1964), 38–50 (erudite, incisive, and well-written essay).

Kirk, Kenneth E. *The Apostolic Ministry; Essays on the History and the Doctrine of Episcopacy.* New York, 1946.

Korn, Hans J. *Die Versuchung des Glaubigen in der Griechischen Bibel.* Stuttgart, 1937.

Kosnetter, Johann. *Die Taufe Jesu. Exegetische und Religionsgeschichtliche Studien.* Wien, 1936.

Lampe, Geoffrey W. H. *The Seal of the Spirit.* London, 1951 (cf. D. Bonhoeffer, *Act and Being,* trans. Bernard Noble, New York, 1956).

Lindblom, Christian Johannes. *The Servant Songs in Deutero-Isaiah.* Lund, 1951 (see also his monograph, *A Study on the Immanuel Section in Isaiah . . . ,* Lund, 1958).

Lohmeyer, Ernst. *Diatheke Untersuchungen zum Neuen Testament.* Leipzig, 1913 (covenant typology).

Lund, Nils Wilhelm. *Chiasmus in New Testament.* Chapel Hill, N.C., 1942 (see further M. D. Goulder, 'The Chiastic Structure of the Lucan Journey,' *Proceedings of the Oxford Congress on the New Testament,* Oxford, 1960).

Lundberg, Per I. *La Typologie Baptismale.* Leipzig, 1942.

Manson, Thomas W. 'The Argument from Prophecy,' *Journal of Theological Studies,* XLVI (1945), 129–36.

Mohrmann, Christine. 'Pascha, Passio, Transitus,' *Ephemerides Liturgicae,* LXVI (1952), 37–52 (see also her 'Sacramentum dans les plus Anciens Textes Chrétiens,' *Harvard Theological Review,* XLVII [1954], 141–52).

Moule, C. F. D. 'Sanctuary and Sacrifice in the Church of the New Testament,' *Journal of Theological Studies,* 2nd ser., I (1950), 29–41 (see further: Hans Joachim Schoeps' very interesting 'The Sacrifice of Isaac in Paul's Theology,' *Journal of Biblical Literature,* LXV [1946], 385–92; Eugene Masure, *The Christian Sacrifice,* London, 1947; and F.C.N. Hicks, *The Fulness of Sacrifice,* London, 1938; and cf.

Thomas Forsyth Torrance's important *Eschatology and the Eucharist*, London, 1952).

Needham, Elizabeth A. *Melchizedek and Aaron as Types of Christ*. New York, 1904.

Nicholson, Wallace B. *The Hebrew Sanctuary: A Study in Typology*. Grand Rapids, Mich., 1951 (see also Isaac M. Halderman, *The Tabernacle, Priesthood and Offerings*, New York, 1925).

Pinsk, Johannes. 'Das Kommen des Herrn in der Liturgie: Adventus —Nativitas—Epiphania Domini,' *Liturgische Zeitschrift*, V (1932– 33), 49–66 (see also Damascus Zähringer, 'Die Schriftlesung in den Messfeiern der Adventsonntage,' *Liturgische Zeitschrift*, III [1930–31], 53–60).

Quasten, Johann. *Monumenta Eucharistica et Liturgica Vetustissima*. 7 vols. Bonn, 1935–37.

Rad, Gerhard von. 'Joseph Geschichte und ältere Chakma,' *Vetus Testamentum Supplement*, I (Brill, 1953), 120–27.

—— *Studies in Deuteronomy*. London, 1953 (see also his more general *Theologie des Alten Testament*, 2 vols. [especially vol. II], München, 1960; influential contemporary typologist).

Rahner, Hugo. *Symbole der Kirche. Die Ecclesiologie der Väter*. Salzburg, 1964 (a distinguished work which discusses, *inter alia*, Odysseus as a type of Christ; see also this author's *Griechische Mythen in christlichen Deutung*. Zurich, 1945, and his series of important essays on the figural meanings of the ship, the masthead, the sea, the Ark, and related images and concepts, in the following issues of *Zeitschrift für Theologie und Kirche*: LXIV [1940], 61–80; LXV [1941],

123–52; LXVI [1942], 89–118 and 196–227; LXVII [1943], 1– 21; LXIX [1947], 1–35; LXXV [1953], 129–73, and 385–410; LXXIX [1957], 129–69; and LXXXVI [1964], 137–79).

Reaser, George W. *Melchizedek; or The Exaltation of the Son of Man*. Boston, 1913.

Reijners, G. Q. *The Terminology of the Holy Cross in Early Christian Literature as based upon Old Testament Typology*. Nijmegen, 1965 (see further: Jean Daniélou, 'La Charrue, Symbole de la Croix,' *Recherches de Science Religieuse*, XLII [1954], 193–203; Erich Dinkler, 'Zur Geschichte des Kreuzsymbols,' *Zeitschrift für Theologie und Kirche*, XLVIII [1951], 148–72 [other articles by this writer on the same subject appear in *Jahrbuch für Antike und Christentum*, V (1962), 93–107, and in *Neutestamentliche Studien für Rudolf Bultmann*, Berlin, 1954]; René Guénon, *Le Symbolisme de la Croix*, Paris, 1957; J. L. Teicher, 'The Christian Interpretation of the Sign X in the Isaiah Scroll,' *Vetus Testamentum*, V [1955], 189–98; and Jan Schouten, *De Slangestef van Asklepios als Symbool van de Geneeskunde*, Utrecht, 1963).

Reik, Theodore. *The Temptation*. New York, 1961.

Reitzenstein, Richard. *Die Vorgeschichte der Christlichen Taufe*. Leipzig, 1929 (baptismal types; cf. Herbert Scheidt, *Die Taufwasserweihegebete*, Münster, 1935, a study of Coptic and Syrian baptism; for lucid presentations of the subject of baptism in general, see Jean Daniélou, *Bible et Liturgie*, Paris, 1951, and Antoine Villien, *The History and Liturgy of the Sacraments*, trans. H. W. Edwards, London,

1932; see further: L. Beinvaert, *The Mythic Dimension in Christian Sacramentalism*, New York, 1951, and O. C. Quick, *The Christian Sacraments*, New York, 1927).

Riesenfeld, Harald. *Jésus Transfiguré*. Paris, 1948.

Rousseau, Olivier. 'La Descent aux Enfers Figura du Baptême Chrétien,' *Mélanges Jules Lebreton*. Paris, 1952 (see also Jean Daniélou, 'Deluge, Baptême, Judgement,' *Dieu Vivant*, VIII [1947], 97–112).

Schelkle, K. H. 'Auslesung als Symbolverständnis,' *Theologische Quartelschrift*, CXXXII (1952), 129–51.

Schnackenburg, R. 'Der Weg der Katholischen Exegese,' *Biblische Zeitschrift*, NF, II (1958), 161–76.

Schoff, Wilfred H. *The Ship 'Tyre'* ... *As Prophesied by Isaiah, Ezekiel, and John, and Fulfilled at Nineveh*. New York, 1920.

Simon, Marcel. *Verus Israël*. Paris, 1948 (on the relations of typological exegesis to the anti-Jewish controversy).

Steffen, Uwe. *Das Mysterium ... Formen und Wandlungen des Jona-Motivs*. Göttingen, 1963 (sums up the vast history of Jonah typology).

Strack, Hermann L., and Paul Billerbeck. *Kommentar zum Neuen Testament aus Talmud und Midrasch*. 4 vols. München, 1922–28.

Thornton, Lionel S. 'The Body of Christ in the New Testament,' in *The Apostolic Ministry*, ed. Kenneth E. Kirk. New York, 1946 (see also his 'The Mother of God in Holy Scripture,' in *The Mother of God*, ed. E. Mas-

call, London, 1949; extensive and rather extreme uses of typology; cf. Ernest Best, *One Body in Christ*, London, 1955).

Vögthe, A. 'Die Adam-Christus Typologie und der "Menschensohn," ' *Trierer Theologische Zeitschrift*, IV (1951), 309–28.

Walvoord, J. F. 'Christological Typology,' *Bibliotheca Sacra*, CV (1948), 404–10.

Wellman, Max. *Der Physiologus: eine religionsgeschichtlichnaturwissenschaftliche Untersuchung*. Leipzig, 1930.

White, Alma. *The Chosen People*. Bound Brook, N.J., 1910 (somewhat eccentric; see also: Jeanette Agnes [pseud.], *The Seventh Seal*, Philadelphia, 1920; Harriet T. Bartlett, *An Esoteric Reading of Biblical Symbolism*, Hollywood, 1920; and Mary Mann, *The Spirit Father*, Chicago, 1901).

Widengren, George. *Sakrales Königtum im Alten Testament und im Judentum*. Stuttgart, 1955 (see also his *The King and the Tree of Life*, Uppsala, 1951).

Zielanski, B. 'De Sensu Transfigurationis,' *Verbum Domini*, XXVI (1948), 340–50.

Zimmerman, W. 'Ecclesia Lignea und Ligneis Tabulis Constructa,' *Bonner Jahrbücher*, CLVIII (1958), 414–53.

d. Art and Architecture

Typology in music (that is, the correspondence between chromatic scales and the figural patterns of liturgical chants) is discussed by Edward E. Lowinsky in *The Secret Chromatic Art in the Netherlands Motet* (New York, 1946). See also in this respect: G. L. Finney, 'A World of Instruments,' *English Literary History*, XX (1953), 87–

120; Manfred Bukofzer, *Studies in Medieval and Renaissance Music* (New York, 1950), and his 'Speculative Thinking in Medieval Music,' *Speculum*, XVII (1942), 165–80; and Leo Spitzer, 'Classical and Christian Ideas of World Harmony,' *Traditio*, II (1944), 409–64, and II (1945), 307–64.

In addition to the art-works discussed below, students of typology should be aware of the illuminated manuscripts (noted in several of the books listed below), such as the sixth-century Joshua Roll of the Vatican, the celebrated eighth-century Commentary on the Book of Revelation by Beatus of Liebana, the often-reprinted illustrations of eighth-century Vienna Genesis, and the famous Biblia Pauperam— attributed to the ninth-century monk St. Ansgar, though the first copies belong to the eleventh century—which was widely circulated after the thirteenth century. Biblical illustration in general makes evident the prevalence of typological readings: see for example *Five Themes from Genesis*, published by the Firestone Library of Princeton University (Princeton, 1972), with brief essays about biblical illustrations on the Creation of Eve, the Flood, the Tower of Babel, Jacob's Ladder, and the story of Joseph, by (respectively) Mary L. Gibbs, F. J. P. Broun, Stephen Gardner, Jeffrey Anderson, and Patricia Krouse.

This listing is limited to twentieth-century studies. However, there is a valuable nineteenth-century literature on the subject, including some notable French studies—such as Abbé Auber's 'Symbolisme du Cantique des Cantiques,' *Revue de l'Art Chrétien*, VI (1862), 132–57; D. Kaufmann's 'Sens et Origines des Symboles Tumulaires de l'Ancien-Testament dans l'Art Chrétien Primitif,' *Revue des Etudes Juives*,

XIV (1887), 33–48 and 217–53; and Augustin J. Crosnier's *Iconographie Chrétienne, ou Etude des Sculptures, Peintures . . . du Moyen-Age* (Paris, 1848)—and an imposing group of German investigations: e.g., Paul J. Ficker, *Der Mitralis des Sicardus, nach seiner Bedeutung für die Ikonographie des Mittelalters* (Leipzig, 1889); Gustav Heider, *Beiträge zur Christlichen Typologie aus Bilderhandschriften des Mittelalters* (Wien, 1861; cf. R. Cruel, *Geschichte der Deutschen Predigt im Mittelalter* [Detmold, 1879]); Fritz Xavier Kraus, *Roma Sotterranea, die römischen Katakomben* (Freiburg, 1879); Heinrich Otte, *Handbuch der Kirchlichen Kunst-Archäologie des deutschen Mittelalters* (Leipzig, 1854); Anton H. Springer, *Der Bilderschmuck in den Sacramentarian des frühen Mittelalters* (Leipzig, 1890; see also his *Genesisbilder in der Kunst des frühen Mittelalters* [Leipzig, 1884], his *Baukunst des christlichen Mittelalters* [Bonn, 1854], and his *Psalter-Illustrationen im frühen Mittelalters* [Leipzig, 1883]); J. Strzygowski, *Ikonographie der Taufe Christi* (Munich, 1885); and Paul Weber, *Geistliches Schauspiel und Kirchliche Kunst in ihrem Verhältnis Erläutert an einer Ikonographie der Kirche und Synagoge* (Stuttgart, 1894).

Anderson, M. D. *The Imagery of British Churches*. London, 1955.

Aubert, Marcel. *French Cathedral Windows of the Twelfth and Thirteenth Centuries*. Oxford, 1947 (see also Hugh Arnold and Lawrence B. Saint, *Stained Glass of the Middle Ages in England and France*, London, 1913).

Beissel, Stephen. 'Zur Geschichte der Thiersymbolik in der Kunst des Abendlandes,' *Zeitschrift für Christliche Kunst*, XIV (1901), 273–83, and XV (1902), 51–60 (cf. his Geschichte der Verehrung Marias im 16. und 17. Jahrhundert. Ein Beitrag zur Religionswissenschaft und Kirchengeschichte, Freiburg, 1910, and his Geschichte der Verehrung Marias im Deutschland während des Mittelalters, Freiburg, 1909; and cf. George Gottfried Dehio, Geschichte der deutschen Kunst, 4 vols., Berlin, 1923–34).

Casel, O. 'Älteste christliche Kunst und Christusmysterium,' Jahrbuch für Literaturwissenschaft, XII (1932), 1–86.

Cook, George Henry. The English Cathedral through the Centuries. London, 1957.

Cornell, Frank. Biblia Pauperum. Stockholm, 1925 (see further Elizabeth Soltész's Introduction and notes to Biblia Pauperum, The Estergom Blockbook of Forty Leaves, Budapest, 1967, and Franz Unterkircher and G. Schmidt, Die Wiener Biblia Pauperum, 3 vols., Graz, 1962).

Didron, Adolph N. Christian Iconography: The History of Christian Art in the Middle Ages. New York, 1965 (2nd edn.; see also I. Speyart van Woerden, 'The Iconography of the Sacrifice of Abraham,' Vigilae Christianae, XV [1961], 214–55; and cf. Samuel C. Chew, The Virtues Reconciled: An Iconographic Study, Toronto, 1947, and Adolf Katzenellenbogen, Allegories of the Virtues and Vices in Medieval Art, New York, 1964).

Ferguson, George. Signs and Symbols in Christian Art. New York, 1954.

Fink, Josef. Noe der Gerechte in der frühchristlichen Kunst. Münster, 1955 (no. 4 of Beihefte zum Archiv für Kulturgeschichte).

Goode, Teresa C., Sister. Gonzalo de Berceo, El Sacrificio de la Misa: A Study of its Symbolism and of its Sources. Washington, 1933 (differentiates typology from other symbolical and allegorical forms).

Goodenough, Erwin R. Jewish Symbols in the Greco-Roman Period. 13 vols. New York, 1953–68 (well known and authoritative; for briefer accounts of Jewish art, see this author's Religious Tradition and Myth, New Haven, 1937; and see further D. Kaufman, 'Sens et origine des symboles tumulaires de l'Ancien Testament dans l'art chrétien primitif,' Revue des Etudes Juives, XIV [1887], 33–48, and Rachael Wischnitzer, The Messianic Theme in the Paintings of the Dura Synagogue, Chicago, 1948).

Grecu, V. 'Darstellungen altheidnischer Denker und Schriftsteller in den Kirchenmalereien des Morgenlandes,' Bulletin de la Section Historique, Académie Roumaine, XI (1924), 1–67 (on the interpretation of pagan and Christian motifs via typology; see also in this respect A. von Premerstein, 'Griechischheidnische Weise als verkünder Christlicher Lehre in Handschriften und Kirchenmalereien,' in Festschrift den Nationalbibliothek in Wien, Vienna, 1926).

Harrison, Kenneth. The Windows of King's College Chapel Cambridge: Notes on Their History. Cambridge, Eng., 1952 (see also Bernard Rackham, The Ancient Glass of Canterbury Cathedral, London, 1949).

Horn, W., and E. Born. 'Two Timbered Medieval Churches of Cheshire,' Art Bulletin, XLIV (1962), 263–78.

Hutter, Herbert. *Medieval Stained Glass.* New York, 1964 (see also Louis Grodeck, *The Stained Glass of French Churches,* Paris, 1948).

Mellinkoff, Ruth. *The Horned Moses in Medieval Art and Thought.* Berkeley, 1970.

James, Montague Rhodes. 'Pictor in Carmine,' *Archaeologia,* XCIV (1951), 246–51 (see also the series of essays by this well-known art-historian in the *Proceedings of the Cambridge Antiquarian Society,* from 1895 to 1901, especially his 'Verses Formerly Inscribed on Twelve Windows in . . . Canterbury Cathedral,' 1901, in Vols. XXXVIII–XL of the *Proceedings;* see further his 'Illustrations of the Old Testament,' in *A Book of Old Testament Illustrations of the Middle of the Thirteenth Century,* ed. Sidney C. Cockerell, Cambridge, Eng., 1927).

Johnson, Clifton. *The Old-Time Schools and School Books.* New York, 1963 (relates the *Primer,* the *Biblia Pauperum,* and the stained glass windows at Canterbury).

Künstle, Karl. *Die Ikonographie der christlichen Kunst.* 2 vols. Freiburg, 1926–28 (impressive both in its breadth and depth of analysis).

Lacroix, Paul. *The Arts in the Middle Ages.* New York, 1964.

Levi D'Anacona, Mirella. *The Iconography of the Immaculate Conception in the Middle Ages and Early Renaissance.* New York, 1957.

Lindblom, Johannes. 'Altchristliche Kreuzessymbolik,' *Societas Orientalis Fennica. Studia Orientalia,* I (1925), 102–13.

Lindet, L. 'Les Représentations Allégoriques du Moulin et du Pressior dans l'Art Chrétien,' *Revue Archeologique,* XXXVI (1900), 403–13.

Lowrie, Walter. *Art in the Early Church.* New York, 1947.

Mâle, Emile. *L'Art Religieux . . . en France.* 1908–32 (a series of important illustrated texts covering the twelfth through the eighteenth centuries, often reprinted [e.g., Paris, 1949, 1951, 1953]; a convenient English translation by D. Nussey of the text on thirteenth-century French religious art appears as *The Gothic Image,* New York, 1958; a selection from the entire multi-volume series in English is *Religious Art from the Twelfth to the Eighteenth Century,* New York, 1958).

Molsdorf, Wilhelm. *Die christliche Symbolik der mittelalterlichen Kunst.* Leipzig, 1926 (see also Karl Krexler, *Der Verduner Altar, ein Emailwerk des 12. Jahrhunderts im Stifte Klosterneuburg,* Wien, 1913).

Morey, Charles P. *Early Christian Art: An Outline of the Evolution of Style and Iconography in Sculpture and Paintings from Antiquity to the Eighth Century.* Princeton, 1962 (see also his 'The Illustrations of Genesis,' in *The Caedmon Poems,* ed. C. W. Kennedy, New York, 1916; and cf. plates 65–91 in Margaret and Ernest Marriage. *The Sculptures of Chartres Cathedral,* Cambridge, Eng., 1909).

Neuss, Wilhelm. *Das Buch Ezekiel in Theologie und Kunst bis zum Ende des XII. Jahrhunderts. Ein Beitrag zur Entwicklungsgeschichte der Typologie der christlichen Kunst.* Münster, 1912 (see further his *Die katalanische Bibelillustrationen um die Wende des ersten Jahrtausends und die altspanische Buchmalerei*, Bonn, 1922).

Panofsky, Erwin. *Meaning in the Visual Arts*. New York, 1957 (see especially the section dealing with the Abbot Suger of St. Denis).

Réau, Louis. *Iconographie de l'Art Chrétien*. Paris, 1956 (see especially the Moses iconography).

Richter, Jean Paul, and A. C. Taylor. *The Golden Age of Classic Christian Art*. London, 1904 (mosaics of the St. Maria Maggiore Chapel in Rome as types of the nave based upon the writings of Justin Martyr).

Riesenfeld, Harald. *The Resurrection in Ezechiel XXXVII and in the Dura-Europos Paintings*. Uppsala, 1948.

Sauer, Joseph. *Symbolik des Kirchengebäudes und seiner Ausstattung in der Auffassung des Mittelalters*. 2 vols. Freiburg, 1924 (cf.: Otto von Simson, *The Gothic Cathedral: Origins of Gothic Architecture and the Medieval Concept of Order*, New York, 1956; Lawrence Stone, *Sculpture in Britain: The Middle Ages*, Baltimore, 1955; and Johannes Schweiterung, 'Mittelalterliche Dichtung und bildende Kunst,' *Zeitschrift für deutsches Altertum und deutsche Literatur*, XLII [1923], 113–27).

Schapiro, Meyer. 'The Image of the Disappearing Christ: The Ascension in English Art Around the Year 1000,' *Gazette des Beaux-Arts*, 6th ser., XXIII (1943), 134–52.

Schütte, Marie. *Geschichte der Bildteppiche und Decken des Mittelalters*. 2 vols., Leipzig, 1927 (see especially vol. I, on tapestries).

Smith, Alison M. 'The Iconography of the Sacrifice of Isaac in Early Christian Art,' *American Journal of Archeology*, XXVI (1922), 159–73.

Smith, Earl Baldwin. *Early Christian Iconography and the School of Ivory Carvers in Provence*. Princeton, 1918 (Princeton Monographs in Art and Archeology, no. 18).

Springer, Anton H. *Handbuch der Kunstgeschichte*. 6 vols. Leipzig, 1923–29 (especially vol. II: *Frühchristliche Kunst und Mittelalter*; and cf. Eric G. Millar's two books on English illuminated manuscripts from the fifth to the fifteenth centuries, Paris, 1926 and 1928).

Truby, Jeffrey. *The Glories of Salisbury Cathedral*. London, 1948.

Tümpel, Christian and Astrid Tümpel. *Rembrandt legt die Bibel aus. Zeichnungen und Radierungen aus dem Kupferstichkabinett der Staatlichen Museen Preussischer Kunst*. Berlin, 1970.

Verplaetse, A. 'L'Architecture en Flandre entre 900 et 1200 d'après les Sources Narratives Contemporaines,' *Cahiers de Civilization Médiévale*, VIII (1956), 37–49 (cf. plates 423, 447–50 in H. Swarzenski, *Monuments of Romanesque Art*, London, 1967).

Vloberg, Maurice. *L'Eucharistie dans l'Art*. 2 vols. Paris, 1946 (cf. plate 54, on baptism, in H. Omont, *Miniatures des Plus Anciens Manuscrits Grecs de la Bibliothèque Nationale du VIe au XIVe Siècle*, Paris, 1929).

Watson, Arthur. *The Early Iconography of the Tree of Jesse*. London, 1934.

——— 'The Imagery of the Tree of Jesse on the West Front of Orvieto Cathedral,' *Fritz Saxl, 1890–1948; A Volume of Memo-*

rial Essays, ed. D. J. Gordon. London, 1957 (see also P. A. Underwood, 'The Fountain of Life,' *Dumbarton Oak Papers*, LI [1950], 43–138).

Wulff, Oscar. *Altchristliche und Byzantinische Kunst*. Berlin, 1922.

e. Literary Analyses

The following list includes several items in which literary texts are of secondary concern and several in which typology figures as only one of several hermeneutical methods under examination; in all cases, however, they are works of literary scholars or critics which tend, at least by implication, toward literary typological analysis.

Abrams, M. H. *Natural Supernaturalism: Tradition and Revolution in Romantic Literature*. New York, 1971 (incisive and far-reaching discussion of the uses of scriptural hermeneutics in the Romantic period; see also Perry Miller, 'Thoreau in the Context of International Romanticism,' *Nature's Nation*, Cambridge, Massachusetts, 1967; and cf. J. P. Hunter, 'Steinbeck's Wine of Affirmation in *The Grapes of Wrath*,' in *Essays in American Literature*, ed. Richard E. Langford, De Land, Florida, 1963 [Stetson Studies in Humanities, no. 1]).

Allen, Don Cameron. 'John Donne's "Paradise and Calvarie," ' *Modern Language Notes*, LX (1945), 398–400.

—— *Mysteriously Meant: The Rediscovery of Pagan Symbolism and Allegorical Interpretation in the Renaissance*. Baltimore, 1970.

Ames, Ruth. *The Fulfillment of the Scriptures. Abraham, Moses, and Piers*. Evanston, Ill., 1970.

Anderson, Mary D. *Drama and Imagery in English Medieval Churches*. Cambridge, Eng., 1963 (important, wide-ranging study; see also Paul Weker, *Geistliches Schauspiel und kirchliche Kunst*, Stuttgart, 1894).

Auerbach, Erich. 'Figura' (1938), trans. R. Manheim, in *Scenes from the Drama of European Literature*, New York, 1959 (deservedly renowned philological, historical, and philosophical interpretation of the subject; see also his *Mimesis: The Representation of Reality in Western Literature*, trans. W. R. Trask. Princeton, 1953).

—— 'Figurative Texts Illustrating Certain Passages of Dante's *Commedia*,' *Speculum*, XXI (1946), 474–89.

—— *Typologische Motive in der mittelalterlichen Literatur*. Krefeld, 1964 (Schriften und Vorträge des Petrarca-Instituta Köln, no. 2; see also his 'Typological Symbolism in Medieval Literature,' *Yale French Studies*, IX, 1952, 3–10; his studies of Dante's *Commedia* in *Italica*, XXII, 19–45, 166–79; and *Modern Language Notes*, LXIV [1949], 166–68, and his recently collected essays in *Literary Language and its Public in Late Latin Antiquity and in the Middle Ages*, trans. Ralph Manheim, New York, 1965).

Bell, Michael Davitt. *Hawthorne and the Historical Romance of New England*. Princeton, 1971.

Bercovitch, Sacvan. 'Endicott's Breastplate: Symbolism and Typology in Hawthorne's "Endicott and the Red Cross," ' *Studies in Short Fiction*, IV (1967), 289–300 (see further his 'Diabolus in Salem: Bunyan and Hawthorne,' *English Language Notes*, IV [1969], 280–85; and cf. his discussions of Hawthorne's *Marble Faun* in *Early American Literature*, I [1966], 5–7, and *New England Quarterly*, XLI [1968], 281–85).

—— 'Milton's "Haemony": Knowledge and Belief,' *Huntington Library Quarterly*, XXXIII (1970), 351–60.

Berry, Boyd M. 'The Doctrine of the Remnant, 1550–1650: A Study in the History of English Puritanism and *Paradise Lost*,' Diss. University of Michigan, 1966.

Bethurum, Dorothy, ed. *Critical Approaches to Medieval Literature*. New York, 1960 (selected Papers of the English Institute; see the essays by E. Talbot Donaldson, R. E. Kaske, and Charles Donahue).

Bloomfield, Morton W. 'Symbolism in Medieval Literature,' *Modern Philology*, LVI (1958), 73–81 (cf.: Robert J. Clements, *Picta Poesis: Literary and Humanistic Theory in Renaissance Emblem Books*, Rome, 1960; Philip Damon, 'The Two Modes of Allegory in Dante's *Convivio*,' *Philological Quarterly*, XL [1961], 144–49; and Edward A. Bloom, 'The Allegorical Principle,' *English Literary History*, XVIII [1951], 163–90).

Bottrall, Margaret. *George Herbert*. London, 1954.

Brown, Norman O. *Love's Body*. New York, 1966 (not entirely reliable but always provocative).

Bruyne, Edgar de. *The Esthetics of the Middle Ages*, trans. E. B. Hennessy. New York, 1969 (abridged from the influential original three-volume edition, Brugge, 1946).

Burlin, Robert S. *The Old English Advent: A Typological Com-*

mentary. New Haven, 1968 (learned and stimulating study; cf. Esther L. Swenson, *An Inquiry into the Composition and Structure of Ludus Coventriae*, Minneapolis, 1914 [University of Minnesota Studies in Language and Literature, no. 1]).

Cannon, Charles K. 'William Whitaker's *Disputatio de Sacra Scriptura*: A Sixteenth-Century Theory of Allegory,' *Huntington Library Quarterly*, XXV (1962), 129–38.

Caplan, Harry. 'The Four Senses of Scriptural Interpretation and the Medieval Theory of Preaching,' *Speculum*, IV (1929), 282–90.

Capone, Vittorio Ugo. *Divino e figura: il tragico e il religioso nella Commedia dantesca*. Napoli, 1967.

Cave, Terence. *Devotional Poetry in France, c. 1570–1613*. Cambridge, 1969 (thorough and stimulating study; see also Henri Lemaire, *Études de Images Littéraire de François de Sales*, Paris, 1969; and cf.: Samuel Berger, *Le Bible au 16ᵉ Siècle*, Paris, 1879 [reprinted 1969]; Leon Gautier, *Tropaires*, Paris, 1886; Jacques Trénel, *L'Elément Biblique dans l'Oeuvre Poetique d'Agrippa D'Aubigné*, Paris, 1904; and Richard Regosin, 'D'Aubigné's *Les Tragiques*: A Protestant Apocalypse,' *Publications of the Modern Language Association*, LXXI [1966], 363–68; there exists a pertinent body of French nineteenth-century scholarship in the drama stimulated in part by M. C. A. Sepet's seminal *Les Prophètes du Christ: Etude sur les Origines du Théâtre au Moyen Age*, Paris, 1867–68, and his later *Le Drame Chrétien au Moyen Age*, Paris,

1878: see, for example, W. Cloetta, 'Le Mystère de l'Epoux,' *Romania*, XXII [1893], 177–229; Edmond Coussemaker, *Drames Liturgiques du Moyen Age*, Paris, 1871; Armand Gaste, *Les Drames Liturgiques de la Cathédrale de Rouen*, Paris, 1893; and L. Petit de Juville, *Histoire du Théâtre en France. Les Mystères*, Paris, 1880).

Charity, Alan C. *Events and their Afterlife; the dialectics of Christian typology in the Bible and Dante*. Cambridge, Eng., 1966 (extremely helpful, beyond its immediate concerns).

Chydenius, Johan. *The Typological Problem in Dante*. Helsingfors, 1958 (Societas Scientiarum Fennica Commentationes Humanarum Litterarum; Finska vetenskapssocieteten, XXV).

Cinquemani, A. M. 'Henry Reynolds' *Mythomystes* and the Continuity of Ancient Modes of Allegoresis in Seventeenth-Century England,' *Publications of the Modern Language Association*, LXXXV (1970), 1041–49 (cf. Frances A. Yates, 'Queen Elizabeth as Astraea,' *Journal of the Warburg and Courtauld Institutes*, X [1947], 27–83).

Craig, Hardin. 'The Origin of the Old Testament Plays,' *Modern Philology*, X (1913), 473–87 (see also Adeline M. Jenney's response to this essay, 'A Further Word as to the Origin of the Old Testament Plays,' *Modern Philology*, XIII [1915–16], 59–64; and cf. Oscar Cargill, *Drama and Liturgy*, New York, 1930, and Howard H. Schless, 'The Comic Element in the Wakefield Noah,' *Studies in Medieval Literature: In Honor of Professor Albert Croll Baugh*, ed. MacEdward Leach, Philadelphia, 1961; pertinent nineteenth-

century studies of the early English drama include: K. L. Bates, *English Religious Drama*, New York, 1893; Rudolf Brotanek, 'Noahs Arche. Ein Misterium aus Newcastle upon Tyne,' *Anglia*, XXI [1898–99], 165–200 [text and commentary]; William Hone, *Ancient Mysteries Described*, London, 1823; and L. Toulmin Smith, 'Play of Abraham and Isaac,' *Anglia*, VII [1884–85], 316–37 [text and commentary on this fifteenth-century mystery play]; pertinent twentieth-century studies of the subject, besides those noted elsewhere in this Bibliography, include: F. W. Cady, 'Liturgical Basis of the Townley Mysteries,' *Publications of the Modern Language Association*, XXIV [1909], 419–69; Edward M. Clarke, 'Liturgical Influences in the Townley Plays,' *Orate Fratres*, XVI [1914], 69–79; P. E. Dunstoor, 'The Origin of the Play of "Moses and the Tables of the Law,"' *Modern Language Review*, XIX [1924], 459–63; S. B. Hemingway, *English Nativity Plays*, New York, 1909; Eleanor Prosser, *Drama and Religion in the English Mystery Plays: A Re-Evaluation*, Stanford, 1961; George C. Taylor, 'The Relation of the English Corpus Christi Play to the Middle English Religious Lyric,' *Modern Philology*, V [1907], 1–38; and Karl Young's 'Observations on the Origin of the Medieval Passion Play,' *Publications of the Modern Language Association* XXV [1910], 309–54; and 'Origin of the Easter Play,' *Publications of the Modern Language Association*, XXIX [1914], 1–58).

Curtius, Ernst R. *European Literature in the Latin Middle Ages*, trans. W. R. Trask. New York, 1953 (see also Pierre de Labriolle, *History and Literature of Christianity from Tertullian to Boethius*, trans. H. Wilson, London, 1924, and Frederick J. E. Raby, *A History of Christian-Latin Poetry*, Oxford, 1927).

Diesenberg, Hans. *Studien zur religiösen Gedankenkwelt in der Spruchdichtung des 13. Jahrhunderts*. Bonn, 1937 (cf. Joseph Faschung, "Beiträge zur Erklärung der Religiösen Dichtungen Walthers von der Vogelweide,' *Germania*, XXIII [1873], 34–46).

Donaldson-Evans, Lance K. *Poésie et Meditations chez Jean de la Ceppède*. Genève, 1969 (important study).

Dunbar, Helen F. *Symbolism in Medieval Thought and its Consummation in the Divine Comedy*. New York, 1961.

Evans, Arthur R., Jr. 'Figural Art in the *Théorèmes* of Jean de la Ceppède,' *Modern Language Notes*, LXXVIII (1963), 278–87.

Fechter, Werner. *Lateinische Dichtkunst und deutsches Mittelalter*. Berlin, 1964.

Fixler, Michael. *Milton and the Kingdoms of God*. Evanston, Ill., 1964.

Fontaine, Jacques. 'Une Clé Littéraire de la Vita Martini de Sulpice Sévère: La Typologie Prophétique,' in *Mélanges Offerts à Mademoiselle Christine Mohrmann*, eds. L. J. Engels, H. W. F. M. Hoppenbrouwers, and A. J. Vermenlen. Utrecht, 1963 (typology and hagiography).

Friedman, Clarence W. *Prefigurations in Meistergesang: Types from the Bible and Nature*. Washington, D.C., 1943 (Catholic University of America, Studies

in German, vol. XVIII; see further vol. II of Max Manitus, *Geschichte der . . . Mittelalters*, Munich, 1911, which discusses the typological applications to nature; and Toni Weber, 'Praefigurationen im geistlichen Drama Deutschlands,' Diss. University of Marburg, 1919; and cf.: Heinrich Lütcke, *Studien zur Philosophe der Meistersinger*, Berlin, 1911; Bado Mergell, *Tristan und Isolde: Ursprung und Entwicklung der Tristansage des Mittelalters*, Mainz, 1949; F. Wolf, *Uber die Lais, Sequenzen und Leiche: Ein Beitrag zur Geschichte der rhythmischen Formen und Singweisen der Volkslieder und der volksmässigen Kirchen-und Kunstlieder im Mittelalter*, Heidelberg, 1841; and Wolfgang Kayser, *Das sprachliche Kunstwerk: Eine Einführung in die Literaturwissenschaft*, Bern, 1967, first published 1948).

Frye, Northrop. 'The Typology of *Paradise Regained*,' *Modern Philology*, LIII (1956), 227–38 (see also the chapter on 'Ethical Criticism: Theory of Symbols,' in Frye's *Anatomy of Criticism*, Princeton, 1957).

Galdon, Joseph A. 'Typology and Seventeenth-Century Literature,' Diss. Columbia University, 1965 (treats particularly the writings of Donne, Herbert, and Milton).

Gardner, Helen. *The Business of Criticism*. Oxford, 1959.

Gillet, J. E. 'The German Dramatist and his Bible,' *Publications of the Modern Language Association*, XXXIV (1919), 465–75 (cf.: R. Froning, *Frankfurter Passions-spiele*, Stuttgart, 1891; Karl von Hase, *Das Geistliche Schauspiel*, Leipzig, 1858, and *Miracle Plays and Sacred Dramas*, trans. A. W. Jackson, London, 1880;

Richard Heinzel, *Beschreibung der Geistlichen Spiele*, Hamburg, 1898; Heinrich Reidt, *Das Geistliche Schauspiel des Mittelalters*, Frankfurt, 1868; and Martin Wickens, *Geschichte der Geistlichen Spiele im Deutschland*, Göttingen, 1872; and Jacob Zeidler, *Studien und Beiträge zur Geschichte der Jesuitenkomödie und des Klosterdramas*, Leipzig, 1891).

Halliburton, David G. 'Blake's French Revolution: the *Figura* and Yesterday's News,' *Studies in Romanticism*, V (1965–66), 158–68.

Hanning, Robert W. *The Vision of History in Early Britain: From Gildas to Geoffrey of Monmouth*. New York, 1966 (brilliant discussion of typology and historiography).

Harris, Victor. 'Allegory to Analogy in the Interpretation of Scriptures,' *Philological Quarterly*, XLV (1966), 1–23 (excellent essay; see also Maurice Evans, 'Metaphor and Symbol in the Sixteenth Century,' *Essays in Criticism*, III [1953], 267–84).

Heider, Andrew Bernard. *The Blessed Virgin Mary in Early Christian Latin Poetry*. Washington, D.C., 1918.

Hellstrom, Ward. 'Time and Type in Browning's Saul,' *English Literary History*, XXXIII (1966), 370–89.

Henss, Rudolf. *Studien zu Hans Folz*. Berlin, 1934 (cf. Hennig Brinckmann, *Geschichte der lateinischen Liebesdichtung im Mittelalter*, Halle, 1925, and Joseph Diemer, *Deutsche Gedichte des 11. und 12. Jahrhunderts*, Wien, 1849).

Henze, Helen. *Die Allegorie bie Hans Sachs*. Halle, 1912.

Hollander, Robert. *Allegory in Dante's 'Commedia.'* Princeton, 1969.

Honig, Edwin. *Dark Conceit: The Making of Allegory*. Evanston, 1959.

Hunter, J. Paul. *The Reluctant Pilgrim: Defoe's Emblematic Method and Quest for Form in 'Robinson Crusoe.'* Baltimore, 1966.

Huppé, Bernard. *Doctrine and Poetry: Augustine's Influence on Old English Poetry*. Albany, 1959.

Jantsch, Heinz Gerhard. *Studien zum Symbolischen in der frühmittelhochdeutschen Literatur*. Tübingen, 1959 (see further: Friedrich Vogt, *Geschichte der mittelhochdeutschen Literatur*, Leipzig, 1922; Karl Raab, *Uber vier allegorische Motive im der lateinischen und deutschen Literatur des Mittelalters*, Lesben, 1885; Anselm Salzer, *Die Sinnbilder und Beiworte Mariens im der deutschen Literatur und lateinischen Hymnenpoesie des Mittelalters*, Linz, 1886–94; George K. W. A. Ebert, *Allgemeine Geschichte der Literatur der Mittelalters im Abendlande*, esp. vol. III, Leipzig, 1874–87; Albert Waag, *Kleinere deutsche Gedichte des XI und XII Jahrhunderts*, Halle, 1890; and U. Ruberg, 'Die Suche in Prosa-Lancelot,' *Zeitschrift für deutsches Altertum*, XCII [1963], 122–57.

Jörso, Lisbeth. *Das Arnsterner Mariengebet und die Sequenzen des Mittelalters*. Marburg, 1920.

Kaske, R. E. 'Two Cruxes in "Pearl": 596 and 609–610,' *Traditio*, XV (1959), 418–28 (see also his 'Gigas the Giant in Piers Plowman,' *Journal of English and Germanic Philology*, LVI

[1957], 177–85; and P. M. Kean, *Pearl: An Interpretation*, London, 1967).

Kaufman, U. Milo. *'The Pilgrim's Progress' and Traditions in Puritan Meditation*. New Haven, 1966.

Knowles, Richard. 'Myth and Type in *As You Like It*,' *English Literary History* XXXIII (1966), 1–22 (cf. Barbara K. Lewalski, 'Biblical Allusion and Allegory in *The Merchant of Venice*,' *Shakespeare Quarterly*, XIII [1962], 327–43).

Kolve, V. A. *The Play Called Corpus Christi*. London, 1966 (illuminating account; cf.: O. B. Hardison, Jr., *Christian Rite and Christian Drama in the Middle Ages*, Baltimore, 1965; H. F. Muller, 'Pre-history of Medieval Drama: The Antecedent of the Tropes and the Conditions of their Appearance,' *Zeitschrift für Romanische Philologie*, XLIV [1924], 544–75; Lily B. Campbell, *Divine Poetry and Drama in Sixteenth-Century England*, Cambridge, Eng., 1959; Grace Frank, *Medieval French Drama*, Oxford, 1954; and Edith Purdie, *The Story of Judith in German and English Literature*, Paris, 1927 [vol. XXXIX of Bibliothèque de la Revue de Littérature Comparée]; a useful bibliography in this area is Edward D. Coleman, *The Bible in English Drama*, New York, 1931).

Korshin, Paul J. 'The Evolution of Neoclassical Poetics: Cleveland, Denham, and Waller as Poetic Theorists,' *Eighteenth-Century Studies*, II (1958), 102–37.

—— 'Swift and Typological Narrative in *A Tale of a Tub*,' in *The Interpretation of Narrative: Theory and Practice*, ed. Morton W. Bloomfield. Cambridge,

Mass., 1970 (Harvard English Studies, vol. I).

Kretzmann, Paul E. *The Liturgical Element in the Earliest Forms of the Medieval Drama, with special reference to the English and German Plays*. Minneapolis, 1916.

Krouse, F. Michael. *Milton's Samson and the Christian Tradition*. Princeton, 1949.

Levine, George R. 'Dryden's "Inarticulate Poesy," Music and the Davidic King in *Absalom and Achitophel*: An Aspect of Style,' *Language and Style*, II, 1969, 330–38 (see also: Edward N. Hooker, 'The Purpose of Dryden's *Annus Mirabilis*,' *Huntington Library Quarterly*, X [1946–47], 49–68; A. L. Korn, 'MacFlecknoe and Cowley's *Davideis*,' *Huntington Library Quarterly*, XIV, [1951], 99–127; Harold E. Toliver's remarks on Dryden in *Marvell's Ironic Vision*, New Haven, 1965; and Barbara K. Lewalski, 'The Scope and function of Biblical Allusion in *Absalom and Achitophel*,' *English Language Notes*, III [1965], 29–35).

Levine, Jay Arnold. 'The Design of *A Tale of A Tub* (With a Digression on a Mad Modern Critic),' *English Literary History*, XXXIII (1966), 198–227 (see also Richard Jacobson, 'A Biblical Allusion in *Gulliver's Travels*,' *Notes & Queries*, CCXV [1970], 286–87).

Lewalski, Barbara K. *Milton's Brief Epic*. Providence, R.I., 1966 (enormously learned and cogently argued).

—— 'Samson Agonistes and the "Tragedy" of the Apocalypse,' *Publications of the Modern Language Association*, LXXXV (1970), 1050–62 (see also Earl

Miner's review article, 'Plundering the Egyptians; or, What We Learn From Recent Books on Milton,' *Eighteenth-Century Studies*, III [1970], 296–305; and cf. Ann Gossman, 'Samson, Job, and "The Exercise of Saints," ' *English Studies*, XLV [1964], 212–24, and Evert M. Clark, 'Milton's Conception of Samson,' *Texas University Studies in English*, VIII [1928], 88–99).

—— 'Structure and the Symbolism of Vision in Michael's Prophecy, *Paradise Lost*, XI–XII,' *Philological Quarterly*, XLII (1963), 25–35.

Lynch, William F. *Christ and Apollo: The Dimensions of the Literary Imagination*. New York, 1960 (see also his 'Theology and the Imagination,' *Thought*, XXIX [1954], 61–87; and 'Theology and the Imagination II: The Evocative Symbol,' *Thought*, XXIX [1954–55], 529–55; and cf. Herbert Musurillo's *Symbolism and the Christian Imagination*, Baltimore, 1962, and 'Symbolism and Kerygmatic Theology,' *Thought*, XXXVI [1961], 59–80).

MacCallum, H. R. 'Milton and the Figurative Interpretation of the Bible,' *University of Toronto Quarterly*, XXXI (1962), 397–415. (The earliest, and still very valuable, demonstration of the exegetical background of the poetry—including typology—appears in Patrick Hume's scholarly edition of Milton, London, 1695.)

—— 'Milton and Sacred History: Books XI and XII of *Paradise Lost*,' *Essays in English Literature from the Renaissance to the Victorian Age, Presented to A. S. P. Woodhouse*, eds. Millar MacLure and F. W. Watt. Toronto, 1964 (see also Arthur E.

Barker, 'Structural and Doctrinal Pattern in Milton's Later Poems,' published in the same volume; and *Milton and the Puritan Dilemma*, Toronto, 1942; and cf.: George W. Whiting, *Milton and this Pendant World*, Austin, 1958; Harold Fisch, *Jerusalem and Albion: The Hebraic Factor in Seventeenth-Century Literature*, London, 1964; Michael Murrin, *The Veil of Allegory: Some Notes Toward a Theory of Allegorical Rhetoric in the English Renaissance*, Chicago, 1969; and Louis L. Martz, *The Paradise Within: Studies in Vaughan, Traherne, and Milton*, New Haven, 1964).

Madsen, William G. *From Shadowy Types to Truth: Studies in Milton's Symbolism*. New Haven, 1968 (excellent study of the subject; cf. Don Cameron Allen, 'Milton and the Descent to Light,' *Journal of English and Germanic Philology*, LX [1961], 614–30, and Jonathan H. Collett, 'Milton's Use of Classical Mythology in *Paradise Lost*,' *Publications of the Modern Language Association*, LXXXV [1970], 88–96).

—— 'Earth as a Shadow of Heaven: Typological Symbolism in *Paradise Lost*,' *Publications of the Modern Language Association*, LXXV (1960), 518–26 (see also his essay 'From Shadowy Types to Truth,' in *The Lyric and Dramatic Milton*, ed. Joseph Summers, New York, 1965).

Mandonnet, Pierre. *Dante le Théologien*. Paris, 1935 (see also Heinrich Naumann, 'Der "Vergleich" bei Dante in Antiker, Mittelaltlicher und Moderner Sicht,' *Wirkendes Wort*, XIV [1964], 314–32).

Manning, Stephen. 'The Meaning

of [Crashaw's] "The Weeper," '
English Literary History, XXII
(1955), 34–47 (see also his
'Herbert's THE PEARL, 38,' *Ex-plicator*, XIV [1955–56], No.
25).

——— 'Nou goth Sonne vnder wod,'
Modern Language Notes,
LXXIV (1959), 578–81 (see
also his 'I Syng of a Myden,'
Publications of the Modern Lan-guage Association, LXXV
[1960], 8–12).

——— *Wisdom and Number: To-wards a Critical Appraisal of the
Middle English Religious Lyric.*
Lincoln, 1962.

Mattheisen, Paul F. *Uproar in the
Echo: The Existential Aesthetic
of Browning's 'The Ring and the
Book.'* Madison, 1970 (*Literary
Monographs*; no. 3; brief but il-luminating comments on Brown-ing's use of typology).

Mazzeo, Joseph A. 'Cromwell as
Davidic King,' *Renaissance and
Seventeenth-Century Studies*,
New York, 1961 (on Marvell's
ode to Cromwell; see also in this
volume 'St. Augustine's Rhetoric
of Silence: Truth vs. Eloquence
and Things vs. Signs"; and see
further Mazzeo's *Structure and
Thought in the Paradiso*, Ithaca,
1958).

McCaffrey, Isabel G. 'The Theme
of *Paradise Lost*, Book III,' in
New Essays on Paradise Lost, ed.
T. Kranidas. Berkeley, 1970.

McGann, Jerome J. 'The Dandy,'
Midway, X (1969), 3–18 (a
study in Romantic iconography
and secular *figurae*; a more recent
general formulation of this re-lationship is McGann's paper,
'Traditional Typology and Ro-mantic Aesthetics,' read at a
Modern Language Association
Seminar, December, 1971, on
'Problems of Neoclassicism:

Typology in the Eighteenth
Century and Afterwards'; other
papers read at the seminar in-clude: Robert E. Reiter, 'Spec-ulations about the Poetic Con-texts of Biblical Typology'; Ste-ven N. Zwicker, 'Political Typol-ogy in Dryden'; and Nancy T.
Stepp, 'Typology and King-ship').

Miller, Robert P. 'Chaucer's Par-doner, the Spiritual Eunuch, and
the Pardoner's Tale,' *Speculum*,
XXX (1955), 180–99.

Miner, Earl. *Dryden's Poetry.*
Bloomington, 1967 (see also his
'Some Characteristics of Dry-den's Use of Metaphor,' *Studies
in English Literature*, II [1962],
309–20).

Mueller, William R. *John Donne:
Preacher.* Princeton, 1962.

Nasser, Eugene. 'Hopkins, *Figura*,
and Grace: God's Better Beauty,'
Renascence, XVII (1964),
120–30, 136.

Nelson, Alan H. ' "Sacred" and
"Secular" Currents in the
Towneley Play of Noah,' *Drama
Survey*, III (1964), 393–401.

Nicholson, Lewis E., ed. *An An-thology of Beowulf Criticism.*
Notre Dame, 1963 (see the essays
by Morton W. Bloomfield,
Allen Cabaniso, Marie P. Hamil-ton, M. B. McNamee, and D. W.
Robertson).

Ohly, Friedrich. 'Goethes Ehrfuch-ten—ein Ordo Caritas,' *Eupho-rion*, LV (1961), 113–45, 405–48 (see further this author's
'Römisches und Biblisches in
Goethes "Märchen," ' *Zeitschrift
für deutsches Altertum*, XCI,
[1961], 147–66, and Wolfgang
Schadewaldt, 'Goethes Knaben-märchen "Der neue Paris," '
Goethestudien; Natur und Alter-tum, Zurich, 1963).

—— 'Vom geistigen Sinn des Wortes in Mittelalter,' Zeitschrift für deutsches Altertum, LXXXIX (1958–59), 1–23 (a later variant treatment of the subject by this author is his 'Die Suche in Dichtungen des Mittelalters,' Zeitschrift für deutsches Altertum, XCIV [1965], 171–84; see further Julius Schwietering, Mystik und höfische Dichtung im Hochmittelalter, Tübingen, 1960, and Wolfgang Stammler, 'Ideenwandel in Sprache und Literatur des Deutschen Mittelalters,' Deutsche Vierteljahrschrift für Literaturwissenschaft und Geistesgeschichte, II [1924], 753–69; cf. Ruth E. Messenger, The Medieval Latin Hymn, Washington, D.C., 1953).

Patrides, Constantinos A. The Phoenix and the Ladder: The Rise and Decline of the Christian View of History. Berkeley, 1964 (cf. Tom F. Driver, The Sense of History in Greek and Shakespearean Drama, New York, 1960).

Pope, Elizabeth M. Paradise Regained: the Tradition and the Poem. Baltimore, 1947.

Quinn, Dennis B. 'John Donne's Principles of Biblical Exegesis,' Journal of English and Germanic Philology, LXI (1962), 313–29.

Raw, Barbara. ' "As Dew in Aprille," ' Modern Language Review, LV (1960), 411–14 (interesting on Mary typology; for some relevant parallel studies, see: J. Vincent Crowne, 'Middle English Poems on the Joys and on the Compassion of the Blessed Virgin Mary,' Catholic University Bulletin, VIII [1902], 304–14; Frank A. Patterson, The Middle English Penitential Lyric, New York, 1911; and George C. Taylor, 'The English Planctus Mariae,' Modern Philology, IV [1906–07], 605–38 [text and commentary]).

Reiter, Robert. 'In Adam's Room: A Study of the Adamic Typology of Christ in Paradise Regained,' Diss. University of Michigan, 1964.

—— 'On Biblical Typology and the Interpretation of Literature,' College English, XXX (1969), 562–71.

Robertson, Durant W., Jr. 'Historical Criticism,' English Institute Essays, ed. Alan S. Downer, New York, 1951.

—— A Preface to Chaucer: Studies in Medieval Perspective. Princeton, 1962 (major work; see also Judson B. Allen, 'The Ironic Fruyt: Chaunticleer as Figura,' Studies in Philology, LXVI [1969], 25–35, and John V. Fleming, The 'Roman de la Rose': A Study in Allegory and Iconography, Princeton, 1969).

—— and Bernard F. Huppé. Piers Plowman and Scriptural Tradition. Princeton, 1951.

Roston, Murray. Biblical Drama in England, from the Middle Ages to the Present Day. Evanston, Ill., 1968 (cf. his Prophet and Poet; the Bible and the Growth of Romanticism. Evanston, Ill., 1965).

Rostvig, Maren-Sofie. 'Images of Perfection,' in Seventeenth-Century Imagery: Essays on the Uses of Figurative Language from Donne to Farquhar, ed. Earl Miner. Berkeley, 1971 (see also in this collection the essay by Pierre Legovis).

Sadler, Lynch Veach. 'Typological Imagery in Samson Agonistes: Noon and the Dragon,' English Literary History, XXXVII (1970), 195–210 (see further

T. S. K. Scott-Craig, 'Concerning Milton's Samson,' *Renaissance News*, V [1952], 45–53).

Salter, Elizabeth. *Medieval Poetry and the Figural View of Reality*. Oxford, 1968 (vol. LIV of Proceedings of the British Academy; excellent brief introduction to the use of typology in poetry; cf. R. W. Frank, 'The Art of Reading Medieval Personification—Allegory,' *English Literary History*, XX [1953], 237–50, and B. G. Koonce, *Chaucer and the Tradition of Fame: Symbolism in 'The House of Fame,'* Princeton, 1966).

Schleiner, Winfried. *The Imagery of John Donne's Sermons*. Providence, 1970.

Schneidau, Herbert N. *Ezra Pound: The Image and the Real*. Baton Rouge, La., 1969.

Singleton, Charles S. *Dante Studies I—Commedia: Elements of Structure*. Cambridge, Mass., 1954 (classic study of formal and theoretical problems; cf. Bruno Nardi, *Nel mondo di Dante*, Roma, 1944).

Smith, Ben H. *Traditional Imagery of Charity in 'Piers Plowman.'* The Hague, 1966 (cf.: Elizabeth Salter, *Piers Plowman: An Introduction*, Cambridge, Mass., 1962; John Lawlor, *Piers Plowman: An Essay in Criticism*, London, 1962; and Morton W. Bloomfield, *Piers Plowman as a Fourteenth-Century Apocalypse*, New Brunswick, N.J., 1962).

Smithers, G. V. 'Two Typological Poems in the Ancrene Riwle,' *Medium Aevum*, XXXIV (1965), 126–28.

Spitzer, Leo. 'Explication de Texte Applied to Three Great Middle English Poems,' *Archivum Linguisticum*, III (1951), 1–23,

136–65 (the latter portion of this essay is especially relevant to figural explication).

Stewart, Stanley. *The Enclosed Garden: The Tradition and the Image in Seventeenth-Century Poetry*. Madison, 1966 (focuses mainly on Canticles; see also his *The Expanded Voice: The Art of Thomas Traherne*, San Marino, 1970).

Summers, Joseph H. *George Herbert, His Religion and Art*. Cambridge, Mass., 1954.

Tayler, Archer. *Literary History of Meistergesang*. New York, 1937 (see also Wolfgang Stammler, 'Die Wurzeln des Meistergesangs,' *Deutsche Vierteljahrsschrift für Literaturwissenschaft und Geistesgeschichte*, I [1923], 529–56).

Tuve, Rosemond. *Allegorical Imagery: Some Medieval Books and their Posterity*. Princeton, 1966.

—— *A Reading of George Herbert*. Chicago, 1952 (brilliant commentary on typology in the poetry; cf. William H. Halewood, *The Poetry of Grace: Reformation Themes and Structures in English Seventeenth-Century Poetry*, New Haven, 1970, which takes issue with Tuve's views; the major poets treated here are Herbert, Marvell, Vaughan, and Milton).

Vriend, Joannes. *The Blessed Virgin Mary in the Medieval Drama of England, with Additional Studies in Middle English Literature*. Purmerend, 1928.

Walker, David. 'The Architectonics of George Herbert's "The Temple," ' *English Literary History*, XXIX (1962), 289–305.

Weber, Sarah A. *Theology and Poetry in the Middle English Lyric: A Study of Sacred History* and *Aesthetic Form*. Columbus, 1969.

Woolf, Rosemary. 'The Effect of Typology on the English Medieval Plays of Abraham and Isaac,' *Speculum*, XXXII (1957), 805–25 (cf. her 'Doctrinal Influences on *The Dream of the Rood*,' *Medium Aevum*, XXVII [1958], 137–53; and see also John R. Elliott, Jr., 'The Sacrifice of Isaac as Comedy and Tragedy,' *Studies in Philology*, LXVI [1969], 36–59).

―――― *The English Religious Lyric in the Middle Ages*. Oxford, 1968 (a penetrating and very useful study).

Young, Karl. *The Drama of the Medieval Church*. 2 vols. Oxford, 1933.

Zwicker, Steven. *Dryden's Political Poetry: The Typology of King and Nation*. Providence, R.I., 1972 (expanded and revised version of his 'Dryden and the Sacred History of the English People: A Study of Typological Imagery in Dryden's Political Poetry, 1660–1688,' Diss. Brown University, 1969; see also the essay by Zwicker on 'The King and Christ: Figural Imagery in Dryden's Restoration Panegyrics,' *Philological Quarterly*, L [1971], 582–98; cf.: Leon M. Guilhamet, 'Dryden's Debasement of Scripture in *Absalom and Achitophel*,' *Studies in English Literature*, IX [1969], 395–413; A. B. Chambers, 'Absalom and Achitophel: Christ and Satan,' *Modern Language Notes*, LXXIV [1959], 592–96; Ruth Nevo, *The Dial of Virtue: A Study of Poems on Affairs of State in the Seventeenth Century*, Princeton, 1963; Gillian Jondorf, *Robert Garnier and the Theory of Political Tragedy in the Sixteenth Century*, Cambridge, Eng., 1969, and Helen W. Randall, "The Rise and Fall of a Martyrology: Sermons of Charles I," *Huntington Library Quarterly*, X [1947], 135–67).

Notes on the Authors

Sacvan Bercovitch teaches English and American Literature at Columbia University. He is now working on a study of the American Puritan imagination.

Ursula Brumm is Professor of American Literature and Intellectual History at the John F. Kennedy Institute of the Free University of Berlin. Her interest in Puritan literature and typology goes back to the years 1953–55 when she studied at Harvard with Perry Miller. She also has published on William Faulkner, the twentieth-century novel, and the interaction of history and fiction, in *Partisan Review, Jahrbuch für Amerikastudien, and Comparative Literature Studies.* In progress is a book on *The American Writer and History.*

Thomas M. Davis is Associate Professor of English at Kent State University. He received his B.S. and M.S. from Kansas State University and his doctorate from the University of Missouri. He has edited several anthologies, including *14 by Emily Dickinson;* has published articles on Old English poetry, J. D. Salinger, and Edward Taylor, and is now working on a study of Taylor's *Preparatory Meditations,* as well as preparing an edition of unpublished Taylor sermons.

Karl Keller, Associate Professor of Comparative and American Literature at San Diego State College, received his degrees from the University of Utah and the University of Minnesota, and has taught literature and religion at the University of Minnesota and the State University College at Cortland, N.Y. He is on the Board of Editors of *Dialogue* and on the staff of *American Literature.* He has written essays on a variety of American writers from Taylor to Robinson Jeffers, on Mormon literature, and on the Bible, as well as two books, *American Literature: Post 1945* and *The Example of Edward Taylor*. In progress with Robert A. Rees is a work on *The Bible in American Literature*.

Mason I. Lowance, Jr. majored in Religion at Princeton. He holds B.A. and M.A. degrees in English from Oxford University, England, and has a Ph.D. from Emory. On the English faculty of the University of Massachusetts, Amherst, he is managing editor of *Early American Literature*. He has written the Twayne volume on Increase Mather, and edited a number of seventeenth-century Puritan works. With Jesper Rosenmeier, he is now preparing several of Jonathan Edwards' writings on typology for the Yale edition of Edwards' works.

Stephen Manning received his A.B. from the Catholic University of America and his Ph.D. from the Johns Hopkins University. He has taught at the Universities of Colorado and Virginia and is now Professor of English at the University of Kentucky. He has published on the Middle English religious lyric, Chaucer, and *Sir Gawain and the Green Knight*, and is currently working on a book on medieval narrative style.

Robert E. Reiter studied at St. Bonaventure University (B.A., 1954), Johannes-Gutenberg University, Mainz, and at the University of Michigan (Ph.D., 1964).

He is now Associate Professor of English at Boston College. His publications include studies on Milton, George Herbert, St. Thomas More, and Flannery O'Connor.

Richard Reinitz received his B.A. from Queens College, his M.A. from Hunter College, and his Ph.D. from the University of Rochester, all in history. He has taught at University College, London, and Wayne State University, and is currently on the faculty of Hobart and William Smith Colleges. In addition to his work on typology, he has edited *Tensions in American Puritanism* and published articles in *The Contemporary Review, The Bulletin of the British Association for American Studies*, and *The Denver Quarterly*.

Jesper Rosenmeier is Associate Professor of English at Tufts University. He received his A.B. from Princeton and his M.A. and Ph.D. from Harvard, under the direction of Perry Miller and Kenneth Murdock. He has published several essays on colonial New England in the *Harvard Library Bulletin* and the *William and Mary Quarterly*, and has edited a number of early American texts. With Mason Lowance, he is now preparing a book for Doubleday entitled *The Language of Canaan: Metaphor in American Thought from 1620 to 1776*. He is also at work on a book, *John Cotton, Preacher of Redemption*.